NETWORK SECURITY AND CRYPTOGRAPHY

NETWORK SECURITY AND CRYPTOGRAPHY

A Self-Teaching Introduction

Second Edition

Sarhan M. Musa, Ph.D.
Prairie View A&M University

MERCURY LEARNING AND INFORMATION
Dulles, Virginia
Boston, Massachusetts
New Delhi

Publisher: David Pallai
MERCURY LEARNING AND INFORMATION
22841 Quicksilver Drive
Dulles, VA 20166
info@merclearning.com
www.merclearning.com
1-800-232-0223

S. M. Musa. *Network Security and Cryptography, Second Edition.*
ISBN: 978-1-68392-883-6

The publisher recognizes and respects all marks used by companies, manufacturers, and developers as a means to distinguish their products. All brand names and product names mentioned in this book are trademarks or service marks of their respective companies. Any omission or misuse (of any kind) of service marks or trademarks, etc. is not an attempt to infringe on the property of others.

Library of Congress Control Number: 2022941507

222324321   Printed on acid-free paper in the United States of America.

Our titles are available for adoption, license, or bulk purchase by institutions, corporations, etc. For additional information, please contact the Customer Service Dept. at 800-232-0223(toll free).

To my wife, Lama and my children,
Mahmoud, Ibrahim, and Khalid

CONTENTS

Preface   *xxiii*

Chapter 1:   **Overview of Computer Networks**   **1**

    1.1   Introduction   1

    1.2   Open Systems Interconnection (OSI) Model   2

    1.3   Transmission Control Protocol/Internetworking
         Protocol (TCP/IP) Model   4

    1.4   Hierarchical Model   9

    1.5   Computer Network Equipment   10

    1.6   Computer Network Types   20

    1.7   Computer Network Topology   21

    1.8   Exercises   26

Chapter 2:   **Mathematical Foundations for Computer Networks**   **29**

    2.1   Introduction   30

    2.2   Probability Fundamentals   32

         2.2.1 Simple Probability   33

         2.2.2 Joint Probability   36

         2.2.3 Conditional Probability   37

         2.2.4 Statistical Independence   38

    2.3   Random Variables   39

         2.3.1 Cumulative Distribution Function   40

         2.3.2 Probability Density Function   41

         2.3.3 Joint Distribution   43

2.4   Discrete Probability Models   45

    2.4.1 Bernoulli Distribution   45

    2.4.2 Binomial Distribution   46

    2.4.3 Geometric Distribution   47

    2.4.4 Poisson Distribution   48

2.5   Continuous Probability Models   50

    2.5.1 Uniform Distribution   50

    2.5.2 Exponential Distribution   51

    2.5.3 Erlang Distribution   52

    2.5.4 Hyperexponential Distribution   53

    2.5.5 Gaussian Distribution   53

2.6   Transformation of a Random Variable   55

2.7   Generating Functions   56

2.8   Central Limit Theorem   58

2.9   Classification of Random Processes   59

    2.9.1 Continuous versus Discrete Random Process   60

    2.9.2 Deterministic versus Non-Deterministic
Random Process   60

    2.9.3 Stationary versus Nonstationary
Random Process   60

    2.9.4 Ergodic versus Nonergodic Random Process   60

2.10   Statistics of Random Processes and Stationarity   61

2.11   Time Averages of Random Processes and Ergodicity   65

2.12   Multiple Random Processes   67

2.13   Sample Random Processes   68

    2.13.1 Random Walks   68

    2.13.2 Markov Processes   70

    2.13.3 Birth-and-Death Processes   71

    2.13.4 Poisson Processes   71

2.14   Renewal Processes   74

2.15   Kendall's Notation   74

2.16   Little's Theorem   76

2.17   M/M/1 Queue   78

2.18	M/M/1 Queue With Bulk Arrivals/Service	85
	2.18.1 M^x/M/1 (Bulk Arrivals) System	85
	2.18.2 M/M^Y/1 (Bulk Service) System	86
	2.18.3 M/M/1/k Queueing System	87
	2.18.4 M/M/k Queueing System	90
	2.18.5 M/M/∞ Queueing System	93
2.19	M/G/1 Queueing SYSTEM	94
2.20	M/E_k/1 Queueing SYSTEM	99
2.21	Networks of Queues	100
	2.21.1 Tandem Queues	101
	2.21.2 Queueing System with Splitting	102
	2.21.3 Queueing System with Feedback	104
2.22	Jackson Networks	104
2.23	Exercises	105
Chapter 3:	**Overview of Cryptography**	**107**
3.1	Introduction	107
3.2	Basic Terms Related to Cryptography	111
	3.2.1 Cryptographic Primitives	112
	3.2.2 Cryptographic Protocols	113
	3.2.3 Encryption (at the Sender's End)	113
	3.2.4 Decryption (at the Recipient's End)	113
3.3	Requirements of Secure Communication	113
3.4	Osi Security Architecture X.800	115
	3.4.1 Security Attacks	115
	3.4.2 Security Services	116
	3.4.3 Security Mechanisms	118
3.5	Categories of Cryptographic Systems	122
3.6	Symmetric (or Conventional) Encryption Model	123
	3.6.1 Types of Attacks on a Conventional Encryption Scheme	125
	3.6.2 Conventional Encryption for Confidentiality	125
	3.6.3 Link Encryption	126
3.7	Exercises	130

Chapter 4: **Mathematical Foundations for Cryptography** 133

4.1 Introduction 134

4.2 Introduction to Groups, Rings, and Fields 134

4.2.1 Groups 134

4.2.2 Ring 138

4.2.3 Field 139

4.3 Modular Arithmetic 139

4.3.1 Residue Classes $(\bmod\, n)$ 142

4.3.2 Properties of Z_n 143

4.3.3 Multiplication within Set Z_n 144

4.4 Introduction to Primes and Co-Primes 147

4.4.1 Prime Numbers 147

4.4.2 Co-Prime Numbers or Relatively Prime Numbers 147

4.5 Euclid's Algorithm To Determine GCD 148

4.6 Extended Euclid's Algorithm 149

4.7 Galols Finite Fields 152

4.7.1 $GF\,(p)$ 153

4.7.2 Set Z_p^* 153

4.7.3 Galois Finite Fields of Order 2^n 154

4.7.4 Arithmetic Operations within GF (2^n) 154

4.7.5 Addition $(+)$ Operation within GF (2^3) 156

4.7.6 Addition Inverse of GF (2^3) 156

4.7.7 Multiplication (x) Operation within GF (2^3) Using $m(x) = x^3 + x^2 + 1$ for Reducing the Polynomials 156

4.7.8 Multiplication Inverse within GF (2^3) 157

4.7.9 Multiplicative Inverses of All Integers in GF (2^3) 158

4.8 Fermat's Little Theorem 159

4.8.1 A Corollary of Fermat's Little Theorem 160

4.9 Euler's Totient Function 161

4.9.1 General Formula for Computation of Totient Function $\phi(n)$ 162

4.10	Euler's Theorem	163
	4.10.1 A Corollary of Euler's Theorem	165
4.11	Prime Numbers	168
	4.11.1 Primitive Roots	169
4.12	Discrete Logarithms	171
	4.12.1 Difficulty of Computing Discrete Logarithms	171
	4.12.2 Algorithm to Determine the Primitive Roots of a Number n	172
	4.12.3 Another Method of Determining the Primitive Roots of a Number n	173
4.13	Primality Testing	174
	4.13.1 Miller and Rabin's Method	175
4.14	Chinese Remainder Theorem	181
	4.14.1 Alternate Interpretation of the Chinese Remainder Theorem	182
4.15	Exercises	187
Chapter 5:	**Classical Cipher Schemes**	**191**
5.1	Introduction	191
5.2	Classical Substitution Ciphers	191
	5.2.1 Caesar Cipher	192
	5.2.2 Mono-Alphabetic Cipher	194
	5.2.3 Hill Cipher	196
	5.2.4 Play-Fair Cipher	199
	5.2.5 Poly-Alphabetic Cipher (Vigenere Cipher)	201
	5.2.6 One-Time Pad	202
5.3	Transposition Ciphers	204
	5.3.1 Rail-Fence Cipher	204
	5.3.2 Rectangular Transposition Cipher	205
5.4	Steganography	206
	5.4.1 Limitation of Steganography	207
	5.4.2 Steganography Combined with Cryptography	207
5.5	Exercises	207

Chapter 6:	**Modern Symmetric Ciphers**	**211**
6.1	Introduction	211
6.2	Some Basic Concepts for Symmetric Ciphers	212
	6.2.1 Concept of Binary Block Substitution	212
	6.2.2 Strength of the Substitution Cipher	214
	6.2.3 Key Size for the Simple Substitution Cipher	215
6.3	Claude Shannon's Theory of Diffusion and Confusion	215
	6.3.1 Diffusion	215
	6.3.2 Confusion	216
6.4	Feistel Cipher	216
	6.4.1 Strength of the Feistel Cipher	219
6.5	Data Encryption Standard (DES)	219
	6.5.1 Description of the Critical Functions of Each Round of DES	225
	6.5.2 S-Box Transformation	228
	6.5.3 Generation of Sub-Keys (K_1... K_{16})	229
	6.5.4 DES Decryption Algorithm	231
6.6	Avalanche Effect	231
	6.6.1 Strength of DES	232
	6.6.2 Possible Attacks on DES	233
	6.6.3 Differential Cryptanalysis vs. Linear Cryptanalysis	237
6.7	Multiple Des	237
	6.7.1 Double DES	237
	6.7.2 Triple DES	240
	6.7.3 Block Cipher vs. Stream Cipher	243
	6.7.4 Block/Stream Cipher Modes of Operation	244
6.8	International Data Encryption Algorithm (IDEA)	257
	6.8.1 Description of IDEA	258
	6.8.2 Generation of Sub-Keys in IDEA	261
	6.8.3 IDEA Modes of Operation	262
6.9	Advanced Encryption Standard (AES)	262
	6.9.1 Processing of Plaintext	263

6.10	Key Management: Symmetric Encryption	269
	6.10.1 Secure Distribution of Keys	269
	6.10.2 Key Distribution Schemes	270
6.11	Pseudo-Random Number Generators	274
	6.11.1 Pseudo-Random Number Generation (PRNG) Algorithms	274
6.12	Exercises	280
Chapter 7:	**Public-Key Cryptography for Data Confidentiality**	**283**
7.1	Introduction	283
7.2	Requirements of Public-Key Cryptography	283
7.3	Data Confidentiality Using Public-Key Cryptography	284
7.4	RSA Algorithm	284
	7.4.1 Main Components	285
	7.4.2 Strength of RSA	288
7.5	Key Management Using Public-Key Cryptography	292
	7.5.1 Diffie-Hellman Algorithm for Key Distribution	292
	7.5.2 Global Parameters	293
	7.5.3 Strength of Diffie-Hellman Key-Exchange Scheme	295
	7.5.4 Types of Attacks against Diffie-Hellman	295
7.6	El-Gamal Encryption Scheme	297
	7.6.1 Determination of Private Key and Public Key (by User "A")	298
7.7	Elliptic Curve Cryptography (ECC)	300
	7.7.1 Elliptic Curves	300
	7.7.2 Elliptic Curves in Cryptography (ECC)	301
	7.7.3 Prime Elliptic Curves	302
	7.7.4 Prime Elliptic Curve Set	302
	7.7.5 Computation of Elliptic Curve Set $E_{11}(1, 1)$	303
	7.7.6 Rules for Addition (+) Operation over $E_p(a, b)$	304
	7.7.7 Multiplication over the Set $E_p(a, b)$	304
	7.7.8 Strength of ECC-Based Schemes	311

		7.7.9 ECC-Based Key-Exchange Algorithm	311
		7.7.10 Strength of ECC Key-Exchange Algorithm	313
		7.7.11 ECC-Based Encryption/Decryption Scheme	313
		7.7.12 Strength of ECC-based Encryption/ Decryption Scheme	315
		7.7.13 ECC Encryption/Decryption vs. RSA	325
		7.7.14 Efficient Hardware Implementation	325
	7.8	Exercises	326
Chapter 8:		**Authentication Schemes**	**329**
	8.1	Introduction	329
	8.2	What is Message Authentication?	329
	8.3	Types of Authentication Services	330
		8.3.1 Different Techniques of Message Authentication	330
		8.3.2 Digital Signatures Using Public-Key Cryptography	333
		8.3.3 Message Authentication Code (MAC)	334
		8.3.4 Many-to-One Relationship between Messages and MAC Values	334
		8.3.5 Use of MAC for Message Authentication	335
		8.3.6 Chosen Plaintext Attack on MAC	336
		8.3.7 Hash Function	337
	8.4	Application Modes of Digital Signatures	340
		8.4.1 Direct Digital Signature	340
		8.4.2 Arbitrated Digital Signature	341
	8.5	Authentication Protocols	343
		8.5.1 Mutual Authentication	343
		8.5.2 Symmetric Encryption Approaches	343
		8.5.3 Needham Schroeder Protocol	344
		8.5.4 Denning Protocol	344
		8.5.5 NEUM Protocol	345
		8.5.6 Public-Key Encryption Approaches	345

8.5.7   One-Way Authentication   346

8.5.8   Symmetric Encryption Approach   346

8.5.9   Public Key Encryption Approach   347

8.5.10 The Birthday Paradox   347

8.5.11 Probability of Two Sets Overlapping   349

8.5.12 Mathematical Basis for Birthday Attack   350

8.5.13 Birthday Attack   351

8.5.14 Verification of the Digital Signature at the
         Recipient End   352

8.5.15 How to Create Many Variants of a Message   352

8.5.16 Weak Collision Resistance   352

8.5.17 Strengths of Hash Functions   353

8.6   Message Digest (Hash Function) Algorithms   354

8.6.1 MD5 Message Digest Algorithm   354

8.6.2 Sequence of Use of Message Words
        in Various Rounds   358

8.6.3 Primitive Logical Functions Used
        in Various Rounds   359

8.6.4 Strength of MD5   360

8.7   Secure Hash Algorithm (SHA-1)   361

8.7.1 Difference between MD5 and SHA-1   365

8.7.2 Various Upgrades of SHA   365

8.8   Digital Signature Schemes   366

8.8.1 RSA Digital Signature Scheme   366

8.8.2 ElGamal's Digital Signature Scheme   368

8.8.3 Digital Signature Algorithm (DSA)   372

8.9   Exercises   377

Chapter 9:   Centralized Authentication Service   381

9.1   Introduction   381

9.2   Centralized Authentication Service   381

9.3   Motivation for Centralized Authentication Service   382

9.4   Simple Authentication Exchange in Open
        Environment   383

	9.4.1 Problems with Simple Authentication Exchange	384
	9.4.2 Full-Service Kerberos Environment (Kerberos Realm)	386
	9.4.3 Kerberos Version 4	386
9.5	Architecture of Kerberos V.4	387
	9.5.1 Inter-Kerberos Authentication	392
	9.5.2 Kerberos Version 5 Authentication Sequence	394
	9.5.3 Differences between Kerberos V.4 and Kerberos V.5	396
9.6	Exercises	397

Chapter 10:	**Public Key Infrastructure (PKI)**	**399**
10.1	Introduction	399
10.2	Format of X.509 Certificate	400
	10.2.1 Version.3 Extensions	402
10.3	Hierarchical Organization of Certification Authorities (CAs)	403
10.4	Creation of Certificates' Chain for CA's Signature Verification	404
10.5	Revocation of X.509 Certificates	404
	10.5.1 Rules for Revocation	405
10.6	Authentication Procedures Defined in X.509	406
10.7	Exercises	407

Chapter 11:	**Pretty Good Privacy**	**409**
11.1	Introduction	409
11.2	Services Supported by Pretty Good Privacy (PGP)	409
	11.2.1 Implementation of the Security Services in PGP	410
	11.2.2 Functions at the Sender End and at the Recipient End	412
	11.2.3 Placement of Compression/Decompression Functions in PGP	414

11.3 Radix-64 (R64) Transformation 414

11.3.1 Segmentation and Reassembly 415

11.4 Concept of the Public Key Ring and Private Key Ring in PGP 415

11.4.1 Fields of the Private Key Ring 416

11.4.2 Generation of Session Keys 416

11.4.3 Use of Key Rings in Authentication 417

11.4.4 Use of Key Rings in Data Confidentiality 418

11.4.5 The Trust Model for Management of Public Keys in PGP 419

11.5 S/Mime (Secure/Multipurpose Internet Mail Extension) 421

11.5.1 S/Mime Functionality 421

11.6 Exercises 424

Chapter 12:   **Internet Security Services**   **425**

12.1 Introduction 425

12.2 Internet Protocol Security (IPSec) 426

12.3 Services Provided by IPSec 426

12.3.1 IPSec Headers 426

12.3.2 Authentication Header (AH) 427

12.3.3 AH Fields 427

12.3.4 Algorithm for Generation of Integrity Check Value (ICV) 428

12.3.5 Encapsulating Security Payload (ESP) 429

12.4 Security Association (SA) 432

12.4.1 SA Parameters 433

12.5 Security Policies 434

12.5.1 Security Policy Database (SPD) 434

12.5.2 Security Association Selectors (SA Selectors) 434

12.5.3 Combining of Security Associations 435

12.5.4 IPSec Protocol Modes 435

12.5.5 Tunnel Mode 436

12.5.6 Anti-Replay Window 438

	12.5.7 IPSec Key Management	439
	12.5.8 Features of Oakley Key-Exchange Protocol	439
12.6	ISAKMP	441
	12.6.1 Payload Types	442
	12.6.2 Important IPSec Documents	443
12.7	Secure Socket Layer/Transport Layer Security (SSL/TLS)	444
	12.7.1 Components of SSL	444
	12.7.2 SSL Handshake Protocol	444
	12.7.3 SSL Change Specs Protocol	444
	12.7.4 SSL Alerts Protocol	445
	12.7.5 SSL Record Protocol	445
	12.7.6 Some Terms Related to SSL	446
	12.7.7 Transport Layer Security (TLS)	447
	12.7.8 TLS Record Protocol	447
	12.7.9 TLS Handshake Protocol	448
12.8	Secure Electronic Transaction	448
	12.8.1 Business Requirements of SET	450
12.9	Key Features of Set	451
	12.9.1 Use of Public Key Certificates in SET	453
	12.9.2 Sequence of Events in SET	453
	12.9.3 Payment Capture	461
12.10	Exercises	462
Chapter 13:	**System Security**	**465**
13.1	Introduction	465
13.2	Intruders	465
13.3	Intrusion Detection	466
	13.3.1 Intrusion Detection Techniques	466
13.4	Password Management	467
13.5	Malicious Programs	467
	13.5.1 Different Phases in the Lifetime of a Virus	468

	13.6	Anti-Virus Scanners	469
		13.6.1 Different Generations of Anti-Virus Scanners	469
	13.7	Worms	469
	13.8	Firewall	470
		13.8.1 Firewall Characteristics	470
		13.8.2 Firewall Techniques to Control Access	471
	13.9	Types of Firewalls	471
		13.9.1 Firewall Configurations	472
	13.10	Trusted Systems	473
	13.11	Exercises	474
Chapter 14:	**Security of Emerging Technology**		**477**
	14.1	Introduction	477
	14.2	Security of Big Data Analytics	478
		14.2.1 Big data analysis can transform security analytics in the following ways:	479
		14.2.2 Big data analytics for security issues and privacy challenges:	480
	14.3	Security of Cloud Computing	481
		14.3.1 Cloud Deployment models:	482
		14.3.2 The three layers of the Cloud computing services model (Software, Platform or Infrastructure (SPI) Model):	483
		14.3.3 Security concerns and challenges of Cloud computing:	485
		14.3.4 Cloud Security as Consumer Service:	485
	14.4	Security of Internet of Things (IoT)	486
		14.4.1 Evolution of IoT	487
		14.4.2 Building Blocks of the Internet of Things (IoT)	487
		14.4.3 Difference between IoT and Machine-to-Machine (M2M)	487
		14.4.4 IoT Layer Models	488

14.4.5 Applications of IoT 489

14.4.6 New Challenges Created by the IoT 491

14.4.7 Security Requirements of the IoT 491

14.4.8 Three Primary Targets of Attack against the IoT 492

14.4.9 Hybrid Encryption Technique 493

14.4.10 Hybrid Encryption Algorithm Based on DES and DSA 494

14.4.11 Advanced Encryption Standard (AES) 495

14.4.12 Requirements for Lightweight Cryptography 496

14.4.13 Lightweight Cryptography in the IoT 497

14.4.14 Prevention of Attacks on IoT 497

14.5 Security of Smart Grids 498

14.5.1 Smart Grid Challenges 498

14.5.2 Smart Grid Layers 499

14.5.3 Information Security Risks and Demands of a Smart Grid 499

14.5.4 Smart Grid Security Objectives 500

14.5.5 The Smart Grid System Can Be Divided into Three Major Systems 500

14.5.6 Types of Security Attacks That Can Compromise the Smart Grid Security 501

14.5.7 Cybersecurity Attacks in a Smart Grid 501

14.6 Security of Scada Control Systems 502

14.6.1 Components of SCADA Systems 503

14.6.2 SCADA System Layers 503

14.6.3 Requirements and Features for the Security of Control Systems 504

14.6.4 Categories for Security Threats to Modern SCADA Systems 505

14.7 Security of Wireless Sensor Networks (WSNs) 505

14.7.1 WSN Layers 506

14.7.2 Security Requirements in WSNs 507

		14.7.3 The Attack Categories in WSNs	507
		14.7.4 Attacks and Defense in WSNs at Different Layers	508
		14.7.5 Security Protocols in WSNs	508
	14.8	Security of Smart City	511
		14.8.1 Challenges and Benefits of Smart City	513
		14.8.2 The security and privacy of information in a smart city	513
	14.9	Security of Blockchain	516
		14.9.1 Features of Blockchain Technology	517
		14.9.2 Benefits and Challenges of Blockchain	518
		14.9.3 Advantages of Blockchain for Security	519
		14.9.4 Security Issues of Blockchain	521
	14.10	Exercises	522
Chapter 15:	**Artificial Intelligence Security**		**525**
	15.1	Introduction	525
	15.2	Machine Learning	526
	15.3	Types of Machine Learning	528
		15.3.1 Supervised Learning	528
		15.3.2 Unsupervised Learning	532
		15.3.3 Semi-supervised Learning	534
		15.3.4 Reinforcement Learning	535
	15.4	Deep Learning	536
		15.4.1 Deep Learning Applications: A Brief Overview	537
		15.4.2 DL Network Layers	538
	15.5	Types of Deep Learning	543
		15.5.1 Multilayer Neural Network	543
		15.5.2 Convolutional Neural Networks (CNN)	544
		15.5.3 Recurrent Neural Networks (RNNs)	550
		15.5.4 Long Short-Term Memory Networks (LSTMs)	551
		15.5.5 Recursive Neural Network (RvNNs)	552

15.5.6 Stacked Autoencoders   553

15.5.7 Extreme Learning Machine (ELM)   554

15.6   AI for Intrusion Detection System   557

15.7   Exercises   560

Bibliography   **563**

Index   **573**

PREFACE

Network Security and Cryptography, Second Edition introduces the basic concepts in computer networks and the latest trends and technologies in cryptography and network security. Primarily intended as a textbook for courses in computer science, electronics and communication, and electrical engineering, the book also serves as a basic reference and refresher for professionals in these areas. Mainly this book is organized into fifteen chapters.

Chapter 1 is an overview of computer networks that defines its various terms and concepts. It also covers the Open Systems Interconnection (OSI) Model, the Transmission Control Protocol/Internetworking Protocol (TCP/IP) Model, the Hierarchical model, computer network equipment, computer network types, and computer network topology.

Chapter 2 covers the mathematical foundations for computer networks including probability fundamentals, random variables, discrete probability models, continuous probability models, transformation of random variables, generating functions, central limit theorem, classification of random processes, statistics of random processes and stationary, time averages of random processes and Ergodicity, multiple random processes, sample random processes, and Kendall's notation.

Chapter 3 is an overview of cryptography that defines its various terms and concepts. It also covers the genetic model of secure communication, OSI security architecture, security attacks, security services, security mechanisms, categorization of security attacks, categorization of cryptographic systems, symmetric encryption model, link encryption, end-to-end encryption, and traffic pattern confidentiality.

Chapter 4 covers the mathematical foundations for cryptography including groups, rings, integral domain and fields, modular arithmetic, residue classes, primes and co-primes, the Euclidean Algorithm and the extended Euclidean Algorithm, the Galois Field, Fermat's little theorem and its corollaries, Euler's totient function, Euler's theorem, prime numbers, discrete logarithms, primitive roots, primality testing, and Chinese remainder theorem.

Chapter 5 provides classical cipher schemes. It contains the Caesar cipher, the mono-alphabetic cipher, Hill cipher, play fair cipher, polyalphabetic cipher, one time pad and rail fence ciphers, rectangular transposition cipher, and steganography.

Chapter 6 discusses modern symmetric ciphers. It covers the concepts of the symmetric cipher, Claude Shannon's theory of diffusion and confusion, the Feistel cipher, the Data Encryption Standard (DES), avalanche effect, differential cryptanalysis attack on the DES, linear cryptanalysis attack on the DES, double DES, meet-in-the-middle attack on double DES, triple DES, block/stream cipher modes of operation, International Data Encryption Algorithm (IDEA), Advanced Encryption Standard (AES), key management in symmetric schemes, and Pseudo-Random Number Generator (PRNG) algorithms.

Chapter 7 addresses public-key cryptography for data confidentiality. It covers requirements of public key cryptography, data confidentiality using public key cryptography, the RSA algorithm, types of attacks against RSA, Diffie-Hellman Key Exchange Algorithm, man-in-the-middle attack against Diffie-Hellman Key exchange algorithm, ElGamal encryption scheme, and elliptic curve cryptography (ECC).

Chapter 8 addresses the authentication schemes including message authentication, authentication services and techniques, digital signature for message authentication; message authentication code (MAC) and secure hash functions, characteristics of hash functions, authentication protocols, birthday paradox, birthday attack against digital signatures, message digest algorithm (MD5), Secure Hash Algorithm (SHA-1), and the Digital Signature Algorithm (DSA).

Chapter 9 covers the concept and details of the Centralized Authentication Service, motivation for the Centralized Authentication Service, the Simple Authentication Exchange in Open Environment, Centralized Authentication Service Kerberos Version 4, Inter-Kerberos Authentication Service, and Authentication Service Kerberos Version 5.

Chapter 10 discusses the public key infrastructure (PKI) including X.509 public key certificate; Hierarchical Organization of Certification Authorities

(CAs), creation of certificates' chain for CA's Signature Verification; revocation of X.509 certificates, and X.509 authentication protocols.

Chapter 11 explains in detail all aspects of Pretty Good Privacy including Email service PGP, services supported by PGP, components of PGP, concept of R64 transformation, the concept of public key ring and private key ring, the trust model of key management in PGP, Email service secure Internet mail extension, and functions supported by S/MIME.

Chapter 12 discusses the Internet Security Services including Internet Protocol Security (IPSec), services provided by IPSec, Authentication Header (AH), Encapsulating Security Payload, the concept of Integrity Check Value (ICV) in IPSec, AH and ESP Packet Formats in IPV.4, the concept of Security Association (SA); Security Policy and Security Policy Database (SPD), combining of SAs; IPSec Protocol Modes e.g., Transport Mode Tunnel Mode, and Wildcard Mode. It covers the Oakley Key Exchange Protocol in IPSec, Secure Socket Layer (SSL) Protocol and its components, Transport Layer Security (TLS) Protocol and its components, the Secure Electronic Transaction (SET) Protocol, and sequence of events in SET message exchange, including concepts of dual signature and payment gateways.

Chapter 13 covers system security including intrusion, intrusion detection techniques, password management, malicious programs, different phases in the life of a virus, types of virus and antivirus scanners, worms, firewalls (characteristics, types, and configurations), and trusted systems.

Chapter 14 provides the security aspects of emerging technology. It contains big data analytics, cloud computing, Internet of Things (IoT), the Smart Grid, supervisory control and data acquisition (SCADA), control systems, and wireless sensor networks (WSN).

Chapter 15 is an overview of perspective and ideas on Artificial Intelligence (AI) security. It covers Machine Learning (ML), types of ML, Deep Learning (DL), and types of DL, AI for Intrusion Detection System (IDS).

Finally, the Bullet Point Reading (BPR) technique is used in the book to simplify the concepts and to enforce the understanding and learning.

Sarhan M. Musa
Cypress, TX
July 2022

CHAPTER 1

OVERVIEW OF COMPUTER NETWORKS

Chapter Outline

1.1 Introduction Signed Numbers

1.2 Open Systems Interconnection (OSI) Model

1.3 Transmission Control Protocol/Internetworking Protocol (TCP/IP) Model

1.4 Hierarchical Model

1.5 Computer Network Equipment

1.6 Computer Network Types

1.7 Computer Network Topology

1.8 Exercises

1.1 INTRODUCTION

Computer networks have grown rapidly in recent years due to critical users' needs in their daily living. A computer network is a collection of devices (nodes) connected to each other (wired or wireless) in order to allow every device to communicate, access, and share its resources with other devices. This chapter gives a basic introduction and overview of computer networking to help in understanding and learning network security.

1.2   OPEN SYSTEMS INTERCONNECTION (OSI) MODEL

The Open Systems Interconnection (OSI) is a reference model that was created by the International Organization for Standardization (ISO). The OSI model defines a networking conceptual framework to implement protocols in seven layers. It is an ideal tool for learning how networks function. The advantages for the OSI model to be a layered network model are to simplify the learning of the network and reduce its complexity, accelerate evolution, standardize interfaces, ensure interoperability, and facilitate modular engineering. Figure 1.1 shows the OSI model.

OSI Model				
Layer Number	Layer Name	Layer Type	Encapsulation / Protocol Data Unit (PDU)	Function
7	Application	Host	Data	Provides network services to user applications. This layer does not provide service to any other layer.
6	Presentation	Host	Data	Ensures common data format between computers. Data representation, encryption and decryption, convert machine dependent data, machine independent data, compression.
5	Session	Host	Data	Establishes, manages, and terminates sessions. Maintains communications sessions between Host layer applications.
4	Transport	Host	Segment	Provides a reliable delivery of segments between points on a network. Provides end-to-end reliable transport, error checking, and flow control.
3	Network	Media	Packet	Provides connectivity and path selection based on IP addresses. Provides addressing, routing, and delivery of packets between points on a network.
2	Data Link	Media	Frame	Provides a reliable direct point-to-point data connection. Provides access to the media and addressing based on physical MAC addresses.

OSI Model				
Layer Number	**Layer Name**	**Layer Type**	**Encapsulation / Protocol Data Unit (PDU)**	**Function**
1	Physical	Media	Bits and Signaling	Converts the data into the stream of electric or analog pulses that will actually cross the transmission medium and oversees the transmission of the data. It is responsible for characteristics of the signaling as voltage levels, timing and clock rates, maximum transmission distances, and the physical connectors used. It activates and deactivates physical link.

FIGURE 1.1 The OSI model.

The Data Link Layer has two sub-layers, the Logical Link Control (LLC) and the Media Access Control (MAC). The Logical Link Control (LLC) is responsible for error correction, flow control, and Service Access Points. The Media Access Control (MAC) is responsible for physical addressing and providing access to shared physical media (wire). It is assigned by the manufacturer. The Ethernet is a standardized way of connecting computers to create a network. Figure 1.2 illustrates the OSI model devices and protocols.

Layer Number	**Layer Name**	**Network Device**	**Protocols**
7	Application	PC	• Simple Mail Transport Protocol (SMTP) • Terminal emulation protocol (Telnet) • File Transfer Protocol (FTP) • Trivial File Transfer Protocol (TFTP) • HyperText transfer Protocol (HTTP)
6	Presentation	PC	• ASCII (text) • EBCDIC (text) • JPEG (image) • GIF (image) • TIFF (image) • MPEG (sound/video) • Quicktime (sound/video)
5	Session	PC	• Session Control Protocol (SPC) • Remote Procedure Call (RPC) from Unix • Zone Information Protocol (ZIP) from AppleTalk

Layer Number	Layer Name	Network Device	Protocols
4	Transport	PC	• Transmission Control Protocol (TCP) from IP • User Datagram Protocol (UDP) from IP • SPX
3	Network	Router or Multi-Layer Switch	• Internet Protocol (IP) • IPX, RIP, IGRP, OSPF
2	Data Link	Switch or Bridge, NIC card	• Ethernet/IEEE 802.3 (includes Fast Ethernet) • 802.3z (Gigabit Ethernet) • Token Ring /IEEE 802.5 • FDDI (from ANSI) • High-Level Data-link Control (HDLC) • Point-to-Point Protocol (PPP) • Frame Relay
1	Physical	Hub or Repeater, Cabling: UTP, coaxial cable, fiber optic cable	• Category 3 cabling • Category 5 cabling • EIA/TIA-232 • EIA/TIA-449 • V.35

FIGURE 1.2 The OSI model devices and protocols.

1.3 TRANSMISSION CONTROL PROTOCOL/ INTERNETWORKING PROTOCOL (TCP/IP) MODEL

The Transmission Control Protocol/Internetworking Protocol (TCP/IP) is the networking model used in today's Internet. The TCP/IP is the basic protocol system by which computers on a network talk to each other. It is a logical address, and without TCP/IP, networks wouldn't work. The TCP/IP consists of four layers—Application, Transport, Internet, and Network Access—as shown in Figure 1.3.

The TCP/IP Model			
Layer Number	Layer Name	Protocols	Function
4	Application layer	FTP, Telnet, SMPT, DNS, SNMP, HTTP	Provides services to user such as electronic email, file transfer, and remote login.
3	Transport	TCP, UDP, SCTP	Provides the delivery of a message from one application program running on the host to another.

The TCP/IP Model			
Layer Number	Layer Name	Protocols	Function
2	Network layer or Internet layer	IP, ICMP, IGMP, ARP, RARP	Provides the delivery of individual packets from the source host to the destination host.
1	Network Interface or Network Access or Physical/Link	Ethernet - IEEE 802.3 10BaseT 100BaseTX 1000BaseT Wifi - IEEE 802.11b/g/n RS232	Provides an interface with the physical network. Formats the data for the transmission medium and addresses data for the subnet based on physical hardware addresses. Provides error control for data delivered on the physical network.

FIGURE 1.3 The TCP/IP model.

A TCP/IP can provide the following operations:

- Responsible for dividing messages into controllable portions of data that will send efficiently through the transmission medium.

- Responsible to interface with the network adapter hardware.

- Capability of addressing data. The source device must be capable of targeting data to a destination. The destination device must be capable of recognizing a message that it is supposed to receive.

- Capability of routing data to the subnet of the destination device, even if the source subnet and the destination subnet are in different physical networks.

- Responsible for performing error control, flow control, and acknowledgment. For reliable communication, the sending and receiving network devices must be able to identify and correct faulty transmissions and control the flow of data.

- Responsible for accepting data from an application and sending it to the network.

- Responsible for receiving data from the network and sending it to an application.

- Figure 1.4 illustrates the TCP/IP model mapped to the OSI model.

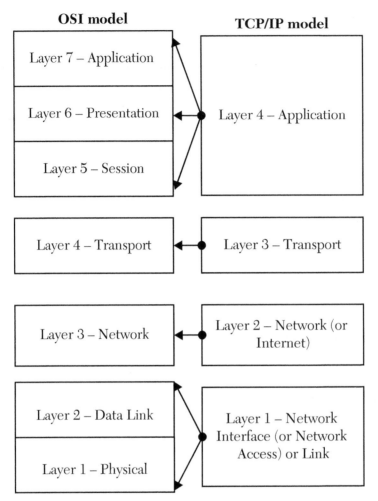

FIGURE 1.4 The TCP/IP model Mapped to the OSI model.

The common protocols can be summarized as below:

- **Domain Name System (DNS):** DNS is the TCP/IP facility that lets us use names rather than numbers to refer to host computers. For example, 74.125.224.147 is www.google.com. DNS allows the IP addresses to change without affecting connectivity.

- **Address Resolution Protocol (ARP):** ARP is used to convert an IP address to a physical address such as an Ethernet address. ARP is a low-level network protocol, operating at Layer 2 of the OSI model. When any device wishes to send data to another target device over the Ethernet, it must first determine the MAC address of that target, given its IP address. ARP resolves or discovers the appropriate destination MAC (layer 2) address to use by using a destination IP address. Map a Layer 3 address to a Layer 2 address.

- **Dynamic Host Configuration Protocol (DHCP):** DHCP automatically configures the IP address for every host on a network, thus ensuring that each host has a valid, unique IP address. DHCP even automatically reconfigures IP addresses as hosts come and go. DHCP can save a network administrator many hours of tedious configuration work.

- **Internet Protocol (IP):** IP is a routable protocol that uses IP addresses to deliver packets to network devices. IP is an intentionally unreliable protocol, so it doesn't guarantee delivery of information.

- **Internet Control Message Protocol (ICMP):** It provides control and feedback messages between IP devices. ICMP sends and receives diagnostic messages. ICMP is the basis of the everywhere ping command. It sends query and error reporting messages.

- **Internet Group Management Protocol (IGMP):** Used to multicast (has more than one destination) messages to multiple IP addresses at once.

- **Layer 2 Protocols** are responsible for providing a reliable link between two directly connected nodes, by detecting and possibly correcting errors that may occur in the physical layer. Some of the common Layer 2 Protocols today are:

  ARP – Address Resolution Protocol
  STP – Spanning Tree Protocol
  SPB – Shortest Path Bridging

- **Layer 3 Protocols** are responsible for providing the functional and procedural means of transferring variable length data sequences (called datagrams) from a source to a destination host connected via one or more networks, while maintaining the quality of service standards.

Some of the common Layer 3 Protocols today are:
IP – Internet Protocol
OSPF – Open Shortest Path First
RIP – Routing Information Protocol
ICMP – Internet Control Message Protocol

These protocols enable routers to route data between networks via the shortest path, or alternate paths, if one path is unavailable. They also define how routers across networks can dynamically share this information so all routers are aware of the available paths.

- **Layer 4 Protocols** are responsible for the reliable transport between nodes on the network. These protocols ensure that a packet makes it to its destination—kind of like a return receipt. TCP is the transport layer protocol for IP.

  Some of the common Layer 4 Protocols today are:
  TCP – Transport Control Protocol; this is the transport layer for IP. It ensures that IP packets are delivered to their destination.
  UDP – Unified Datagram Protocol; this is a lighter weight transport layer for IP. It does not provide the overhead of error checking for simple queries like DNS or NTP.
  SPX – Sequenced Package Exchange; this is the transport layer for IPX. It ensures that IPX packets are delivered to their destination.

- **Open Shortest Path First (OSPF):** Link-state, hierarchical IGP routing algorithm proposed as a successor to RIP in the Internet community. OSPF features include least-cost routing, multipath routing, and load balancing. OSPF was derived from an early version of the Intermediate System to Intermediate System (IS-IS) protocol.

- **Intermediate System-Intermediate System (ISIS):** One of a family of IP Routing protocols, it is an Interior Gateway Protocol (IGP) for the Internet, used to distribute IP routing information throughout a single Autonomous System (AS) in an IP network. IS-IS is a link-state routing protocol, which means that the routers exchange topology information with their nearest neighbors. The topology information is flooded throughout the AS, so that every router within the AS has a complete picture of the topology of the AS. This picture is then used to calculate end-to-end paths through the AS, normally using a variant of the Dijkstra algorithm. Therefore, in a link-state routing protocol, the next hop address to which data is forwarded is determined by choosing the best end-to-end path to the eventual destination.

- **Autonomous System (AS):** Collection of networks under a common administration sharing a common routing strategy. Autonomous systems are subdivided by areas.

- **Spanning Tree Protocol (STP):** It is a Layer 2 Protocol that runs on bridges and switches. The specification for STP is IEEE 802.1D. The primary purpose of STP is to ensure that the network does not create redundant loops.

- **Shortest Path Bridging (SPB):** SPB is the IEEE 802.1aq specification for enabling multipath routing in the data center. It allows all paths to be active with multiple equal cost paths, provides much larger layer 2 topologies, supports faster convergence times, and improves the efficiency by allowing traffic to load share across all paths of a mesh network.

1.4 HIERARCHICAL MODEL

A Hierarchical model simplifies design, implementation, and management of the network. As shown in Figure 1.5, a Hierarchical model consists of three layers: Core, Distribution, and Access.

Hierarchical model		
Layer Number	Layer Name	Function
3	Core or Backbone	It is a high-speed backbone that is designed to switch packets as quickly as possible to optimize communication transport within the network. It provides fast and efficient data transport. It represents the enterprise in a network that is available to end users (clients). Network devices used in the core layer are: High-speed routers or Multi-layer switches.
2	Distribution or Aggregation	It is a separation layer between the access and core layers and a connection point between the diverse access sites and the core layer. It determines the quickest, shortest, and least expensive route the data need to pass through to arrive at the destination. It defines the local policies and local routing. Distribution layer devices control access to resources that are available at the core layer in order to use bandwidth efficiently. Network devices used in the distribution layer are Routers.

Hierarchical model		
Layer Number	Layer Name	Function
1	Access	It represents the end users' connection to the network. The end users' data transmissions access the network at the access layer. It is used to control user (client) access to the network resources. Access layer devices control traffic by localizing service requests to the access media. Network devices used in the access layer are Switches, Bridges, or Hubs.

FIGURE 1.5 The Hierarchical model.

1.5 COMPUTER NETWORK EQUIPMENT

Network equipment includes network devices that connect directly to a network segment. There are two types of devices (equipment):

▪ **End devices or user devices**

User devices are network devices that provide services directly to the user (host), Examples of end devices are scanners, fax machines, PCs, laptops, printers, servers, iPhones, smart TVs, and iPads.

▪ **Network Devices (Hardware)**

Network devices provide transport for the data that needs to be transferred between end users' devices.

▪ **Network interface cards (NICs)**

- Network interface cards (NICs) are printed circuit boards that are installed in workstations to enable systems to connect to the network.

- They provide the physical connection between the network cable and the workstation. In addition, they possess the circuitry necessary to gain access to the network.

- The NIC formats information from the workstation so that it can be transmitted across the network. The NIC operates at the physical layer (Layer 1) of the OSI model, and it is also considered a data link layer device. Part of the NIC's function is to format information between the workstation and the network, and also to control the transmission of data onto the wire.

FIGURE 1.6 NIC card.

- The NIC converts the data to electrical impulses if copper wire is used, or to light signals if a fiber-optic cable is used. Each NIC carries a unique Media Access Control (MAC) address. The NIC controls user (host) access to the networking medium. Figure 1.6 shows a NIC card.

Repeaters

Repeaters work against attenuation (degradation of signal) by cleaning and repeating signals that they receive on a network, as shown in Figure 1.7. A repeater enables signals to travel longer distances over a network.

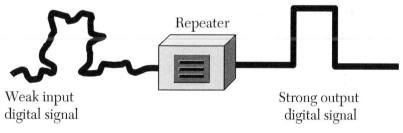

Weak input
digital signal

Repeater

Strong output
digital signal

FIGURE 1.7 A Repeater.

Repeaters operate at the Physical layer (Layer 1) of the OSI model. They cannot connect different network architectures. Also, they can't reformat, resize, or manipulate the data signal. A repeater is used to re-time, re-shape, and re-amplify the data signal to its original shape. A repeater receives data on one port and repeats them on the other port. It can be used as a connection device on a network. Figure 1.8 shows a repeater on a network.

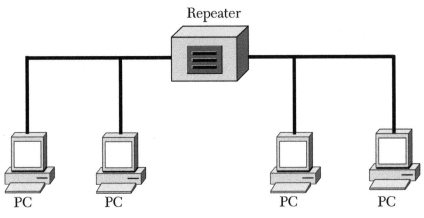

FIGURE 1.8 Repeater in the network.

- **Hub**

  - A hub is a multiple port repeater. It generates and re-times network signals. A hub connects devices on an Ethernet twisted pair network.

  - It forms a central point on a network where the cables of other network devices come together at its ports.

  - Hubs operate at the physical layer (Layer 1) of the OSI model.

  - A hub does not perform any tasks besides signal regeneration. A hub receives data on one port and transmits it on all the other ports. Figure 1.9 shows a network with a hub in the center.

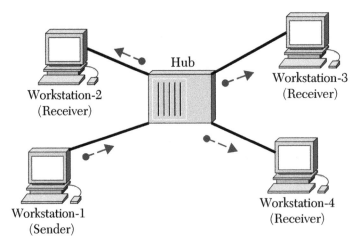

FIGURE 1.9 A hub in the network.

There are two types of Hubs:

- **Active hub:** It amplifies or repeats signals that pass through it; it provides a path for the data signals and regenerates the signal before it forwards it to all of the connected devices.

- **Passive hub:** It just connects cables on a network and provides no signal regeneration; it provides only a pathway for the electrical signals to travel along.

Bridges

- A Bridge is a network device that connects multiple network segments. It breaks networks into separate segments and directs the transmission to the appropriate segment in order to filter traffic between network segments. Bridges reduce network traffic by keeping local traffic on the local segment. A Bridge examines the destination Media Access Control (MAC) address (hardware address) in order to either forward or discard the frame. It operates at the Data Link layer (Layer 2) of the OSI model.

- Network Bridging allows two or more communication networks or network segments to create and aggregate a Network. Bridging is different than routing, which allows networks to communicate independently as separate networks.

- A Bridge is more intelligent than a hub. A Bridge maintains a MAC address table known as a "Bridge Table," which is stored on the Bridge memory.

Switches

- A switch is a multi-port bridge, and it creates a network.

- A switch is a network device with several inputs and outputs leading to and from the hosts that the switch interconnects.

- A switch allows multiple physical LAN segments to be interconnected into single larger networks.

- A switch connects devices on twisted pair networks, and it forwards data to its destination by using the MAC address embedded in each packet.

- A switch takes packets that arrive on an input and forwards them to the right output so that they will reach their appropriate destination.

- A switch increases network performance by reducing the number of frames transmitted to the rest of the network. It operates at the Data Link layer (Layer 2) of the OSI model.

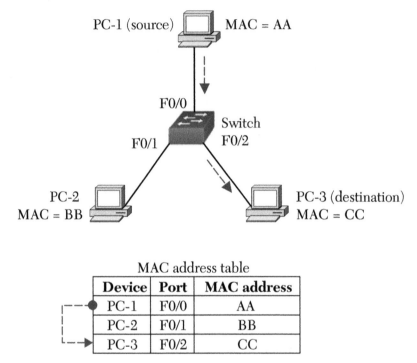

MAC address table

Device	Port	MAC address
PC-1	F0/0	AA
PC-2	F0/1	BB
PC-3	F0/2	CC

FIGURE 1.10 Sending data through a switch.

- **Routers**

  - Routers connect networks.

  - A router acts as a dispatcher, choosing the best path for information to travel so it is received quickly.

  - They connect multiple segments and multiple networks.

  - Routers provide filtering and network traffic control on LANs and WANs.

  - They operate at the Network layer (Layer 3) of the OSI model.

  - Routers use the logical address (IP Address).

  - Internetworks are Networks connected by multiple routers.

- A router is a type of internetworking device that passes data packets between networks based on layer 3 addresses.

▪ **Gateways**

- Gateways are usually a combination of hardware and software.

- They translate between different protocol suites; that is, they convert information from one protocol stack to another.

- Gateways have the most negative effect on network performance.

- Packets must be rebuilt not just at the lower levels but at the very upper levels so that actual data content can be converted into a format the destination can process.

- Gateways create the most latency.

▪ **Firewalls**

- Firewalls act as a security guard between the Internet and your local area network (LAN). All network traffic into and out of the LAN must pass through the firewall, which prevents unauthorized access to the network.

- Firewalls protect a private network's resources from users in other networks.

- They provide controlled data access between networks. Firewalls can be hardware or software.

▪ **Access points (APs)**

- An AP is a wireless LAN transceiver that can act as a center point of a standalone wireless network or as connection point between wireless and wired networks.

- It provides cell-based areas where hosts can connect to the network by associating with the AP.

- An AP operates at the Physical layer (Layer 1) and Data Link layer (Layer 2) of the OSI model.

▪ **Servers**

- A server is a device that handles user requests for access to computer and network resources.

- It provides authentication, authorization, and accounting services for an enterprise.

Media Access Control (MAC)

- A MAC address may be called a "Physical address" or "Hardware address" or "Ethernet address."

- It is found at the Data Link layer (Layer 2) of the OSI model.

- Bridges and switches use the MAC address to make forwarding decisions within a network or subnetwork.

- The MAC address consists of six bytes.

Carrier Sense Multiple Access with Collision Detection (CSMA/CD):

- CSMA/CD is used by the Ethernet to prevent data packets from colliding on the network.

- CSMA/CD allows any station connected to a network to transmit anytime there is not already a transmission on the wire.

- The *collision domain* is the physical area in which a frame collision might occur; for example, routers, switches, bridges, and gateways do segment networks, and thus they create separate collision domains.

- A Hub does not divide the collision domain.

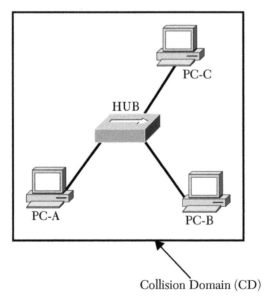

FIGURE 1.11 A Hub does not divide the collision domain.

- A switch divides the collision domains. Therefore, every computer connected to the switch exists in its own collision domain. This will enhance the network performance.

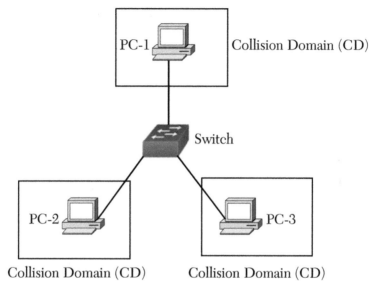

FIGURE 1.12 The switch divides the collision domain.

- **Internet Protocol (IP) address**

  - The IP address may be called the "Logical address."

  - It is called the logical address when TCP/IP is used on an internetwork.

  - Routers use the IP address to route packets to the correct network segment.

  - It is found at the Network layer (Layer 3) of the OSI model.

  - The IP address is formed of 4 Bytes (32 bits).

  - 1 Byte = 1 Octet = 8 bits.

  - IP addresses are written using decimal numbers separated by dots.

IP address format:

Byte • Byte • Byte • Byte

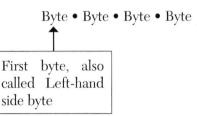

First byte, also called Left-hand side byte

- Every byte of the IP address is equal to a decimal number in the range of 0 (minimum value) to 255 (maximum value).

- The IP address is a combination of the Host Portion (H) and Network Portion (N).

- **IP Classes:**

  - IP addresses are grouped into five different IP classes (A, B, C, D, and E) depending on the value of the first byte on the left-hand side in every IP address.

  - Only classes A, B, and C are available for commercial use. From the class of the IP address, the N and H portions can be determined.

  - The *network IP* and the *broadcast IP* of the IP address can be determined by the N and H portions of the IP address.

Class A:

Format: N • H • H • H

In Binary: 0 is the leading bit pattern, also called the high order bit

$$\underbrace{\mathbf{0}\text{xxx xxxx}}_{N} • \underbrace{\text{xxxx xxxx} • \text{xxxx xxxx} • \text{xxxx xxxx}}_{H}$$

Where x = 0 or 1

In Decimal: $\underbrace{0-127}_{N} • \underbrace{0-255 • 0-255 • 0-255}_{H}$

Subnet Mask: 255 • 0 • 0 • 0

Purpose: reserved for governments or large organizations
               127 is reserved for loopback address and testing

Number of bits of network / number of bits of host = 7 / 24

Maximum number of supported hosts = $2^{\#H} - 2 = 2^{24}\text{-}2$

Class B:

Format: N • N • H • H

In Binary: 10 is the leading bit pattern, also called the high order bit

$$\underbrace{\mathbf{10}xx\ xxxx \bullet xxxx\ xxxx}_{N} \bullet \underbrace{xxxx\ xxxx \bullet xxxx\ xxxx}_{H}$$

Where x = 0 or 1

In Decimal: $\underbrace{128 - 191 \bullet 0 - 255}_{N} \bullet \underbrace{0 - 255 \bullet 0 - 255}_{H}$

Subnet Mask: 255 • 255 • 0 • 0

Purpose: reserved for medium size organizations

Number of bits of network / number of bits of host = 14 / 16

Maximum number of supported hosts = $2^{\#H} - 2 = 2^{16} - 2$

Class C:

Format: N • N • N • H

In Binary: 110 is the leading bit pattern, also called the high order bit

$$\underbrace{\mathbf{110}x\ xxxx \bullet xxxx\ xxxx \bullet xxxx\ xxxx}_{N} \bullet \underbrace{xxxx\ xxxx}_{H}$$

Where x = 0 or 1

In Decimal: $\underbrace{192 - 223 \bullet 0 - 255 \bullet 0 - 255}_{N} \bullet \underbrace{0 - 255}_{H}$

Subnet Mask: 255 • 255 • 255 • 0

Purpose: reserved for relatively small organizations

Number of bits of network / number of bits of host = 22 / 8

Maximum number of supported hosts = $2^{\#H} - 2 = 2^{8} - 2$

Class D:

In Binary: 1110 is the leading bit pattern, also called the high order bit

$$\mathbf{1110}\ xxxx \bullet xxxx\ xxxx \bullet xxxx\ xxxx \bullet xxxx\ xxxx$$

Where x = 0 or 1

In Decimal: 224 – 239 • 0 – 255 • 0 – 255 • 0 – 255

Purpose: reserved for multicast (not for commercial)

Class E:

In Binary: 1111 is the leading bit pattern, also called the high order bit

$$\mathbf{1111}\ xxxx \bullet xxxx\ xxxx \bullet xxxx\ xxxx \bullet xxxx\ xxxx$$

Where x = 0 or 1

In Decimal: 240 – 255 • 0 – 255 • 0 – 255 • 0 – 255

Purpose: reserved for research and experimental

1.6   COMPUTER NETWORK TYPES

- **Personal Area Network (PAN)**

  - A PAN is a computer network that provides data transmission among devices that are located typically within a 10-meter radius close to a single user for a location on a body or in a room.

- **Local Area Network (LAN)**

  - A LAN is a data communications network which is in a geographically limited region (typically within a 1-mile radius—buildings/campus) allowing many users to access high bandwidth media.

  - A LAN connects different devices and provides full-time connectivity.

  - LAN traffic is transmitted in three ways:

    1. Broadcast: data packets that are sent to all nodes on a network.

    2. Multicast: single packets copied by the network and sent to a specific subset of network addresses.

    3. Unicast: message sent to a single network destination.

- **Virtual Local Area Network (VLAN)**

  - The VLAN groups hosts with a common set of requirements (common broadcast domain) regardless of their physical location in the internetwork.

  - It has the same attributes as a physical LAN, but is configured via software (virtual).

  - To physically replicate the functions of a VLAN would require a separate, parallel collection of network equipment.

  - The VLAN improves performance and security in the switched network by controlling the broadcast propagation.

  - It is a logical broadcast domain that can cover multiple physical LAN segments.

  - It enables switches to create multiple broadcast domains within a switched network.

- **Metropolitan Area Network (MAN)**

  - MAN is a network that covers a distance typically 10 km greater than LAN but lesser than WAN for a location such as a city or town.

- **WAN-Wide Area Network**

  - WAN covers a large distance, typically up to a 100 km away for one or more cities or countries.

  - The speeds are limited by cost and bandwidth.

- **SAN-Storage Area Network**

  - SAN is a high-speed network of storage devices that connects them to servers.

1.7 COMPUTER NETWORK TOPOLOGY

Computer networks are connected based on a topology. Topology means how network equipment is arranged in order to communicate. It defines the structure of the network. There are two types of topology: physical topology and logical topology.

- **Physical topology:** the way in which the devices of the network are physically connected. It is the actual layout of the wires or media.

- **Logical topology:** the way the hosts access the media to send data. It shows the flow of data on a network.

The most common topologies are described as follows:

1. Point-to-Point Topology:

A point-to-point link is simply topology in which one device has one connection (link) to another device. Each device can add a secondary link connection, but if the device fails, then there will be no connectivity. It is used mainly for WAN links.

Router-A

Router-B

FIGURE 1.13 Point to Point topology.

2. Bus Topology:

Bus topology is a topology in which all devices are connected to a single thick backbone cable. If the backbone cable fails, then the network goes down. If a cable linking the device to the backbone cable fails, then only that device will lose connection.

10Base-2 (ThinNet) and 10Base-5 (ThickNet) are popular Ethernet cabling options in bus topology.

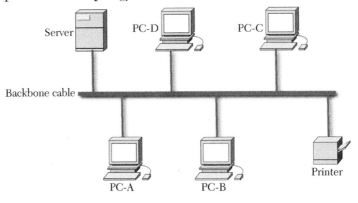

FIGURE 1.14 Bus topology.

3. Star Topology:

Each network device in a star topology is connected to a central device such as a hub or switch or router. If one of the cables to the devices fails, then only that device becomes disconnected. Devices typically connect to the hub with the Unshielded Twisted Pair (UTP) Ethernet. It is the most commonly used physical topology in the Ethernet LANs.

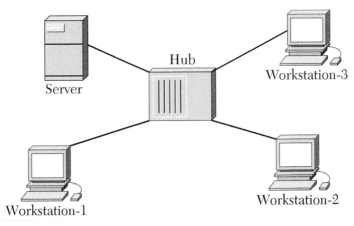

FIGURE 1.15 A Star topology.

4. Ring Topology:

A ring topology connects hosts in the form of a ring or a circle. Every device in the ring topology has exactly two neighbors for communication purposes. All messages travel through a ring in the same direction (either clockwise or counter-clockwise). A failure in any device or any cable breaks the loop and can take down the entire network.

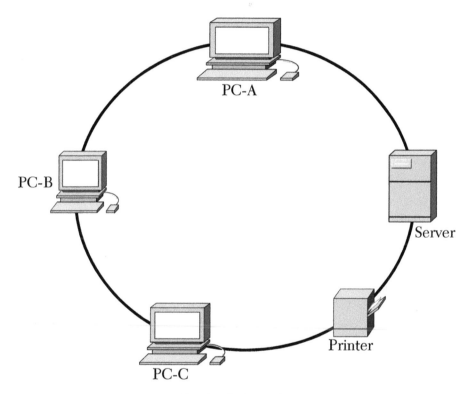

FIGURE 1.16 Ring topology.

5. Mesh Topology:

A mesh topology allows multiple access links between network devices. A mesh topology provides network reliability because whenever one network device fails, the network does not stop operations; it finds a bypass to the failed node, and the network continues to operate. A mesh topology can handle high amounts of traffic, because multiple devices can transmit data simultaneously. In a mesh topology, every device has a directed point-to-point link to every other device. The link carries traffic only between the two devices it connects.

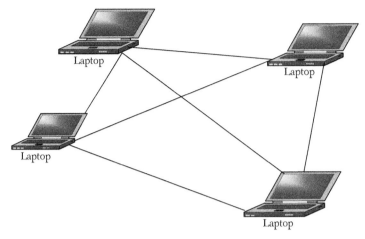

FIGURE 1.17 Mesh Network topology.

6. Tree (Hierarchical) Topology:

A tree topology puts the network devices in a hierarchical structure. A Central device on the top level of the hierarchy is connected to one or more other devices that are one level lower in the hierarchy. A tree topology is a combination of a Bus and a Star topology.

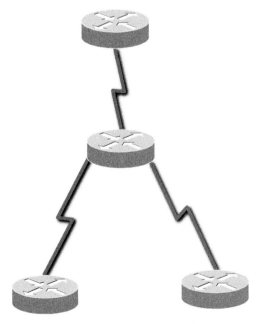

FIGURE 1.18 Tree Network topology.

7. Hybrid Topology:

A hybrid topology is an integration of two or more different previously illustrated topologies connected to each other.

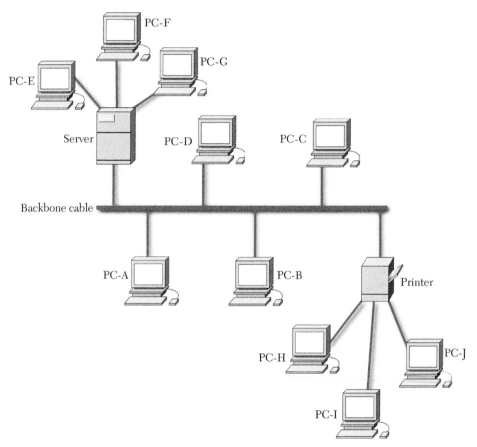

FIGURE 1.19 Hybrid topology.

Simplex, Half-Duplex, and Full-Duplex Communications modes:

- **Half-duplex communications:** Devices can send and receive signals, but not at the same time.
- **Full-duplex communications:** Devices can send and receive signals simultaneously.
- **Simplex:** One of the devices is always the sender, while the other device is always the receiver.

1.8 EXERCISES

1. What are the seven layers of the OSI model?

2. What are the four layers of the TCP/IP model?

3. What are the three layers of the hierarchical model?

4. Find the Protocol data unit (PDU)—encapsulation—of each layer of the TCP/IP model.

5. Match each layer of the TCP/IP and OSI models in correct layer order.

6. Number of bits in an IP address = _____

7. Number of octets in an IP address = _____

8. Name the class reserved for research and experiment: _____

9. Identify the communication between two devices which can be simplex, half-duplex, or full-duplex, as shown in the following figures:

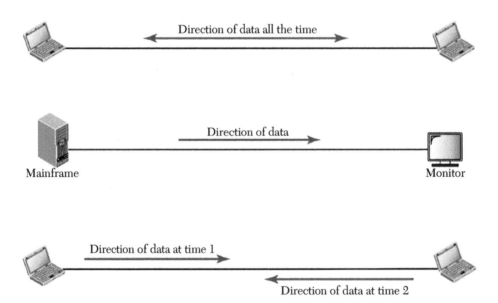

10. What is the difference between LAN and WAN?

11. For Class A:

    A. Range of network number in decimal _____

    B. Most left-hand binary numbers start with _____.

    C. The 127 is used for _____.

    D. Write the IP address in N and H form

    ____ • _____ • _____ • _____

    E. Write the default subnet Mask address

    _____ • _____ • _____ • _____

    F. Number of Network bits = _____

    G. Number of Host bits = _____

12. For Class B:

    A. Range of network number in decimal _____

    B. Most left-hand binary numbers start with _____

    C. Write the IP address in N and H form:

    ____ • _____ • _____ • _____

    D. Default subnet Mask address:

    E. _____ • _____ • _____ • _____

    F. Number of Network bits = _____

    G. Number of Host bits = _____

13. For Class C:

    A. Range of network number in decimal _____

    B. Most left-hand binary numbers start with _____

    C. Write the IP address in N and H form:

    ____ • _____ • _____ • _____

    D. Write the default subnet Mask address:

    _____ • _____ • _____ • _____

    E. Number of Network bits = _____

    F. Number of Host bits = _____

14. Identify the type of topology in each of the following connections:

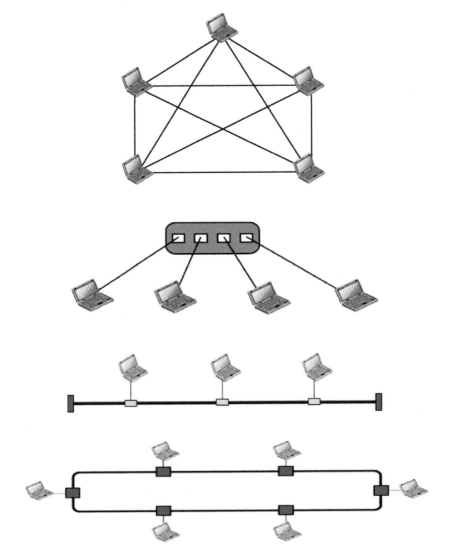

15. What is the meaning of the CSMA/CD and the collision domain?

16. At what layer of the OSI model do the following devices function: routers, switches, and hubs?

17. What is the difference between the MAC address and the IP address?

18. At what layer of the OSI model do the MAC address and the IP address operate?

CHAPTER 2

MATHEMATICAL FOUNDATIONS FOR COMPUTER NETWORKS

Chapter Outline

2.1 Introduction

2.2 Probability Fundamentals

2.3 Random Variables

2.4 Discrete Probability Models

2.5 Continuous Probability Models

2.6 Transformation of Random Variables

2.7 Generating Functions

2.8 Central Limit Theorem

2.9 Classification of Random Processes

2.10 Statistics of Random Processes and Stationary

2.11 Time Averages of Random Processes and Ergodicity

2.12 Multiple Random Processes

2.13 Sample Random Processes

2.14 Kendall's Notation

2.15 Queueing Networks

2.16 Exercises

2.1 INTRODUCTION

The most essential branches of mathematical concepts in computer networks security are probability and random variables, stochastic process, and queueing theory. The *theory of probability* is used to quantify uncertainty, and it provides essential techniques in analyzing telecommunications, computer network systems, and network security.

Most network communications signals we deal with in practice are random (unpredictable or erratic) and not deterministic. Random signals are encountered in one form or another in every practical communication system. They occur in network communications both as information-conveying signals and as unwanted noise signals.

A *random quantity* is one having values which are regulated in some probabilistic way.

Therefore, our work with random quantities must begin with the theory of probability, which is the mathematical discipline that deals with the statistical characterization of random signals and random processes.

The concept of *random* (or *stochastic*) *process* is the generalization of a random variable to include another dimension—time. While a random variable depends on the outcome of a random experiment, a random process depends on both the outcome of a random experiment and time. In other words, if a random variable X is time-dependent, $X(t)$ is known as a *random process*. Thus, a random process may be regarded as any process that changes with time and is controlled by some probabilistic law. For example, the number of customers N in a queueing system varies with time; hence $N(t)$ is a random process.

Figure 2.1 portrays typical *realizations* or *sample functions* of a random process. From this figure, we notice that a random process is a mapping from the sample space into an ensemble (family, set, collection) of time functions known as sample functions. Here $X(t, s_k)$ denotes the sample function or a realization of the random process for the s_k experimental outcome. It is customary to drop the s variable and use $X(t)$ to denote a random process. For a fixed time t_1, $X(t_1) = X_1$ is a random variable. Thus,

A *random* (or *stochastic*) *process* is a family of a random variables $X(t)$, indexed by the parameter t and defined on a common probability space.

It should be noted that the parameter t does not have to always represent time; it can represent any other variable such as space.

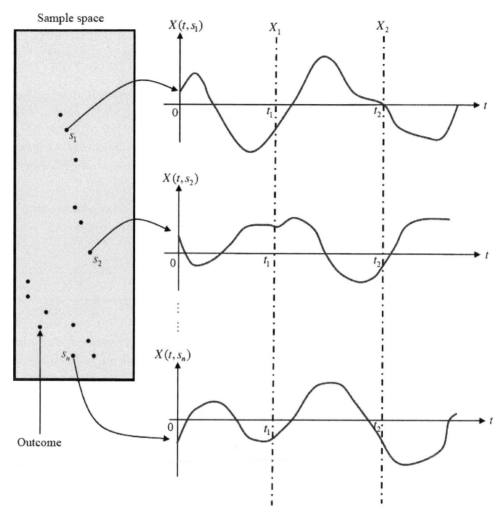

FIGURE 2.1 Realizations of a random process.

Queueing is simply waiting in lines, such as stopping at the toll booth, waiting in line for a bank cashier, stopping at a traffic light, waiting to buy stamps at the post office, and so on.

A *queue* consists of a line of customers or things waiting to be served and a service center with one or more servers.

For example, there would be no need of queueing in a bank if there were an infinite number of people serving the customers. But that would be very expensive and impractical.

Queueing theory is applied in several disciplines such as computer systems, traffic management, operations, production, and manufacturing. It plays a significant role in modeling computer communication networks.

Reduced to its most basic form, a computer network consists of communication channels and processors (or nodes). As messages flow from node to node, queues begin to form different nodes. For high traffic intensity the waiting or queueing time can be dominant, so that the performance of the network is dictated by the behavior of the queues at the nodes. Analytical derivation of the waiting time requires the knowledge of queueing theory.

This chapter provides a cursory review of the basic mathematical concepts needed throughout this book for computer networking and security. A reader already well-versed in these concepts may skip this chapter.

2.2   PROBABILITY FUNDAMENTALS

A fundamental concept in probability theory is the idea of an *experiment*. An experiment (or trial) is the performance of an operation that leads to results called *outcomes*. In other words, an outcome is a result of performing the experiment once. An *event* is one or more outcomes of an experiment. The relationship between outcomes and events is shown in the Venn diagram of Figure 2.2. Thus,

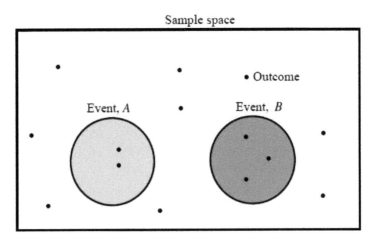

FIGURE 2.2 Sample space (rectangle) illustrating the relationship between outcomes (dots) and events (cirles).

An *experiment* consists of making a measurement or observation.

An *outcome* is a possible result of an experiment.

An *event* is a collection of outcomes.

An experiment is said to be *random* if its outcome cannot be predicted. Thus, a random experiment is one that can be repeated a number of times but yields unpredictable outcomes at each trial. Examples of random experiments are tossing a coin, observing the number of cars arriving at a toll booth, and keeping track of the number of telephone calls on your iPhone.

2.2.1 Simple Probability

We now define the probability of an event. The probability of event A is the number of ways event A can occur divided by the total number of possible outcomes. Suppose we perform n trials of an experiment and we observe that outcomes satisfying event A occur n_A times. We define the probability $P(A)$ of event A occurring as

$$P(A) = \lim_{n \to \infty} \frac{n_A}{n} \tag{2.1}$$

This is known as the *relative frequency* of event A. Two key points should be noted from Equation (2.1). First, we note that the probability P of an event is always a positive number and that

$$0 \le P \le 1 \tag{2.2}$$

where $P = 0$ (0%) when an event is not possible (never occurs or is impossible) and $P = 1$ (100%) when the event is sure (always occurs or is certain). Second, observe that for the probability to have meaning, the number of trials n must be large.

For a finite number of outcomes of any sample space S with events A_1, A_2, ..., A_f is always the total probability of all events equal to 1, that is,

$$\sum_{i=1}^{f} P(A_f) = 1 \tag{2.3}$$

Let A and B be two events. Then, the following are true.

- Intersection probability: $P(A \cap B)$ occurs when the probability of both A and B occurs;

- Union probability: $P(A \cup B)$ occurs when the probability of A or B occurs; and

- Complement of probability: $P(\overline{A})$ occurs when the probability of A does not occur.

The events A and B are *mutually exclusive* events if they are disjoint, that is, $A \cap B = \emptyset$, so

$$P(A \cap B) = 0 \tag{2.4}$$

If events A and B are *independent*, then the probability of event A and event B occurring is equal to multiplying the probability of event A with the probability of event B, that is

$$P(A \text{ and } B) = P(A \cap B) = P(A)P(B) \tag{2.5}$$

If events A and B are *disjoint* or *mutually exclusive*, it follows that the two events cannot occur simultaneously or that the two events have no outcomes in common, as shown in Figure 2.3. In this case, the probability that either event A or B occurs is equal to the sum of their probabilities, that is,

$$P(A \text{ or } B) = P(A \cup B) = P(A) + P(B) \tag{2.6}$$

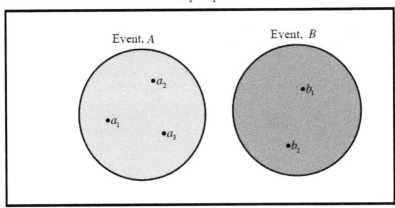

FIGURE 2.3 Mutually exclusive or disjoint events.

To prove this, suppose in an experiment with n trials, event A occurs n_A times, while event B occurs n_B times. Then event A or event B occurs $n_A + n_B$ times, and

$$P(A \text{ or } B) = \frac{n_A + n_B}{n} = \frac{n_A}{n} + \frac{n_B}{n} = P(A) + P(B) \qquad (2.7)$$

This result can be extended to the case when all possible events in an experiment are A, B, C, ..., Z. If the experiment is performed n times and event A occurs n_A times, event B occurs n_B times, and so on. Since some event must occur at each trial,

$$n_A + n_B + n_C + \cdots + n_Z = n$$

Dividing by n and assuming n is very large, we obtain

$$P(A) + P(B) + P(C) + \cdots + P(Z) = 1 \qquad (2.8)$$

which indicates that the probabilities of mutually exclusive events must add up to unity. A special case of this is when two events are complimentary, that is, if event A occurs B must not occur, and vice versa. In this case,

$$P(A) + P(B) = 1 \qquad (2.9)$$

or

$$P(A) = 1 - P(B) \qquad (2.10)$$

For example, in tossing a coin, the event of a head appearing is complementary to that of a tail appearing. Since the probability of either event is ½, their probabilities add up to 1.

The sum of the probability of any event A and its complement must be equal to 1, that is,

$$P(A) + P(\overline{A}) = 1 \qquad (2.11)$$

Or

$$P(\text{not } A) = P(\overline{A}) = 1 - P(A) \qquad (2.12)$$

2.2.2 Joint Probability

Next, we consider when events A and B are not mutually exclusive. Two events are non-mutually exclusive if they have one or more outcomes in common, as illustrated in Figure 2.4. The probability of the union event A or B (or $A \cup B$) is

$$P(A \cup B) = P(A) + P(B) - P(A \cap B) \tag{2.13}$$

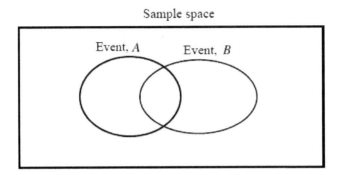

Sample space

Event, A Event, B

FIGURE 2.4 Non-mutually exclusive events.

where $P(A \cap B)$ is called the *joint probability* of events A and B, that is, the probability of the intersection of joint event $A \cap B$.

The probability of event A occurs, but not B; that is,

$$P(A - B) = P(A) - P(A \cap B) \tag{2.14}$$

Example 2.1

Consider two events A and B with $P(A) = 0.6$, $P(B) = 0.3$, and $P(A \cap B) = 0.1$.

Find: (a) the probability of A does not occur, (b) the probability of A or B occurs, and (c) the probability of A but not B occurs.

Solution

A. $P(\text{not } A) = P(\overline{A}) = 1 - P(A) = 1 - 0.6 = 0.4$

B. $P(A \text{ or } B \text{ occurs}) = P(A \cup B) = P(A) + P(B) - P(A \cap B) = 0.6 + 0.2 - 0.1 = 0.9$

C. $P(A \text{ but not } B) = P(A - B) = P(A) - P(A \cap B) = 0.6 - 0.1 = 0.5$

2.2.3 Conditional Probability

Sometimes we are confronted with a situation in which the outcome of one event depends on another event. The dependence of event B on event A is measured by the *conditional probability* $P(B|A)$ given by

$$P(B \mid A) = \frac{P(A \cap B)}{P(A)} \tag{2.15}$$

where $P(A \cap B)$ is the joint probability of events A and B. The notation $B|A$ stands for "B given A." In case events A and B are mutually exclusive, the joint probability $P(A \cap B) = 0$ so that the conditional probability $P(B|A) = 0$. Similarly, the conditional probability of A given B is

$$P(A \mid B) = \frac{P(A \cap B)}{P(B)} \tag{2.16}$$

From Equations (2.15) and (2.16), we obtain

$$P(A \cap B) = P(B|A)P(A) = P(A|B)P(B) \tag{2.17}$$

Eliminating $P(AB)$ gives

$$P(B \mid A) = \frac{P(A \mid B)P(B)}{P(A)} \tag{2.18}$$

which is a form of *Bayes' theorem*.

Example 2.2

A box contains 10 balls of which 7 are yellow and 3 are orange. Three balls are drawn at random one after the other. Find the probability $P(E)$ that all three are yellow.

Solution

The probability that the first ball is yellow is 7/10, since 7 of the 10 balls are yellow. So, if the first ball is yellow, then the probability that the second ball is yellow is 6/9, since only 6 of the remaining 9 balls are yellow. If the first two drawn balls are yellow, then the probability that the third ball is yellow is 5/8, since only 5 of the remaining balls are yellow. Therefore, by using the multiplication theory of conditional probability,

$$P(E) = (7/10)\ (6/9)\ (5/8) = 210/720 = 0.292$$

2.2.4 Statistical Independence

Lastly, suppose events A and B do not depend on each other. In this case, events A and B are said to be *statistically independent*. Since B has no influence on A or vice versa,

$$P(A|B) = P(A),\ P(B|A) = P(B) \tag{2.19}$$

From Equations (2.12) and (2.14), we obtain

$$P(A \cap B) = P(A)P(B) \tag{2.20}$$

indicating that the joint probability of statistically independent events is the product of the individual event probabilities. This can be extended to three or more statistically independent events

$$P(A \cap B \cap C \ldots) = P(A)P(B)P(C)\ldots. \tag{2.21}$$

Example 2.3

Roll three fair dice separately one time. Find the probability of getting a five and a two and a three.

Solution

Let a five event $= A$, a two event $= B$, and a three event $= C$.

The probability of event A is $P(A) = \dfrac{1}{6}$, the probability of event B is $P(B) = \dfrac{1}{6}$, and the probability of event C is $P(C) = \dfrac{1}{6}$.

A, B, and C are independent, because the occurrence of one event is not influenced by the occurrence of another.

Therefore, the probability for all events to occur is multiplying together the probabilities of the individual events, that is, $P(A \text{ and } B) = P(A \text{ and } B \text{ and } C) = P(A \cap B \cap C) = P(A)P(B)P(C) = \dfrac{1}{6} \times \dfrac{1}{6} \times \dfrac{1}{6} = \dfrac{1}{216}$.

2.3 RANDOM VARIABLES

Random variables are used in probability theory for at least two reasons. First, the way we have defined probabilities earlier in terms of events is awkward. We cannot use that approach in describing sets of objects such as cars, apples, and houses. It is preferable to have numerical values for all outcomes. Second, mathematicians and communication engineers in particular deal with random processes that generate numerical outcomes. Such processes are handled using random variables.

The term "random variable" is a misnomer; a random variable is neither random nor a variable. Rather, it is a function or rule that produces numbers from the outcome of a random experiment. In other words, for every possible outcome of an experiment, a real number is assigned to the outcome. This outcome becomes the value of the random variable. We usually represent a random variable by uppercase letters such as X, Y, and Z, while the value of a random variable (which is fixed) is represented by a lowercase letter such as x, y, and z. Thus, X is a function that maps elements of the sample space S to the real line $-\infty \leq x \leq \infty$, as illustrated in Figure 2.5.

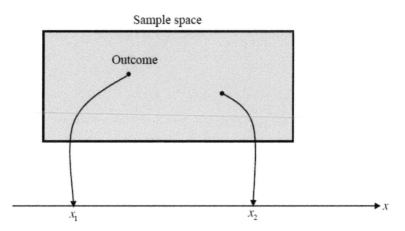

FIGURE 2.5 Random variable X maps elements of the sample space to the real line.

A *random variable* X is a single-valued real function that assigns a real value $X(t)$ to every point x in the sample space S.

Random variable X may be either discrete or continuous. X is said to be a discrete random variable if it can take only discrete values. It is said to be continuous if it takes continuous values. An example of a discrete random variable is the outcome of rolling a die. An example of a continuous random variable is one that is Gaussian distributed, to be discussed later.

2.3.1 Cumulative Distribution Function

Whether X is discrete or continuous, we need a probabilistic description of it in order to work with it. All random variables (discrete and continuous) have a cumulative distribution function.

The *cumulative distribution function* is a function given by the probability that the random variable X is less than or equal to x, for every value x.

Let us denote the probability of the event $X \leq x$, where x is given as $P(X \leq x)$. The *cumulative distribution function* of X is given by

$$F_X(x) = P(X \leq x), \ -\infty \leq x \leq \infty \tag{2.22}$$

for a continuous random variable X. Note that $F_X(x)$ does not depend on the random variable X, but on the assigned value of X. $F_X(x)$ has the following five properties:

1. $F_X(-\infty) = 0$ (2.23a)

2. $F_X(\infty) = 1$ (2.23b)

3. $0 \leq F_X(x) \leq 1$ (2.23c)

4. $F_X(x_1) \leq F_X(x_2)$, if $x_1 < x_2$ (2.23d)

5. $P(x_1 < X \leq x_2) = F_X(x_2) - F_X(x_1)$ (2.23e)

The first and second properties show that $F_X(-\infty)$ includes no possible events and $F_X(\infty)$ includes all possible events. The third property follows from the fact that $F_X(x)$ is a probability. The fourth property indicates that $F_X(x)$ is a nondecreasing function. And the last property is easy to prove since

$$P(X \leq x_2) = P(X \leq x_1) + P(x_1 < X \leq x_2)$$

or

$$P(x_1 < X \leq x_2) = P(X \leq x_2) - P(X \leq x_1) = F_X(x_2) - F_X(x_1) \tag{2.24}$$

If X is discrete, then

$$F_X(x) = \sum_{i=0}^{N} P(x_i) \tag{2.25}$$

where $P(x_i) = P(X = x_i)$ is the probability of obtaining event x_i, and N is the largest integer such that $x_N \leq x$ and $N \leq M$, and M is the total number of points in the discrete distribution. It is assumed that $x_1 < x_2 < x_3 < \cdots < x_M$.

2.3.2 Probability Density Function

It is sometimes convenient to use the derivative of $F_X(x)$, which is given by

$$f_X(x) = \frac{dF_x(x)}{dx} \tag{2.26}$$

1. $f_X(x) \geq 0$ $\tag{2.26a}$

where $f_X(x)$ is known as the *probability density function*. Note that $f_X(x)$ has the following properties:

1. $f_X(x)^3 0$ $\tag{2.27a}$

2. $\displaystyle\int_{-\infty}^{\infty} f_X(x)dx = 1$ $\tag{2.27b}$

3. $\displaystyle F_X(x) = \int_{-\infty}^{x} f_X(x)dx$ $\tag{2.27c}$

4. $\displaystyle P(x_1 \leq x \leq x_2) = \int_{x_1}^{x_2} f_X(x)dx$ $\tag{2.27d}$

Properties 1 and 2 follow from the fact that $F_X(-\infty) = 0$ and $F_X(\infty) = 1$ respectively. As mentioned previously, since $F_X(x)$ must be nondecreasing, its derivative $f_X(x)$ must always be nonnegative, as stated by Property 1. Property 3 follows from Equation (2.26). Property 4 follows from Equation (2.24):

$$P(x_1 < X \leq x_2) = F_X(x_2) - F_X(x_1)$$

$$= \int_{-\infty}^{x_2} f_X(x)dx - \int_{-\infty}^{x_1} f_X(x)dx = \int_{x_1}^{x_2} f_X(x)dx \tag{2.28}$$

which is typically illustrated in Figure 2.6 for a continuous random variable. For discrete X,

$$f_X(x) = \sum_{i=1}^{M} P(x_i)\delta(x - x_i) \tag{2.29}$$

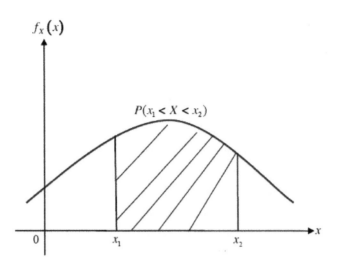

FIGURE 2.6 A typical probability density function (PDF).

where M is the total number of discrete events, $P(x_i) = P(x = x_i)$, and $d(x)$ is the impulse function. Thus,

The *probability density function* of a continuous or discrete random variable is a function which can be integrated or summed to obtain the probability that the random variable takes a value in a given interval.

Example 2.4

Let the random variable X have distribution density function

$$
f(x) = \begin{cases} \dfrac{1}{3}x, & 0 \le x \le 4 \\ 0, & otherwise \end{cases}
$$

Find the probability density function $f_x(x)$.

Solution

The area under the curve $f(x)$ must be 1. This area is

$$
f_X(x) = P(0 \le X \le 4) = \int_0^4 \frac{1}{3}x\,dx = \left(\frac{1}{6}x^2 \right)_0^4 = \frac{8}{3}
$$

2.3.3 Joint Distribution

We have focused on cases when a single random variable is involved. Sometimes several random variables are required to describe the outcome of an experiment. Here we consider situations involving two random variables X and Y; this may be extended to any number of random variables. The *joint cumulative distribution function* of X and Y is the function

$$F_{XY}(x,y) = P(X \leq x, Y \leq y) \tag{2.30}$$

where $-\infty < x < \infty$, and $-\infty < y < \infty$. If $F_{XY}(x, y)$ is continuous, the *joint probability density function* of X and Y is given by

$$f_{XY}(x,y) = \frac{\partial^2 F_{XY}(x,y)}{\partial x \partial y} \tag{2.31}$$

where $f_{XY}(x, y) \geq 0$. Just as we did for a single variable, the probability of event $x_1 < X \leq x_2$ and $y_1 < Y \leq y_2$ is

$$P(x_1 < X \leq x_2, y_1 < Y \leq y_2) = F_{XY}(x,y) = \int_{x_1}^{x_2}\int_{y_1}^{y_2} f_{XY}(x,y)dxdy \tag{2.32}$$

From this, we obtain the case where the entire sample space is included as

$$F_{XY}(\infty,\infty) = \int_{-\infty}^{\infty}\int_{-\infty}^{\infty} f_{XY}(x,y)dxdy = 1 \tag{2.33}$$

since the total probability must be unity.

Given the joint *cumulative distribution function* of X and Y, we can obtain the individual CDFs of the random variables X and Y. For X,

$$F_X(x) = P(X \leq x, -\infty < Y < \infty) = F_{XY}(x,\infty) = \int_{-\infty}^{x}\int_{-\infty}^{\infty} f_{XY}(x,y)dxdy \tag{2.34}$$

and for Y,

$$F_Y(y) = P(-\infty < x < \infty, y \leq Y) = F_{XY}(\infty,y) = \int_{-\infty}^{\infty}\int_{-\infty}^{y} f_{XY}(x,y)dxdy \tag{2.35}$$

$F_X(x)$ and $F_Y(y)$ are known as the *marginal cumulative distribution functions*.

Similarly, the individual *probability density functions* of the random variables X and Y can be obtained from their joint *probability density function*. For X,

$$f_X(x) = \frac{dF_X(x)}{dx} = \int_{-\infty}^{\infty} f_{XY}(x,y)dy \qquad (2.36)$$

and for Y,

$$f_Y(y) = \frac{dF_Y(y)}{dy} = \int_{-\infty}^{\infty} f_{XY}(x,y)dx \qquad (2.37)$$

$f_X(x)$ and $f_Y(y)$ are known as the *marginal probability density functions*.

As mentioned earlier, two random variables are independent if the values taken by one do not affect the other. As a result,

$$P(X \leq x, Y \leq y) = P(X \leq x)P(Y \leq y) \qquad (2.38)$$

or

$$F_{XY}(x,y) = F_X(x)F_Y(y) \qquad (2.39)$$

This condition is equivalent to

$$f_{XY}(x,y) = f_X(x)f_Y(y) \qquad (2.40)$$

Thus, two random variables are independent when their joint distribution (or density) is the product of their individual marginal distributions (or densities).

Finally, we may extend the concept of conditional probabilities to the case of continuous random variables. The conditional probability density function of X given the event $Y = y$ is

$$f_X(x \mid Y = y) = \frac{f_{XY}(x,y)}{f_Y(y)} \qquad (2.41)$$

where $f_Y(y)$ is the marginal *probability density function* of Y. Note that $f_X(x|Y=y)$ is a function of x with y fixed. Similarly, the conditional *probability density functions* of Y given $X = x$ is

$$f_Y(y \mid X = x) = \frac{f_{XY}(x,y)}{f_X(x)} \tag{2.42}$$

where $f_X(x)$ is the marginal PDF of X. By combining Equations (2.40) and (2.42), we get

$$f_Y(y \mid X = x) = \frac{f_X(x \mid Y = y) f_Y(y)}{f_X(x)} \tag{2.43}$$

which is Bayes' theorem for continuous random variables. If X and Y are independent, combining Equations (2.40) and (2.42) gives

$$f_X(x \mid Y = y) = f_X(x) \tag{2.44a}$$

$$f_Y(y \mid X = x) = f_Y(y) \tag{2.44b}$$

indicating that one random variable has no effect on the other.

2.4   DISCRETE PROBABILITY MODELS

Based on experience and usage, several probability distributions have been developed by engineers and scientists as models of physical phenomena. These distributions often arise in communication problems and deserve special attention. It is needless to say that each of these distributions satisfies the axioms of probability covered in Section 2.2. In this section, we discuss four discrete probability distributions; continuous probability distributions will be covered in the next section.

2.4.1 Bernoulli Distribution

A Bernoulli trial is an experiment that has two possible outcomes. Examples are tossing a coin with the two outcomes (heads and tails) and the output of a half-wave rectifier which is 0 or 1. Let us denote the outcome of the ith trial as 0 (failure) or 1 (success) and let X be a Bernoulli random variable with $P(X = 1) = p$ and $P(X = 0) = 1\text{-}p$. Then the probability mass function (PMF) of X is given by

$$P(x) = \begin{cases} p, & x = 1 \\ 1-p, & x = 0 \\ 0, & \text{otherwise} \end{cases} \tag{2.45}$$

which is illustrated in Figure 2.7. The parameters of the Bernoulli distribution are easily obtained as

$$E[X] = p \tag{2.46a}$$

$$E[X^2] = p \tag{2.46b}$$

$$\text{Var}(X) = p(1\text{-}p) \tag{2.46c}$$

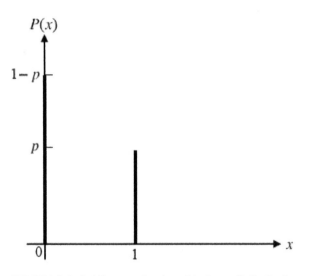

FIGURE 2.7 Probability mass function of the Bernoulli distribution.

2.4.2 Binomial Distribution

This is an extension of the Bernoulli distribution. A random variable follows a Binomial distribution when: (a) n Bernoulli trials are involved, (b) the n trials are independent of each other, and (c) the probabilities of the outcome remain constant as p for success and $q = 1\text{-}p$ for failure. The random variable X for Binomial distribution represents the number of successes in n Bernoulli trials.

In order to find the probability of k successes in n trials, we first define different ways of combining k out of n things, which is

$$C_k^n = \binom{n}{k} = \frac{n!}{k!(n-k)!} \tag{2.47}$$

Note that $\binom{n}{k} = \binom{n}{n-k}$. Hence, the probability of having k successes in n trials is

$$P(k) = \binom{n}{k} p^k (1-p)^{n-k} \tag{2.48}$$

since there are k successes each with probability p and n-k failures each with probability $q = 1$-p and all the trials are independent of each other. If we let $x = k$, where $k = 0, 1, 2, ..., n$, the PDF of the Binomial random variable X is

$$f_X(x) = \sum_{k=0}^{n} P(k)\delta(x-k) \tag{2.49}$$

From $f_X(x)$, we can obtain the mean and variance for X as

$$E(X) = np \tag{2.50a}$$

$$\text{Var}(X) = npq = np(1\text{-}p) \tag{2.50b}$$

2.4.3 Geometric Distribution

The geometric distribution is related to Bernoulli trials. A geometric random variable represents the number of Bernoulli trials required to achieve the first success. Thus, a random variable X has a geometric distribution if it takes the values of 1, 2, 3, ... with probability

$$P(k) = pq^{k-1}, \qquad k = 1, 2, 3, ... \tag{2.51}$$

where p = probability of success $(0 < p < 1)$ and $q = 1$-p = probability of failure. This forms a geometric sequence so that

$$\sum_{k=1}^{\infty} pq^{k-1} = \frac{p}{1-q} = 1 \tag{2.52}$$

The mean and variance of the geometric distribution are

$$E(X) = \frac{1}{p} \tag{2.53a}$$

$$\mathrm{Var(X)} = \frac{q}{p^2} \tag{2.53b}$$

The geometric distribution is somehow related to binomial distribution. They are both based on independent Bernoulli trials with equal probability of success p. However, a geometric random variable is the number of trials required to achieve the first success, whereas a binomial random variable is the number of successes in n trials.

2.4.4 Poisson Distribution

The Poisson distribution is perhaps the most important discrete probability distribution in engineering. It can be obtained as a special case of Binomial distribution when n is very large and p is very small. Poisson distribution is commonly used in engineering to model problems such as queueing (birth-and-death process or waiting on line), radioactive experiments, the telephone calls received at an office, the emission of electrons from a cathode, and natural hazards (earthquakes, hurricanes, or tornados). A random variable X has a Poisson distribution with parameter l if it takes the values 0, 1, 2, ... with

$$P(k) = \frac{\lambda^k}{k!} e^{-\lambda}, \qquad k = 0, 1, 2, \cdots \tag{2.54}$$

The corresponding PDF is

$$f_X(x) = \sum_{k=0}^{\infty} P(k)\delta(x-k) \tag{2.55}$$

The mean and variance of X are

$$E[X] = \lambda \tag{2.56a}$$

$$\mathrm{Var}(X) = l \tag{2.56b}$$

Note from Equation (2.56a) that the parameter l represents the average rate of occurrence of X. A summary of the properties of the four discrete probability distributions is provided in Table 2.1.

TABLE 2.1 Properties of Discrete Probability Distributions

Name	P(k)	PDF	Mean	Variance
Bernoulli	$P(x) = \begin{cases} p, & x = 1 \\ 1-p, & x = 0 \\ 0, & \text{otherwise} \end{cases}$	$f_X(x) = \sum_{k=0}^{1} P(k)\delta(x-k)$	p	$p(1\text{-}p)$
Binomial	$P(k) = \binom{n}{k} p^k (1-p)^{n-k}$	$f_X(x) = \sum_{k=0}^{n} P(k)\delta(x-k)$	np	$np(1\text{-}p)$
Geometri	$P(k) = pq^{k-1}$	$f_X(x) = \sum_{k=0}^{n} P(k)\delta(x-k)$	$1/p$	q/p^2
Poisson	$P(k) = \dfrac{\lambda^k}{k!} e^{-\lambda}$	$f_X(x) = \sum_{k=0}^{\infty} P(k)\delta(x-k)$	λ	λ

Example *2.5*

Verify Equation (2.56).

Solution

First, we notice that

$$\sum_{k=0}^{\infty} P(k) = \sum_{k=0}^{\infty} \frac{\lambda^k}{k!} e^{-\lambda} = e^{-\lambda} \sum_{k=0}^{\infty} \frac{\lambda^k}{k!} = e^{-\lambda}(e^{\lambda}) = 1$$

We obtain the mean value of X as

$$E[X] = \sum_{k=0}^{\infty} kP(k) = \sum_{k=0}^{\infty} k \frac{\lambda^k}{k!} e^{-\lambda} = 0 + \sum_{k=1}^{\infty} \frac{\lambda^{k-1}}{(k-1)!} \lambda e^{-\lambda}$$

If we let $n = k\text{-}1$, we get

$$E[X] = \lambda e^{-\lambda} \sum_{n=0}^{\infty} \frac{\lambda^n}{n!} = \lambda e^{-\lambda}(e^{\lambda}) = \lambda$$

The second moment is handled the same way.

$$E[X^2] = \sum_{k=0}^{\infty} k^2 P(k) = \sum_{k=0}^{\infty} k^2 \frac{\lambda^k}{k!} e^{-\lambda} = 0 + \sum_{k=1}^{\infty} k \frac{\lambda^{k-1}}{(k-1)!} \lambda e^{-\lambda}$$

Since, $k = k\text{-}1 + 1$

$$E[X^2] = \sum_{k=1}^{\infty} (k-1+1) \frac{\lambda^{k-1}}{(k-1)!} \lambda e^{-\lambda} = \lambda^2 e^{-\lambda} \sum_{k=1}^{\infty} \frac{\lambda^{k-2}}{(k-2)!} + \lambda e^{-\lambda} \sum_{k=1}^{\infty} \frac{\lambda^{k-1}}{(k-1)!} = \lambda^2 + \lambda$$

Hence

$$\text{Var}(X) = E[X^2] - E^2[X] = \lambda^2 + \lambda - \lambda^2 = \lambda$$

as expected.

2.5 CONTINUOUS PROBABILITY MODELS

In this section, we consider five continuous probability distributions: uniform, exponential, Erlang, hyperexponential, and Gaussian distributions.

2.5.1 Uniform Distribution

This distribution, also known as *rectangular distribution*, is very important for performing pseudo random number generation used in simulation. It is also useful for describing quantizing noise that is generated in pulse-code modulation. It is a distribution in which the density is constant. It models random events in which every value between a minimum and maximum value is equally likely. A random variable X has a uniform distribution if its PDF is given by

$$f_X(x) = \begin{cases} \dfrac{1}{b-a}, & a \leq x \leq b \\ 0, & \text{otherwise} \end{cases} \tag{2.57}$$

which is shown in Figure 2.8. The mean and variance are given by

$$E(X) = \frac{b+a}{2} \tag{2.58a}$$

$$\text{Var}(X) = \frac{(b-a)^2}{12} \tag{2.58b}$$

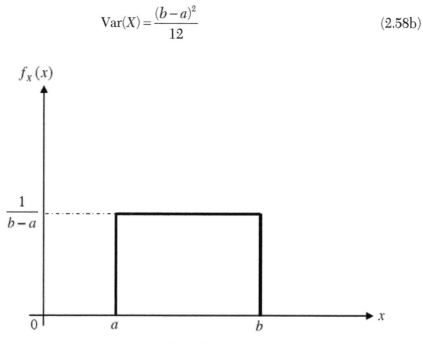

FIGURE 2.8 PDF for a uniform random variable.

A special uniform distribution for which $a = 0$, $b = 1$, called the standard uniform distribution, is very useful in generating random samples from any probability distribution function. Also, if $Y = A\sin X$, where X is a uniformly distributed random variable, the distribution of Y is said to be a *sinusoidal distribution*.

2.5.2 Exponential Distribution

This distribution, also known as *negative exponential distribution*, is important because of its relationship to the Poisson distribution. It is frequently used in simulation of queueing systems to describe the interarrival or interdeparture times of customers at a server. Its frequent use is due to the lack of conditioning of remaining time on past time expended. This peculiar characteristic is known variably as Markov, *forgetfulness*, or *lack of memory* property. For a given Poisson process, the time interval X between occurrence of events has an exponential distribution with the following PDF

$$f_X(x) = \lambda e^{-\lambda x} u(x) \tag{2.59}$$

which is portrayed in Figure 2.9. The mean and the variance of X are

$$E(X) = \frac{1}{\lambda} \tag{2.60a}$$

$$\text{Var}(X) = \frac{1}{\lambda^2} \tag{2.60b}$$

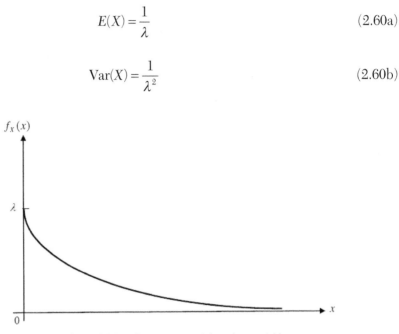

FIGURE 2.9 PDF for an exponential random variable.

2.5.3 Erlang Distribution

This is an extension of the exponential distribution. It is commonly used in queueing theory to model an activity that occurs in phases, with each phase being exponentially distributed. Let $X_1, X_2, \cdots, X_n$ be independent, identically distributed random variables having exponential distribution with mean $1/\lambda$. Then their sum $X = X_1 + X_2 + \cdots X_n$ has n-stage Erlang distribution. The PDF of X is

$$f_X(x) = \frac{\lambda^k x^{k-1}}{(n-1)!} e^{-\lambda x} \tag{2.61}$$

with mean

$$E(X) = \frac{n}{\lambda} \tag{2.62a}$$

and variance

$$\mathrm{Var}(X) = \frac{n}{\lambda^2} \qquad (2.62\mathrm{b})$$

2.5.4 Hyperexponential Distribution

This is another extension of the exponential distribution. Suppose X_1 and X_2 are two exponentially distributed random variables with means $1/\lambda_1$ and $1/\lambda_2$ respectively. If the random variable X assumes the value X_1 with probability p, and the value of X_2 with probability $q = 1\text{-}p$, then the PFD of X is

$$f_X(x) = p\lambda_1 e^{-\lambda_1 x} + q\lambda_2 e^{-\lambda_2 x} \qquad (2.63)$$

This is known as a two-stage hyperexponential distribution. Its mean and variance are given by

$$E(X) = \frac{p}{\lambda_1} + \frac{q}{\lambda_2} \qquad (2.64)$$

$$\mathrm{Var}(X) = \frac{p(2-p)}{\lambda_1^2} + \frac{1-p^2}{\lambda_2^2} - \frac{2p(1-p)}{\lambda_1 \lambda_2} \qquad (2.65)$$

2.5.5 Gaussian Distribution

This distribution, also known as *normal* distribution, is the most important probability distribution in engineering. It is used to describe phenomena with symmetric variations above and below the mean m. A random variable X with Gaussian distribution has its PDF of the form

$$f_X(x) = \frac{1}{\sigma\sqrt{2\pi}} \exp\left[-\frac{1}{2}\left(\frac{x-\mu}{\sigma}\right)^2 \right], \qquad -\infty < x < \infty \qquad (2.66)$$

where the mean

$$E(X) = \mu \qquad (2.67\mathrm{a})$$

and the variance

$$\mathrm{Var}(X) = \sigma^2 \qquad (2.67\mathrm{b})$$

are themselves incorporated in the PDF. Figure 1.9 shows the Gaussian PDF. It is a common practice to use the notation $X \approx N(\mu, \sigma^2)$ to denote a normal random variable X with mean μ and variance σ^2. When $\mu = 0$ and $s = 1$, we have $X = N(0,1)$, and the *normalized* or *standard normal* distribution function with

$$f_X(x) = \frac{1}{\sqrt{2\pi}} e^{-x^2/2} \tag{2.68}$$

which is widely tabulated.

It is important that we note the following points about the normal distribution, which make the distribution the most prominent in probability and statistics and also in communication.

1. The binomial probability function with parameters n and p is approximated by a Gaussian PDF with $\mu = np$ and $\sigma^2 = np(1-p)$ for large n and finite p.

2. The Poisson probability function with parameter λ can be approximated by a normal distribution with $\mu = \sigma^2 = \lambda$ for large λ.

3. The normal distribution is useful in characterizing the uncertainty associated with the estimated values. In other words, it is used in performing statistical analysis on simulation output.

4. The justification for the use of normal distribution comes from the *central limit theorem*.

5. The *central limit theorem* states that the distribution of the sum of n independent random variables from any distribution approaches a normal distribution as n becomes large.

Thus, the normal distribution is used to model the cumulative effect of many small disturbances, each of which contributes to the stochastic variable X. It has the advantage of being mathematically tractable. Consequently, many statistical analyses such as those of regression and variance have been derived assuming a normal density function. In several communication applications, we assume that noise is Gaussian distributed in view of the central limit theorem, because noise is due to the sum of several random parameters. A summary of the properties of the five continuous probability distributions is provided in Table 2.2.

TABLE 2.2 Properties of Continuous Probability Distributions

Name	PDF	CDF	Mean	Variance
Uniform	$f_X(x) = \dfrac{1}{b-a}$	$F_X(x) = \dfrac{x-a}{b-a}$	$\dfrac{b+a}{2}$	$\dfrac{(b-a)^2}{12}$
Exponential	$f_X(x) = \lambda e^{-\lambda x} u(x)$	$F_X(x) = 1 - e^{-\lambda x}$	$\dfrac{1}{\lambda}$	$\dfrac{1}{\lambda^2}$
Erlang	$f_X(x) = \dfrac{\lambda^k x^{k-1}}{(n-1)!} e^{-\lambda x}$	$F_X(x) =$ $1 - e^{-\lambda x} \sum\limits_{k=0}^{n-1} \dfrac{(\lambda x)^k}{k!}$	$\dfrac{n}{\lambda}$	$\dfrac{n}{\lambda^2}$
Hyper-exponential	$f_X(x) = p\lambda_1 e^{-\lambda_1 x} +$ $q\lambda_2 e^{-\lambda_2 x}$	$F_X(x) = p(1 - e^{-\lambda_1 t}) +$ $q(1 - e^{-\lambda_2 t})$	$\dfrac{p}{\lambda_1} + \dfrac{q}{\lambda_2}$	$\dfrac{p(2-p)}{\lambda_1^2} + \dfrac{1-p^2}{\lambda_2^2} -$ $\dfrac{2p(1-p)}{\lambda_1 \lambda_2}$
Gaussian	$f_X(x) = \dfrac{1}{\sigma\sqrt{2\pi}}$ $\exp\left[-\dfrac{1}{2}\left(\dfrac{x-\mu}{\sigma}\right)^2 \right]$	$F_X(x) =$ $\dfrac{1}{2}\left[1 + \mathrm{erf}\left(\dfrac{x-\mu}{\sigma\sqrt{2}}\right) \right]$	μ	σ^2

where erf(.) is the error function.

2.6 TRANSFORMATION OF A RANDOM VARIABLE

It is sometimes required in system analysis that we obtain the PDF $f_Y(y)$ of the output random variable Y, given that the PDF $f_X(x)$ for the input random variable X is known and the input-output transformation function

$$Y = g(X) \tag{2.69}$$

is provided. If we assume that $g(X)$ is continuous or piecewise continuous, then Y will be a random variable. Our goal is to get $f_Y(y)$. We begin with the distribution of Y.

$$F_Y(y) = P[Y \le y] = P[g(X) \le y] = P[X \le g^{-1}(y)] = F_X(g^{-1}(y))$$

Hence,

$$f_Y(y) = \frac{d}{dy} F_X(g^{-1}(y)) = \frac{d}{dx} F_X(g^{-1}(y)) \frac{dx}{dy}$$

or

$$f_Y(y) = \frac{f_X(x)}{\left|\dfrac{dy}{dx}\right|} \tag{2.70}$$

where $x = g^{-1}(y)$. In case $Y = g(X)$ has a finite number of roots X_1, X_2, ..., X_n such that

$$Y = g(X_1) = g(X_2) = \cdots = g(X_n)$$

then the PDF of y becomes

$$f_X(y) = \frac{f_X(x_1)}{\left|\dfrac{dy}{dx_1}\right|} + \frac{f_X(x_2)}{\left|\dfrac{dy}{dx_2}\right|} + \cdots + \frac{f_X(x_n)}{\left|\dfrac{dy}{dx_n}\right|} \tag{2.71}$$

Once the PDF of Y is determined, we can find its mean and variance using the regular approach.

2.7   GENERATING FUNCTIONS

It is sometimes more convenient to work with generating functions. A probability generating function, often called the *z-transform*, is a tool for manipulating infinite series. Generating functions are important for at least two reasons. First, they may have a closed form. Second, they may be used to generate probability distribution and the moments of the distributions.

If $p_0, p_1, p_2, \cdots$ form a probability distribution, the probability generating function is

$$G(z) = E[z^i] = \sum_{i=0}^{\infty} z^i p_i \qquad (2.72)$$

Notice that $G(1) = 1$ since the probabilities must sum up to 1. The generating function $G(z)$ contains all the information that the individual probabilities have. We can find the individual probabilities from $G(z)$ by repeated differentiation as

$$p_n = \frac{1}{n!} \frac{d^n G(z)}{dz^n}\bigg|_{z=0} \qquad (2.73)$$

The moments of the random variable can be obtained from $G(z)$. For example, for the first moment,

$$E[X] = \sum_{i=0}^{\infty} i p_i = \sum_{i=0}^{\infty} i p_i z^{i-1}\bigg|_{z=1} = \frac{d}{dz} \sum_{i=0}^{\infty} p_i z^i \bigg|_{z=1} = G'(1) \qquad (2.75)$$

For the second moment,

$$\begin{aligned} E[X^2] &= \sum_{i=0}^{\infty} i^2 p_i = \sum_{i=0}^{\infty} i(i-1)p_i + \sum_{i=0}^{\infty} i p_i \\ &= \sum_{i=0}^{\infty} i(i-1)p_i z^{i-2}\bigg|_{z=1} + \sum_{i=0}^{\infty} i p_i z^{i-1}\bigg|_{z=1} \\ &= G''(1) + G'(1) \end{aligned} \qquad (2.76)$$

Example 2.6

Find the generating function for geometric distribution.

Solution

For geometric distribution, $q = 1-p$ and $p_i = pq^{i-1}$. Hence,

$$G(z) = \sum_{i=1}^{\infty} pq^{i-1} z^i = pz \sum_{i=1}^{\infty} (qz)^{i-1} = \frac{pz}{1-qz}$$

For $n \geq 1$,

$$\frac{d^n G(z)}{dz^n} = \frac{n! pq^{n-1}}{(1-qz)^{n+1}}$$

Thus,

$$E[X] = G'(1) = \frac{p}{(1-q)^2} = \frac{1}{p}$$

and

$$E[X^2] = G'(1) + G''(1) = \frac{1}{p} + \frac{2q}{p^2} = \frac{1+q}{p^2}$$

so that variance is

$$\mathrm{Var(X)} = E[X^2] - E^2[X] = \frac{q}{p^2}$$

2.8 CENTRAL LIMIT THEOREM

This is a fundamental result in probability theory. The theorem explains why many random variables encountered in nature have distributions close to the Gaussian distribution. To derive the theorem, consider the binomial function

$$B(M) = \frac{N!}{M!(N-M)!} p^M q^{N-M} \qquad (2.76)$$

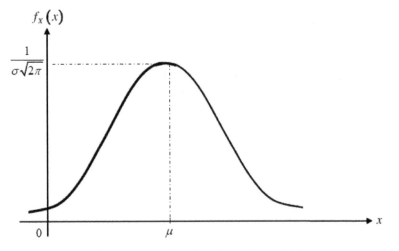

FIGURE 2.10 PDF for a Gaussian random variable.

which is the probability of M successes in N independent trials. If M and N-M are large, we may use Stirling's formula

$$n! \cong n^n e^{-n} \sqrt{2n\pi} \tag{2.77}$$

Hence,

$$B(M) = f(x) = \frac{1}{\sigma\sqrt{2\pi}} \exp\left[-\frac{(x-\mu)^2}{2\sigma^2}\right] \tag{2.78}$$

which is a normal distribution, $\mu = Np$ and $\sigma = \sqrt{Npq}$. Thus, as $N \to \infty$, the sum of a large number of random variables tends to be normally distributed. This is known as the *central limit theorem*.

The *central limit theorem* states that the PDF of the sum of a large number of individual random variables approaches a Gaussian (normal) du = distribution regardless of whether or not the distribution of the individual variables is normal.

Although the derivation above is based on binomial distribution, the central limit theorem is true for all distributions. A simple consequence of the theorem is that any random variable which is the sum of n independent identical random variables approximates a normal random variable as n becomes large.

2.9   CLASSIFICATION OF RANDOM PROCESSES

It is expedient to begin our discussion of random (stochastic) processes by developing the terminology for describing random processes. An appropriate way of achieving this is to consider the various types of random processes. Random processes may be classified as:

- Continuous or discrete

- Deterministic or nondeterministic

- Stationary or nonstationary

- Ergodic or nonergodic

2.9.1 Continuous versus Discrete Random Process

A *continuous-time random process* is one that has both a continuous random variable and continuous time. Noise in transistors and wind velocity are examples of continuous random processes. So are the Wiener process and Brownian motion. A *discrete-time random process* is one in which the random variables are discrete, that is, it is a sequence of random variables. The binomial counting and random walk processes are discrete processes. It is also possible to have a mixed or hybrid random process which is partly continuous and partly discrete.

2.9.2 Deterministic versus Non-Deterministic Random Process

A *deterministic random process* is one for which the future value of any sample function can be predicted from a knowledge of the past values. For example, consider a random process described by

$$X(t) = A\cos(\omega t + \Phi) \tag{2.79}$$

where A and ω are constants and Φ is a random variable with a known probability distribution. Although $X(t)$ is a random process, one can predict its future values and hence $X(t)$ is deterministic. For a *nondeterministic random process*, each sample function is a random function of time and its future values cannot be predicted from the past values.

2.9.3 Stationary versus Nonstationary Random Process

A *stationary random process* is one in which the probability density function of the random variable does not change with time. In other words, a random process is stationary when its statistical characteristics are time-invariant, that is, not affected by a shift in time origin. Thus, the random process is stationary if all marginal and joint density functions of the process are not affected by the choice of time origin. A *nonstationary random process* is one in which the probability density function of the random variable is a function of time.

2.9.4 Ergodic versus Nonergodic Random Process

An ergodic random process is one in which every member of the ensemble possesses the same statistical behavior as the entire ensemble. Thus, for ergodic processes, it is possible to determine the statistical characteristic by examining only one typical sample function; that is, the average value and moments can be determined by time averages as well as by ensemble averages. For example, the nth moment is given by

$$\overline{X^n} = \int_{-\infty}^{\infty} x^n f_X(x)dx = \lim_{T \to \infty} \frac{1}{2T} \int_{-T}^{T} X^n(t)dt \qquad (2.80)$$

This condition will only be satisfied if the process is stationary. This implies that ergodic processes are stationary as well. A nonergodic process does not satisfy the condition in Equation (2.80). All non-stationary processes are nonergodic, but a stationary process could also be nonergodic. Figure 2.11 shows the relationship between stationary and ergodic processes. These terms will become clearer as we move along in the chapter.

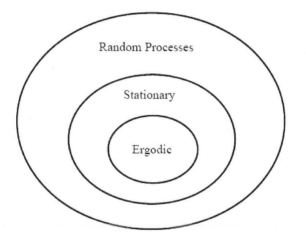

FIGURE 2.11 Relationship between stationary and ergodic random processes.

2.10 STATISTICS OF RANDOM PROCESSES AND STATIONARITY

Since a random process specifies a random variable at any given time, we can find the statistical averages for the process through the statistical averages of the corresponding random variables. For example, the first-order probability density function (PDF) for a random process $X(t)$ is $f_X(x; t)$, while the corresponding first-order cumulative distribution function (CDF) of $X(t)$ is

$$F_X(x;t) = P[X(t) \le x] = \int_{-\infty}^{x} f_X(\lambda;t)d\lambda \tag{2.81}$$

or

$$f_X(x;t) = \frac{\partial F_X(x;t)}{\partial x} \tag{2.82}$$

Similarly, if $X(t_1) = X_1$ and $X(t_2) = X_2$ represent two random variables of a random process $X(t)$, then their joint distributions are known as second-order PDF and CDF, which are related as

$$F_X(x_1, x_2; t_1, t_2) = P[X(t_1) \le x_1, X(t_2) \le x_2] = \int_{-\infty}^{x_2} \int_{-\infty}^{x_1} f_X(\lambda_1, \lambda_2; t_1, t_2)d\lambda_1 d\lambda_2 \tag{2.83}$$

or

$$f_X(x_1, x_2; t_1, t_2) = \frac{\partial F_X(x_1, x_2; t_1, t_2)}{\partial x_1 \partial x_2} \tag{2.84}$$

In general, the joint distributions of n random variables $X(t_1) = X_1$, $X(t_2) = X_2, \ldots, X(t_n) = X_n$ provide the nth-order PDF and CDF of a random process $X(t)$ and are related as

$$F_X(x_1, x_2, \ldots, x_n; t_1, t_2, \ldots, t_n) = P[X(t_1) \le x_1, X(t_2) \le x_2, \ldots, X(t_n) \le x_n]$$
$$= \int_{-\infty}^{x_n} \ldots \int_{-\infty}^{x_2} \int_{-\infty}^{x_1} f_X(\lambda_1, \lambda_2, \ldots, \lambda_n; t_1, t_2, \ldots, t_n)d\lambda_1 d\lambda_2 \ldots d\lambda_n \tag{2.85}$$

or

$$f_X(x_1, x_2, \ldots, x_n; t_1, t_2, \ldots, t_n) = \frac{\partial F_X(x_1, x_2, \ldots, x_n; t_1, t_2, \ldots, t_n)}{\partial x_1 \partial x_2 \ldots \partial x_n} \tag{2.86}$$

A random process $X(t)$ is said to be *strictly stationary of order n* if its nth-order PDF and CDF are time-invariant, that is,

$$F_X(x_1, x_2, \ldots, x_n; t_1 + \tau, t_2 + \tau, \ldots, t_n + \tau) = F_X(x_1, x_2, \ldots, x_n; t_1, t_2, \ldots, t_n) \tag{2.87}$$

That is, the CDF depends only on the relative location of $t_1, t_2, \ldots, t_n$ and not on their direct values.

We say that $\{X_k\}$, $k = 0,1,2,\cdots,n$ is an independent process if and only if

$$F_X(x_0, x_1, \cdots, x_n; t_0, t_1, \cdots, t_n) = F_{X_0}(x_0; t_0) F_{X_1}(x_1; t_1) \cdots F_{X_n}(x_n; t_n)$$

In addition, if all random variables are drawn from the same distribution, the process is characterized by a single CDF, $F_{X_k}(x_k; t_k)$, $k = 0,1,2,\cdots,n$. In this case, we call $\{X_k\}$ a sequence of independent and identically distributed (IID) random variables.

Having defined the CDF and PDF for a random process $X(t)$, we are now prepared to define the statistical (or ensemble) averages—the mean, variance, autocorrelation, and autocovariance of $X(t)$. As in the case of random variables, these statistics play an important role in practical applications.

The *mean* or *expected value* of the random process $X(t)$ is

$$m_X(t) = \overline{X(t)} = E[X(t)] = \int_{-\infty}^{-\infty} x f_X(x; t) dx \tag{2.88}$$

where $E[\cdot]$ denotes ensemble average, $f_X(x;t)$ is the PDF of $X(t)$, and $X(t)$ is regarded as a random variable for a fixed value of t. In general, the mean $m_X(t)$ is a function of time.

The *variance* of a random process $X(t)$ is given by

$$\text{Var}(X) = \sigma_X^2 = E\left[\left(X(t) - m_X(t)\right)^2\right] = E[X^2] - m_X^2 \tag{2.89}$$

The *autocorrelation* of a random process $X(t)$ is the joint moment of $X(t_1)$ and $X(t_2)$, that is,

$$R_X(t_1, t_2) = E[X(t_1)X(t_2)] = \int_{-\infty}^{\infty} \int_{-\infty}^{\infty} x_1 x_2 f_X(x_1, x_2; t_1, t_2) dx_1 dx_2 \tag{2.90}$$

where $f_X(x_1, x_2; t_1, t_2)$ is the second-order PDF of $X(t)$. In general, $R_X(t_1, t_2)$ is a deterministic function of two variables t_1 and t_2. The autocorrection function is important because it describes the power-spectral density of a random process.

The *covariance* or *autocovariance* of a random process $X(t)$ is the covariance of $X(t_1)$ and $X(t_2)$, that is,

$$\text{Cov}\left[X(t_1), X(t_2)\right] = C_X(t_1, t_2) = E\left[\left\{X(t_1) - m_X(t_1)\right\}\left\{X(t_2) - m_X(t_2)\right\}\right] \quad (2.91a)$$

or

$$\text{Cov}\left[X(t_1), X(t_2)\right] = R_X(t_1, t_2) - m_X(t_1)m_X(t_2) \quad (2.91b)$$

indicating that the autocovariance can be expressed in terms of the auto-correlation and the means. Note that the variance of $X(t)$ can be expressed in terms of its autocovariance, that is,

$$\text{Var}(X(t)) = C_X(t, t) \quad (2.92)$$

The *correlation coefficient* of a random process $X(t)$ is the correlation coefficient of $X(t_1)$ and $X(t_2)$, that is,

$$\rho_X(t_1, t_2) = \frac{C_X(t_1, t_2)}{\sqrt{C_X(t_1, t_1)C_X(t_2, t_2)}} \quad (2.93)$$

where $|\rho_X(t_1, t_2)| \leq 1$.

Finally, we define the *nth joint moment* of $X(t)$ as

$$E[X(t_1)X(t_2)\dots X(t_n)] = \int_{-\infty}^{\infty}\dots\int_{-\infty}^{\infty}\int_{-\infty}^{\infty} x_1 x_2 \dots x_n f_X(x_1, x_2, \dots, x_n; t_1, t_2, \dots, t_n) dx_1 dx_2 \dots dx_n \quad (2.94)$$

We should keep in mind that the mean, variance, autocorrelation, auto-covariance, and nth joint moment are good indicators of the behavior of a random process but only partial characterizations of the process.

In terms of these statistics, a random process may be classified as follows:

1. A random process is *wide-sense stationary* (WSS) or weakly stationary if its mean is constant, that is,

$$E[X(t)] = E[X(t_1)] = E[X(t_2)] = m_x = \text{constant} \quad (2.95)$$

and its autocorrelation depends only on the absolute time difference $\tau = |t_1 - t_2|$, that is,

$$E[X(t)X(t + \tau)] = R_X(\tau) \quad (2.96)$$

Note that the autocovariance of a WSS process depends only on the time difference τ

$$C_X(\tau) = R_X(\tau) - m_x^2 \qquad (2.97)$$

and that by setting $\tau = 0$ in Equation (1.96), we get

$$E[X^2(t)] = R_X(0) \qquad (2.98)$$

indicating that the mean power of a WSS process $X(t)$ does not depend on t. The autocorrelation function has its maximum value when $\tau = 0$ so that we can write

$$-R_X(0) \le R_X(\tau) \le R_X(0) \qquad (2.99)$$

2. A random process is said to be *strict-sense stationary* (SSS) if its statistics are invariant to a shift in the time axis. Hence,

$$F_X(x_1, x_2, \ldots, x_n; t_1 + \tau, t_2 + \tau, \ldots, t_n + \tau) = F_X(x_1, x_2, \ldots, x_n; t_1, t_2, \ldots, t_n) \qquad (2.100)$$

An SSS random process is also WSS, but the converse is not generally true.

In general terms, a random process is a *stationary* if all its statistical properties do not vary with time.

2.11 TIME AVERAGES OF RANDOM PROCESSES AND ERGODICITY

For a random process $X(t)$, we can define two types of averages: ensemble and time averages. The ensemble averages (or statistical averages) of a random process $X(t)$ may be regarded as "averages across the process" because they involve all sample functions of the process observed at a particular instant of time. The time averages of a random process $X(t)$ may be regarded as "averages along the process" because they involve long-term sample averaging of the process.

To define the time averages, consider the sample function $x(t)$ of random process $X(t)$, which is observed within the time interval $-T \le t \le T$. The *time average* (or *time mean*) of the sample function is

$$\overline{x} = <x(t)> = \lim_{T \to \infty} \left(\frac{1}{2T} \int_{-T}^{T} x(t)dt \right) \tag{2.101}$$

where $<\;>$ denotes a time-averaging operation. Similarly, the *time autocorrelation* of the sample function $x(t)$ is given by

$$\overline{R}_X(\tau) = <x(t)x(t+\tau)> = \lim_{T \to \infty} \frac{1}{2T} \int_{-T}^{T} x(t)x(t+\tau)dt \tag{2.102}$$

Note that both $\overline{x}$ and $\overline{R}_X(\tau)$ are random variables, since their values depend on the observation interval and on the sample function $x(t)$ used.

If all time averages are equal to their corresponding ensemble averages, then the stationary process is *ergodic*, that is,

$$\overline{x} = <x(t)> = E[X(t)] = m_X \tag{2.103}$$

$$\overline{R}_X(\tau) = <x(t)x(t+\tau)> = E[X(t)X(t+\tau)] = R_X(\tau) \tag{2.104}$$

An *ergodic* process is one for which time and ensemble averages are interchangeable.

The concept of ergodicity is a very powerful tool and it is always assumed in many engineering applications. This is due to the fact that it is impractical to have a large number of sample functions to work with. Ergodicity suggests that if a random process is ergodic, only one sample function is necessary to determine the ensemble averages. This seems reasonable because over infinite time each sample function of a random process would take on, at one time or another, all the possible values of the process. We will assume throughout this text that the random processes we will encounter are ergodic and WSS.

Basic quantities such as dc value, rms value, and average power can be defined in terms of time averages of an ergodic random process as follows:

1. $\overline{x} = m_X$ is the dc value of $x(t)$.

2. $\left[\overline{x}\right]^2 = m_X^2$ is the normalized dc power.

3. $\overline{R}_X(0) = \overline{x^2}$ is the total average normalized power.

4. $\sigma_X^2 = \overline{x^2} - \left[\overline{x}\right]^2$ is the average normalized power in the ac or time-varying component of the signal.

5. $X_{rms} = \sqrt{\overline{x^2}} = \sqrt{\overline{\sigma}_X^2 + \left[\overline{x}\right]^2}$ is the rms value of $x(t)$.

2.12 MULTIPLE RANDOM PROCESSES

The joint behavior of two or more random processes is dictated by their joint distributions. For example, two random processes $X(t)$ and $Y(t)$ are said to be *independent* if for all t_1 and t_2, the random variables $X(t_1)$ and $Y(t_2)$ are independent. That means that their nth order joint PDF factors, i.e.

$$F_{XY}(x_1, y_1, x_2, y_2, \ldots, x_n, y_n; t_1, t_2, \ldots, t_n) = F_X(x_1, x_2, \ldots, x_n; t_1, t_2, \ldots, t_n)$$

$$F_Y(y_1, y_2, \ldots, y_n; t_1, t_2, \ldots, t_n) \tag{2.105}$$

The *crosscorrelation* between two random processes $X(t)$ and $Y(t)$ is defined as

$$R_{XY}(t_1, t_2) = E[X(t_1)Y(t_2)] \tag{2.106}$$

Note that

$$R_{XY}(t_1, t_2) = R_{YX}(t_2, t_1) \tag{2.107}$$

The processes $X(t)$ and $Y(t)$ are said to be *orthogonal* if

$$R_{XY}(t_1, t_2) = 0 \qquad \text{for all } t_1 \text{ and } t_2 \tag{2.108}$$

If $X(t)$ and $Y(t)$ are jointly stationary, then their crosscorrelation function becomes

$$R_{XY}(t_1, t_2) = R_{XY}(\tau)$$

where $\tau = t_2 - t_1$. Other properties of the crosscorrelation of jointly stationary processes are:

1. $R_{XY}(-\tau) = R_{XY}(\tau)$, that is, it is symmetric.

2. $|R_{XY}(\tau)| \leq \sqrt{R_X(0)R_Y(0)}$, that is, it is bounded.

3. $|R_{XY}(\tau)| \leq \frac{1}{2}[R_X(0) + R_Y(0)]$, that is, it is bounded

The *crosscovariance* of $X(t)$ and $Y(t)$ is given by

$$C_{XY}(t_1,t_2) = E\left[\{X(t_1)-m_X(t_1)\}\{Y(t_2)-m_Y(t_2)\}\right] = R_{XY}(t_1,t_2)-m_X(t_1)m_Y(t_2) \quad (2.109)$$

Just like with random variables, two random processes $X(t)$ and $Y(t)$ are *uncorrelated* if

$$C_{XY}(t_1,t_2) = 0 \qquad \text{for all } t_1 \text{ and } t_2 \quad (2.110)$$

which implies that

$$R_{XY}(t_1,t_2) = m_X(t_1)m_Y(t_2) \quad \text{for all } t_1 \text{ and } t_2 \quad (2.111)$$

Finally, for jointly ergodic random processes $X(t)$ and $Y(t)$,

$$\overline{R}_{XY}(\tau) = \lim_{T\to\infty}\frac{1}{2T}\int_{-T}^{T} x(t)x(t+\tau)\,dt = R_{XY}(\tau) \quad (2.113)$$

Thus, two random processes $X(t)$ and $Y(t)$ are:

1. **Independent** if their joint PDF factors;
2. **Orthogonal** if $R_{XY}(t_1,t_2)=0$ $\qquad$ for all t_1 and t_2; and
3. **Uncorrelated** if $R_{XY}(t_1,t_2)=m_X(t_1)m_Y(t_2)$ $\quad$ for all t_1 and t_2.

2.13   SAMPLE RANDOM PROCESSES

We have been discussing random processes in general. Specific random processes include the Poisson counting process, the Wiener process or Brownian motion, the random walking process, the Bernoulli process, the birth-and-death process, and the Markov process. In this section, we consider some of these specific random processes.

2.13.1 Random Walks

A random walk (or drunkard's walk) is a stochastic process in which the states are integers X_n representing the position of a particle at time n. Each state changes according to

$$X_n = X_{n-1} + Z_n \quad (2.113)$$

where Z_n is a random variable which takes values of 1 or –1. If $X_0 = 0$, then

$$X_n = \sum_{i=1}^{n} Z_i \qquad (2.114)$$

A *random walk* on X corresponds to a sequence of states, one for each step of the walk. At each step, the walk switches from its current state to a new state or remains at the current state. Thus, Random walks constitute a random process consisting of a sequence of discrete steps of fixed length.

Random walks are usually *Markovian*, which means that the transition at each step is independent of the previous steps and depends only on the current state. Although random walks are not limited to one-dimensional problems, the one-dimensional random walk is one of the simplest stochastic processes and can be used to model many gambling games. A typical one-dimensional random walk is illustrated in Figure 2.12.

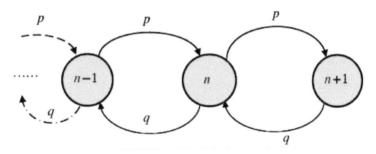

FIGURE 2.12 A typical random walk.

Example 2.7

Consider the following standard Markovian random walk on the integers over the range $\{0, ..., N\}$ that models a simple gambling game, where a player bets the same amount on each hand (i.e., step). We assume that if the player ever reaches 0, he has lost all his money and stops, but if he reaches N, he has won a certain amount of money and stops. Otherwise, at each step, one moves from state i (where $i \neq 0, N$) to $i + 1$ with probability p (the probability of winning the game), to i-1 with probability q (the probability of losing the game), and stays at the same state with probability 1-p-q (the probability of a draw).

2.13.2 Markov Processes

If the future state of a process depends only on the present (and is independent of the past), the process is called a *Markov process*. A Markov process is made possible only if the state time has a memoryless (exponential) distribution. This requirement often limits the applicability of Markov processes.

Formally, a stochastic process $X(t)$ is a Markov process if

$$\text{Prob}\big[X(t) = x \,|\, X(t_n) = x_n, X(t_{n-1}) = x_{n-1} \cdots, X(t_o) = x_o\big] = \text{Prob}\big[X(t) = x \,|\, X(t_n) = x_n\big]$$

$$\text{for } t_o < t_1 < \cdots < t_n < t \tag{2.115}$$

A discrete-state Markov process is called a *Markov chain*. We use the state transition diagram to represent the evolution of a Markov chain. An example of three-state Markov chain is shown in Figure 2.13. The conditional probability

$$\text{Prob}[X_{n+1} = i \,|\, X_n = j] = p_n(i, j) = p_{ij}$$

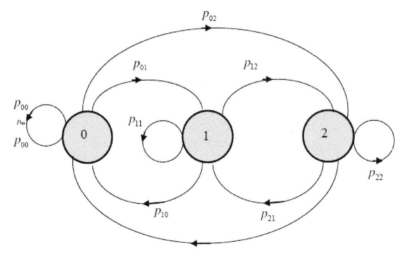

FIGURE 2.13 State transition diagram for a three-state Markov chain.

is called the *transition probability* from state i to state j. Since a Markov chain must go somewhere with a probability of 1, the sum of $p_n(i,j)$'s over all j's is equal to 1. If $p_n(i,j)$ is independent of n, the Markov chain is said to be time-homogeneous and, in this case, the transition probability becomes $p(i,j)$.

When we arrange $p(i,j)$ into an square array, the resulting matrix is called the *transition matrix*.

For a simple example, consider four possible states as 0, 1, 2, 3, and 4. The transition matrix is

$$P = \begin{bmatrix} p(0,0) & p(0,1) & p(0,2) & p(0,3) & p(0,4) \\ p(1,0) & p(1,1) & p(1,2) & p(1,3) & p(1,4) \\ p(2,0) & p(2,1) & p(2,2) & p(2,3) & p(2,4) \\ p(3,0) & p(3,1) & p(3,2) & p(3,3) & p(3,4) \\ p(4,0) & p(4,1) & p(4,2) & p(4,3) & p(4,4) \end{bmatrix} \qquad (2.116)$$

2.13.3 Birth-and-Death Processes

Birth-death processes describe the stochastic evolution in time of a random variable whose value increases or decreases by one in a single event. These are discrete-space Markov processes in which the transitions are restricted to neighboring states only. A typical example is shown in Figure 2.14. For example, the number of jobs in a queue with a single server and the individual arrivals can be represented as a birth-death process. An arrival to the queue (a birth) causes the state to change by +1, while a departure (a death) causes the state to change by –1. Although the birth-death processes are used in modeling population, they are useful in the analysis of communication networks. They are also used in physics, biology, sociology, and economics.

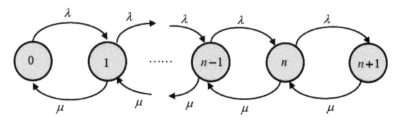

FIGURE 2.14 The state transition diagram for a birth-and-death process.

2.13.4 Poisson Processes

From an application point of view, Poisson processes are very useful. They can be used to model a large class of stochastic phenomena. A Poisson process is one in which the number of events which occur in any time interval t is distributed according to a Poisson random variable, with mean λt. In this process, the interarrival time is distributed exponentially. A process is called a *Poisson process* when the time intervals between successive events are exponentially distributed.

Given a sequence of discrete events occurring at times $t_0, t_1, t_2, t_3, \ldots$, the intervals between successive events are $\Delta t_1 = (t_1 - t_0)$, $\Delta t_2 = (t_2 - t_1)$, $\Delta t_3 = (t_3 - t_2)$, $\ldots$, and so on. For a Poisson process, these intervals are treated as independent random variables drawn from an exponentially distributed population, that is, a population with the density function $f(x) = \lambda e^{-\lambda x}$ for some fixed constant λ. The interoccurrence times between successive events of a Poisson process with parameter λ are independent identical distributed (IID) exponential random variables with mean $1/\lambda$.

The Poisson process is a counting process for the number of randomly occurring point-events observed in a given time interval. For example, suppose the arrival process has a Poisson type distribution. If $N(t)$ denotes the number of arrivals in time interval $(0,t]$, the probability mass function for $N(t)$ is

$$p_n(t) = P[N(t) = n] = \frac{(\lambda t)^n}{n!} e^{-\lambda t} \tag{2.117}$$

Thus, the number of events $N(t)$ in the interval $(0,t]$ has a Poisson distribution with parameter λt and the parameter λ is called the arrival rate of the Poisson process.

Two properties of the Poisson process are the superposition property and decomposition property.

The superposition (additive) property states that the superposition of Poisson processes is also a Poisson process, as illustrated in Figure 2.15. Thus, the sum of n independent Poisson processes with parameters $\lambda_k, k = 1, 2, \cdots, n$ is a Poisson process with parameter $\lambda = \lambda_1 + \lambda_2 + \cdots + \lambda_n$.

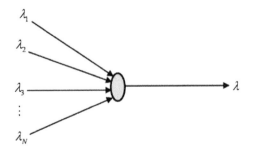

FIGURE 2.15 Superposition of Poisson streams.

The decomposition (splitting) property is just the reverse of the superposition property. If a Poisson stream is split into k substreams, each substream is also Poisson, as illustrated in Figure 2.16.

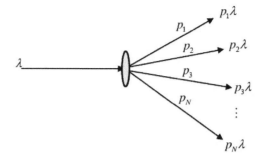

FIGURE 2.16 Decomposition of a Poisson stream.

The Poisson process is related to the exponential distribution. If the interarrival times are exponentially distributed, the number of arrival-points in a time interval is given by the Poisson distribution and the process is a Poisson arrival process. The converse is also true—if the number of arrival-points in any interval is a Poisson process, the interarrival times are exponentially distributed. The relationship among various types of stochastic (random) processes is shown in Figure 2.17.

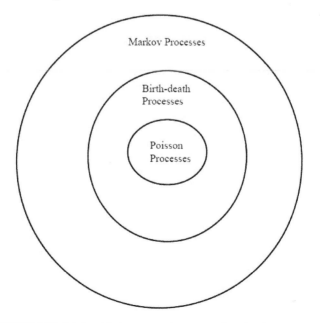

FIGURE 2.17 Relationship between various types of stochastic processes.

2.14 RENEWAL PROCESSES

A renewal process generalizes the notion of a Markov process. In a Markov process, the times between state transitions are exponentially distributed. Let $X_1, X_2, X_3, \cdots$ be times of successive occurrences of some phenomenon and let $Z_i = X_i - X_{i-1}$ be the times between $(i-1)$th and ith occurrences, and then if $\{Z_i\}$ are independent and identically distributed (IID), the process $\{X_i\}$ is called a *renewal process*. The study of renewal processes is called *renewal theory*.

One common example of a renewal process is the arrival process to a queueing system. The times between successive arrivals are IID. In a special case where the interarrival times are exponential, the renewal process is a Poisson process. Poisson processes, binomial processes, and random walk processes are special cases of renewal processes.

2.15 KENDALL'S NOTATION

In view of the complexity of a data network, we first examine the properties of a single queue. The results from a single queue model can be extended to model a network of queues. A single queue is comprised of one or more servers and customers waiting for service. As shown in Figure 2.18, the queue is characterized by three quantities:

- the input process,
- the service mechanism, and
- the queue discipline.

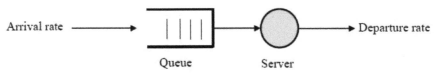

Arrival rate   Departure rate

Queue   Server

FIGURE 2.18 A typical queueing system.

The *input process* is expressed in terms of the probability distribution of the interarrival times of arriving customers. The *service mechanism* describes the statistical properties of the service process. The *queue discipline* is the rule used to determine how the customers waiting get served. To avoid ambiguity in specifying these characteristics, a queue is usually described in terms of a well-known shorthand notation devised by D. G. Kendall. In Kendall's notation, a queue is characterized by six parameters as follows:

$$A/B/C/K/m/z \tag{2.118}$$

where the letters denote:

A: Arrival process, that is, the interarrival time (t) distribution

(M = exponential, D = deterministic, G= general, arrival rate $= \lambda = 1 / E(\tau)$)

B: Service process, that is, the service time (s) distribution

(M = exponential, D = deterministic, G = general, service rate $= \mu = 1 / E(s)$)

C: Number of servers (1 server, c servers, ∞)

K: Maximum capacity of the queue (default $= \infty$)

m: Population of customers (default $= \infty$)

z: Service discipline (default = FIFO)

The letters A and B represent the arrival and service processes and assume the following specific letters, depending on which probability distribution law is adopted:

D: Constant (deterministic) law, that is, interarrival/service times are fixed

M: Markov or exponential law, that is, interarrival/service times are exponentially distributed

G: General law, that is, nothing is known about the interarrival/service time distribution

GI: General independent law, that is, all interarrival/service times are independent

E$_k$: Erlang's law of order k ($k = 1,2,.....$)

H$_k$: Hyperexponential (Mixture of k exponentials) law of order k

The most commonly used service (queue) disciplines are:

FIFO: first-in first-out

FCFS: first-come first-served

LCFS: last-come first-served

LIFO: last-in first-out

FIRO: first-in random-out

PR: priority

GD: general-discipline

It is common in practice to represent a queue by specifying only the first three symbols of Kendall's notation. In this case, it is assumed that $K = \infty$, $m = \infty$, and z = FIFO. Thus, for example, the notation M/M/1 represents a queue in which arrival times are exponentially distributed, service times are exponentially distributed, there is one server, the queue length is infinite, the customer population is infinite, and the service discipline is FIFO. In the same way, an M/G/n queue is one with Poisson arrivals, general service distribution, and n servers.

Example 2.8

A single-queue system is denoted by M/G/5/20/100/FCFS. Explain what the operation of the system is.

Solution

The system can be described as follows:

1. The interval arrival times are exponentially distributed.

2. The services times follow a general probability distribution.

3. There are five servers.

4. The buffer size of the queue is 20.

5. The population of customers to be served is 100; that is, only 100 customers can occupy this queue.

6. The service discipline is first come, first served.

2.16 LITTLE'S THEOREM

To obtain the waiting or queueing time, we apply a useful result, known as *Little's theorem*, after the author of the first formal proof in 1961. The theorem relates the mean number of customers in a queue to the mean arrival rate and the mean waiting time. It states that a queueing system, with average arrival rate λ and mean waiting time per customer $E(W)$, has a mean number of customers in the queue (or average queue length) $E(N_q)$ given by

$$E(N_q) = \lambda E(W) \tag{2.119}$$

The theorem is very general and applies to all kinds of queueing systems. It assumes that the system is in a statistical equilibrium or steady state, meaning that the probabilities of the system being in a particular state have settled down and are not changing with time.

It should be noted that Equation (2.119) is valid irrespective of the operating policies of the queueing system. For example, it holds for an arbitrary network of queues and servers. It also applies to a single queue, excluding the server.

The graphical proof of the theorem will be given here. Suppose we keep track of arrival and departure times of individual customers for a long time t_o. If t_o is large, the number of arrivals would approximately equal to the number of departures. If this number is N_a, then

$$\text{Arrival Rate} = \lambda = \frac{N_a}{t_o} \tag{2.120}$$

Let $A(t)$ and $D(t)$ be respectively the number of arrivals and departures in the interval $(0, t_o)$. Figure 2.18 shows $A(t)$ and $D(t)$. If we subtract the departure curve from the arrival curve at each time instant, we get the number of customers in the system at that moment. The hatched area in Figure 2.19 represents the total time spent inside the system by all customers.

If this is represented by J,

$$\text{Mean time spent in system} = T = \frac{J}{N_a} \tag{2.121}$$

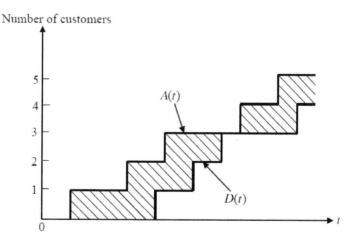

FIGURE 2.19 Plot of arrival time and departure time.

From Equations (2.120) and (2.121),

$$\text{Mean number of customers in the system} = N = \frac{J}{t_o} = \left(\frac{N_a}{t_o}\right) \times \left(\frac{J}{N_a}\right) \tag{2.122}$$

or

$$N = \lambda T \tag{2.123}$$

which is *Little's theorem*.

2.17   M/M/1 QUEUE

Consider the M/M/1 queue shown in Figure 2.20. This is a single-server system with infinite queue size, Poisson arrival process with arrival rate λ, and exponentially distributed service times with service rate μ. The queue discipline is FCFS.

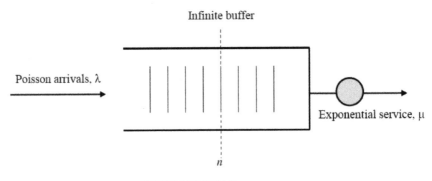

FIGURE 2.20 M/M/1 queue.

The probability of k arrivals in a time interval t is given by the Poisson distribution:

$$p(k) = \frac{(\lambda t)^k}{k!} e^{-\lambda t}, \qquad k = 0, 1, 2, \cdots \tag{2.124}$$

(Note that the Poisson arrival process has exponential arrival times.) It is readily shown that the mean or expected value and variance are given by

$$E(k) = \sum_{k=0}^{\infty} kp(k) = \lambda t \qquad (2.125a)$$

$$\mathrm{Var}(k) = E[(k - E(k))^2] = \lambda t \qquad (2.125b)$$

One way of analyzing such a queue is to consider its state diagram in Figure 2.21. We say that the system is in state n where there are n customers in the system (in the queue and the server). Notice from Figure 2.21 that λ is the rate of moving from state n to $n+1$ due to an arrival in the system, whereas μ is the rate of moving from state n to $n-1$ due to departure when service is completed. If $N(t)$ is the number of customers in the system (in the queue and the server) at time t, the probability of the queue being in state n at a steady state is given by

$$p_n = \lim_{t \longrightarrow \infty} \mathrm{Prob}[N(t) = n], \qquad n = 0, 1, 2, \cdots \qquad (2.126)$$

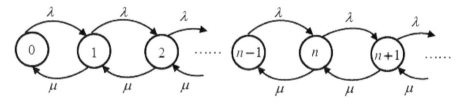

FIGURE 2.21 State diagram for M/M/1 queue.

Our goal is to find p_n and use it to find some performance measures of interest.

Consider when the system is in state 0. Due to an arrival, the rate at which the process leaves state 0 for state 1 is λp_o. Due to a departure, the rate at which the process leaves state 1 for state 0 is μp_1. In order for stationary probability to exist, the rate of leaving state 0 must equal the rate of entering it. Thus

$$\lambda p_o = \mu p_1 \qquad (2.127)$$

when the system is in state 1. Since p_1 is the proportion of time in which the system is in state 1, the total rate at which arrival or departure occurs is $\lambda p_1 + \mu p_1$, which is the rate at which the process leaves state 1. Similarly, the total rate at which the process enters state 1 is $\lambda p_0 + \mu p_2$. Applying the rate-equality principle gives

$$\lambda p_1 + \mu p_1 = \lambda p_0 + \mu p_2 \tag{2.128}$$

We proceed in this manner for the general case of the system being in state n and obtain

$$(\lambda + \mu)p_n = \lambda p_{n-1} + \mu p_{n+1}, \quad n \geq 1 \tag{2.129}$$

The right-hand side of this equation denotes the rate of entering state n, while the left-hand side represents the rate of leaving state n. Equations (2.127) to (2.129) are called *balance equations*.

We can solve Equation (2.129) in several ways. An easy way is to write Equation (2.129) as

$$\begin{aligned}
\lambda p_n - \mu p_{n+1} &= \lambda p_{n-1} - \mu p_n \\
&= \lambda p_{n-2} - \mu p_{n-1} \\
&= \lambda p_{n-3} - \mu p_{n-2} \\
&\vdots \quad \vdots \\
&= \lambda p_0 - \mu p_1 = 0
\end{aligned} \tag{2.130}$$

Thus

$$\lambda p_n = \mu p_{n+1} \tag{2.131}$$

or

$$p_{n+1} = \rho p_n, \quad \rho = \lambda / \mu \tag{2.132}$$

If we apply this repeatedly, we get

$$p_{n+1} = \rho p_n = \rho^2 p_{n-1} = \rho^3 p_{n-2} = \cdots = \rho^{n+1} p_0, \quad n = 0, 1, 2, \cdots \tag{2.133}$$

We now apply the probability normalization condition,

$$\sum_{n=0}^{\infty} p_n = 1 \tag{2.134}$$

and obtain

$$p_0 \left[1 + \sum_{n=1}^{\infty} \rho^n \right] = 1 \tag{2.135}$$

If $\rho < 1$, we get the probability of zero jobs in the system

$$p_0 \frac{1}{1-\rho} = 1 \tag{2.136}$$

or

$$p_0 = 1 - \rho \tag{2.137}$$

From Equations (2.132) and (2.137), we get the probability of n jobs in the system

$$p_n = (1-\rho)\rho^n, \quad n = 1, 2, \cdots \tag{2.138}$$

which is a geometric distribution.

Having found p_n, we are now prepared to obtain some performance measures or measures of effectiveness. These include utilization, throughput, the average queue length, and the average service time.

The *utilization* U of the system is the fraction of time that the server is busy. In other words, U is the probability of the server being busy. Thus

$$U = \sum_{n=1}^{\infty} p_n = 1 - p_0 = \rho$$

or

$$U = \rho \tag{2.139}$$

The *throughput* R of the system is the rate at which customers leave the queue after service, that is, the departure rate of the server. Thus,

$$R = \mu(1 - p_0) = \mu\rho = \lambda \tag{2.140}$$

This should be expected because the arrival and departure rates are equal at a steady state for the system to be stable.

The average number of customers in the system is

$$\begin{aligned}
E(N) &= \sum_{n=0}^{\infty} np_n = \sum_{n=0}^{\infty} n(1-\rho)\rho^n = (1-\rho)\sum_{n=0}^{\infty} n\rho^n \\
&= (1-\rho)\frac{\rho}{(1-\rho)^2} = \frac{\rho}{1-\rho}
\end{aligned} \tag{2.141}$$

The *variance of the number of jobs in the system* is

$$\text{Var}(N) = E(N^2) - [E(N)]^2 = \left(\sum_{n=1}^{\infty} n^2 (1-\rho)\rho^n \right) - [E(N)]^2 = \frac{\rho}{(1-\rho)^2}$$

Applying Little's formula, we obtain the *average response time* or *average delay* as

$$E(T) = \frac{E(N)}{\lambda} = \frac{1}{\lambda} \frac{\rho}{1-\rho} \tag{2.142}$$

or

$$E(T) = \frac{1}{\mu(1-\rho)} \tag{2.143}$$

Using $\rho = \dfrac{\lambda}{\mu}$, we have $E(T) = \dfrac{1}{\mu - \lambda}$.

The *variance of response time* is $\text{Var}(T) = \dfrac{1}{\mu^2 (1-\rho)^2}$

This is the mean value of the total time spent in the system (i.e., queue and the server).

As shown in Figure 2.22, the average delay $E(T)$ is the sum of the average waiting time $E(W)$ and the average service time $E(S)$, that is,

$$E(T) = E(W) + E(S) \tag{2.144}$$

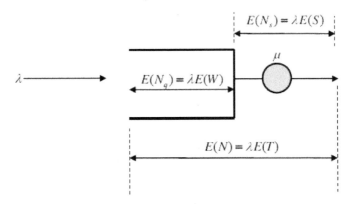

FIGURE 2.22 Little's formula applied to M/M/1 queue thrice.

Equivalently, the average number of customers $E(N)$ in the system equals the sum of the average of customers waiting $E(N_q)$ in the queue and the average number of customers $E(N_s)$ being served, that is,

$$E(N) = E(N_q) + E(N_s) \tag{2.145}$$

But the mean service $E(S) = \dfrac{1}{\mu}$. Thus, *average waiting time* is

$$E(W) = E(T) - \frac{1}{\mu} \tag{2.146}$$

or

$$E(W) = \frac{\rho}{\mu(1-\rho)} = \frac{\rho}{\mu - \lambda} \tag{2.147}$$

The *variance of the waiting time*,

$$\mathrm{Var}(W) = \frac{2\rho - \rho^2}{\mu^2(1-\rho)^2}$$

We now apply Little's theorem to find the *average queue length* or the average number of customers waiting in the queue, that is,

$$E(N_q) = \lambda E(W) = \frac{\rho^2}{1-\rho} \tag{2.148}$$

The *variance of number of jobs in the queue*,

$$\mathrm{Var}(N_q) = \frac{\rho^2\left(1+\rho-\rho^2\right)}{\left(1-\rho\right)^2}$$

Finally, since $E(N) = lE(T)$, it is evident from Equations (2.126) and (2.127) that

$$E(N_s) = \lambda E(S) = \lambda\frac{1}{\mu} = \rho \tag{2.149}$$

Notice from Equations (2.142), (2.147), and (2.149) that the Little's theorem is applied three times. This is also shown in Figure 2.22.

Example 2.9

Service at a bank may be modeled as an M/M/1 queue at which customers arrive according to the Poisson process. Assume that the mean arrival rate is 1 customer/minute and that the service times are exponentially distributed with a mean of 50 seconds/customer. (a) Find the average queue length. (b) How long does a customer have to wait in line? (c) Determine the average queue size and the waiting time in the queue if the service time is increased to 55 seconds/customer.

Solution

As an M/M/1 queue, we obtain the mean arrival rate as

$\lambda = 1$ customer/minute

and the mean service rate as

$$E(S) = \frac{1}{\mu} = 50 \text{ seconds/customer } = \frac{50}{60} = \frac{5}{6} \text{ minute/customer}$$

Hence, the traffic intensity is

$$\rho = \frac{\lambda}{\mu} = (1)(50/60) = \frac{5}{6}$$

A. The mean queue size is

$$E[N_q] = \frac{\rho^2}{1-\rho} = \frac{(5/6)^2}{1-5/6} = \frac{0.694}{0.167} = 4.156 \text{ customers}$$

B. The mean waiting time is

$$E[W] = \frac{\rho}{\mu(1-\rho)} = \frac{5/6(5/6)}{(1-5/6)} = 4.158 \text{ minutes}$$

C. If the mean service time $E(S) = 55$ seconds/customer $= 55/60$ minutes/customer, then

$$\rho = \frac{\lambda}{\mu} = (1)(55/60) = 0.917$$

$$E[N_q] = \frac{\rho^2}{1-\rho} = \frac{(55/60)^2}{1-55/60} = \frac{0.840}{0.083} = 10.120 \text{ customers}$$

$$E[W] = \frac{\rho}{\mu(1-\rho)} = \frac{55/60(55/60)}{(1-55/60)} = \frac{0.840}{0.083} = 10.120 \text{ minutes}$$

We expect the queue size and waiting time to increase if it takes a longer time for customers to be served.

2.18   M/M/1 QUEUE WITH BULK ARRIVALS/SERVICE

In the previous section, it was assumed that customers arrive individually (or one at a time) and are provided service individually. In this section, we consider the possibility of customers arriving in bulk (or in groups or batch) or being served in bulk. Bulk arrivals/service occur in practice because it is often more economical to collect a number of items (jobs, orders, etc.) before servicing them.

2.18.1 M^x/M/1 (Bulk Arrivals) System

Here we consider the situation where arrivals occur in batches of more than one customer, that is, in bulk. Although the process is not a birth-and-death process, the arrival instants still occur as a Poisson process with constant rate λ. Each of the arriving customers is served in standard fashion (first-come, first served, one at a time) by a server with exponentially distributed service times with parameter μ. Suppose the size of the batch is fixed at $m \geq 1$ customers. Then only two transitions can occur as

$$n \quad \longrightarrow \quad n+m \quad \text{(arrival)}$$

or

$$n+1 \quad \longrightarrow \quad n \quad \text{(departure)}$$

The state transition diagram is shown in Figure 2.23 for $m = 2$. The balance equation for $n = 0$ is

$$\lambda p_0 = m\mu p_1 \tag{2.150}$$

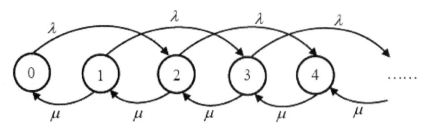

FIGURE 2.23 Transition diagram of MX/M/1 queue with $m = 2$.

and for $n \geq 1$ is

$$(\lambda + \mu m)p_n = \mu m p_{n+1} + \lambda p_{n-m} \tag{2.151}$$

We now apply the method of z-transforms to solve for p_n. We define the generating function

$$G(z) = \sum_{i=0}^{\infty} p_n z^n \tag{2.152}$$

Multiplying the balance equation for state n by z^n and summing, we obtain

$$\sum_{n=1}^{\infty} (\lambda + \mu m)p_n z^n = \sum_{n=1}^{\infty} \mu m p_{n+1} z^n + \sum_{n=1}^{\infty} \lambda p_{n-m} z^n \tag{2.153}$$

Simplifying yields

$$G(z) = \frac{\mu m(1-z)p_0}{\mu m + \lambda z^{m+1} - z(\lambda + \mu m)} \tag{2.154}$$

The value of p_0 is obtained using the condition $G(1) = 1$.

$$p_0 = 1 - \frac{\lambda m}{\mu} = 1 - \rho, \quad \rho = \frac{\lambda m}{\mu} \tag{2.155}$$

2.18.2 M/M^Y/1 (Bulk Service) System

This kind of model is used to analyze systems that wait until a certain message size is reached before releasing the data for transmission. We will assume that customers are served in bulk of size m, that is, customers are served m at a time. At equilibrium, the balance equations are:

$$(\lambda + \mu)p_n = \lambda p_{n-1} + \mu p_{n+m}, \quad n \geq 1 \qquad (2.156a)$$

$$\lambda p_0 = \mu p_m + \mu p_{m-1} + \cdots + \mu p_1 \qquad (2.156b)$$

Equation (2.156a) can be written in terms of an operator D so

$$\left[\mu D^{m+1} - (\lambda + \mu)D + \lambda \right] p_n = 0, \quad n \geq 0 \qquad (2.157)$$

If the roots of the characteristic equation are $r_1, r_2, \cdots, r_{m+1}$, then

$$p_n = \sum_{I=1}^{m+1} C_i r_i^n, \quad n \geq 0 \qquad (2.158)$$

Using the fact that $\sum_{n=0}^{\infty} p_n = 1$, we obtain

$$p_n = (1 - r_0)r_0^n, \quad n \geq 0, 0 < r_0 < 1 \qquad (2.159)$$

where r_0 is the one and only one root of Equation (2.157) that is less than one. Comparing this with Equation (2.138) shows the similarity between this solution and that of M/M/1. Hence,

$$E[N] = \frac{r_0}{1 - r_0} \qquad (2.160)$$

$$E[T] = \frac{r_0}{\lambda(1 - r_0)} \qquad (2.161)$$

2.18.3 M/M/1/k Queueing System

In this case, we have situations similar to M/M/1, but the number of customers that can be queued is limited to k. In other words, this is a system with limited waiting space. If an arriving customer finds the queue full, it is lost or blocked, as shown in Figure 2.24. Hence,

$$\lambda_n = \begin{cases} \lambda, & \text{if } 0 \leq n < k \\ 0, & n \geq k \end{cases} \qquad (2.162)$$

$$\mu_n = \mu, \quad 0 \leq n \leq k \qquad (2.163)$$

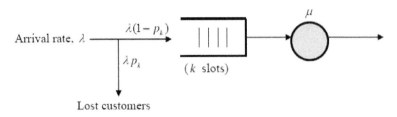

FIGURE 2.24 M/M/1/k queueing system.

The state transition diagram is given in Figure 2.25. The balance equations are

$$\lambda p_0 = \mu p_1$$

$$\lambda p_n + \mu p_n = \lambda p_{n-1} + \mu p_{n+1}, \quad 1 \le n \le k-1 \tag{2.164}$$

$$\lambda p_{k-1} = \mu p_k$$

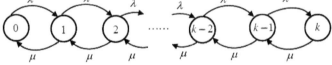

FIGURE 2.25 State transition diagram for the M/M/1/k queue.

The probability of zero customers in the system, p_0 can be obtained from

$$p_0 = \frac{1}{1 + \sum_{n=1}^{\infty} \left(\dfrac{\lambda_0 \ldots \lambda_{n-1}}{\mu_1 \ldots \mu_n} \right)}, \text{ thus } p_0 = \left(1 + \sum_{n=1}^{k} \left(\frac{\lambda}{\mu} \right)^n \right)^{-1}$$

The sum is a finite geometric series which can be obtained as

$$\sum_{n=1}^{k} \left(\frac{\lambda}{\mu} \right)^n = \frac{\left(\dfrac{\lambda}{\mu} \right) \left(1 - \left(\dfrac{\lambda}{\mu} \right)^k \right)}{1 - \left(\dfrac{\lambda}{\mu} \right)}$$

Now, we get

$$p_0 = \frac{1 - \rho}{1 - \rho^{k+1}}$$

We solve these equations recursively and apply the normalization condition. If we define $\rho = \lambda / \mu$, the state probabilities at a steady state are given by

$$p_n = \begin{cases} \dfrac{(1-\rho)\rho^n}{1-\rho^{k+1}}, & 0 \leq n \leq k \\ \\ 0, & n > k \end{cases} \qquad (2.165)$$

The utilization of the server is given by

$$U = 1 - p_0 = \frac{\rho(1-\rho^k)}{1-\rho^{k+1}} \qquad (2.166)$$

The average number of customers in the system is

$$E(N) = \sum_{n=0}^{k} np_n = \frac{\rho}{1-\rho^{k+1}}\left[\frac{1-\rho^k}{1-\rho} - k\rho^k\right] \qquad (2.167)$$

Since there can be blocking in this system, the blocking probability is

$$P_B = p_k = \frac{(1-\rho)\rho^k}{1-\rho^{k+1}} \qquad (2.168)$$

This is the probability that an arriving customer is blocked, that is, is lost because the queue is full.

Example 2.10

A system consists of a packet buffer and a communication server and can hold not more than three packets. Arrivals are Poisson with a rate of 30 packets/ms and the server follows exponential distribution with a mean of 60 packets/ms. Determine the blocking probability of the system.

Solution

This is an M/M/1/k system with $k = 4$.

$$\rho = \lambda \frac{1}{\mu} = \frac{60}{60} = 0.5$$

The probability is

$$P_B = \frac{(1-\rho)\rho^k}{1-\rho^{k+1}} = \frac{(1-0.5)0.5^4}{1-0.5^5} = 0.0323$$

which is about 3 percent.

2.18.4 M/M/k Queueing System

This is the case where we have k servers, as shown in Figure 2.26. Upon arrival, a customer is served by any available server. The arriving customer is queued when all servers are found busy, that is, no customer is queued until the number of arrivals exceeds k. The state transition diagram is shown in Figure 2.27. The system can be modeled as a birth-and-death process with

$$\lambda_n = \lambda \tag{2.169}$$

$$\mu_m = \begin{cases} n\mu, & 0 \le n \le k \\ k\mu, & n \ge k \end{cases}$$

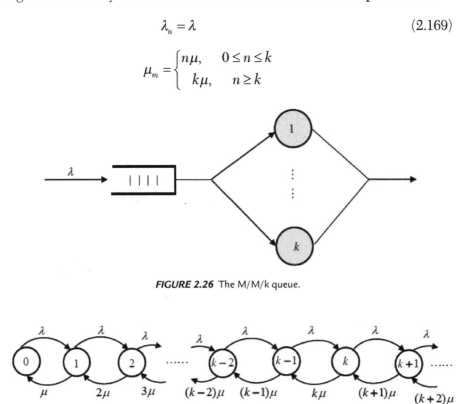

FIGURE 2.26 The M/M/k queue.

FIGURE 2.27 State transition diagram for M/M/k system.

At a steady state,

$$\lambda p_{n-1} = n\mu p_n, \quad n \le k \tag{2.170a}$$

$$\lambda p_{n-1} = k\mu p_n, \quad n > k \tag{2.170b}$$

From these, we obtain the state probabilities as

$$p_n = \begin{cases} p_0 \dfrac{(k\rho)^n}{n!}, & n \le k \\[3mm] p_0 \dfrac{\rho^n k^k}{k!}, & n \ge k \end{cases}$$

(2.171)

where $\rho = \dfrac{\lambda}{k\mu} < 1$. Solving for p_0, we get

$$p_0 = \left[\sum_{n=0}^{k-1} \frac{(k\rho)^n}{n!} + \left(\frac{k^k \rho^k}{k!} \right) \frac{1}{1-\rho} \right]^{-1}$$

(2.172)

Measures of effectiveness for this model can be obtained in the usual manner. The probability that an arriving customer joins the queue is

$$\text{Prob[queueing]} = P_Q = \sum_{n=k}^{\infty} p_n = \sum_{n=k}^{\infty} \frac{p_0 k^k \rho^n}{k!} = \frac{p_0 (k\rho)^k}{k!} \sum_{n=k}^{\infty} \rho^{n-k} = \frac{k^k \rho^k}{k!} \left(\frac{p_0}{1-\rho} \right)$$

or

$$P_Q = \frac{k^k \rho^k}{k!} \left(\frac{p_0}{1-\rho} \right)$$

(2.173)

This formula is known as Erlang's C formula. It is widely used in telephony; it gives the probability that no trunk (or server) is available for an arriving call.

The average number of customers waiting in queue in the system can be obtained as $E(N_q) = \dfrac{P_Q \rho}{1-\rho}$.

The average waiting time in queue of customers in the system can be obtained as $E(W) = \dfrac{E(N_q)}{\lambda} = \dfrac{\rho P_Q}{\lambda(1-\rho)}$

The average queue length in the system can be obtained as is

$$E[N] = \sum_{n=0}^{\infty} n p_n = k\rho + \frac{\rho}{(1-\rho)} P_Q$$

(2.174)

The *variance of number of customers* in the system can be obtained as

$$Var(N) = k\rho + \rho P_Q \left(\frac{1 + \rho - \rho P_Q}{(1-\rho)^2} + k \right)$$

The *average number of customers in the queue* in the system can be obtained as

$$E(N_q) = \frac{\rho P_Q}{1-\rho}$$

The *variance of number of customers in the queue* in the system can be obtained as s

$$Var(N_q) = \frac{\rho P_Q \left(1 + \rho - \rho P_Q\right)}{(1-\rho)^2}$$

The average utilization of each server in the system can be obtained as

$$U = \frac{\lambda}{k\mu} = \rho$$

The *average number of customers in service* can be obtained as

$$E(N_s) = k\rho$$

Using Little's theorem, the average time spent $E[T]$ in the system can be obtained as

$$E[T] = \frac{E[N]}{\lambda} = \frac{1}{\mu} + \frac{1}{\mu k} \frac{P_Q}{(1-\rho)} \tag{2.175}$$

The variance of response time in the system can be obtained as

$$Var(T) = \frac{1}{\mu^2} \left(1 + \frac{P_Q \left(2 - P_Q\right)}{k^2 \left(1-\rho\right)^2} \right)$$

Example 2.11

Customers arrive at a computer center in a Poisson way at an average rate of 30/hour. Each customer spends an average of 10 minutes at the terminal, assuming the time is exponentially distributed. The center has 20 terminals. Find the traffic intensity (Utilization), ρ.

Solution

The center can be modeled as an M/M/20. The arrival rate $\lambda = \dfrac{30}{60} = 0.5$ per minute and the service rate of $\mu = \dfrac{1}{10}$ per minute

The traffic intensity $\rho = \dfrac{\lambda}{k\mu} = \dfrac{0.5}{20(1/10)} = 0.25$

2.18.5 M/M/∞ Queueing System

This is the case in which we have an infinite number of servers so that an arriving customer can always find a server and need not queue. This model can be used to study the effect of delay in large systems. The state transition diagram for the M/M/∞ system is shown in Figure 2.28. Like we did before, we assume a Poisson arrival at rate λ and exponentially distributed service times with mean $1/\mu$. We adopt a birth-and-death process with parameters

$$\lambda_n = \lambda, \quad n = 0, 1, 2, \cdots \tag{2.176}$$

$$\mu_n = n\mu, \quad n = 0, 1, 2, \cdots \tag{2.177}$$

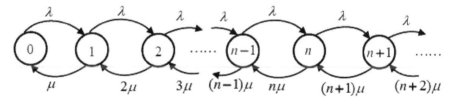

FIGURE 2.28 State transition diagram for M/M/ ∞ queueing system.

The balance equation is

$$\lambda p_n = (n+1)\mu p_{n+1} \tag{2.178}$$

which can be solved to give

$$p_n = \frac{\rho^n}{n!} p_0, \quad n = 0, 1, 2, \cdots \tag{2.179}$$

where $\rho = \lambda / \mu$. Applying the normalization condition $\sum_{n=0}^{\infty} p_n = 1$ gives

$$p_0 = e^{-\rho} \tag{2.180}$$

The utilization of the server is

$$U = 1 - p_0 = 1 - e^{-\rho} \tag{2.181}$$

The average number of customers in the system is

$$E[N] = \sum_{n=0}^{\infty} np_n = \rho \tag{2.182}$$

We apply Little's theorem in finding the average time spent in the system.

$$E[T] = \frac{E[N]}{\lambda} = \frac{1}{\mu} \tag{2.183}$$

Also,

$$E[N_q] = 0 = E[W_q] \tag{2.184}$$

that is, the average waiting time and the average number of customers waiting in the queue are both zero.

2.19   M/G/1 QUEUEING SYSTEM

The M/G/1 queueing system, the simplest non-Markovian system, is shown in Figure 2.29. We analyze it assuming that it is in the steady state. An M/G/1 system assumes a FIFO service discipline, an infinite queue size, a Poisson input process (with arrival rate λ), general service times (with arbitrary but known distribution function H, mean $\tau = 1 / \mu$, and variance σ^2), and one server.

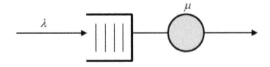

FIGURE 2.29 The M/G/1 queue system has a general service time distribution.

In order to find the waiting time of the M/G/1 model, we apply the method *of z-transform* or generating functions.

The probability of having k arrivals during the service time t is

$$p_k = \int_0^\infty p(k)dH(t) = \int_0^\infty \frac{(\lambda t)^k}{k!} e^{-\lambda t} dH(t) \qquad (2.185)$$

where $H(t)$ is the service time distribution.

Let N be the number of customers present in the system and Q be the number of customers in the queue. Let the probability that an arriving customer finds j other customers present be

$$\Pi_j = \text{Prob}(N = j), \quad j = 0,1,2,... \qquad (2.186)$$

It can be shown using the theorem of total probability and the equilibrium imbedded-Markov-chain that

$$\Pi_j = p_j \Pi_0 + \sum_{i=1}^{j+1} p_{j-i+1} \Pi_i, \quad j = 0,1,2,... \qquad (2.187)$$

We define the probability-generating functions

$$g(z) = \sum_{j=0}^\infty \Pi_j z^j \qquad (2.188a)$$

$$h(z) = \sum_{j=0}^\infty p_j z^j \qquad (2.188b)$$

Substituting Equation (2.188a) into Equation (2.187) results in

$$g(z) = \frac{(z-1)h(z)}{z - h(z)} \Pi_0 \qquad (2.189)$$

The normalization equation

$$\sum_{j=0}^\infty \Pi_j = 1 \qquad (2.190)$$

implies that $g(1) = 1$. With a single application of L'Hopital's rule, we find

$$\Pi_0 = 1 - \rho \qquad (2.191)$$

where $\rho = \lambda / \mu = \lambda \tau$. If we define $\eta(s)$ as the Laplace-Stieltjes transform of the service-time distribution function $H(t)$,

$$\eta(s) = \int_0^\infty e^{-st} dH(t) \tag{2.192}$$

Substitution of Equation (2.185) into Equation (2.188b) yields

$$h(z) = \eta(\lambda - \lambda z) \tag{2.193}$$

and substitution of Equation (2.191) and Equation (2.193) into Equation (2.189) leads to

$$g(z) = \frac{(z-1)\eta(\lambda - \lambda z)}{z - \eta(\lambda - \lambda z)}(1 - \rho) \tag{2.194}$$

Differentiating this and applying the L'Hopital rule twice, we obtain

$$g'(1) = \frac{\rho^2}{2(1-\rho)}\left(1 + \frac{\sigma^2}{\tau^2}\right) + \rho \tag{2.195}$$

The mean values of the number of customers in the system and queue are respectively given by

$$E(N) = \sum_{j=0}^\infty j\Pi_j = g'(1) \tag{2.196a}$$

$$E(Q) = E(N) - \rho \tag{2.196b}$$

By applying Little's theorem, the mean value of the response time is

$$E(T) = \frac{E(N)}{\lambda} = \frac{\rho\tau}{2(1-\rho)}\left(1 + \frac{\sigma^2}{\tau^2}\right) + \tau \tag{2.197}$$

$$= E(W) + \tau$$

Thus, we obtain the mean waiting time as

$$E(W) = \frac{E(Q)}{\lambda} = \frac{\rho\tau}{2(1-\rho)}\left(1 + \frac{\sigma^2}{\tau^2}\right) \tag{2.198}$$

where $\rho = \lambda / \mu = \lambda\tau$. This is known as the *Pollaczek-Khintchine formula* after two Russian mathematicians Pollaczek and Khintchine who derived the formula independently in 1930 and 1932 respectively. The average number of customers $E(N_q)$ in the queue is

$$E(N_q) = \lambda E(W) = \frac{\rho^2}{2(1-\rho)}\left(1 + \frac{\sigma^2}{\tau^2}\right) \tag{2.199}$$

The average response time is

$$E(T) = E(W) + \tau = \frac{\rho\tau}{2(1-\rho)}\left(1 + \frac{\sigma^2}{\tau^2}\right) + \tau \tag{2.200}$$

and the mean number of customers in the system is

$$E(N) = \lambda E(T) = E(N_q) + \rho \tag{2.201}$$

or

$$E(N) = \frac{\rho^2}{2(1-\rho)}\left(1 + \frac{\sigma^2}{\tau^2}\right) + \rho \tag{2.202}$$

We may now obtain the mean waiting time for the M/M/1 and M/D/1 queue models as special cases of the M/G/1 model.

For the M/M/1 queue model, a special case of the M/G/1 model, the service times follow an exponential distribution with mean $\tau = 1/\mu$ and variance σ^2. That means,

$$H(t) = \text{Prob}[X \le t] = 1 - e^{-\mu t} \tag{2.203}$$

Hence,

$$\sigma^2 = \tau^2 \tag{2.204}$$

Substituting this in the Pollaczek-Khintchine formula in Equation (2.198) gives the mean waiting time as

$$E(W) = \frac{\rho\tau}{(1-\rho)} \tag{2.205}$$

The M/D/1 queue is another special case of the M/G/1 model. For this model, the service times are constant with the mean value $\tau = 1/\mu$ and variance $\sigma = 0$. Thus, the Pollaczek-Khintchine formula in Equation (2.198) gives the mean waiting time as

$$E(W) = \frac{\rho\tau}{2(1-\rho)} \tag{2.206}$$

It should be noted from Equations (2.205) and (2.206) that the waiting time for the M/D/1 model is one-half that for the M/M/1 model, that is,

$$E(W)_{M/D/1} = \frac{\rho\tau}{2(1-\rho)} = \frac{1}{2}E(W)_{M/M/1} \qquad (2.207)$$

Example 2.12

In the M/G/1 system, prove that:

1. Prob (the system is empty) $= 1 - \rho$

2. Average length of time between busy periods $= 1/\lambda$

3. Average number of customers served in a busy period $= \dfrac{1}{1-\rho}$

    where $\rho = \lambda\overline{X}$ and $\overline{X}$ is the mean service time.

Solution

1. Let p_b = Prob. that the system is busy. Then p_b is the fraction of time that the server is busy. At a steady state,

$$\text{arrival rate} = \text{departure rate}$$

$$\lambda = p_b\mu$$

or

$$p_b = \frac{\lambda}{\mu} = \rho$$

The Prob. that the system is empty is

$$p_e = 1 - p_b = 1 - \rho$$

2. The server is busy only when there are arrivals. Hence the average length of time between busy periods = average interarrival rate = $1/\lambda$. Alternatively, we recall that if t is the interarrival time,

$$f(t) = \lambda e^{-\lambda t}$$

Hence $E(t) = 1/\lambda$.

3. Let $E(B)$ = average busy period, $E(I)$ = average idle period. From part (1),

$$p_b = \rho = \frac{E(B)}{E(B) + E(I)}$$

From part (2),

$E(I)$ = average length of time between busy periods = $1/\lambda$

Hence,

$$\rho = \frac{E(B)}{E(B) + \dfrac{1}{\lambda}}$$

Solving for $E(B)$ yields

$$E(B) = \frac{\rho}{\lambda(1-\rho)} = \frac{\overline{X}}{1-\rho}$$

as required.

The average number of customers served in a busy period is

$$N_b = \frac{\text{Average length of busy period}}{\text{Average service time}}$$

Hence,

$$N_b = \frac{E(B)}{\overline{\overline{X}}} = \frac{1}{1-\rho}$$

2.20   M/E$_K$/1 QUEUEING SYSTEM

In this case, the service time distribution is an Erlang distribution with parameters μ and k, that is,

$$f_X(x) = \frac{\mu(\mu x)^{k-1}}{(k-1)!} e^{-\mu x}, \quad x \geq 0 \tag{2.208}$$

with mean and variance

$$E[X] = \frac{k}{\mu}, \qquad \text{Var}[X] = \frac{k}{\mu^2} \tag{2.209}$$

This should be regarded as another special case of the M/G/1 system so that the Pollaczek-Khintchine formula in Equation (2.198) applies. Thus,

$$E[W_q] = \frac{1+k}{2k} \frac{\lambda}{\mu(\mu - \lambda)} = \frac{1+k}{2k} \frac{\rho}{\mu(1 - \rho)} \tag{2.210}$$

$$E[N_q] = \lambda E(W_q) = \frac{1+k}{2k} \frac{\lambda^2}{\mu(\mu - \lambda)} = \frac{1+k}{2k} \frac{\rho^2}{1 - \rho} \tag{2.211}$$

$$E[T] = E[W_q] + \frac{1}{\mu} \tag{2.212}$$

$$E[N] = \lambda E[T] \tag{2.213}$$

where $\rho = \lambda / \mu$.

2.21 NETWORKS OF QUEUES

The queues we have considered so far are isolated. In real life, we have a network of queues interconnected such as shown in Figure 2.30. Such networks of queues are usually complicated and are best analyzed using simulation.

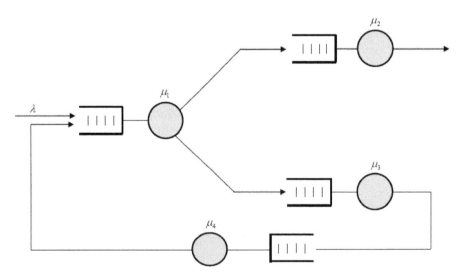

FIGURE 2.30 A typical network of queues.

2.21.1 Tandem Queues

Consider two M/M/1 queues in tandem, as shown in Figure 2.31. This is an example of an open queueing network. The state diagram is shown in Figure 2.32. From the state diagram, we can obtain the balance equations. Let

$$p_{i,j} = \text{Prob}[\text{ i jobs at server 1 and j jobs at server 2}]$$

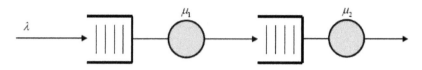

FIGURE 2.31 Two M/M/1 queues in tandem.

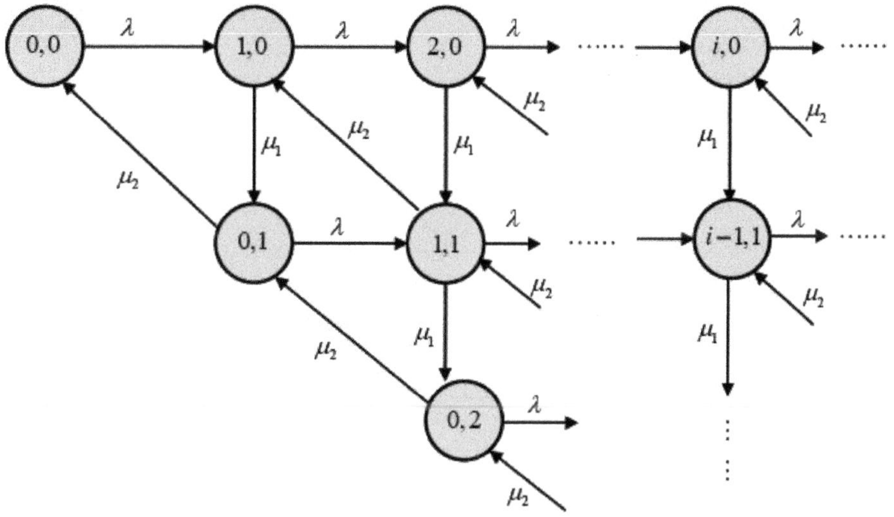

FIGURE 2.32 The state diagram for two M/M/1 queues in tandem.

For state $(0,0)$,

$$\lambda p_{0,0} = \mu_2 p_{0,1} \tag{2.214}$$

For state $(i,0)$, $\quad i > 0$,

$$\lambda p_{i-1,0} + \mu_2 p_{i,1} - (\lambda + \mu_1) p_{i,0} = 0 \tag{2.215}$$

For state $(0, j)$, $\quad j > 0$,

$$\mu_1 p_{1,j-1} + \mu_2 p_{0,j+1} - (\lambda + \mu_2) p_{0,j} = 0 \tag{2.216}$$

For state (i,j),

$$\lambda p_{i-1,j} + \mu_1 p_{i+1,j-1} + \mu_2 p_{i,j+1} - (\lambda + \mu_1 + \mu_2)p_{i,j} = 0 \tag{2.217}$$

Since queue 1 is unaffected by what happens at queue 2, the marginal probability of i jobs

at queue 1 is

$$p_i = (1 - \rho_1)\rho_1^i, \qquad \rho_1 = \frac{\lambda}{\mu_1} \tag{2.218}$$

Similarly, for queue 2

$$p_j = (1 - \rho_2)\rho_2^j, \qquad \rho_2 = \frac{\lambda}{\mu_2} \tag{2.219}$$

A simple product form solution for this two-node network is

$$p_{i,j} = (1 - \rho_1)(1 - \rho_2)\rho_1^i \rho_2^j, \qquad \rho_1 = \frac{\lambda}{\mu_1}, \qquad \rho_2 = \frac{\lambda}{\mu_2} \tag{2.220}$$

The average number of customers in the system is given by

$$E(N) = \sum_{i,j}(i+j)p_{i,j} = \sum_i i\left(\frac{\lambda}{\mu_1}\right)^i\left(1 - \frac{\lambda}{\mu_1}\right) + \sum_j j\left(\frac{\lambda}{\mu_2}\right)^j\left(1 - \frac{\lambda}{\mu_2}\right)$$

$$= \frac{\lambda}{\mu_1 - \lambda} + \frac{\lambda}{\mu_2 - \lambda} \tag{2.221}$$

From this we find the average time a customer spends in the system is given by

$$E(W) = \frac{E(N)}{\lambda} = \frac{1}{\mu_1 - \lambda} + \frac{1}{\mu_2 - \lambda} \tag{2.222}$$

2.21.2 Queueing System with Splitting

Splitting a Poisson distribution is shown in Figure 2.33. Suppose that a proportion p of the departures from an M/M/1 system (or an M/M/k or an M/M/∞) joined a second system, and the remainder depart altogether. The input to the second system is a Poisson distribution with rate $p\lambda$. Let $X_1(t)$ be the number of departures from the first system and $Y_2(t)$ be the number of arrivals to the second system by time t. Then

$$P\left(Y_2(t) = k \mid X_1(t) = n\right) = \binom{n}{k} p^k (1-p)^{n-k} \qquad (2.223)$$

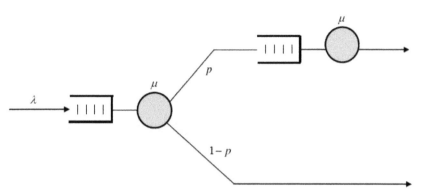

FIGURE 2.33 A queueing system with Splitting.

Thus,

$$P\left(Y_2(t) = k\right) = \sum_{n=k}^{\infty} P\left(Y_2(t) = k \mid X_1(t) = n\right) P\left(X_1(t) = n\right) \qquad (2.224)$$

Where n has to be at least as large as k. Therefore,

$$
\begin{aligned}
P\left(Y_2(t) = k\right) &= \sum_{n=k}^{\infty} e^{\lambda t} \frac{(\lambda t)^n}{n!} \frac{n!}{k!(n-k)!} p^k (1-p)^{n-k} \\
&= \frac{p^k e^{-\lambda t} (\lambda t)^k}{k!} \sum_{n=k}^{\infty} \frac{\left[\lambda t (1-p)\right]^{n-k}}{(n-k)!} \\
&= \frac{(p\lambda t)^k e^{-\lambda t}}{k!} e^{\lambda t (1-p)} \\
&= \frac{(p\lambda t)^k e^{-p\lambda t}}{k!}
\end{aligned}
\qquad (2.225)
$$

Thus, $Y_2(t)$ forms a Poisson distribution with input rate $p\lambda$.

2.21.3 Queueing System with Feedback

Queueing systems with feedback are applicable to a fairly limited set of circumstances. A typical example is shown in Figure 2.34. The problem here is that the combination of the external Poisson process and the feedback process is not Poisson because the processes being superposed are not independent due to the feedback. However, consideration of the steady state diagram shows us that, as far as queue length is concerned, the system behaves like an M/M/1 queue with arrival rate λ and service rate $p\mu$. Also, the traffic equation for this network is

$$\lambda_1 = \lambda + \lambda_1 p \qquad \longrightarrow \qquad \lambda_1 = \frac{\lambda}{1-p} \qquad (2.226)$$

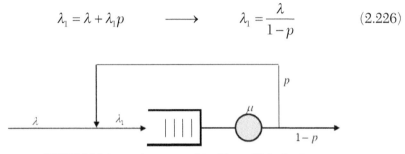

FIGURE 2.34 A queueing system with a (Bernoulli) feedback.

2.22   JACKSON NETWORKS

A Jackson network has a steady state solution in product form. Such product-form queueing networks can be open or closed. The nature of such networks allows us to decouple the queues, analyze them separately as individual systems, and then combine the results. For example, consider a series of k single-server queues with exponential service time and Poisson arrivals, as shown in Figure 2.35. Customers entering the system join a queue at each stage. It can be shown that each queue can be analyzed independently of other queues. Each queue has an arrival and a departure rate of λ. If the ith server has a service rate of μ_i, the utilization of the ith server is

$$\rho_i = \frac{\lambda}{\mu_i} \qquad (2.227)$$

and

$$\text{Prob}[n_i \text{ customers in the ith queue}] = P(n_i) = (1-\rho_i)\rho_i^{n_i} \qquad (2.228)$$

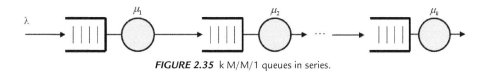

FIGURE 2.35 k M/M/1 queues in series.

The joint probability of queue lengths of k queues is the product of individual probabilities.

$$
\begin{aligned}
P(n_1, n_2, \cdots, n_k) &= (1 - \rho_1)\rho_1^{n_1}(1 - \rho_2)\rho_2^{n_2}\cdots(1 - \rho_k)\rho_k^{n_k} \\
&= P_1(n_1)P_2(n_2)\cdots P_k(n_k)
\end{aligned}
\tag{2.229}
$$

This is known as the *Jackson theorem* after J. R. Jackson who first proved the property. The queueing network is therefore a product-form network. A network to which Jackson's theorem is applicable is known as the *Jackson network*. In general, for a product-form network

$$
P(n_1, n_2, \cdots, n_k) = \frac{1}{G}\prod_{i=1}^{k}\rho_i^{n_i}
\tag{2.230}
$$

where G is a normalization constant and is a function of the total number of jobs in the system. The product-form networks are easier to solve than non-product-form networks.

2.23 EXERCISES

1. Suppose the following three boxes are given:

    Box A has 12 microchips of which 4 are defective,

    Box B has 10 microchips of which 3 are defective, and

    Box C has 8 microchips of which 1 is defective.

    A box is chosen at random, and then a microchip is randomly selected from the chosen box. Find the probability that the microchip is non-defective. If the microchip is non-defective, find the probability that it came from box C.

2. An electronic device in a data center consists of two components which function independently. Component 1 has probability 0.03, and component 2 has probability 0.01 of failing. In order for the device to work, at least one of the components must not have failed. What is the probability that the device works?

3. Assume that the arrivals at a telephone booth form a Poisson process with a mean of 14/hour. An exponential distribution with mean 2 minutes has also been found to be a good fit for the distribution of the length of the telephone calls. What is the probability that an arrival will find the telephone occupied? What is the average length of the queue when it forms?

4. The probability that a queueing process is idle in a steady state is 0.4. Find the expected number in the system.

5. In a three-server Bernoulli queueing process, the probability that arrival occurs from each is 0.15, and the probability that a busy server completes service is 0.20. Find the transition probabilities for the system.

6. On a network device, the packets arrive at a mean rate of 150 packets/second and the device takes about 3 milliseconds to forward them. Using an M/M/1 model, what is the probability of buffer overflow if the device had only 12 buffers?

7. Consider an M/M/1 queue with parameters λ and μ. A customer in the queue will defect with probability $c\Delta t + o(\Delta t)$ in any interval of duration Δt. Express p_{k+1} in terms of k.

8. A plane takes almost 10 minutes to land after it has been given the signal to land by traffic control. Planes arrive at random at an average rate of 12/hour. How long can a plane expect to circle before getting the signal to land?

9. An M/E$_k$/1 queue has an arrival rate of 16 customers/second and a service rate of 28 customers/second. Assuming that $k = 4$, find the mean waiting time.

CHAPTER 3

OVERVIEW OF CRYPTOGRAPHY

Chapter Outline

3.1 Introduction

3.2 Basic Terms Related to Cryptography

3.3 Requirements of Secure Communication

3.4 OSI Security Architecture X.800

3.5 Categories of Cryptographic Systems

3.6 Symmetric (or Conventional) Encryption Model

3.7 Exercises

3.1 INTRODUCTION

In the olden days, Cryptography was used for converting plain messages (called *plaintext*) to an unintelligible form (called *Cipher-text*). The idea was to render the messages incomprehensible. The messages, in such an unintelligible form, were communicated to the intended recipients. The recipients, with the prior knowledge of the decryption key, could decrypt the messages.

The process of transforming the messages from a plaintext form to a cipher-text form is called *Encryption*, and the process of transforming the cipher-text to plaintext is called *Decryption*. This decryption is possible only with the use of a *Decryption Key*, which has to be communicated to the recipients prior to the transmission of encrypted messages. Then the recipients will be able to extract the original plaintexts from the received cipher-texts. The encryption/decryption keys and the transformation algorithms are pre-decided and known to the communicating parties.

There are some classical cipher schemes that were in vogue in the olden days. These schemes can be categorized as Transposition Ciphers and Substitution Ciphers. In Transposition Ciphers, the message contents are systematically scrambled (reordered) so as to make the message unintelligible. For example, the word "object" may be scrambled to "boejtc." In the substitution ciphers, message letters are systematically replaced by other letters in the alphabet. For example, in the classical *Caesar Cipher*, each letter in the plaintext is substituted by a letter three positions down in the alphabetic order, in a cyclic manner.

For example, "a" is substituted by "d," "b" is substituted by "e," and "x" is replaced by "a" ("a" is three positions down from "x" in the alphabet, in a cyclic manner). Julius Caesar is believed to have used this cipher in his confidential communications. But such classical ciphers are only of academic interest today, as they are extremely easy to break. The cipher-texts in such ciphers contain sufficient statistical information about the plaintext, which betrays their secrecy.

The act of breaking the ciphers is known as *Cryptanalysis* (also known as *Hacking*). Hacking is attempted by adversaries with the ulterior motive of gaining unauthorized access to encrypted messages. These days, the cipher designers also employ a kind of hacking called *Ethical Hacking*, with the aim of determining weaknesses in their cipher schemes so that such weaknesses can be effectively plugged, and so the cipher schemes do not remain vulnerable to unethical hacking.

Cryptography has been used for maintaining the secrecy of military plans. The success of military operations depends largely on surprising the adversary. During World War II, the Germans used a complex electromechanical cipher machine known as the *Enigma Machine*.

With the development of digital computers after World War II, a sea change was observed in the development of sophisticated and highly secure cipher systems. The computers enabled data to be represented in a binary form, and highly complex encryption/decryption algorithms came into form. Each scheme involved the use of one or more secret keys which were kept confidential among the communicating parties. As long as the confidentiality of the keys was maintained, the cipher schemes would remain secured even if the underlying encryption algorithms were made publicly known.

The modern encryption schemes can be broadly classified into two categories—Symmetric Schemes and Asymmetric (or *Public Key*) Schemes. In symmetric schemes, there is only one key that is kept secret between the sender and recipient of secure messages. The secret key is used both for encryption and decryption. In asymmetric schemes, each user generates a pair of related keys, one that is made public and one that is kept secret (*private*) by the owner. The public key is used by others for encryption of messages that are intended to be received by the owner of the related private key. The related private key is used for decryption. Thus, if a user "A" has to send a message M to another user "B," then "A" will encrypt the message using "B"'s public key and then send the resulting cipher-text to "B." Since only "B" has the related private key for decryption of this message, no one except "B" can decrypt the *cipher-text*. Once encrypted, even "A" cannot decrypt it. The Public-key algorithms are based on certain computational difficulties. The popular RSA algorithm (a public key encrypter) is based on the difficulty of factorizing a very large composite number into its prime factors. Some other schemes are based on the difficulty of computing Discrete Logarithms.

New areas have emerged in the field of cryptography. One such area is digital signing of electronic documents. The electronic documents exchanged through the Internet need authentication, that is, surety that the document has been initiated by the party claiming to be the sender. The digital signature should be such that it could have been created only by the initiator of the document, and it should be possible for the recipient to verify that the document has been signed only by the initiator. There is another aspect of non-repudiation. This implies that the signer of a document should not be able to later deny having signed the document. If the signer disowns a signature, the recipient should be able to prove that the signer is lying. This is feasible only with *Public Key Cryptography*. The signatory of a document uses a private key to encrypt the signature. The recipient would use the associated public key to decrypt the signature (called verification of the signature). Now, since the private key is known only to the owner of the key, the signer cannot refute having signed a document. If the signer denies having sent the message, then the recipient will be able to rebut the denial.

The advancement of computers has also enhanced the capabilities of cryptanalysis. A continuous fight goes on between the designers of cipher schemes and the cryptanalysts (called *hackers*). The cryptanalysts who break the cipher with malicious intentions of cheating and fraud are called *unethical hackers*; the hackers who perform cryptanalysis with good intentions of improving the systems and making it difficult for unethical hackers to break the ciphers are called *ethical hackers*. Whenever a scheme is believed to have become vulnerable to successful hacking, the system designers try to counter it by increasing the key-size. A larger key-size makes it more difficult to break the cipher. But a larger key-size also increases the encryption/decryption over-heads. Finally, when the key-size becomes unduly large, the designers look for more efficient technologies that can afford higher security with smaller key-sizes and lower overheads. As in the area of Public Key Cryptography, the popular RSA scheme is likely to be replaced by the more efficient *Elliptic Curve Cryptography (ECC)*, which needs a much smaller key-size for a given security level supported by RSA.

In general, the encryption/decryption overheads of Symmetric Ciphers are much lower than Public Key Ciphers. Due to this reason, most of the existing Cipher Systems are hybrid, involving both Symmetric and Asymmetric Cryptography. Public Key Cryptography is used to exchange only a secret key among the communicating parties. This is followed by Symmetric Cryptography to communicate the actual message, which is encrypted using the secret key that has been already exchanged using Public Key Cryptography.

Modern-day cryptography also encompasses some other aspects like *Digital Signatures*. In today's scenario, when more and more critical information is being exchanged through the Internet, the confidentiality and security of such information has gained paramount importance. The databases of commercial banks can be accessed through the Internet from anywhere across the globe. Suppose a client has a bank account in a branch located in Texas. Through Internet Banking, the client can transfer funds from one account to another account that may be located elsewhere (say in Boston). While doing this transfer, the client may be physically sitting elsewhere, say in New Jersey. All this has been made possible through the Internet. But all such communications are likely to be intercepted by unscrupulous elements trying to gain an unauthorized access to such transmissions (called *hacking*). Now, imagine a scenario wherein a hacker captures a message pertaining to the transfer of money. The *hacker* may modify the message to effect transfer of money to a different account by altering the destination account number in the message. So, the end results can be catastrophic. Imagine another scenario, wherein a hacker hacks into someone's account and transfers funds to a different account. So, there is the need to ensure the security of databases and also to secure the communication of critical messages through the Internet. This is where cryptography plays its role to make the communications more and more secure and trusted. There is a never-ending fight between the designers of secure systems and the hackers. The hackers attempt to find loopholes in the cryptographic systems and the designers of such systems attempt to plug such loopholes. For designers to detect the loopholes, they have to employ hacker's techniques (called *ethical hacking*).

3.2   BASIC TERMS RELATED TO CRYPTOGRAPHY

Cryptology: Cryptology in Greek means "A Hidden Secret." Though sometimes the terms Cryptography and Cryptology are used interchangeably, strictly speaking Cryptology encompasses two areas: Cryptography and Cryptanalysis.

1. **Cryptography** primarily deals with design of techniques for ensuring data confidentiality and/or data origin authentication. In a nutshell, cryptography deals with the design of Ciphers.

2. **Cryptanalysis** deals with techniques for the breaking of ciphers. A cryptanalyst attempts to defeat cryptographic means. It attempts to obtain unauthorized access to information and/or attempts to forge the authentication sequence of others. Cryptanalysis is also known as hacking, which is divided into two categories:

   A. Ethical hacking, which is used by the cipher designers to determine weaknesses existing in cipher schemes and to eliminate these to make the cipher schemes more robust against attacks.

   B. Unethical hacking, which is performed by antisocial elements with the aim of having unauthorized access to protected information.

Plaintext: It refers to a message in plain form that is readily intelligible. If transmitted in this form, it is highly prone to unauthorized disclosure, since a message in transit can be easily captured by adversaries.

Cipher-text: It refers to the encrypted form of a message. Prior to transmission, a plaintext M is encrypted so that it does not remain readily intelligible. The message travels from the sender to the intended recipients in cipher-text form. The cipher-text should be such that adversaries should find it extremely difficult to decipher it. The intended recipients will have the necessary keys to decipher it easily.

Encryption Algorithm: The Algorithm used for transforming plaintext to cipher-text is called an "Encryption (or Enciphering) Algorithm." It performs complex substitutions and/or permutations on the plaintext using an encryption key to produce the resulting cipher-text.

$$C = f(M, K_1) = E_{K_1}[M] \tag{3.1}$$

where C is Cipher-text, M is Plaintext, K_1 is the Encryption Key, and E is the Encryption algorithm.

The encryption process must be reversible so as to enable deciphering of the cipher-text by the intended recipients.

- **Decryption Algorithm:** It transforms cipher-text C back to the original plaintext M. The Decryption process is the reverse of the Encryption process. The intended recipients of cipher-text C will perform the decryption process using Decryption Key K_2 and recover plaintext message M from the received cipher-text C.

$$M = f(C, K_2) = D_{K_2}[C] \tag{3.2}$$

where D is the Decryption algorithm.

The Key Distribution mechanism should be so secure that only the intended recipients get the decryption key and no adversary is able to lay hands on it. The authorized recipients of the key must keep it highly secure.

Since Decryption is reverse of Encryption, the following holds true:

$$D_{K_2}[C] = D_{K_2}[E_{K_1}[M]] = \left(E_{K_1}\right)^{-1}[E_{K_1}[M]] = M \tag{3.3}$$

In the case of Symmetric Cryptography, the Decryption Key is same as the Encryption Key. However, in the case of Asymmetric or Public Key Cryptography, the Decryption Key is different from the Encryption Key; the Decryption Key is related to the Encryption Key, but knowing the Encryption Key it is still extremely difficult (or computationally infeasible) to determine the Decryption Key.

3.2.1 Cryptographic Primitives

Encryption and Decryption Algorithms, Cryptographic Hash Functions, and Pseudo-Random Number Generators are basic building blocks of Crypto Systems. These are called *Cryptographic Primitives*.

3.2.2 Cryptographic Protocols

A single building block (or *Cryptographic Primitive*) may not be sufficient to provide a complete solution to achieve secrecy, validation, and integrity of data. It may require a series of basic building blocks to accomplish the task. Such a well-defined series of steps is called *a Cryptographic Protocol*. Figure 3.1 shows a generic model of secure communication.

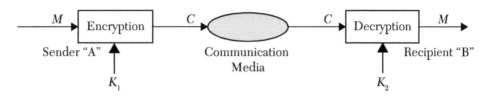

FIGURE 3.1 Generic model of secure communication (*M*: Plaintext Message, *C*: Cipher-text, K_1: Encryption Key, K_2: Decryption Key).

3.2.3 Encryption (at the Sender's End)

$$C = E_{K_1}[M] \tag{3.4}$$

3.2.4 Decryption (at the Recipient's End)

$$D_{K_2}[C] = D_{K_2}\left[E_{K_1}[C]\right] = \left(E_{K_1}\right)^{-1}\left[E_{K_1}[M]\right] = M \tag{3.5}$$

3.3 REQUIREMENTS OF SECURE COMMUNICATION

Cryptography meets the following requirements of secure communication:

- The sender of a confidential message should be able to encrypt the message easily. What travels from the sender to the intended recipient is the cipher-text.

- It is presumed that adversaries can easily capture the cipher-text from the transmission media. The encryption should be such that an adversary should not be able to easily extract the plaintext from the cipher-text.

- The intended recipient should be able to decipher the received cipher-text easily and recover the plaintext using the decryption keys available with the recipient. For this to be feasible, the sender and the intended recipient first exchange some keys that are needed for encryption and decryption. The Decryption Key may be same as the Encryption Key (as in the case of Symmetric Cryptography) or the two keys may be different (as in the case of Public Key Cryptography).

- The exchange of keys is done prior to the exchange of messages. In the case of Symmetric Cryptography, the exchange of a secret key (shared between the two parties) has to be done by the most secure means. The sender of a message will encrypt the message using the secret key and the intended recipient will use the same key for decryption. Since the key is known only to the sender and the intended recipient, no eavesdropper should be able to recover the plaintext easily. However, in the case of Public Key Cryptography, each party will generate a pair of keys that will be related to each other. One of the keys, known as the Private Key, is kept secret by the party generating it, and the other key, known as the Public Key, is made public, that is, made known to all other users. Any message to be transmitted is encrypted using the Public Key of the intended recipient. The intended recipient will be able to decrypt the cipher-text using the Private Key. Since the Private Key is kept secret by each party, only the intended recipient will be able to recover the plaintext from the received cipher-text; an attacker will find it extremely hard to decipher the cipher-text.

- If a cipher-text gets modified in transit (either intentionally by an attacker or unintentionally due to some system error), the intended recipient should be able to detect that the cipher-text has been modified in transit, and the recipient should be able to take appropriate recovery action.

- If some entity (say "A") impersonates some other entity (say "B") and sends a message to entity "C" with the intention of making "C" feel as if the message has been sent by "B," it is called a "masquerade." In this case, "C" should be able to detect the impersonation and take appropriate corrective action. For this to be feasible, "C" should have the means to authenticate the source of the received message to ascertain that the message has been sent by the alleged sender ("B" in this case) or someone else.

- The sender of a message should not be able to later deny having sent the message. In case the sender denies having sent a message, the recipient should be able to prove that the message has been sent by the alleged sender and no one else. It is not feasible to prove in Symmetric Cryptography, but it is easy to prove in Public Key Cryptography. This function is known as "Source Non-Repudiation."

- The recipient of a message should not be able to later deny having received a message. In case a recipient denies this, the sender of the message should be able to prove that the message has been received by the alleged recipient. Recipient acknowledgement would be needed to prove the Recipient Non-Repudiation.

3.4 OSI SECURITY ARCHITECTURE X.800

Open Systems Interconnection (OSI) Architecture X.800 is a set of standards relating to Security of Information. These standards have been developed by the International Telecom Union (ITU-T), UN-sponsored body that is responsible for the development of standards relating to telecommunications. The standards pertain to Security Attacks, Security Mechanisms, and Security Services.

Security Attacks – Security Attacks refer to the actions intending to compromise the security of information belonging to an organization.

Security Mechanisms – Security Mechanisms refer to the processes (or devices incorporating the processes) that are designed to prevent, detect, or recover from Security Attacks.

Security Services – Security Services refer to the services that make use of Security Mechanisms to counter Security Attacks.

3.4.1 Security Attacks

Security Attacks are divided into the following categories:

1. **Passive Attacks** – A Passive Attack is in the form of eavesdropping or monitoring the communications by an adversary. The goal of the adversary is to capture information or to obtain the pattern of information flow. Since the intruder is only listening to the communications and does not alter any information, the passive attacks are very difficult to detect; therefore, the emphasis should be on preventing such attacks. The passive attacks can be divided into two sub-categories:

   A. **Unauthorized Disclosure of Message Contents** – The adversary may capture the cipher-text by tapping the communication media and attempt to decipher it either by brute force or by sophisticated cryptanalysis techniques.

B. **Traffic Pattern Analysis –** The attacker may attempt to determine the traffic pattern, like frequency and length of messages being transmitted. This may provide some leads to the nature of information being transmitted. For example, in the defense scenario, if the frequency of messages suddenly goes up, it may indicate that some operations are imminent.

2. **Active Attacks –** Active attacks involve the modification of data streams or the creation of false data streams. The Active attacks can be subdivided into the following four categories:

   A. **Masquerade –** It refers to a scenario, wherein an entity (Say "A") pretends to be another entity (say "B") and sends a message to Entity "C." This is possible if "A" is able to capture the authentication sequences of entity "B" and replay them in order to send an unauthorized message to entity "C." The recipient "C" will tend to believe that the message has been sent by "B."

   B. **Replay –** It involves the capturing of a data unit and its subsequent retransmission to produce an unauthorized effect. Suppose a message **"ARRIVING TODAY AT 4:00 PM"** is captured on July 15, 2009 and replayed on July 17, 2009. The recipient will wrongly believe that the alleged sender of the message is arriving on July 17th.

   C. **Modification of Messages –** It involves capturing a data stream, altering the data stream, and then transmitting it to the intended recipient to produce an unauthorized effect. The altering may involve modification, deletion, appending, or reordering of the data stream.

   D. **Denial of Service –** It refers to preventing or inhibiting normal use of communication services; for example, the adversary may suppress all the messages meant for a particular destination or saturate the network by flooding it with spurious messages that degrade the network's performance. If the network is saturated, then the transmission of valid messages will get unduly delayed, and some messages may even get lost in transit. Such a type of attack means a denial of service.

3.4.2 Security Services

X.800 defines the Security Services under the following categories:

1. **Authentication –** Authentication is of two kinds:

   A. **Peer-to-Peer Authentication –** This service is specific to a connection-oriented environment and attempts to provide confidence to the recipient against masquerade, that is, against unauthorized replay of previous connections.

B. Data Origin Authentication – It is specific to a connection-less environment and provides data source authentication; that is, it ensures the recipient that the received message has been sent by the alleged sender only.

2. **Access Control** – This service controls and limits the client's access to the host systems (on the Internet) and to the applications running on the host systems. Each entity attempting to access a host system or an application running on a host system must first identify and authenticate itself; only then is it granted access. The access is granted only to the extent authorized for that entity.

3. **Data Confidentiality** – This service protects the transmitted data against passive attacks. This is achieved by encrypting the data in such a way that only the intended recipient, having access to the decryption key, can decrypt the cipher-text; any adversary should find it extremely difficult to decrypt it.

4. **Data Integrity** – In a connection-oriented environment, the Data Integrity Service assures that the messages are delivered to the intended recipient without any duplication, insertion, modification, reordering, or replay. Any destruction of data is also considered a loss of data integrity. In a connectionless communication, the Data Integrity Service is provided at an individual datagram level. The service attempts to assure the recipient against any alteration of message in transit. This can be achieved by computing the Cyclic Redundancy Check (CRC) value of the message at the sender end and appending it to the message prior to its transmission. At the recipient end, the message CRC is re-computed and compared with the CRC value received along with the message; if both the values match, then the message is considered to be received without any alteration in transit and data integrity is considered to be preserved.

5. **Non-repudiation** – This service prevents the sender of a message from refuting having sent the message. If a sender refutes having sent a message, the service enables the recipient to prove beyond doubt that the message was sent only by the alleged sender. This can be achieved by requiring the sender to sign the message using its private key. The signature can be verified by the recipient using the sender's public key. The recipient can save the sender's signature along with the received message for ensuring source non-repudiation. The service should also prevent the

recipient from later denying having received the message. When a message has been delivered to the intended recipient, the sender can prove that the message was in fact received by the alleged recipient; this can be achieved by requiring the recipient to acknowledge receipt of message. The acknowledgement can be saved by the sender for ensuring the recipient non-repudiation.

6. **Availability** – The availability service assures that system resources are made available to the authorized entities, as per the accepted specs, as and when the authorized entities request those resources. It provides protection against "Denial-of-Service" Attacks. For its functioning, the service relies on the proper management and control of the system resources, and thus makes use of access control and other security mechanisms.

3.4.3 Security Mechanisms

In X.800, the security mechanisms are defined under two major categories:

- Specific Mechanisms
- Pervasive Mechanisms

1. **Specific Security Mechanisms** – A Security Mechanism that pertains to a particular layer of protocol is called a specific security mechanism. The specific security mechanisms are further subdivided into following sub-categories:

   A. **Enciphering/Deciphering:** The mechanism of Enciphering (Encryption) refers to the use of mathematical algorithms that along with a key transform plaintext to cipher-text. Deciphering refers to the mathematical algorithms that along with a secret key transform cipher-text to plaintext. Only one key is used for enciphering and deciphering in case of symmetric cryptography and two different (but related) keys are used for enciphering and deciphering for public key cryptography. The mathematical operations performed in enciphering and deciphering are mainly substitution and permutation.

   B. **Digital Signature:** It refers to the block of data that comprises a hash value (called a message digest) of the message, encrypted using the sender's private key and appended to the message at the sender's end prior to its transmission. It is feasible only in Public Key Cryptography (not in Symmetric Cryptography). The digital signature serves the following purposes:

- It proves the identity of the sender (called data origin); that is, it attempts to assure the recipient about the identity of the alleged sender of data. The recipient verifies the signature by deciphering it using sender's public key.

- It proves integrity of the data unit to the recipient; that is, it assures the recipient that the received data unit has not been altered in transit either intentionally by an adversary or unintentionally by a system malfunction like a noisy channel.

- It protects the data unit against forgery (by the recipient). The recipient cannot alter the received document, since then its hash value will not match with the encrypted hash value in the signature. Also, the recipient cannot alter the signature, since it is created using a sender's private key, which is known only to the sender.

- It assures source non-repudiation. The sender cannot refute having sent the message, since the recipient can prove it by deciphering the signature by the sender's public key. This proves that the signature has been generated by using only the sender's private key.

C. **Access Control:** The access control mechanism limits and controls the access of system resources by the authorized entities. An entity attempting to gain access to system resources has to first identify and authenticate itself; only then is access granted to it, to the extent authorized for that entity.

D. **Data Integrity:** It refers to the mechanisms that assure the recipient about integrity of a data unit or a data stream. To achieve this, a checksum or CRC is computed at the sender end and appended to the data unit. At the recipient's end, a checksum/CRC is again computed by the recipient and compared with that received from the sender. If both the values match, the data unit is assumed to have been received correctly.

E. **Traffic Padding:** It refers to the insertion of dummy bits into the gaps among the data units so that eavesdroppers are not able to determine the length and frequency of messages. It protects the communication against "Traffic Analysis Attacks."

F. Routing Control: It refers to the mechanisms that enable the sender to select physically secure routes for communicating certain sensitive data and change the routes whenever any security breach is suspected.

G. Notarization: It refers to the use of a trusted Third Party for the provisioning of certain functions related to data security, such as "key distribution," and so on.

2. **Pervasive Security Mechanisms** – The following pervasive security mechanisms are the ones that do not pertain to any particular protocol layers:

A. Trusted Functionality: It refers to the functionality of a system resource, as perceived to be correct with respect to accepted specifications and norms.

B. Security Label: It refers to the designation of security attributes of a resource (like Top-Secret, Secret, Confidential, etc.), which are used for access control. A security label indicates the class of entities to whom the access can be granted.

C. Event Detection: It refers to the detection of security-related events, like intrusion detection.

D. Security Audit Trail: It refers to the data that is gathered for carrying out a Security Audit, that is, to carry out an independent review and examination of system records and activities with respect to security.

E. Security Recovery: It refers to the mechanisms that enable recovery in case of security failures, to reduce the damage caused by such failures.

Attack Categorization is based on the extent of information available to the adversaries:

1. Cipher-text only attack

2. Known Plaintext attack

3. Chosen Plaintext attack

4. Adaptively-chosen plaintext attack

5. Chosen and adaptively chosen cipher-text attack

1. **Cipher-Text Only Attack** – It is presumed that when the cipher-text is transiting in the media from the sender to the recipients, it can be easily captured by the adversaries by tapping the media. In a "Cipher-text Only Attack," the adversary has access only to the Cipher-text and attempts to extract the plaintext from the captured cipher-text. For a reasonably secure cipher scheme, the attacker would find it extremely difficult to determine plaintext from the captured cipher-text.

2. **Known Plaintext Attack** – The adversary may be able to obtain plaintexts of some captured cipher-texts. This is feasible if the adversary gets access to the encryption equipment for some time. From the plaintext-cipher-text pairs, the adversary would attempt to determine the decryption key by using sophisticated cryptanalysis techniques. If successful, the adversary would have the capability to decipher all captured cipher-texts.

3. **Chosen Plaintext Attack** – An adversary may have the ability to obtain cipher-texts of chosen plaintexts. This is slightly different than the known plaintext Attack. Here, the adversary may not have access to the Encryption Equipment, but may send some interesting plaintext messages to the Encryption Side, hoping that the Encryption Side will encrypt the received messages and send the cipher-text back. Then the adversary may gather the corresponding Cipher-text. Using information from plaintext-cipher-text pairs, the adversary may attempt to determine the decryption key and use it to decipher all captured cipher-texts.

4. **Adaptively Chosen Plaintext Attack** – This attack is the same as the Chosen Plaintext Attack, except that the adversary may do some analysis on the gathered plaintext-cipher-text pairs and subsequently get more pairs to further refine the analysis. Then, the adversary may use the refined information to decrypt the cipher-texts for which plaintext is not available. The adversary may periodically switch over to refining the analysis.

5. **Chosen and Adaptively Chosen Cipher-Text Attack** – Here the adversary has access to the Decryption Device. The adversary can choose Cipher-texts and obtain corresponding plaintexts. By analyzing the gathered cipher-text-plaintext pairs, the attacker attempts to determine the decryption key. Then the attacker obtains more pairs of cipher-text and plaintext to refine the analysis process, till the decryption key is recovered.

3.5 CATEGORIES OF CRYPTOGRAPHIC SYSTEMS

Cryptographic Systems can be categorized on the basis of the following parameters:

1. **Type of mathematical operations used for Encryption/Decryption**

   A. Substitution Ciphers: Cipher-text is obtained by mapping each plaintext element to another element in the alphabet; for example, in Caesar's Cipher, each letter is substituted by a letter three places down in the alphabet sequence.

   B. Transposition Ciphers: The cipher-text is obtained by rearranging (scrambling or permuting) the plaintext elements.

   The fundamental requirement is that no information should be lost, that is, all operations must be reversible. Practical Systems would comprise multiple stages of substitution and transposition.

2. **Number of keys used in encryption/decryption**

   A. Single-Key Scheme

   It is also called the Symmetric Cipher or Conventional Cipher. In this scheme, only one key is used for both encryption and decryption. The decryption process is exactly the inverse of the encryption process, using the same key.

   B. Double-Key Scheme (Asymmetric or Public-Key Encryption)

   In Public Key Cryptography, the Sender and Recipient of a message use different keys. Due to this reason, the scheme is called the Asymmetric Encryption Scheme. Each User (say "A") has a pair of keys (PU_A, PR_A) where PU_A is called the public key of "A" and PR_A is called the private key of "A." Though the private key PR_A is related to the public key PU_A, it is not easy to determine PR_A from PU_A. The private key PR_A is kept private (secret) by the user "A" and the public key PU_A is made public, that is, sent to all other users who are to send messages to user "A." The other users will use PU_A to encrypt messages meant for user "A." Once a message is encrypted using PU_A, it can be decrypted only by using the related private key PR_A. Since the private key PR_A is available only to user "A," only "A" can decrypt the messages encrypted with PU_A. Thus, once a plaintext M has been transformed to cipher-text C using public key PU_A, only "A" can transform it back to M; even the originator of the message M cannot transform the cipher-text back to M.

A message encrypted with the private key of a user can be decrypted using the same user's public key. This mode is used to perform digital signatures of messages, which provides source authentication and source non-repudiation. This is possible only in public key encryption, since the private key is known only to its owner.

The Public Key Encryption has very large overheads as compared to Symmetric Encryption. Due to this reason, public key encryption is used only to encrypt short messages like "secret keys" or digital signatures, while symmetric encryption is used for bulk encryption of large chunks of data.

3. **Method of processing the plaintext**

A. **Block Cipher:** The plaintext is divided into blocks of fixed size and encryption/decryption is performed block-by-block. A plaintext block of size N will result in a cipher-text block of the same size.

B. **Stream Cipher:** The Stream Cipher processes a continuous stream of plaintext, one element at a time, and produces cipher-text one element at a time. It is suitable for real-time systems where information is produced as a stream.

3.6 SYMMETRIC (OR CONVENTIONAL) ENCRYPTION MODEL

A Conventional Encryption Scheme (also known as a Symmetric Encryption Scheme or a Single-Key Encryption Scheme) involves the following:

1. A common Secret Key K, shared by the sender and the intended recipients.

2. A secure mechanism for distribution of the Secret Key K to the sender and to the intended recipients. Only the sender and the intended recipients should know the key. To keep it secure against leakage, the key must be replaced periodically.

3. An Encryption Algorithm to transform plaintext M to cipher-text C, as illustrated in Figure 3.2. The algorithm should be such that a hostile party, not knowing the secret K, is not able to decipher the cipher-text C.

4. A Decryption Algorithm to transform cipher-text C back to plaintext M. The algorithm will also make use of the common secret key K to recover the plaintext M from the cipher-text C.

5. The adversaries may perform an unauthorized capture of the cipher-text from the communication media and perform cryptanalysis for determining the decryption key.

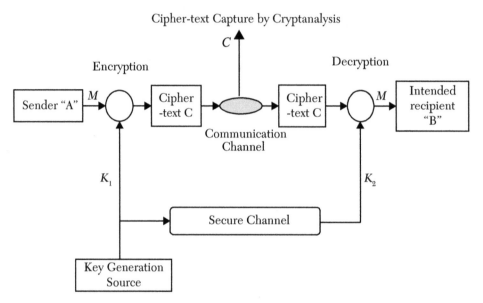

FIGURE 3.2 Conventional encryption model.

Let $M = [M_1, M_2, \dots, M_n]$ be plaintext, where $M_1, M_2, \dots, M_n$ are letters in some alphabet (these could be 0s and 1s in binary), and $K = [K_1, K_2, \dots, K_j]$ is the secret key. The secret key is generated at the sender end and is also communicated to the intended receiver via a secure channel. Alternatively, the key could be generated by a third party and then communicated to both sender and receiver via secure channels.

With plaintext M and Secret Key K as inputs, the Encryption Algorithm would generate Cipher-text $C = [C_1, C_2, \dots, C_n]$. We express the Encryption Process as $C = E_k(M)$.

The Decryption Algorithm would take Cipher-text C and Key K as inputs and produce Plaintext M as output. The Decryption can be expressed as $M = D_k(C)$.

3.6.1 Types of Attacks on a Conventional Encryption Scheme

In general, it is presumed that the Cipher-text C is prone to tapping by an adversary during the transit of Cipher-text from Sender to Intended Receiver. Also, it can be presumed that characteristics of the Encryption/Decryption Algorithm may be known to an adversary. An adversary may employ the following approaches to attack a conventional encryption scheme:

1. **Cryptanalysis** – For this type of attack, it is presumed that the attacker has full knowledge of the characteristics of the Encryption Algorithm. The attacker in this case attempts to analyze a captured cipher-text by exploiting the characteristics of the algorithm and attempts to deduce the corresponding plaintext and the key used for encryption. That is, a Cryptanalyst may capture cipher-text C from the communication media and may attempt to recover M *(plaintext estimate)* and K *(Key estimate)*. If an attacker is successful in deducing the key K, the results will be catastrophic. All the messages encrypted with that key will be presumed to be compromised.

2. **Brute Force Attack** – The attacker tries every possible key on a captured cipher-text until an intelligible translation is obtained, which is presumed to be the corresponding plaintext. On the average, half the possible keys would need to be tried to attain success. To defeat this approach, the key-space, that is, the set of possible keys, must be made very large. For example, if the key-size is 128 bits, then the attacker must try an average of 2^{127} keys, which is extremely large, that is, on the order of 10^{38}.

3.6.2 Conventional Encryption for Confidentiality

One of the major goals of information security is Confidentiality. A plaintext message is first encrypted and then transmitted to the intended recipients. The cipher-text generated by encryption is considered to meet confidentiality criteria if it satisfies the following requirements:

- An adversary, not having knowledge of the decryption key, must find it extremely difficult to decrypt the cipher-text. An adversary may be able to capture cipher-text from the communication media.

- The intended recipients, possessing the decryption key, should be able to easily decrypt the received cipher-text.

Consider a message transiting from the sender "A" to the intended recipient "B" via the Internet. En route the message will pass through many Routers/Switches. The Routers/Switches will make use of the destination IP address, stored in the message (packet) header, for routing the message from "A" to "B," as given in the schematic in Figure 3.3.

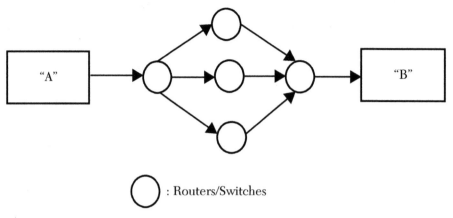

: Routers/Switches

FIGURE 3.3 A schematic diagram showing the routing of message from "A" to "B."

The various approaches for the placement of Encryption/Decryption Devices could be categorized into the following three categories:

- Link Encryption
- End-to-End Encryption
- Combined End-to-End and Link Encryption

3.6.3 Link Encryption

In Link Encryption, the entire message including the header is encrypted as illustrated in Figure 3.4.

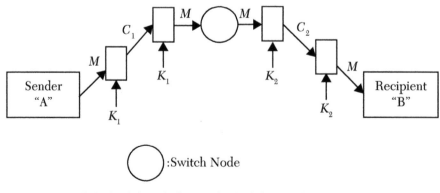

:Switch Node

FIGURE 3.4 Schematic diagram showing link encryption.

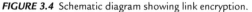

Each link is equipped with an Encryption/Decryption Device on both ends and has a secret key shared between the link-nodes. This key is used for the encryption/decryption of the messages routed on the link.

The message is decrypted at each switch node, since the switch needs to access the destination address from the message header for further routing of the message. After making a decision on routing, the switch node encrypts the message and sends it on to the next link.

Let Message $M = H\|PL$, where H is a Header containing the Destination IP address, and PL is the Payload.

Let $K_1, K_2, \ldots$ be the link encryption/decryption keys. Then, Cipher-text $C_1 = E_{K_1}[M]$ and Cipher-text $C_2 = E_{K_2}[M]$.

Advantage

- The link encryption covers the entire message. Thus, the entire message is protected from adversaries, except while at the switch nodes.

Disadvantages

- At the switch nodes, the messages are completely unprotected and the switch nodes are not under user control.

- The scheme needs a large number of encryption/decryption keys to be provided—one for each link. Thus, management of keys is a big task.

- Since the message needs to be decrypted and encrypted at each switch node, it adds to delays in message delivery.

3.6.3.1 End-to-End Encryption

- The encryption/decryption is performed only at the end points (sender and recipient ends).

- The sender encrypts the data and transmits. In this scheme, only the data portion of a packet (called the payload) is encrypted; the header is left clear so that the en route switches can access the destination address from the packet header for routing.

Let Message $M = H\|PL$, and let K_{ab} be the secret key shared between nodes A and B. Then, Cipher-text $C = H\|E_{K_{ab}}[PL]$.

- The data in the cipher-text form travels unaltered through the network to the destination.

- The destination shares a secret key with the source node (like K_{ab} shared between the nodes A and B), which is used to decrypt the data.

Advantages

- This scheme requires fewer keys as compared to link encryption; thus, key management is simpler.

- Since the encryption/decryption is performed only at the end nodes, there are fewer delays than with the link encryption scheme.

- The payload portion of the message is protected throughout the travel of the message from the source to the destination.

- Since the message is encrypted using a key that is shared between the sender and the recipient, it provides source authentication.

Disadvantage

- Since the message-header is not encrypted, any adversary can monitor source and destination addresses. Thus, the messages are vulnerable to traffic analysis attacks.

3.6.3.2 Combined End-to-End and Link Encryption

- To achieve greater security, both link and end-to-end encryption schemes may be implemented.

- The Link Encryption is implemented at the Data Link Layer and the end-to-end encryption is implemented at the Network Layer.

- The sender at the source node first encrypts the payload portion of the message, leaving the header clear, using the end-to-end encryption key that it shares with the destination node. Then the source applies link encryption, which covers the entire message including the header.

- As the packet traverses the network, each switch decrypts using the link decryption key to access its header and then encrypts the entire packet again, using another link encryption key prior to its retransmission on another link. At the switch nodes, only the Packet Header is vulnerable to attack.

- At the destination node, first the link encryption is removed using the link key and then the end-to-end encryption is removed using the key that is shared with the source node.

- The scheme has the advantages and disadvantages of both link encryption and end-to-end encryption.

3.6.3.3 Traffic-Pattern Confidentiality

The following information can be derived by an adversary from the Traffic-Pattern:

- Identities of the communicating partners. This can be determined from the Source and Destination IP addresses stored in the Packet Header.

- Frequency and length of the messages among different communicating partners.

- The adversary will also monitor the events correlating with the exchange of information.

3.6.3.4 Schemes to Achieve Traffic-Pattern Confidentiality

- **Link Encryption:** In Link Encryption, the Network Layer Headers (Packet Headers) are encrypted, reducing the opportunity of Traffic Analysis. However, it is still possible for an attacker to get the number and frequency of messages. Protection against this analysis can be provided by *Traffic Padding*. Traffic Padding produces a continuous stream of cipher-text, filling the gaps among messages with encrypted random data. This dummy data is recognized and ignored at the recipient end. So, an attacker cannot assess the quantum computing of traffic and the message's length.

- **End-to-End Encryption:** In End-to-End Encryption, the traffic analysis can be prevented by inserting some dummy messages randomly at the Network Layer. At the other end, such messages should be easily recognizable to avoid confusion.

3.6.3.5 Security Level of Encryption Schemes

The security level of an encryption scheme can be defined as follows:

1. **Unconditionally Secure Schemes:** An Encryption Scheme is said to be unconditionally secure if the cipher-text generated by that scheme does not contain enough information for uniquely determining the corresponding plaintext, irrespective of how much of cipher-text may be available to an adversary.

2. **Computationally Secure Schemes:** An Encryption Scheme is said to be computationally secure if it satisfies either of the following two conditions:

   A. The cost of breaking the cipher far exceeds the value of the encrypted information.

   B. The time required to break the cipher far exceeds the useful lifetime of the encrypted information.

3.6.3.6 Cipher Designers vs. Cryptanalysts

Strictly speaking, no cipher scheme is unconditionally secure. Given an unlimited memory space and unlimited processing speed, any cipher can be broken in a reasonable timeframe. The commercially available cipher schemes are considered only to be *"Computationally Secure"* till someone succeeds to break it. Then the designers attempt to make the scheme more secure either by refining the algorithm or by increasing the key size. As the speed of computers and the refinement of cryptanalysis algorithms are also improving at a matching pace, there is ongoing competition between the cipher designers and the hackers. The hackers look for loopholes in the schemes that make the latter vulnerable to attacks and the cipher designers are using their ingenuity to plug those loopholes to make the schemes computationally secure. With increasing key sizes, the enormous overheads of encryption/decryption are making some of the schemes unviable to use; therefore, the cipher designers are looking for alternate technologies like Elliptic Curve Cryptography (ECC).

3.7 EXERCISES

1. Differentiate among Cryptology, Cryptography, and Cryptanalysis.

2. What are the requirements of Secure Communication?

3. Differentiate between a "known plaintext attack" and a "chosen plaintext attack." Which one is easier to perform?

4. Differentiate between "Source Authentication" and "Source Non-Repudiation." Is it possible to provide Source Non-Repudiation in Symmetric Cryptography?

5. What are the services provided by "Digital Signatures"? Is it feasible to sign a message using symmetric cryptography?

6. What are the relative merits and demerits of link encryption and end-to-end encryption?

7. Differentiate among the following:

   A. Plaintext and Cipher-text

   B. Source Authentication and Source Non-Repudiation

   C. Symmetric and Public Key Ciphers

   D. Block Ciphers and Stream Ciphers

   E. Substitution Ciphers and Transposition Ciphers

   F. Unconditionally Secure and Computationally Secure Cipher Schemes

8. Given a cipher-breaking machine with infinitely large RAM and infinitely high computational power, will any crypto system be secure? Justify your answer.

9. In a Symmetric Cipher, can a cipher produced using a key K_1 be decrypted using another key $K_2 \neq K_1$?

10. Determine the Security Services required to counter various types of Active and Passive Attacks.

11. Determine the security mechanisms required to provide various types of Security Services.

12. "Passive attacks are easier to prevent but difficult to detect. On the other hand, active attacks are difficult to prevent but easy to detect." Justify this assertion.

13. Explain why encryption of only short messages is performed using Public Key Encryption and bulk encryption of large chunks of data is performed using Symmetric Encryption.

CHAPTER 4

MATHEMATICAL FOUNDATIONS FOR CRYPTOGRAPHY

Chapter Outline

4.1 Introduction

4.2 Introduction to Groups, Rings, and Fields

4.3 Modular Arithmetic

4.4 Introduction to Primes and Co-Primes

4.5 Euclid's Algorithm to Determine GCD

4.6 Extended Euclid's Algorithm

4.7 Galois Finite Fields

4.8 Fermat's Little Theorem

4.9 Euler's Totient Function

4.10 Euler's Theorem

4.11 Prime Numbers

4.12 Discrete Logarithms

4.13 Primality Testing

4.14 Chinese Remainder Theorem

4.15 Exercises

4.1   INTRODUCTION

This chapter covers the mathematical concepts of finite fields, co-primes, primes, discrete logarithms, primitive roots, and the Chinese Remainder Theorem, which form the foundation of cryptography. It also covers modular arithmetic, without the knowledge of which it would be difficult to grasp the concepts of cryptography.

4.2   INTRODUCTION TO GROUPS, RINGS, AND FIELDS

4.2.1 Groups

A Group $\{G, \bullet\}$ is a set of elements G with a binary operator $\bullet$ that obeys the following axioms:

(A_1) **Closure:** For each pair of elements $(a,b) \in G$, $a \bullet b$ also belong to G.

(A_2) **Associative:** For all a,b,c in G, then $a \bullet (b \bullet c) = (a \bullet b) \bullet c$.

(A_3) **Identity Element:** There exists an element $e \in G$ (called the identity element), which satisfies $e \bullet a = a \bullet e = a$ for each $a \in G$.

(A_4) **Inverse Element:** For each element $a \in G$, there exists an element $a' \in G$ such that $a \bullet a' = a' \bullet a = e$. Element a' is called the inverse of element a.

Finite Group – A group having a finite number of elements is called a *Finite* Group and the number of elements in the Group is called the *Order* of the Group. Otherwise, the Group is an Infinite Group.

Example 4.1

1. The set of all integers (positive, negative, and 0) forms a group with respect to the addition operator; that is, $(I,+)$ is a group. It obeys all axioms of a group. Zero will be the identity operator; for each integer $k, -k$ will be its additive inverse. However, the set of all integers does not form a group with respect to the multiplication operator, since it does not satisfy the requirement of "Inverse Element." For a given integer, its multiplicative inverse will not be an integer; also, no inverse exists for the integer 0.

2. Let N_n be a set of n integers $\{1, 2, 3, ..., n\}$.
   Let S_n be a set of all possible permutations of N_n.
   The size of set S_n, that is, $|S_n| = n!$.

Let a and b be any two elements belonging to set S_n.

Let us define a binary operation on the elements of S_n, called composite permutation $a \bullet b$, which permutes the element b in accordance with elements of a, as illustrated in the following:

Let $N = 3$

Then $N_3 = \{1,2,3\}$

And

$$S_3 = \{(1,2,3),(13,2),(2,1,3),(2,3,1),(3,1,2),(3,2,1)\}$$
$$|S_3| = 3! = 3 \times 2 \times 1 = 6$$

Let $a = (3,1,2)$ and $b = (2,3,1)$, then $a \bullet b = (3,2,1) \bullet (2,3,1) = (1,3,2)$

Since the first element of a is 3, this implies that the first element of the result should be the third element of b (i.e., 1).

Similarly, since the second element in a is 2, this implies that the second element of the result should be the second element of b (i.e., 3).

And since the third element in a is l, this implies that the third element of the result should be the first element of b (i.e., 2).

Thus, $a \bullet b = (1,3,2)$.

The set S_n forms a group under the Binary-operation Composite Permutation ($\bullet$), defined previously, as it satisfies the following axioms:

(A_1) **Closure:** For each $a,b \in S_n$, then $a \bullet b$ will also be in S_n.

(A_2) **Associative:** For each $a,b,c \in S_n$, then $a \bullet (b \bullet c) = (a \bullet b) \bullet c$ will hold.

Example 4.2

Let

$$a = (1,3,2)$$
$$b = (3,1,2)$$
$$c = (2,3,1)$$
$$a \bullet (b \bullet c) = (1,3,2) \bullet (1,2,3) = (1,3,2)$$
$$(a \bullet b) \bullet c = (3,2,1) \bullet (2,3,1) = (1,3,2)$$
$$a \bullet (b \bullet c) = (a \bullet b) \bullet c = (1,3,2) \text{ holds.}$$

(A_3) **Identity Elements:** The identity element is $e = (1,2,3,...,n) \in S_n$, which satisfies $e \bullet a = a \bullet e = a$ for each $a \in S_n$.

Example 4.3

Let

$a = (3,1,2)$ and $e = (1,2,3)$

$$e \bullet a = (3,1,2)$$
$$a \bullet e = (3,1,2)$$

Thus,

$$e \bullet a = a \bullet e = a = (3,1,2)$$

(A_4) **Inverse Element:** for each element $a \in S_n$, there exists an element $a' \in S_n$ which satisfies that $a \bullet a' = a' \bullet a = e$.

Let $a = (3,1,2)$

Now,

$$(2,3,1) \bullet (3,1,2) = (1,2,3) = e$$

Therefore,

$$a' = (2,3,1)$$

Also,

$$a \bullet a' = (3,1,2) \bullet (2,3,1) = (1,2,3) = e$$

S_n forms a group under the "Composite Permutation" operation, as defined here.

Abelian Group:

A Group is called an *Abelian Group* if it is a Group (i.e., obeys axioms 1 through 4 obeyed by a group) and also obeys the following additional axiom:

(A_5) **Commutative:** $a \bullet b = b \bullet a$, for all $a,b \in G$

The Set of all Integers (positive, negative, and 0) is an Abelian Group under "Addition" with 0 as the identity element. The Set of non-zero real numbers is an Abelian Group with respect to "Multiplication," with 1 as the identity element. The element 0 is not included in the group, since it does not have a multiplicative inverse.

For "Addition" the identity element is 0, and the additive inverse of an element a is $-a$. *Subtraction* is defined by $a - b = a + (-b)$.

For "Multiplication" the identity element is 1, and the multiplicative inverse of an element a is a^{-1}.

Division is defined as $a / b = ab^{-1}$.

4.2.1.1 Exponentiation within a Group

Exponentiation in a Group is defined as repeated application of the Group Operator.

For example, if element $a \in \{G, \bullet\}$ then $a^k = a \bullet a \bullet a \dots$ (k times), with $a^0 = e$ (the identity element) and $a^{-n} = (a')^n$.

$$\text{For } \{G,+\}, \quad a^k = a + a + a + \dots + a \ (k \text{ times})$$
$$= kn$$
$$a^0 = 0n = 0 \text{ (additive identity element)}$$
$$\text{For } \{G,\times\}, \quad a^k = a + a + a + \dots + a \ (k \text{ times})$$
$$= a^k$$
$$a^0 = 1 \text{ (multiplicative identity element)}$$

Example 4.4

For $\{G,+\}$, $\ 1^n = 1 + 1 + 1 \dots (n \text{ times}) \ = n$

For $\{G,\times\}$, $\ 2^5 = 2 \times 2 \times 2 \times 2 \times 2 = 32$

4.2.1.2 Cyclic Group

A Group $\{G, \bullet\}$ is said to be cyclic if each element in G is generated as a^k, where k is an integer and a is a fixed element from G. The element a is called the Generator of the Cyclic Group G. A Cyclic Group is always an abelian group; it may be a finite abelian group or an infinite abelian group.

The set of all integers is an infinite cyclic group with respect to addition, with element 1 as the group generator. All positive integers are defined as $(1)^n$. For example, $5 = (1)^5 = 1+1+1+1+1$ (5 times). In addition, all negative integers are generated as $(-1)^n$. For example, $-3 = (-1)^3 = (-1)+(-1)+(-1)$; 0 is generated as $(1)^0$, that is, by adding 1 zero times.

4.2.2 Ring

A *Ring* is denoted as $\{R,+,\times\}$ where R is a set of elements, $+$ is an addition operator, and $\times$ is a multiplication operator. It obeys the following axioms:

(M_0) **Axiom (A_1) to (A_5):** A ring R is an *Abelian Group* with respect to the "Addition" operation.

(M_1) **Closure under Multiplication:** If a and b are in R then ab also will be in R.

(M_2) **Associative under Multiplication:** $a(bc) = (ab)c$ for all a,b,c in R.

(M_3) **Distributive:** $a(b+c) = ab + ac$

$$(a+b)c = ac + bc$$

For all a,b,c in R.

Commutative Ring: A Ring R is said to be a Commutative Ring if it is a Ring (i.e., obeys all axioms that are obeyed by a Ring) and also obeys the following additional Axiom:

(M_4) **Commutative under Multiplication:** $ab = ba$ for all a,b in R.

A Ring is a set in which we can perform addition, subtraction, and multiplication without leaving the set. A Set of all "Even" Integers (positive, negative, and zero) is a Ring and is also a Commutative Ring.

Integral Domain: An *Integral Domain* is a *Commutative Ring*, obeying the following additional axioms:

(M_5) **Multiplicative Identity:** There exists an element 1 in R such that $a \times 1 = 1 \times a = a$ for all a in R.

(M_6) **Non-Zero Divisor:** If $a,b \in R$ and $ab = 0$, then either $a = 0$ or $b = 0$.

The Set of all Integers (positive, negative, and zero) is an Integral Domain.

4.2.3 Field

A Field F, denoted as $\{F,+,\times\}$, is a set of elements F with two binary opera-tors, Addition (+) and Multiplication ($\times$), which obeys the following Axioms:

(M_7) **Axioms (A_1) to (M_6):** F is an integral Domain that satisfies Axioms A_1 to M_6 defined previously.

(M_8) **Multiplicative Inverse:** For each element $a \in F$ (except 0), there exists a multiplicative inverse a^{-1} in F such that $a \times a^{-1} = a^{-1} \times a = 1$.

A Field is a set of elements in which we can perform addition, subtrac-tion, multiplication, and division without leaving the set. Division is defined as $a/b = a \times (b)^{-1}$ where $b \neq 0$.

Example 4.5

The following are examples of Infinite fields:

1. A set of all rational numbers. A rational number is a number of the form a/b, where a and b are integers with $b \neq 0$.

2. A set of all real numbers.

3. A set of all complex numbers.

The set of integers does not form a field, since the multiplicative inverse of an integer is not an integer, but a real number.

4.3 MODULAR ARITHMETIC

If an integer a (positive, negative, or 0) is divided by a positive integer n, then we get an integer quotient q and an integer remainder r such that:

$$a = nq + r, \text{ for } 0 \leq r < n \text{ and } q = (a/n) \tag{4.1}$$

The remainder r is called *residue*.

Example 4.6

1. For $a = 11, n = 7 \Rightarrow q = 1, r = 4$
2. For $a = -11, n = 7 \Rightarrow q = -2, r = 3$
3. For $a = -21, n = 5 \Rightarrow q = -5, r = 4$

Modulus – If an integer a is divided by a positive integer n such that

$$a = nq + r, \text{ for } 0 \le r < n \text{ and } q = (a / n), \text{ then } r = a \bmod n. \qquad (4.2)$$

Example 4.7

1. $11 \bmod 7 = 4$
2. $-11 \bmod 7 = 3$
3. $-23 \bmod 5 = 2$
4. $23 \bmod 5 = 3$

Congruent Modulo – Two integers a and b are said to be congruent modulo n, if $a \bmod n = b \bmod n$. It is expressed as

$$a \equiv b (\bmod n) \qquad (4.3)$$

Example 4.8

1. $23 \equiv 2 (\bmod 7)$
2. $18 \equiv 3 (\bmod 5)$
3. $-18 \equiv 2 (\bmod 5)$
4. $-23 \equiv 5 (\bmod 7)$

Divisor: A non-zero integer b is said to divide an integer a (expressed as $b \mid a$), if there exists an integer m such that $a = mb$. Here, b is called a divisor of a. If b divides a, the remainder is 0.

Example 4.9

Positive divisors of 105 are 3, 5, 7, 15, 21, 35, and 105.

Some Properties of Divisors

1. If $a \mid 1$, then $a = \pm 1$

2. If $a \mid b$ and $b \mid a$, then $a = \pm b$

3. Any integer $b \neq 0$ divides 0

4. If $b \mid g$ and $b \mid b$, then $b \mid (mg + nb)$, where m and n are some integers

5. If $a \equiv 0 \bmod n$, then $n \mid a$, that is, n divides a.

Properties of the Modulo Operator

1. $a \equiv b \bmod n \Rightarrow n \mid (a - b)$

2. $a \equiv b \bmod n \Rightarrow b \equiv a \bmod n$

3. $a \equiv b \bmod n$ and $b \equiv c \bmod n \Rightarrow a \equiv c \bmod n$

Properties of Modular Arithmetic

1. $\left[(a \bmod n) + (b \bmod n) \right] \bmod n = (a + b) \bmod n$

2. $\left[(a \bmod n) - (b \bmod n) \right] \bmod n = (a - b) \bmod n$

3. $\left[(a \bmod n) \times (b \bmod n) \right] \bmod n = (a \times b) \bmod n$

4. Exponentiation is performed by repeated multiplication $\bmod n$, that is,
$\left[a^k \right] \bmod n = \left[(a \bmod n) \times (a \bmod n) \times ... k \text{ times} \right] \bmod n$

Example 4.10

Prove that $[(a \bmod n) + (b \bmod n)] \bmod n = (a + b) \bmod n$

Solution

Let $a = kn + r_a$, where k is some integer and r_a is the remainder and $b = tn + r_b$, where t is some integer and r_b is the remainder

By definition $r_a = a \bmod n$ and $r_b = b \bmod n$

$$(a + b) \bmod n = (kn + r_a + tn + r_b) \bmod n$$

$$= \left[(k + t)n + r_a + r_b \right] \bmod n$$

$$= (r_a + r_b) \bmod n \text{, since } \left[(k+t)n\right] \bmod n = 0$$

$$= (a \bmod n + b \bmod n) \bmod n$$

Thus, $[(a \bmod n) + (b \bmod n)] \bmod n = (a + b) \bmod n$

Similarly, we can have proof of other properties of modular arithmetic.

4.3.1 Residue Classes (mod *n*)

The $\bmod n$ operator maps all integers onto the finite set $\{0, 1, ..., (n-1)\}$.

Let us denote this set as Z_n, that is, the set of non-negative integers less than n.

$Z_n = \{0, 1, ..., (n-1)\}$.

This set is also known as the *Set of Residues* ($\bmod n$) or *Residue Classes* ($\bmod n$).

Each integer in Z_n represents a Residue Class ($\bmod n$).

We can label the Residue Classes Modulo n as:

$$[0] = \{..., -2n, -n, 0, n, 2n, ...\}$$
$$[1] = \{..., -2n+1, -n+1, 1, n+1, 2n+1, ...\}$$
$$[2] = \{..., -2n+2, -n+2, 2, n+2, 2n+2, ...\}$$

And so on …

Example 4.11

The Residue Classes ($\bmod n$) are:

$$[0] = \{..., -8, -4, 0, 4, 8, ...\}$$
$$[1] = \{..., -7, -3, 1, 5, 9, ...\}$$
$$[2] = \{..., -6, -2, 2, 6, 10, ...\}$$
$$[3] = \{..., -5, -1, 3, 7, 11, ...\}$$

Thus, of all the integers in a Residue Class, the smallest positive integer represents the modulo class.

4.3.2 Properties of Z_n

The properties of Z_n are summarized in Table 4.1.

TABLE 4.1 Properties of Z_n

Property	Expression
Commutative Laws	$(w + x) \bmod n = (x + w) \bmod n$ $(w \times x) \bmod n = (x \times w) \bmod n$
Associative Laws	$[(w + x) \bmod n + y] \bmod n = [w + (x + y) \bmod n] \bmod n$ $[(w \times x) \bmod n \times y] \bmod n = [w \times (x \times y) \bmod n] \bmod n$
Distributive Laws	$[w(x + y) \bmod n] \bmod n = [(w \times x) \bmod n + (w \times y) \bmod n] \bmod n$
Identities	$(0 + w) \bmod n = w \bmod n$ $(1 \times w) \bmod n = w \bmod n$
Additive Inverse	For each $w \in Z_n$ there exists an additive inverse x of w such that $(w + x) \equiv 0 \bmod n$
Multiplicative Inverse	For $w \in Z_n$, if w is relatively prime to n, then there exists a multiplicative inverse x of w such that $(wx) \equiv 1 \bmod n$

Thus Z_n forms an Integral Domain.

Example 4.12

Consider set $Z_8 = \{0, 1, 2, 3, 4, 5, 6, 7\}$

1. $(\bmod\, 8)$ Addition

Table 4.2 illustrates the $(\bmod\, 8)$ Addition as follows.

TABLE 4.2 (mod8) Addition

+	0	1	2	3	4	5	6	7
0	0	1	2	3	4	5	6	7
1	1	2	3	4	5	6	7	0
2	2	3	4	5	6	7	0	1
3	3	4	5	6	7	0	1	2
4	4	5	6	7	0	1	2	3
5	5	6	7	0	1	2	3	4
6	6	7	0	1	2	3	4	5
7	7	0	1	2	3	4	5	6

2. (mod 8) Multiplication

Table 4.3 illustrates the (mod 8) Multiplication as follows.

TABLE 4.3 (mod 8) Multiplication

◊	0	1	2	3	4	5	6	7
0	0	0	0	0	0	0	0	0
1	0	1	2	3	4	5	6	7
2	0	2	4	6	0	2	4	6
3	0	3	6	1	4	7	2	5
4	0	4	0	4	0	4	0	4
5	0	5	2	7	4	1	6	3
6	0	6	4	2	0	6	4	2
7	0	7	6	5	4	3	2	1

3. Additive and Multiplicative Inverses (mod 8)

Table 4.4 illustrates the Additive and Multiplicative Inverses (mod 8) as follows:

TABLE 4.4 Additive and Multiplicative Inverses (mod 8)

w	−w	$w^{\wedge 1}$
0	0	-
1	7	1
2	6	-
3	5	3
4	4	-
5	3	5
6	2	-
7	1	7

The following observations can be made from the above tables (4.2–4.4):

- Additive Inverses exist for all $w \in Z_n$.

- Multiplicative inverses exist only for $w \in Z_n$, if w is relatively prime to n. For example, the multiplicative inverses (mod 8) exist for 1, 3, 5, and 7 that are relatively prime to 8. However, multiplicative inverses do not exist for 2, 4, and 6 that are not relatively prime to 8. The multiplicative inverse for 0 is not defined.

4.3.3 Multiplication within Set Z_n

- $Z_n = \{0, 1, 2, \ldots, (n-1)\}$
- Let K be any integer from the set Z_n

- If all elements of Z_n are multiplied by K, we get a set L of n integers

- If K is relatively prime to n, then the set L will be a permutation of set Z_n and the multiplication within the set will be reversible, as demonstrated here:

Let $K = 5$ and $n = 8$.

$Z_8 = \{0,1,2,3,4,5,6,7\}$

$L = (KXJ) \bmod 8 = (0,5,2,7,4,1,6,3)$, for $J = 0...7$

Each element of Z_8 appears only once in L.

Thus, set L is just a permutation of set Z_8.

Mapping from set Z_8 to set L for $K = 5$ and $n = 8$ is indicated as follows in Table 4.5:

TABLE 4.5 Mapping from Set Z_8 to Set L for $K = 5$ and $n = 8$

Set Z_8	Set L
0	0
1	5
2	2
3	7
4	4
5	1
6	6
7	3

In this case reverse transformation from set L to set Z_8 is feasible, as shown Table 4.6 as follows:

TABLE 4.6 Reverse Transformation from Set L to Set Z_8

Set L	Set Z_8
0	0
1	5
2	2
3	7
4	4
5	1
6	6
7	3

Thus, the multiplication of Z_n elements, with an integer relatively prime to n, is reversible.

If K is not relatively prime to n then set L will be a subset of Z_n and the multiplication will not be reversible. Some of the elements of Z_n will appear repetitively in L as demonstrated in the following:

Take $K = 4$ and $n = 8$.

$$Z_8 = \{0, 1, 2, 3, 4, 5, 6, 7\}$$

$$L = (KXJ) \bmod 8 = (0, 4, 0, 4, 0, 4, 0, 4), \text{ for } J = 0...7$$

Set L has only two elements of Z_8, that is, 0 and 4, which are repeated again and again.

Mapping from set Z_8 to set L for $K = 4$ and $n = 8$ is indicated as follows in Table 4.7:

TABLE 4.7 Mapping from Set Z_8 to Set L for $K = 4$ and $n = 8$

Set Z_8	Set L
0	0
1	4
2	0
3	4
4	0
5	4
6	0
7	4

In this case reverse transformation back to J is not feasible, as demonstrated as follows in Table 4.8:

TABLE 4.8 Reverse Transformation from Set L to Set Z_8

Set L	Set Z_8
0	0 or 2 or 4 or 6
4	1 or 3 or 5 or 7

Thus, the multiplication of Z_n elements with an integer that is not relatively prime to integer value n is not reversible.

Example 4.14

Determine the multiplicative inverse of $18 \bmod 1761$.

Solution

For $18 \bmod 1761$, $x = 18; m = 1761$.

Table 4.10 illustrates the multiplicative inverse of $18 \bmod 1761$.

TABLE 4.10 Multiplicative Inverse of 18 mod 1761

(A_1, A_2, A_3)	(B_1, B_2, B_3)	(T_1, T_2, T_3)	$Q = A_3 \text{ DIV } B_3$
(1,0,1761)	(0,1,18)	(1,-97,15)	97
(0,1,18)	(1,-97,15)	(-1,98,3)	1
(1,-97,15)	(-1,98,3)	(6,-587,0)	5
(-1,98,3)	(6,-587,0)	-	-

$GCD(18,1761) = A_3 = 3$

Since $B_3 = 0$, Therefore, $18^{-1} \bmod 1761$ does not exist

Example 4.15

Determine the multiplicative inverse of $18 \bmod 557$.

Solution

For $18 \bmod 557$, $x = 18; m = 557$.

Table 4.11 illustrates the multiplicative inverse of $18 \bmod 557$.

TABLE 4.11 Multiplicative Inverse of 18 mod 557

(A_1, A_2, A_3)	(B_1, B_2, B_3)	(T_1, T_2, T_3)	$Q = A_3 \text{ DIV } B_3$
(1,0,557)	(0,1,18)	(1,-30,17)	30
(0,1,18)	(1,-30,17)	(-1,31,1)	1
(1,-30,17)	(-1,31,1)	-	-

Since $B_3 = 1$

$\therefore B_2 = 31 = 18^{-1} \bmod 557$

$\therefore 18^{-1} \bmod 557 = 31$

Verification

$$31 \times 18 \bmod 557 = 558 \bmod 557 = 1$$

$\therefore 18^{-1} \bmod 557 = 31$, stands verify.

Example 4.16

Determine the multiplicative inverse of $37 \bmod 1023$.

Solution

For $37 \bmod 1023$, $x = 37; m = 1023$.

Table 4.12 illustrates the multiplicative inverse of $37 \bmod 1023$.

TABLE 4.12 Multiplicative Inverse of 37 mod 1023

(A_1, A_2, A_3)	(B_1, B_2, B_3)	(T_1, T_2, T_3)	$Q = A_3$ DIV B_3
(1,0,1023)	(0,1,37)	(1,–27,24)	27
(0,1,37)	(1,–27,24)	(–1,28,13)	1
(1,–27,24)	(–1,28,13)	(2,–55,11)	1
(–1,28,13)	(2,–55,11)	(–3,83,2)	1
(2,–55,11)	(–3,83,2)	(5,–470,1)	5
(–3,83,2)	(5,–470,1)	-	-

Since $B_3 = 1$

$\therefore$ Multiplicative Inverse $37^{-1} \bmod 1023 = (-470) \bmod 2023 = 553$

Verification

$$xx^{-1} \bmod 1023 = (37 \times 553) \bmod 1023$$

$$= 20461 \bmod 1023$$

$$= 1$$

$\therefore 37^{-1} \bmod 1023 = 553$, stands verify.

4.7 GALOLS FINITE FIELDS

The Galois Finite Fields are named in honor of mathematician Évariste Galois, who invented the finite fields. There are two kinds of Galois Fields:

- Galois Fields of order p^n denoted as $GF(p^n)$, where p is a prime number and n is a positive integer. A special case that is of interest to us from a cryptography point of view is where $n = 1$, that is, $GF(p^n)$ where order of the finite field is p.

- Galois Fields of order 2^n denoted as $GF(2^n)$ where n is a positive integer

4.7.1 GF (p):

$Z_p = \{0,1,2,3,4,...(p-1)\}$ is a Galois Field of order p, where p is a prime number.

Z_p is also called a set of residues ($\bmod p$).

Proof:

- For any integer n, the set residue ($\bmod p$), that is, Z_p, forms an integral domain of size n. But Z_p may not be a field, since a multiplicative inverse exists only for those elements of Z_p that are relatively prime to n.

- But all elements in Z_p (except 0) are relatively prime to p. Therefore, multiplicative inverses ($\bmod p$) exist for all the elements of Z_p (except 0).

- Thus, Z_p satisfies all the properties of a Field.

- $\therefore Z_p$ is a field of size p.

4.7.2 Set Z_p^*

Z_p^* is a set of residues (excluding 0) $\bmod p$ where p is a prime number.

$Z_p^* = \{1,2,3,4,...(p-1)\}$

Each element in Z_p^* has its unique multiplicative inverse ($\bmod p$). Thus, multiplication within Z_p^* is reversible, which is an important property of a finite set from a cryptography point of view.

Example 4.17

Prove that there exists a Reversible Multiplication of elements within the Set Z_p^*.

Solution

Each element of Z_p^* will be relatively prime to p, since p is a prime number.

Therefore, if all the elements of Z_p^* are multiplied by any element $a \in Z_p^*$, the result will be a set of integers that will be a permutation of set Z_p^*.

Thus, the multiplication of elements within the set Z_p^* is reversible.

4.7.3 Galois Finite Fields of Order 2^n

- A Galois Field GF (2^n) is a finite field of order 2^n. It comprises 2^n distinct integers $\{0, 1, 2, \ldots (2^n - 1)\}$.
- There exist 2^n distinct polynomials of degree $\leq n - 1$ that are used to represent the integers in the field GF (2^n).

Example 4.18

If $n = 3$, the integers 0 through 7 can be represented by 8 distinct polynomials of degree ≤ 7 as shown in Table 4.13:

TABLE 4.13 A Galois Field GF (2^n) for $n = 3$

Integer	3-bit binary value	Equivalent Polynomial
0	000	0
1	001	1
2	010	x
3	011	$x + 1$
4	100	x^2
5	101	$x^2 + 1$
6	110	$x^2 + x$
7	111	$x^2 + x + 1$

Each integer in the range $0, \ldots (2^3 - 1)$ is represented by a distinct polynomial.

4.7.4 Arithmetic Operations within GF (2^n)

- The arithmetic operations like addition, subtraction, multiplication, and division are performed within the finite field GF (2^n), using the usual polynomial arithmetic, with the following additional rules:

1. The coefficients of the polynomials are reduced (mod 2). Thus, the additive inverse of an integer "w" belonging to GF (2^n) will be "w" itself.

2. If the multiplication of two polynomials within GF (2^n) results in a polynomial of degree greater than ($n-1$), then the resultant polynomial is the reduced modulo of some irreducible polynomial $m(x)$ of degree n.

3. A polynomial $m(x)$ of degree n is said to be irreducible if it cannot be expressed as a product of two polynomials of degrees lower than n.

Example 4.19

- Let us consider GF (2^3) and let $m(x) = x^3 + x^2 + 1$ be the irreducible polynomial of degree 3. The polynomial $m(x)$ does not have any factors of degree 1 or 2.

- The order of the finite field GF (2^3) will be $2^3 = 8$.

- There will be $2^3 = 8$ distinct polynomials of degree "2 that are used to represent the integers in the range from 0 to 7.

- If multiplication results in a polynomial of degree greater than 2, then the resultant polynomial is the reduced modulo $m(x) = x^3 + x^2 + 1$. This operation is demonstrated here:

Let $f(x) = x^2 + x + 1$ and $g(x) = x^2 + x$; $m(x) = x^3 + x^2 + 1$

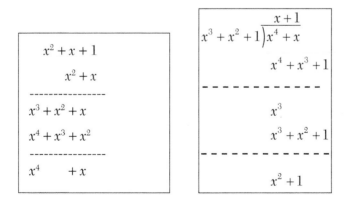

4.7.5 Addition (+) Operation within GF (2^3)

Table 4.14 demonstrates the addition (+) operation within GF (2^3).

TABLE 4.14 Addition (+) Operation within GF (2^3)

(+)	0 000 (0)	1 001 (1)	2 010 (x)	3 011 (x+1)	4 100 (x^2)	5 101 (x^2+1)	6 110 (x^2+x)	7 111 (x^2+x+1)
0 (0)	0 (0)	1 (1)	2 (x)	3 (x+1)	4 (x^2)	5 (x^2+1)	6 (x^2+x)	7 (x^2+x+1)
1 (1)	1 (1)	0 (0)	3 (x+1)	2 (x)	5 (x^2+1)	4 (x^2)	7 (x^2+x+1)	6 (x^2+x)
2 (x)	2 (x)	3 (x+1)	0 (0)	1 (1)	6 (x^2+x)	7 (x^2+x+1)	4 (x^2)	5 (x^2+1)
3 (x+1)	3 (x+1)	2 (x)	1 (1)	0 (0)	7 (x^2+x+1)	6 (x^2+x)	5 (x^2+1)	4 (x^2)
4 (x^2)	4 (x^2)	5 (x^2+1)	6 (x^2+x)	7 (x^2+x+1)	0 (0)	1 (1)	2 (x)	3 (x+1)
5 (x^2+1)	5 (x^2+1)	4 (x^2)	7 (x^2+x+1)	6 (x^2+x)	1 (1)	0 (0)	3 (x+1)	2 (x)
6 (x^2+x)	6 (x^2+x)	7 (x^2+x+1)	4 (x^2)	5 (x^2+1)	2 (x)	3 (x+1)	0 (0)	1 (1)
7 (x^2+x+1)	7 (x^2+x+1)	6 (x^2+x)	5 (x^2+1)	4 (x^2)	3 (x+1)	2 (x)	1 (1)	0 (0)

4.7.6 Addition Inverse of GF (2^3):

Since addition in GF (2^3) is performed ($\bmod 2$), the additive inverse of any integer "w" belonging to GF (2^3) will be "w" itself, since $(w+w) \bmod 2 = 0$.

4.7.7 Multiplication (x) Operation within GF (2^3) Using $m(x) = x^3 + x^2 + 1$ for Reducing the Polynomials

Table 4.15 demonstrates the multiplication (x) operation within GF (2^3) using $m(x) = x^3 + x^2 + 1$.

TABLE 4.15 Multiplication ($\times$) Operation within GF(2^3) Using $m(x) = x^3 + x^2 + 1$

	0	1	2	3	4	5	6	7
(+)	000	001	010	011	100	101	110	111
	(0)	(1)	(x)	($x+1$)	(x^2)	(x^2+1)	(x^2+x)	(x^2+x+1)
0 (0)	0 (0)	0 (0)	0 (0)	0 (0)	0 (0)	0 (0)	0 (0)	0 (0)
1 (1)	0 (0)	1 (1)	2 (x)	3 ($x+1$)	4 (x^2)	5 (x^2+1)	6 (x^2+x)	7 (x^2+x+1)
2 (x)	0 (0)	2 (x)	4 (x^2)	6 (x^2+x)	5 (x^2+1)	7 (x^2+x+1)	1 (1)	3 ($x+1$)
3 ($x+1$)	0 (0)	3 ($x+1$)	6 (x^2+x)	5 (x^2+1)	1 (1)	2 (x)	7 (x^2+x+1)	4 (x^2)
4 (x^2)	0 (0)	4 (x^2)	5 (x^2+1)	1 (1)	7 (x^2+x+1)	3 ($x+1$)	2 (x)	6 (x^2+x)
5 (x^2+1)	0 (0)	5 (x^2+1)	7 (x^2+x+1)	2 (x)	3 ($x+1$)	6 (x^2+x)	4 (x^2)	1 (1)
6 (x^2+x)	0 (0)	6 (x^2+x)	1 (1)	7 (x^2+x+1)	2 (x)	4 (x^2)	3 ($x+1$)	5 (x^2+1)
7 (x^2+x+1)	0 (0)	7 (x^2+x+1)	3 ($x+1$)	4 (x^2)	6 (x^2+x)	1 (1)	5 (x^2+1)	2 (x)

4.7.8 Multiplication Inverse within GF (2^3)

The multiplicative inverse of a polynomial $f(x) \bmod m(x)$, that is, $f(x)^{-1} \bmod m(x)$, is determined by Euclid's Extended Algorithm:

$$\text{Euclid}\left(f(x), m(x)\right) \quad /^*\text{Determine } f(x)^{-1} \bmod m(x) \,^*/$$

$$/^*\text{where } f(x) \text{ is a polynomial of degree } \leq n-1 \,^*/$$

$$/^*\text{and } m(x) \text{ is irreducible polynomial of degree } n \,^*/$$

Step 1: $\left(A_1, A_2, A_3\right) \leftarrow \left(1, 0, m(x)\right); \left(B_1, B_2, B_3\right) \leftarrow \left(0, 1, f(x)\right)$

Step 2: If $\left(B_3 = 0\right)$ then Return $f(x)^{-1} \bmod m(x)$ does not exist)

Step 3: If $\left(B_3 = 1\right)$ then Return $B_2 = f(x)^{-1} \bmod m(x)$

Step 4: $Q = A_3 \text{ DIV } B_3$

Step 5: $\left(T_1, T_2, T_3\right) \leftarrow \left(A_1 - QB_1, A_2 - QB_2, A_3 - QB_3\right)$

Step 6: $\left(A_1, A_2, A_3\right) \leftarrow \left(B_1, B_2, B_3\right)$

Step 7: $\left(B_1, B_2, B_3\right) \leftarrow \left(T_1, T_2, T_3\right)$

Step 8: GOTO Step 2

Example 4.20

Let $f(x) = x^2 + 1$ and $m(x) = x^3 + x^2 + 1$. Determine $f(x)^{-1} \bmod m(x)$.

Solution

For $f(x) = x^2 + 1$ and $m(x) = x^3 + x^2 + 1$.

Table 4.16 illustrates the computation of $f(x)^{-1} \bmod m(x)$

TABLE 4.16 Computational of Multiplicative Inverse of $f(x)$ mod $m(x)$

(A_1, A_2, A_3)	(B_1, B_2, B_3)	(T_1, T_2, T_3)	$Q = A_3 \text{ DIV } B_3$
$(1, 0, m(x))$	$(0, 1, f(x))$	-	-
$(1, 0, (x^3 + x^2 + 1))$	$(0, 1, (x^2 + 1))$	$(1, x, (x^2 + x + 1))$	x
$(0, 1, (x^2 + 1))$	$(1, x, (x^2 + x + 1))$	$(1, (x + 1), x)$	1
$(1, x, (x^2 + x + 1))$	$(1, (x + 1), x)$	$(x, (x^2 + x + 1), 1)$	$x + 1$
$(1, (x + 1), x)$	$(x, (x^2 + x + 1), 1)$	-	-

Since in the last iteration of Table 4.16 $B_3 = 1$, the value of $B_2 = x^2 + x + 1$ represents the multiplicative inverse of $f(x) \bmod m(x)$

$\therefore f(x)^{-1} \bmod m(x) = x^2 + x + 1$.

4.7.9 Multiplicative Inverses of All Integers in GF (2^3)

Using the Extended Euclid Algorithm as indicated previously, we can determine the multiplicative inverse of all integers in GF (2^3) as shown in Table 4.17:

TABLE 4.17 Computational of Multiplicative Inverse of $f(x)$ mod $m(x)$

w	$w(x)$	$w(x)^{-1} \bmod m(x)$	w^{-1}
0	0	-	-
1	1	1	1
2	x	$x^2 + x$	6
3	$x + 1$	x^2	4
4	x^2	$x + 1$	3
5	$x^2 + 1$	$x^2 + x + 1$	7
6	$x^2 + x$	x	2
7	$x^2 + x + 1$	$x^2 + 1$	5

Each integer except 0 in GF (2^n) has a unique multiplicative inverse.

Thus, GF(2^3) satisfies all the properties of a finite field of order 2^3.

The Advanced Encryption Standard (AES) makes use of GF (2^8) finite fields with reducing polynomial $m(x) = x^8 + x^4 + x^3 + x + 1$, which is an irreducible polynomial of order 8.

4.8 FERMAT'S LITTLE THEOREM

Fermat's Little Theorem states that if p is a prime number and a is a positive integer not divisible by p then $a^{p-1} \equiv 1 \bmod p$ will hold.

Proof:

$$Z_p^* = \left\{1, 2, \dots (p-1)\right\}$$

Since integer a is a positive integer not divisible by p, $(a \bmod p) \in Z_p^*$ and thus will be relatively prime to p. If each element of Z_p^* is multiplied by $(a \bmod p)$, we get a set L that will have exactly same set of integers as set Z_p^* but permuted.

$$L = \left\{a \bmod p, 2a \bmod p, \dots, (p-1)a \bmod p\right\}$$

Since L is a permutation of Z_p^*, the product of all elements of L will be congruent to the product of all elements of $Z_p^* (\bmod p)$.

$$\therefore \left[a \bmod p \times 2a \bmod p \times \dots \times (p-1)a\right] \bmod p \equiv \left[1 \times 2 \times 3 \dots \times (p-1)\right] \bmod p.$$

Using the identity $(A \bmod p \times B \bmod p) \equiv (A \times B) \bmod p$, we get

$$\left[a \times 2a \times \dots \times (p-1)a\right] \equiv \left[1 \times 2 \times \dots \times (p-1)\right] \bmod p$$

$$\therefore \left[1 \times 2 \times \dots \times (p-1)\right] a^{p-1} \equiv \left[1 \times 2 \times \dots \times (p-1)\right] \bmod p$$

$$\therefore (p-1)! \, a^{p-1} \equiv (p-1)! \bmod p \qquad (4.6)$$

Since $(p-1)!$ is the product of integers relatively prime to p, $(p-1)!$ will also be relatively prime to p. Therefore, we can divide the previous congruence by $(p-1)!$ on both sides and get:

$$\therefore a^{p-1} \equiv 1 \bmod p \qquad (4.7)$$

This proves Fermat's Little Theorem.

Example 4.21

Determine a^{p-1} using Fermat's Little Theorem when $p = 11$ and $a = 8$.

Solution

Table 4.18 illustrates the calculation of $(k \times a) \bmod p$.

TABLE 4.18 Calculation of $(k \times a)$ mod p

$(k \times a)$ mod p	$k = 0..10$
0	0
1	8
2	5
3	2
4	10
5	7
6	4
7	1
8	9
9	6
10	3

Thus, the set of values in the second column is a permutation of the set of values in the first column, thus making possible the reverse transformation from the second column to the first column without any ambiguity.

$$a^{p-1} = 8^{10} \bmod 11 = \left(8^2 \bmod 11\right)^5 \bmod 11 = 9^5 \bmod 11$$

4.8.1 A Corollary of Fermat's Little Theorem

$$a^p \equiv a \bmod p , \tag{4.9}$$

where p is a prime number and a is any positive integer.

Proof:

There are two possibilities:

1. **Case I: Integer relatively prime to** p **, that is, does not divide integer** a **.**

Then by Fermat's Little Theorem,

$$a^{p-1} \equiv 1 \bmod p$$

Multiplying both sides of the above congruence by integer a:

$$a^p \equiv a \bmod p$$

2. **Case II:** p **divides integer** a **.**

Let $a = cp$ for some integer p.

Then $a^p \equiv (cp)^p \bmod p \equiv 0 \bmod p$

Also, $a \bmod p = (cp) \bmod p \equiv 0 \bmod p$

$\therefore a^p \equiv a \bmod p$

Thus, the corollary stands proven for both cases.

4.9 EULER'S TOTIENT FUNCTION

Euler's Totient Function $\phi(n) = (p-1)(q-1)$ of a positive integer n is defined as the number of non-negative integers less than n and relatively prime to n.

For a prime number p, $\phi(n) = p-1$, since all positive integers less than p will be relatively prime to p.

Example 4.22

A. $\phi(1) = 1$, Integer 0 is relatively prime to 1.

B. $\phi(11) = 10$, Integer 11 is a prime.

C. $\phi(12) = 4$, $\{1,5,7,11\}$

Example 4.23

If $n = pq$ where p and q are prime numbers, then prove that $\phi(n) = (p-1)(q-1)$.

Solution

To prove that $\phi(pq) = \phi(p) \times \phi(q)$, where p and q are prime numbers.

The set of residues $Z_n = \{0,1,2,3,..(pq-1)\}$.

The elements in Z_n that are not relatively prime to n are:

$\{0,\{p,2p,3p,...,(q-1)p\}$ and $\{q,2q,3q,...,(p-1)q\}\}$.

The number of elements in Z_n that are not relatively prime to n are equal to $[1+(p-1)+(q-1)]$.

$$\therefore \phi(n) = pq - [1+(p-1)+(q-1)]$$
$$= pq - [p+q-1]$$
$$= pq - p - q + 1$$
$$= (p-1)(q-1)$$
$$= \phi(p) \times \phi(q)$$

$\phi(pq) = \phi(p) \times \phi(q)$, where p and q are prime numbers. $\qquad$ (4.10)

Example 4.24

If n equals p^2, prove that $\phi(n) = p\phi(p)$

Solution

The set of residues $Z_n = \{0,1,2,3,..(p^2-1)\}$.

The elements in Z_n that are not relatively prime to n are:

$\{0,\{p,2p,3p,...,(p-1)p\}\}$.

The number of elements in Z_n that are not relatively prime to n are equal to $[1+(p-1)]=p$.

$$\therefore \phi(n) = p^2 - p = (p)(p-1)$$
$$= p \times \phi(p)$$

Example 4.25

$\phi(49) = \phi(7 \times 7) = 7 \times \phi(7) = 7 \times 6 = 42$.

4.9.1 General Formula for Computation of Totient Function ϕ(*n*)

Let n be any positive integer > 1.

It can be expressed as a product of prime numbers as follows:

$n = p_1^{a_1} \times p_2^{a_2} \times ... \times p_k^{a_k} = \prod_{i=1}^{i=k} (p_i^{a_i})$, where $p_1, p_2, .., p_k$ are prime numbers and $a_1, a_2, ..., a_k$ are positive integers.

Then Euler's Totient Function of n will be:

$$\phi(n) = p_1^{a_1-1}\phi(p_1) \times p_2^{a_2-1}\phi(p_2) \times ... \times p_k^{a_{k-1}}\phi(p_k) = \prod_{i=1}^{i=k}\left(p_i^{a_i-1} \times\right)\phi(p_i) \qquad (4.11)$$

Example 4.26

Determine $\phi(n)$ for the following values of n:

A. 735

B. 400

C. 3375

Solution

A. $735 = 7^2 \times 5 \times 3$

$$\begin{aligned}
\phi(735) &= \phi(7^2) \times \phi(5) \times \phi(3) \\
&= 7 \times \phi(7) \times 4 \times 2 \\
&= 7 \times 6 \times 4 \times 2 \\
&= 336
\end{aligned}$$

B. $400 = 2^4 \times 5^2$

$$\begin{aligned}
\phi(400) &= \phi(2^4) \times \phi(5^2) \\
&= 2^3 \times \phi(2) \times 5 \times \phi(5) \\
&= 8 \times 1 \times 5 \times 4 \\
&= 160
\end{aligned}$$

C. $3375 = 5^3 \times 3^3$

$$\begin{aligned}
\phi(3375) &= \phi(5^3) \times \phi(3^3) \\
&= 5^2 \times \phi(5) \times 3^2 \times \phi(3) \\
&= 25 \times 4 \times 9 \times 2 \\
&= 1800
\end{aligned}$$

4.10   EULER'S THEOREM

If a and n are two integers relatively prime to each other, then $a^{\phi(n)} \equiv 1 \bmod n$.

Proof:

By definition of Euler's Totient Function, an integer n will have precisely $\phi(n)$ positive integers less than n and relatively prime to n. Let the set of those $\phi(n)$ integers be:

$$X = \left\{x_1, x_2, ..., x_{\phi(n)}\right\}$$

Multiplying the elements of X by $(a \bmod n)$, we get set Y:

$$Y = \left\{ax_1 \bmod n, ax_2 \bmod n, ..., ax_{\phi(n)} \bmod n\right\}$$

Since all $x_i\,(i = 1...\phi(n))$ are relatively prime to n and also integer a is relatively prime to n, all the elements of set Y will be less than n and relatively prime to n.

Also, since all $x_i\,(i = 1...\phi(n))$ are distinct and a is relatively prime to n, all elements of set Y will be distinct.

Therefore, Y is a set of $\phi(n)$ distinct integers less than n and relatively prime to n. This is the precise definition of set X. Thus, set Y is a permutation of set X.

Therefore, the product of all elements of set Y will be congruent to the product of all elements of set X.

$$\therefore Y = \left[\left(ax_1 \bmod n\right) \times \left(ax_2 \bmod n\right) \times ... \times \left(ax_{\phi(n)} \bmod n\right)\right] \equiv \left(x_1, x_2, ..., x_{\phi(n)}\right) \bmod n$$

Using the identity $\left(A \bmod p \times B \bmod p\right) \equiv \left(A \times B\right) \bmod p$, we get:

$$\left[\left(ax_1\right) \times \left(ax_2\right) \times ... \times \left(ax_{\phi(n)}\right)\right] \equiv \left(x_1, x_2, ..., x_{\phi(n)}\right) \bmod n$$

$$\therefore a^{\phi(n)} \left(\prod_{i=1}^{i=\phi(n)} x_i\right) \equiv \left(\prod_{i=1}^{i=\phi(n)} x_i\right) \bmod n$$

Since $\left(\prod_{i=1}^{i=\phi(n)} x_i\right)$ is the product of integers relatively prime to n, $\left(\prod_{i=1}^{i=\phi(n)} x_i\right)$ will also be relatively prime to n. Therefore, we can divide the above congruence by $\left(\prod_{i=1}^{i=\phi(n)} x_i\right)$ on both sides and get:

$$\therefore a^{\phi(n)} \equiv 1 \bmod n \tag{4.12}$$

Thus, Euler's Theorem stands proven.

4.10.1 A Corollary of Euler's Theorem

Let $n = p \times q$, where p and q are two prime numbers.

And let M be any integer such that $0 < M < n$.

Then, $M^{\phi(n)} \equiv M \bmod n$, will hold true for and M that may not be relatively prime to n.

Proof:

There are two cases:

1. **Case I: *M* is relatively prime to *n*, that is, GCD (M, n) = 1**
   Then, by Euler's Theorem:

   $$M^{\phi(n)} \equiv 1 \bmod n$$

   Multiplying both sides of the above congruence by M

   $$M^{\phi(n)+1} \equiv M \bmod n$$

2. **Case II: *M* is not relatively prime to n, that is, $\mathbf{GCD}(M,n) \neq 1$**
   Since $0 < M < n$ and n are products of p and q, it is not possible for M to have both p and as its factors; thus, there are two possibilities:

   A. M is a multiple of p, but is relatively prime to q, $\mathrm{GCD}(M,q) = 1$.
   Or

   B. M is a multiple of q, but is relatively prime to p, $\mathrm{GCD}(M,\mathrm{p}) = 1$.
   Case II (a): *M* is a multiple of p and $GCD(M,q) = 1$

   Let $M = cp$ where c is an integer > 0. M will not have q as its factor;
   $\therefore GCD(\mathrm{m},\mathrm{q}) = 1$

   Therefore, by Euler's Theorem

   $$M^{\phi(q)} \equiv 1 \bmod q$$

   Raising both sides of the above congruence to power $\phi(p)$

   $$\left[M^{\phi(q)}\right]^{\phi(p)} \equiv (1)^{\phi(p)} \bmod q$$

$$\therefore M^{\phi(q)\phi(p)} \equiv (1)^{\phi(p)} \bmod q$$

$$\therefore M^{\phi(n)} \equiv 1 \bmod q$$

Thus, there will be some integer k such that:

$$M^{\phi(n)} \equiv kq + 1$$

Multiplying both sides by $M = cp$

$$M^{\phi(n)+1} \equiv kcpq + cp = kcn + M$$

$\therefore M^{\phi(n)+1} \equiv M \bmod n$, which holds when p is a factor of M.

Case II (b): M **is a multiple of** q **and** $GCD(M,p) = 1$.

Then $GCD(m,p) = 1$. The proof is similar to case II(a).

Thus, $M^{\phi(n)+1} \equiv M \bmod n$, with $n = pq$, where p and q are prime numbers and $0 < M < n$.

Example 4.27

Suppose G is a finite cyclic group of order $|G|$. Prove that it will have exactly $\phi(|G|)$ Generators.

Solution

Let $G = \{0,1,2,3,4,...,(n-1)\}$ be a finite cyclic group of order $|G| = n$. With respect to Addition Operation $(\bmod n)$, any integer $a \in G$ will be a generator of G provided a is relatively prime to n, that is, $GCD(a,n) = 1$.

Now, the number of integers in G that are relatively prime to $n = \phi(n) = \phi(|G|)$.

Example 4.28

Let $G = \{0,1,2,3,4,5\}$ be a cyclic group of order 6. Determine the Generators of G.

Solution

$|G| = 6$. The group is called cyclic, since all its elements can be generated as a power $a^k \bmod 6$, where $a^k \bmod 6 = \underbrace{(a + a + ... + a)}_{k\text{-times}} \bmod 6 = (k \times a) \bmod 6$

Where $a^0 = 0$ and $a^{-k} = (-a)^k$

Let us now check for generators of G.

As is obvious, 0 is not a generator of G.

Let us check 1, 2, 3, 4, and 5.

$1^0 \bmod 6 = 0$

$1^1 \bmod 6 = 1 \bmod 6 = 1$

$1^2 \bmod 6 = (1+1) \bmod 6 = 2$

$1^3 \bmod 6 = (1+1+1) \bmod 6 = 3$

$1^4 \bmod 6 = (1+1+1+1) \bmod 6 = 4$

$1^5 \bmod 6 = (1+1+1+1+1) \bmod 6 = 5$

$1^6 \bmod 6 = (1+1+1+1+1+1) \bmod 6 = 0$

The cycle repeats after $1^5 \bmod 6$, and all elements of G appear in the cycle.

$\therefore$ 1 is a generator of G.

Let us now check for 2.

$2^0 \bmod 6 = 0$

$2^1 \bmod 6 = 2 \bmod 6 = 2$

$2^2 \bmod 6 = (2+2) \bmod 6 = 4$

$2^3 \bmod 6 = (2+2+2) \bmod 6 = 0$

$2^4 \bmod 6 = (2+2+2+2) \bmod 6 = 2$

$2^5 \bmod 6 = (2+2+2+2+2) \bmod 6 = 4$

In this case the cycle repeats after $2^2 \bmod 6$ itself, and some elements of G do not appear in the cycle.

Therefore, 2 is not a generator of G, because 2 is not relatively prime to 6.

Similarly, we can determine that 3 and 4 are not generators of G since these integers are not relatively prime to 6.

But 5 is generator of G, as indicated in the following:

$5^0 \bmod 6 = 0$

$$5^1 \bmod 6 = 5 \bmod 6 = 5$$

$$5^2 \bmod 6 = (5+5) \bmod 6 = 10 \bmod 6 = 4$$

$$5^3 \bmod 6 = (5+5+5) \bmod 6 = 15 \bmod 6 = 3$$

$$5^4 \bmod 6 = (5+5+5+5) \bmod 6 = 20 \bmod 6 = 2$$

$$5^5 \bmod 6 = (5+5+5+5+5) \bmod 6 = 25 \bmod 6 = 1$$

$$5^6 \bmod 6 = (5+5+5+5+5+5) \bmod 6 = 30 \bmod 6 = 0$$

The cycle repeats after $5^5 \bmod 6$ itself, and some elements of G appear in the cycle.

$\therefore$ 5 is a generator of G.

Thus, the generators of $G = \{1,5\}$. The number of generators of $G = 2 = \phi(6) = \phi(|G|)$.

4.11 PRIME NUMBERS

An integer $p > 1$ is called a prime number if its only divisors are ± 1 and $\pm p$. The following are prime numbers: $2, 3, 5, 7, 11, 13, 17, 19, 23, 29, 31, 37, 41, \ldots$. An integer $a > 1$ can be uniquely expressed as product of primes:

$a = p_1^{a_1} \times p_2^{a_2} \times \ldots \times p_n^{a_n}$, where $p_1 < p_2 < \ldots < p_n$ are prime numbers and $a_1 \ldots a_n$ are non-negative integers. For example, $324 = 2^2 \times 3^4$.

Formally, it can be stated that if P is the set of all prime numbers, then any positive integer can be uniquely expressed as:

$$a = \prod_{p \in P} p^{a_p} \quad , \text{where } a_p \geq 0 \text{ for all } p \in P. \tag{4.13}$$

The a_p values for a product of two positive integers can be obtained by adding up the corresponding a_p values of two integers, that is,

If $K = mn$, then $k_p = m_p + n_p$ for all $p \in P$.

Example 4.29

$84 = 2^2 \times 3^1 \times 7^1$ and $300 = 2^2 \times 3^1 \times 5^2$

$84 \times 300 = 2^{2+2} \times 3^{1+1} \times 5^{0+2} \times 7^{1+0} = 2^4 \times 3^2 \times 5^2 \times 7^1$

Divides: a **divides** b **(expressed as** $a \mid b$**) will hold, if** $a_p \leq b_p$ **for all** $p \in P$.

GCD (Greatest Common Divisor): The GCD of two integers can be defined as the product of common prime factors of the two integers.

It can be easily determined if the two numbers are expressed as a product of primes, and then common primes are located.

Example 4.30

$$540 = 2^2 \times 3^3 \times 5^1$$

$$525 = 3^1 \times 5^2 \times 7^1$$

$$GCD(540,525) = \text{ Product of common factors of } 540 \text{ and } 525$$

$$= 3^1 \times 5^1 = 15$$

Relative Primes: Two integers a and b are said to be relatively prime, if their Greatest Common Denominator is 1, that is, $GCD\ (a,b) = 1$.

Example 4.31

8 and 21 are relative primes since $GCD\ (8,\ 21) = 1$, though none of them is a prime number.

4.11.1 Primitive Roots

- By Euler's Theorem, $g^{\phi(n)} \equiv 1 \bmod n$ holds if g and n are relatively prime, where $\phi(n)$ is Euler's Totient Function of n, which is defined as the number of non-negative integers less than n and relatively prime to n.

- In addition, there may exist some integers $m < \phi(n)$ that satisfy $gm \equiv 1 \bmod n$.

- The lowest value of m that satisfies $g^m \equiv 1 \bmod n$ is called the "Order of $g(\bmod n)$."

- If the "Order of $g(\bmod n)$" equals $\phi(n)$, then integer g is called a "Primitive Root of n."

4.11.1.1 Significance of Primitive Roots

If $g(1 < g < \phi(n))$ is a primitive of positive integer n, then its powers $\{g, g^2, g^3, ..., g^{\phi(n)}\}(\bmod n)$ will all be distinct integers relatively prime to n.

Conversely, we can say that a positive integer g is called a primitive root of positive integer n, if its powers $\{g, g^2, g^3, ..., g^{\phi(n)}\}(\bmod n)$ are all distinct and relatively prime to n.

If p is a prime number and g is a primitive root of p, then the powers $g, g^2, g^3, ..., g^{p-1} \pmod{p}$ will all be distinct and relatively prime to p. The set of these values will be a permutation of set $Z_p^* = \{1, 2, 3, .., (p-1)\}$.

Example 4.32

Let $n = 7$. Is $g = 2$ a primitive root of n?

Solution

$\phi(n) = n - 1 = 6$. Table 4.19 illustrates the calculation of $y = g^x \pmod{n}$ for $n = 7$ and $g = 2$.

TABLE 4.19 Calculation of $y = g^x \pmod{n}$ for $n = 7$ and $g = 2$

X	g^x	$y = g^x \pmod{n}$
1	2	2
2	4	4
3	8	1
4	16	2
5	32	4
$6 = \phi(n)$	64	1

2 is not a primitive root of 7, since its powers 2, 2^2, 2^3, ... , 2^6 are not distinct $\pmod{7}$.

Example 4.33

Let $n = 7$. Is $g = 3$ a primitive root of n?

Solution

$\phi(n) = n - 1 = 6$. Table 4.20 illustrates the calculation of $y = g^x \pmod{n}$ for $n = 7$ and $g = 3$.

TABLE 4.20 Calculation of $y = g^x \pmod{n}$ for $n = 7$ and $g = 3$

X	g^x	$y = g^x \pmod{n}$
1	3	3
2	9	2
3	27	6
4	81	4
5	243	5
$6 = \phi(n)$	729	1

3 is a primitive root of 7, since its powers $3, 3^2, 3^3, \ldots, 3^6$ are all distinct $(\bmod 7)$.

4.12 DISCRETE LOGARITHMS

Let p be a prime number and g be one of its primitive roots, and let x be an integer $(0 < x < p)$; then $y = g^x (\bmod p)$ will be an integer $(0 < y < p)$.

In addition, $x = \log_g y (\bmod p)$ is called a Discrete Logarithm of y to the base $g (\bmod p)$. Sometimes x is also denoted as $ind_{g,p}(y)$, that is, index of y to base $g (\bmod p)$.

4.12.1 Difficulty of Computing Discrete Logarithms

Given g, X and p, it is considered easy to compute $y = g^x \bmod p$. However, given y, g and p, when p is large, it is considered extremely difficult to compute x, that is, take the discrete logarithm of y to the base $g (\bmod p)$.

Example 4.34

Determine Discrete Logarithms to the base 3 mod 7.

Solution

$n = 7$. $g = 3$ is a primitive root of 7.

Table 4.20 illustrated the calculation of $y = g^x (\bmod n)$ for $n = 7$ and $g = 3$ as in Example 4.33.

The Distinct Logarithms to the base $3 \bmod 7$ are shown in Table 4.21.

TABLE 4.21 Calculation of $x = ind_{3,7}(y)$ for $n = 7$ and $g = 3$

y	$x = ind_{3,7}(y)$
1	6
2	2
3	1
4	4
5	5
6	3

Example 4.35

Determine Discrete Logarithms to the base $5 \bmod 7$.

Solution

For $5 \bmod 7$, $n = 7$ and $g = 5$.

$\phi(n) = n - 1 = 6$. Table 4.22 illustrates the calculation of $y = g^x \pmod{n}$ for $n = 7$ and $g = 5$.

TABLE 4.22 Calculation of $y = g^x \pmod{n}$ for $n = 7$ and $g = 5$

X	g^x	$y = g^x \pmod{n}$
1	5	5
2	25	4
3	125	6
4	625	2
5	3125	3
$6 = \phi(n)$	15625	1

Then, the Distinct Logarithms to the base $5 \bmod 7$ are shown in Table 4.23.

TABLE 4.23 Calculation of $x = ind_{5,7}(y)$ for $n = 7$ and $g = 5$

y	$x = ind_{5,7}(y)$
1	6
2	4
3	5
4	2
5	1
6	3

4.12.2 Algorithm to Determine the Primitive Roots of a Number n

Step 1: Determine $\phi(n)$

Step 2: Determine the prime factors of $\phi(n)$. Let these be $p_1, p_2, ..., p_k$.

Step 3: For each $m \in \{2, 3, ..., n - 1\}$ do

{ Determine $(m)^{\phi(n)/p_1}, (m)^{\phi(n)/p_2}, ..., (m)^{\phi(n)/p_k} \pmod{n}$

If none of the k values determined previously is 1, then m is a primitive root of n, else it is not }.

Example 4.36

Determine the primitive roots of $n = 7$.

Solution

$n = 7$, $\phi(n) = 6$. The prime factors of $\phi(n)$ are $p_1 = 2$ and $p_2 = 3$.

Table 4.24 shows the primitive roots of the $n = 7$ calculation.

TABLE 4.24 Calculation of Primitive Roots of **n** = 7

M	2	3	4	5	6
M^3 mod 7	2	6	1	6	6
M^2 mod 7	-	2	-	4	1
Is M Primitive Root?	No	Yes	No	Yes	No

Thus, the Primitive Roots of 7 are 3 and 5.

Example 4.37

Determine the primitive roots of $n = 11$.

Solution

$n = 11$, $\phi(n) = 10$. The prime factors of $\phi(n)$ are $p_1 = 2$ and $p_2 = 5$.

Table 4.25 shows the primitive roots of the $n = 11$ calculation.

TABLE 4.25 Calculation of Primitive Roots of **n** = 11

M	2	3	4	5	6	7	8	9	10
M^3 mod 11	10	1	1	1	10	10	10	1	10
M^2 mod 11	4	-	-	-	3	5	9	-	1
Is M Primitive Root?	Yes	No	No	No	Yes	Yes	Yes	No	No

Thus, the Primitive Roots of 11 are 2, 6, 7, and 8.

4.12.3 Another Method of Determining the Primitive Roots of a Number *n*

Step 1: Determine integer $g(1 < g < \phi(n))$ such that $\{g^1 \bmod n, g^2 \bmod n, ..., g^{\phi(n)} \bmod n\}$ are all distinct and relatively prime to n. The g is one of the primitive roots of n.

Step 2: Determine positive integers $< \phi(n)$ and relatively prime to $\phi(n)$. Let the set of such integers be $\{x_1, x_2, ..., x_k\}$.

Step 3: Determine the primitive roots of n by the following algorithm:

For $i = 1$ to k do

Primitive roots of $[i] = (g)^{x_i} \bmod n$

Thus, the primitive roots of $[1],...,$ primitive roots of $[k]$ represent the k primitive roots of n.

Example 4.38

Determine all the primitive roots of $p = 17$.

Solution

$\phi(p) = \phi(17) = 16$.

$g = 3$ is a primitive root of 17.

The other primitive roots of 17 can be determined as follows in Table 4.26.

TABLE 4.26 Calculation of Other Primitive Roots of 17

X such that GCD(X, 16) = 1	Primitive Root = (3)^x mod17
3	10
5	5
7	11
9	14
11	7
13	12
15	6

4.13 PRIMALITY TESTING

Most of the Public Key Cryptographic Systems make use of very large prime numbers. It is a major issue to choose very large prime numbers. All prime numbers larger than 2 are odd integers. In cryptography, it is a major problem to determine whether a given large odd integer is a prime number or not. Many probabilistic algorithms exist that determine with a very high degree of certainty whether a given odd integer is likely to be prime or not.

4.13.1 Miller and Rabin's Method

The Miller-Rabin Method determines whether a given odd number n is likely to be prime or not. It works as follows:

1. Choose a large odd integer n

2. Determine integer k and q, which satisfy $(n-1) = 2^k q$, where q is an odd integer. For a given value of n, the values of k and q will be unique. Let $p_0 = 2^0 q$, $p_1 = 2^1 q$, $p_2 = 2^2 q, ..., p_{k-1} = 2^{k-1} q$ and $p_k = 2^k q$.

   Choose a random number a such that $1 < a < n-1$.

   Now, consider the series:

   $a^{p_0} \bmod n, a^{p_1} \bmod n, a^{p_2} \bmod n, ..., a^{p_{k-1}} \bmod n, a^{p_k} \bmod n$

   that is, $\left\{ a^{p_j} \bmod n \mid 0 \le j \le k \right\}$

   Let the above series be represented by:

   $$X_0, X_1, X_2, ..., X_{k-1}, X_k$$
   $$p_0 = 2^0 q = q$$
   $$\therefore X_0 = a^q \bmod n$$
   $$p_k = 2^k q = n-1$$
   $$\therefore X_k = a^{n-1} \bmod n$$

   In general, $X_i = \left(X_{i-1} \right)^2 \bmod n$ for $1 \le i \le k$, that is, each term in the series is a square of the previous term ($\bmod n$).

3. If n is a prime then $X_k = a^{n-1} \bmod n = 1$ (by Fermat's Theorem).

4. If n is a prime and "a" is not a primitive root of n, then some other term lower than X_k will also be equal to 1.

   Let $X_j \left(j < k \right)$ be the lowest term equal to 1.

   Then there are two possibilities:

   Case I: $j = 0$

   $$X_0 = a^q \bmod n = 1$$

   Case II: $1 \le j \le k$

   When $X_j = 1$,

$$X_j \bmod n = 1, \text{ implies that } \left(X_{j-1}\right)^2 \bmod n = 1$$

$$\therefore \left(X_{j-1}\right) \bmod n = \pm 1$$

$\left(X_{j-1}\right) \bmod n$ cannot be equal to $+1$, since we have assumed that X_j is the lowest term equal to 1.

$$\therefore \left(X_{j-1}\right) \bmod n = -1 \text{ will hold.}$$

$\left(X_{j-1}\right) \bmod n = -1$ implies that $\left(X_{j-1}\right) \bmod n = (n-1)$

Note: If $X_j \bmod n = 1$, then all terms X_{j+1} onward will be equal to 1, since $\left(X_{j+1}\right) \bmod n = \left(X_j\right)^2 \bmod n$.

5. It can be concluded from the preceding arguments that an Integer n is likely to be prime if either $X_0 = 1$ OR any of the terms (other than X) is equal to $(n-1)$; if not, n will be a composite integer.

4.13.1.1 Miller-Rabin Algorithm

Test (n) //where n is an odd integer ≥ 3.

Step 1: Find integers k, q such that $(n-1) = 2^k q$, // q is an odd integer and $k > 0$

Step 2: Select random integer a such that $1 < a < (n-1)$

Step 3: Compute $X_0 \leftarrow a^q \bmod n$

Step 4: If $\left(X_0 = 1\right)$ or $\left(X_0 = (n-1)\right)$ then return ("n likely to be Prime")

Step 5: For $j = 1$ or $k-1$ do

    Begin

$$X_j \leftarrow \left(X_{j-1}\right)^2 \bmod n;$$

      If $\left(X_j = (n-1)\right)$ then return ("n likely to be Prime");

    End;

Step 6: Return ("n is Composite")

Algorithm to determine k and q

Function *get-kq* (n : integer)

Step 1: $q \leftarrow n-1; k \leftarrow 0;$

Step 2: Temp $\leftarrow q \bmod 2;$

Step 3: If $(\text{Temp} = 1)$ then return k and q

Step 4: $k \leftarrow k + 1;$

Step 5: $q \leftarrow q$ div $2;$

Step 6: GOTO step 2

Example 4.39

Use the Miller-Rabin Method to determine whether a given odd number $n = 13$ is likely to be prime or not.

Solution

$n = 13$; $(n-1) = 12 = 2^2 \times 3$

$\therefore k = 2$ and $q = 3$

Choose $a = 5$

$X_0 = a^3 \bmod 13 = 5^3 \bmod 13 = 8 \neq 1$

$X_1 = a^6 \bmod 13 = (8)^2 \bmod 13 = 12 = (n-1)$

$\therefore$ Test returns: "13 is likely to be prime".

Example 4.40

Use the Miller-Rabin Method to determine whether a given odd number $n = 9$ is likely to be prime or not.

Solution

$n = 91$; $(n-1) = 8 = 2^3 \times 1$

$\therefore k = 3$ and $q = 1$

Choose $a = 5$

$X_0 = a^1 \bmod 9 = 5^1 \bmod 9 = 5 \neq 1$

$X_1 = a^2 \bmod 9 = 5^2 \bmod 9 = 7 \neq (n-1)$

$X_2 = a^4 \bmod 9 = (7)^2 \bmod 9 = 4 \neq (n-1)$

$\therefore$ It returns: "9 is Composite".

Example 4.41

Use the Miller-Rabin Method to determine whether a given odd number $n = 17$ is likely to be prime or not.

Solution

$n = 17$; $(n-1) = 16 = 2^4 \times 1$

$\therefore k = 4$ and $q = 1$

Choose $a = 5$

$X_0 = a^1 \bmod 17 = 5^1 \bmod 17 = 5 \neq 1$

$X_1 = a^2 \bmod 17 = 5^2 \bmod 17 = 8 \neq (n-1)$

$X_2 = a^4 \bmod 17 = (8)^2 \bmod 17 = 13 \neq (n-1)$

$X_3 = a^8 \bmod 17 = (13)^2 \bmod 17 = 16 = (n-1)$

$\therefore$ Test returns: "17 is likely to be prime".

When an integer passes Miller-Rabin's Test, why does it return "Likely to be prime" and not "Certainly Prime"?

- If n is prime then it will pass the Miller-Rabin Test for all possible values of "a" $(1 < a < (n-1))$. But it is only a one-way implication.

- If any integer n passes the Miller-Rabin Test, there is a likelihood that n may not be prime, since a composite number may also pass the Miller-Rabin Test for certain values, but not for all possible values of "a" $(1 < a < (n-1))$.

- If an integer n passes the Miller-Rabin Test for one value of "a" $(1 < a < (n-1))$ then the probability that n is not prime is less than $\frac{1}{4}$ and the probability that n is prime is greater than $\left(1 - \frac{1}{4}\right)$.

- If an integer passes the Miller-Rabin Test with t random values of "a," then the probability that n is prime is greater than $1 - \left(\frac{1}{4}\right)^t$.

Example 4.42

Show that a composite number $n = 25$ passes the Miller-Rabin test for some value of a.

Solution

When $n = 25$, then $n - 1 = 24 = 2^3 \times 3$.

$\therefore k = 3$ and $q = 3$

Let $a = 7$

$X_0 = a^q \bmod n = 7^3 \bmod 25 = (49 \times 7) \bmod 25 = (24 \times 7) \bmod 25 = 18$

$$X_1 = (X_0)^2 \bmod 25 = (18 \times 18) \bmod 25 = 24 = (n-1)$$

$\therefore$ 25 returns "Likely to be prime" with $a = 7$.

Thus, 25, a composite number, passes the test with $a = 7$.

Let us try with $a = 11$

$$X_0 = a^3 \bmod n = 11^3 \bmod 25 = (121 \times 11) \bmod 25 = (21 \times 11) \bmod 25 = 6 \neq 1$$

$$X_1 = a^6 \bmod 25 = (36) \bmod 25 = 11 \neq (n-1)$$

$$X_2 = a^{12} \bmod 25 = (11 \times 11) \bmod 25 = 21 \neq (n-1)$$

$\therefore$ 25 returns "Composite" with $a = 11$.

Thus, 25 does not pass the test with $a = 11$.

Procedure to determine a Prime Number with very high degree of certainty (using the Miller-Rabin Algorithm repeatedly):

If the Miller-Rabin Test is invoked repeatedly for a given value of n, each time selecting a different randomly selected value of "a", and the test returns "Likely to be prime" contiguously t times, then the probability that n is prime is greater than $1 - \left(\dfrac{1}{4}\right)^t$. If $t = 10$, then the probability that n is prime is greater than 0.999999.

The Flow Chart in Figure 4.1 can be explained by the following steps:

Step 1: Choose a very large odd integer n

Step 2: Choose an integer "a" such that $1 < a < n-1$

Step 3: Perform Miller-Rabin Test

Step 4: If the Miller-Rabin test does not pass, then reject the current value of n since it is a composite number, and go back to Step 1 and choose another odd integer n.

Step 5: If the Miller-Rabin Test is passed, then check whether the current value of n has passed the Miller-Rabin Test with "t" $(t \geq 10)$ different randomly selected values of "a." If "No," then go back to Step 2 and choose another value of "a" for the Miller-Rabin Test.

Step 6: If the current value of n has passed the Miller-Rabin Test with "t" randomly selected values of "a," then "n is a prime number, with very high degree of certainty."

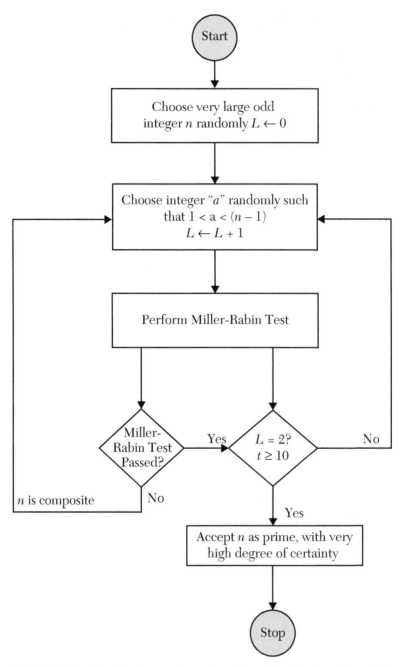

FIGURE 4.1 Flow chart for the procedure to determine a Prime Number with very high degree of certainty (using Miller-Rabin Algorithm repeatedly).

4.14   CHINESE REMAINDER THEOREM

Given two co-prime integers p and q, each integer "N" $\left(0 \leq N \leq (pq-1)\right)$ can be uniquely represented by a pair of residues $\left(N \bmod p, N \bmod q\right)$.

Example 4.43

Show that $p = 3$ and $q = 4$ are two co-prime integers, and then that each integer in the range 0–11 can be uniquely represented by a pair of residues $(\bmod\, 3)$ and $(\bmod\, 4)$.

Solution

Table 4.27 illustrates the calculation of ($N \bmod 3$) and ($N \bmod 4$).

TABLE 4.27   Calculation of (**N** mod 3) and (**N** mod 4)

N	N mod 3	N mod 4
0	0	0
1	1	1
2	2	2
3	0	3
4	1	0
5	2	1
6	0	2
7	1	3
8	2	0
9	0	1
10	1	2
11	2	3

- As illustrated in Table 4.27, each integer N in the range $(0$–$11)$ is represented by a unique ordered pair of values ($N \bmod 3$, $N \bmod 4$); for example, 5 can be represented by (2, 1) and 9 can be represented by (0, 1).

- This implies that each integer N in the range $(0, \ldots, 11)$ can be reconstructed from the distinct ordered pair of values ($N \bmod 3$, $N \bmod 4$).

- The set of values in the previous table will be repeated for the ranges (12–23), (24–35), and so on. For example, 13 in the range (12–23) will be represented by unique pair of values (1, 1) and 25 in the range (24–35) will also be represented by $(1, 1)$. All integers in a given range can be uniquely reconstructed from their residues $(\mathrm{mod}\, 3)$ and $(\mathrm{mod}\, 4)$.

4.14.1 Alternate Interpretation of the Chinese Remainder Theorem

Suppose $m_1, m_2, ..., m_n$ are n positive integers, pair-wise relatively prime to each other, that is, $GCD(m_i, m_j)$ where $i \leq j$.

Let $m = m_1 \times m_2 \times ... \times m_n$

Then, the following set of congruence has a unique solution $(\mathrm{mod}\, m)$, that is, $\times$ has a unique solution in the range $0 \leq x \leq m$.

$x \equiv a_1 \bmod m_1$

$x \equiv a_2 \bmod m_2$

$------$

$x \equiv a_n \bmod m_n$

Proof:

Let $M_k = m / m_k, (1 \leq k \leq n)$, that is, M_k is the product of all the moduli, except m_k. Since m_k is relatively prime to all the other moduli in the previous set, m_k will be relatively prime to their product M_k too.

$\therefore GCD(M_k, m_k) = 1$

Thus, there exists a multiplicative inverse y_k of $M_k (\mathrm{mod}\, m_k)$.

$\therefore y_k \equiv M_k^{-1} \bmod m_k$

$\therefore M_k y_k \equiv 1 \bmod m_k, (1 \leq k \leq n)$

Multiplying both sides by a_k

$a_k M_k y_k \equiv a_k \bmod m_k$

Thus, we have

$a_1 M_1 y_1 \equiv a_1 \bmod m_1$

$a_2 M_2 y_2 \equiv a_2 \bmod m_2$

$----------$

$A_n M_n y_n \equiv a_n \bmod m_n$

But M_k will not be relatively prime to any other modulus in previous set, except m_k, since M_k is the product of all the moduli except m_k.

$\therefore M_k \equiv 0 \bmod m_i, (1 \le i \le n)$ and $i \le k$.

Then, the simultaneous solution to all the congruence will be:

$$X \equiv \left(a_1 M_1 y_1 + a_2 M_2 y_2 + a_3 M_3 y_3 + \ldots + a_n M_n y_n\right) \bmod m \ldots \ldots "A"$$

Since for each modulus m_k, the kth term of "A" represents solution to the kth congruence, and all the other terms are congruent to 0 $(\bmod m_k)$.

$\therefore$ The n terms of "A," combined, represent a simultaneous solution to the congruence $(\bmod m)$.

Example 4.44

Solve the following simultaneous congruence using the Chinese Remainder Theorem:

$X \equiv 2 \bmod 3$

$X \equiv 3 \bmod 5$

$X \equiv 2 \bmod 7$

Solution

$m_1 = 3, m_2 = 5, m_3 = 7$

$a_1 = 2, a_2 = 3, a_3 = 2$

$m = m_1 \times m_2 \times m_3 = 3 \times 5 \times 7 = 105$

$M_1 = m / m_1 = 35$

$M_2 = m / m_2 = 21$

$M_3 = m / m_3 = 15$

$y_1 \equiv M_1^{-1} \bmod m_1 \equiv (35)^{-1} \bmod 3$

Table 4.28 shows the calculated values for $\left(A_1, A_2, A_3\right)$, $\left(B_1, B_2, B_3\right)$, $\left(T_1, T_2, T_3\right)$, and $Q = A_3$ DIV B_3.

TABLE 4.28 The calculated values for (A_1, A_2, A_3), (B_1, B_2, B_3), (T_1, T_2, T_3), and $\textbf{\textit{Q}} = A_3$ DIV $\textbf{\textit{B}}_3$

(A_1, A_2, A_3)	(B_1, B_2, B_3)	(T_1, T_2, T_3)	$Q = A_3$ DIV B_3
(1,0,3)	(0,1,35)	(1,0,3)	0
(0,1,35)	(1,0,3)	(−11,1,2)	11
(1,0,3)	(−11,1,2)	(12,−1,1)	1

$y_1 \equiv (-1)^{-1} \bmod 3 = 2$

Similarly, we can determine y_2 and y_3.

$$y_2 \equiv M_2^{-1} \bmod m_2 \equiv (21)^{-1} \bmod 5 = 1$$

$$y_3 \equiv M_3^{-1} \bmod m_3 \equiv (15)^{-1} \bmod 7 = 1$$

Now, the simultaneous solution to the n congruent is:

$$X \equiv (a_1 \times M_1 \times y_1 + a_2 \times M_2 \times y_2 + a_3 \times M_3 \times y_3 + \ldots + a_n \times M_n \times y_n) \bmod m$$

$$\equiv (2 \times 35 \times 2 + 3 \times 21 \times 1 + 2 \times 15 \times 1) \bmod 105$$

$$\equiv (140 + 63 + 30) \bmod 105$$

$$\equiv (233) \bmod 105$$

$$\therefore X = 23, 128, 233, \ldots.$$

Example 4.45

Solve the following simultaneous congruence using the Chinese Remainder Theorem:

$$X \equiv 1 \bmod 2$$
$$X \equiv 1 \bmod 3$$
$$X \equiv 1 \bmod 5$$
$$X \equiv 1 \bmod 7$$

Solution

$$m_1 = 2, m_2 = 3, m_3 = 5, m_4 = 7$$
$$a_1 = 1, a_2 = 1, a_3 = 1, a_4 = 1$$
$$m = m_1 \times m_2 \times m_3 \times m_4 = 2 \times 3 \times 5 \times 7 = 210$$
$$M_1 = m / m_1 = 105$$
$$M_2 = m / m_2 = 70$$
$$M_3 = m / m_3 = 42$$
$$M_4 = m / m_4 = 30$$

$$y_1 \equiv M_1^{-1} \bmod m_1 \equiv (105)^{-1} \bmod 2 = 1$$

$$y_2 \equiv M_2^{-1} \bmod m_2 \equiv (70)^{-1} \bmod 3 = 1$$

$$y_3 \equiv M_3^{-1} \bmod m_3 \equiv (42)^{-1} \bmod 5 = 3$$

$$y_4 \equiv M_4^{-1} \bmod m_4 \equiv (30)^{-1} \bmod 7 = 4$$

$$\therefore X \equiv \left(a_1 \times M_1 \times y_1 + a_2 \times M_2 \times y_2 + a_3 \times M_3 \times y_3 + \dots + a_n \times M_n \times y_n \right) \bmod m$$

$$\equiv (105 + 70 + 126 + 120) \bmod 210$$

$$\equiv (421) \bmod 210$$

$$\equiv 1$$

$$\therefore X = 1, 211, 421, \dots .$$

Example 4.46

Solve the following simultaneous congruence using the Chinese Remainder Theorem:

$$X \equiv 3 \bmod 5$$

$$X \equiv 2 \bmod 7$$

$$X \equiv 1 \bmod 3$$

Solution

$$m_1 = 5, m_2 = 7, m_3 = 3$$

$$a_1 = 3, a_2 = 2, a_3 = 1$$

$$m = m_1 \times m_2 \times m_3 = 5 \times 7 \times 3 = 105$$

$$M_1 = m / m_1 = 21$$

$$M_2 = m / m_2 = 15$$

$$M_3 = m / m_3 = 35$$

Since $GCD(M_1, m_1) = 1$

$M_1 y_1 \equiv 1 \bmod m_1$, where y_1 is the multiplicative inverse of $M_1 (\bmod m_1)$.

Determine y_1 by the extended Euclid's Algorithm as in Table 4.29.

TABLE 4.29 The calculated values for (A_1, A_2, A_3), (B_1, B_2, B_3), (T_1, T_2, T_3), and $Q = A_3$ DIV B_3 for y_1

(A_1, A_2, A_3)	(B_1, B_2, B_3)	(T_1, T_2, T_3)	$Q = A_3$ DIV B_3
(1,0,5)	(0,1,21)	(1,0,5)	0
(0,1,21)	(1,0,5)	(−4,1,1)	4

$$\therefore y_1 = 1$$

Similarly, we can determine y_2 by the extended Euclid's Algorithm as in Table 4.30.

TABLE 4.30 The calculated values for (A_1, A_2, A_3), (B_1, B_2, B_3), (T_1, T_2, T_3), and $Q = A_3$ DIV B_3 for y_2

(A_1, A_2, A_3)	(A_1, A_2, A_3)	(T_1, T_2, T_3)	$Q = A_3$ DIV B_3
(1,0,7)	(0,1,15)	(1,0,7)	0
(0,1,15)	(1,0,7)	(−2,1,1)	2

$$\therefore y_2 = 1$$

In addition, we can determine y_3 by the extended Euclid's Algorithm as in Table 4.31.

TABLE 4.31 The Calculated Values for (A_1, A_2, A_3), (B_1, B_2, B_3), (T_1, T_2, T_3), and $Q = A_3$ DIV B_3 for y_3

(A_1, A_2, A_3)	(B_1, B_2, B_3)	(T_1, T_2, T_3)	$Q = A_3$ DIV B_3
(1,0,3)	(0,1,35)	(1, 0, 3)	0
(0,1,35)	(1,0,3)	(−11, 1, 2)	11
(1,0,3)	(−11,1,2)	(12, −1, 1)	1

$$\therefore y_3 = (-1) \bmod 3 = 2$$

Therefore, the solution is:

$$X \equiv \left(a_1 \times M_1 \times y_1 + a_2 \times M_2 \times y_2 + a_3 \times M_3 \times y_3\right) \bmod m$$

$$X \equiv \left(3 \times 21 \times 1 + 2 \times 15 \times 1 + 1 \times 35 \times 2\right) \bmod 105$$

$$\equiv \left(63 + 30 + 70\right) \bmod 105$$

$$\equiv \left(163\right) \bmod 105$$

$$\equiv 58$$

$$\therefore X = 58, 163, 268, 373, \ldots.$$

4.15   EXERCISES

1. Differentiate between a Group and an Abelian Group.

2. What are the additional requirements of an Integral Domain compared to a Commutative Ring?

3. Is a set of all integers a cyclic group with respect to addition? If so, what is its generator?

4. Does a set of all integers form a field? If no, then list the properties of a field that it does not satisfy.

5. Do multiplicative inverses exist for all integers $(\bmod n)$ where n is a positive integer? If n is prime will all integers in the range $1...\phi(n)$ have their multiplicative inverses defined $(\bmod n)$?

6. If $Z_p^* = \{1,2,3,...,\phi(p)\}$, will multiplication within the set be reversible? Explain its significance. Is this question related to Question 5?

7. Differentiate between primes and co-primes. Can two non-prime positive integers be co-primes of each other? Give an example.

8. What is a primitive root? Will each positive integer n less than a prime number p be its primitive root?

9. Given a prime number p, its primitive root g, and integer "x" $\left(1 < x < \phi(p)\right)$, why is it easier to compute $y = g^x \bmod p$ but difficult to compute discrete logarithm $x = \log_x y \left(\bmod p\right)$?

10. Briefly explain Group, Ring, and Field.

11. Does a commutative ring with unity and without a zero divisor form a field?

12. Determine GCD (1970, 1066).

13. Using the Extended Euclid's Algorithm, determine the multiplicative inverse of $1234 \bmod 4321$.

14. Why is $GCD(n, n+1) = 1$ for two consecutive integers n and $n+1$?

    Hint: Integers n and $n+1$ will always be relatively prime to each other. Therefore, $GCD(n, n+1) = 1$.

15. Explain and prove the Extended Euclid's Algorithm. Using this algorithm, determine the following:

A. $37^{-1} \bmod 101$

B. $23^{-1} \bmod 57$

Verify the results.

16. Will the following be defined? If no, then why?

A. $15^{-1} \bmod 25$

B. $17^{-1} \bmod 51$

17. State and prove Fermat's Little Theorem.

18. What is Euler's Totient Function? Determine Euler's Totient Function $\phi(n)$ of the following numbers:

A. 61

B. 60

C. 1024

D. 1000

E. 101

19. Prove that $a^p \equiv a \bmod p$, where p is a prime number and a is any integer.

Hint: a is any integer that may not be relatively prime to p.

20. If $a \equiv 1023 \bmod 27$, then determine $a \equiv 1023 \bmod 27$ such that $(0 \le a \le 27)$.

21. If $(3)^{220} \equiv x \bmod 23$, then determine x such that $(0 \le x \le 23)$.

22. If $(7)^{49} \equiv x \bmod 17$, then determine x such that $(0 \le x \le 17)$.

23. If p is a prime number, then prove that $\phi(p^i) = p^i - p^{i-1}$.

Hint: There will be p^{i-1} integers less than p^i and having a common factor with p. Therefore, $\phi(p^i) = p^i - p^{i-1}$.

24. For $n > 2$, then $\phi(n)$ is always even. Explain why.

Hint: If a is an integer less than n and relatively prime to n, then $(n - a)$ will be another integer less than n and relatively prime to n, since $GCD(a,n) = GCD((n-a),n)$. Also, the two integers "a" and $(n-a)$ will be distinct, because $a = n - a$ implies $n = 2a$, which is not possible since $GCD(a,n) = 1$. Therefore, for $n > 2$ there will be pairs of integers less than n; thus, $\phi(n)$ will have even value.

25. State and prove Euler's Theorem. Using Euler's Theorem, determine " a " $(1 \le a \le 10)$ if $a \equiv 7^{400} \bmod 10$.

26. What is a primitive root? Explain an algorithm to determine primitive roots. Determine all the primitive roots of:

    A. 19

    B. 25

    C. 23

27. Explain the Miller-Rabin Primality Testing Algorithm. Using the Miller-Rabin Algorithm, test whether the following integers are likely to be prime:

    A. 101

    B. 111

    C. 229

    D. 1023

28. If an integer passes the Miller-Rabin Primality Test, why it is only likely to be prime (why not surely prime)? Give an example wherein a non-prime integer passes the Miller-Rabin Primality Test.

29. Explain and prove the Chinese Remainder Theorem (CRT).

30. Using CRT, solve the following to determine x :

    A. $x \equiv 2 (\bmod 3)$
       $x \equiv 3 (\bmod 5)$
       $x \equiv 2 (\bmod 7)$

    B. $x \equiv 1 (\bmod 2)$
       $x \equiv 1 (\bmod 3)$
       $x \equiv 1 (\bmod 5)$
       $x \equiv 1 (\bmod 7)$

    C. $x \equiv 2 (\bmod 5)$
       $x \equiv 3 (\bmod 7)$
       $x \equiv 5 (\bmod 9)$

CHAPTER 5

CLASSICAL CIPHER SCHEMES

Chapter Outline

5.1 Introduction

5.2 Classical Substitution Ciphers

5.3 Transposition Ciphers

5.4 Steganography

5.5 Exercises

5.1 INTRODUCTION

In classical cryptography, primarily two kinds of crypto-systems were in vogue, that is, the Substitution Ciphers and the Transposition Ciphers. In the Transposition Cipher, the plaintext letters are systematically scrambled (reordered) so as to make the plaintext unintelligible. For example, the word "software" may be scrambled to read as "fosawter," that is, letters are swapped with each other. In the transposition ciphers, the letters in the plaintext are systematically replaced by other letters. In this chapter, we discuss some of the popular classical cipher schemes.

5.2 CLASSICAL SUBSTITUTION CIPHERS

In classical substitution Ciphers, the letters of the plaintext are replaced by other letters or by numbers or symbols; or if plaintext is viewed as a sequence of bits, then substitution involves replacing the plaintext bit patterns with cipher-text bit patterns. There are six types of classical substitution Ciphers:

- Caesar Cipher

- Mono-Alphabetic Cipher

- Hill Cipher

- Play-Fair Cipher

- Poly-Alphabetic Cipher (Vigenere Cipher)

- One-Time Pad

5.2.1 Caesar Cipher

It is believed to have been used by Julius Caesar for communication of secret messages. The Caesar Cipher is used to transform messages coded in the English alphabet (letters "A" . . . "Z"). Each letter in the plaintext is replaced by a letter three places down in the alphabetic sequence, in a cyclic manner, as explained in the following:

- Each letter in the alphabet is coded as its numeric equivalent, that is, "A": 0, "B": 1, "C": 2, . . . "Y": 24, and "Z": 25.

- Let $M[O...n-1]$ represent plaintext comprising n alphabetic characters and let $C[O...n-1]$ represent its cipher-text.

- Then $C[i]=(M[i]+3)\bmod 26$ for $0<i<n$.

- "A" will be substituted by "D", "B" will be substituted by "E", . . . ,"X" will be substituted by "A", "Y" will be substituted by "B" and "Z" will be substituted by "C".

- The Caesar cipher can be made more robust if each letter in the plaintext is substituted by a letter that falls k places down in the alphabetic sequence ($O<k<26$) in a cyclic manner, and if the value of k is kept confidential between the sender and the recipient. The value of k may be changed from time to time for security reasons. Whenever k is changed, the recipient of the message must be informed in advance in a secure manner. Now, the encryption process can be expressed as:

$$C[i]=(M[i]+k)\bmod 26, \text{ for } 0<i<n \text{ and } 0<k<26 \qquad (5.1)$$

and

$$M[i] = \left(C[i] - k\right) \bmod 26, \text{ for } 0 < i < n \text{ and } 0 < k < 26 \qquad (5.2)$$

Example 5.1

Plaintext: MEET ME TODAY
Cipher-text: PHHW PH WRGDB $(k = 3)$

Example 5.2

Caesar Scheme with $k = 6$.
Look up Table 5.1 for the Caesar Cipher (for $k = 6$).

TABLE 5.1 Encryption/Decryption Using Caesar Cipher with $k = 6$

Plaintext	Cipher-text	Plaintext	Cipher-text
A	G	N	T
B	H	O	U
C	I	P	V
D	J	Q	W
E	K	R	X
F	L	S	Y
G	M	T	Z
H	N	U	A
I	O	V	B
J	P	W	C
K	Q	X	D
L	R	Y	E
M	S	Z	F

Table 5.1 can be used for encryption/decryption using the Caesar Cipher with $k = 6$.

Plain text: MEET ME TODAY
Cipher-text: SKKZ SK ZUJGE $(k = 6)$

Weakness of the Caesar Cipher: The size of the key space is limited to just 25 values. In a brute force attack, an adversary has to try only 25 possible keys. The attacker will attempt to find the value of key that produces an intelligible output. Then the adversary can confirm the key on other cipher-texts. Thus, the cipher scheme can be broken in a short time frame.

5.2.2 Mono-Alphabetic Cipher

In the mono-alphabetic cipher, each plaintext letter is mapped onto a cipher-text letter. To make the encryption process reversible, the mapping from plaintext alphabets co cipher-text alphabets is one-to-one, that is, mapping is unique both ways. To implement this scheme, a look-up table is created defining the mapping from plaintext alphabets to cipher-text alphabets, and that table acts as a key for encryption and decryption. The table is kept confidential between the sender and the intended recipients. For example, Table 5.2 may form the encryption/decryption key:

TABLE 5.2 Encryption/Decryption key

Plaintext Alphabet	Cipher-Text Alphabet	Plaintext Alphabet	Cipher-Text Alphabet
A	J	N	G
B	E	O	D
C	N	P	I
D	A	Q	W
E	C	R	L
F	K	S	Q
G	S	T	O
H	F	U	Z
I	B	V	M
J	H	W	Y
K	U	X	T
L	V	Y	R
M	P	Z	X

The mapping between plaintext and cipher-text alphabets is one-to-one. For example, the letter "C" in plaintext maps only to the letter "N" in cipher-text, and the letter "N" in cipher-text maps only to the letter "C" in plaintext.

Example 5.3

Plaintext: ATTACKTIGER HILL AT SEVEN AM

Cipher-text: JOOJNU OBSCL FBW JO QCMCG JP

5.2.2.1 Key Space of Mono-Alphabetic Cipher

The letter "A" in plaintext can be mapped to any of the 26 letters in the cipher-text alphabet (say "X"); the letter "B" in the plaintext can be mapped onto any of the remaining 25 letters (except "X") in the cipher-text, and so on.

$$\text{Number of possible keys} = 26 \times 25 \times 24 \times ... \times 2 \times 1$$
$$= 26!$$

Thus, 26! is the size of the key space in a mono-alphabetic cipher. This works out to be more than 4×10^{26}, which is a very large figure as compared to the Caesar Cipher.

5.2.2.1.1 Strength of the Mono-Alphabetic Cipher

Since the size of the key space is very large ($> 4 \times 10^{26}$), it is extremely hard to determine the key by brute force attack.

5.2.2.1.2 Weaknesses of the Mono-Alphabetic Cipher

The Mono-alphabetic cipher is prone to a statistical analysis attack. Extensive research has established that any English text of reasonable length has the following relative frequency of occurrence of different letters as in Table 5.3.

TABLE 5.3 Relative Frequency of Occurrence of Different Alphabets

Alphabet	Relative Frequency	Alphabet	Relative Frequency
A	8.167	N	6.749
B	1.492	O	7.507
C	2.782	P	1.929
D	4.253	Q	0.095
E	12.702	R	5.987
F	2.228	S	6.327
G	2.015	T	9.056
H	6.094	U	2.758
I	6.996	V	0.978
J	0.153	W	2.360
K	0.772	X	0.150
L	4.025	Y	1.974
M	2.406	Z	0.074

- An adversary can analyze a captured cipher-text to determine the relative frequency of occurrence of different letters in the cipher-text, and from that the adversary can attempt to predict the corresponding plaintext letters. For example, if the letter "Q" is found to be occurring with the highest frequency in a cipher-text, then the letter "Q" appearing in the cipher-text may be representing the letter "E" in the plain-text, since "E" is expected to have the highest frequency of occurrence in any text. Similarly, if the letter "P" has the lowest frequency of occurrence in a cipher-text, then it may be representing the letter "Z" or "Q" in the corresponding plaintext, since the letters "Z" and "Q" are expected to have the lowest frequency of occurrence in any text. This way, the cryptanalyst can attempt to decipher the cipher-text without resorting to the brute force approach.

- A cipher should be such that the statistical structure of the plaintexts should not be reflected in the corresponding cipher-texts. The statistical structure of the plaintexts must be dissipated (or diffused) into the long-term statistics of cipher-texts.

5.2.3 Hill Cipher

The Hill Cipher is a substitution cipher in which the statistical structure of the plaintext is not transferred to the resulting cipher-text. Rather, the statistical structure of the plaintext is diffused in the resulting cipher-text. The encryption algorithm uses a non-singular square matrix of size $n \times n$ as an encryption key. It takes n successive letters of plaintext and substitutes for them n cipher-text letters. Each letter in the alphabet is assigned a numerical value, that is, "A" = 0, "B" = 1, . . . "Z" = 25.

Encryption: The encryption process is defined as:

$$C = KP \bmod 26 \tag{5.3}$$

where

P: Plaintext—a column matrix of size n. It contains the equivalent numeric values of the plaintext letters to be encrypted.

K: $n \times n$ key matrix—the values have to be so chosen that a matrix should be non-singular.

G: Cipher-text—a column matrix of size n. It contains numeric values of the cipher-text letters obtained after encryption.

For $n = 3$, C and P are column vectors of length 3, representing the plaintext and cipher-text, and K is a 3×3 matrix, representing the encryption key. Operations are performed mod 26. The system can be described in terms of column vectors and matrices as follows:

$$\begin{bmatrix} c_1 \\ c_2 \\ c_3 \end{bmatrix} = \begin{bmatrix} k_{11} & k_{12} & k_{13} \\ k_{21} & k_{22} & k_{23} \\ k_{31} & k_{32} & k_{33} \end{bmatrix} \times \begin{bmatrix} p_1 \\ p_2 \\ p_3 \end{bmatrix} \bmod 26$$

This can be expressed in terms following equations:

$$c_1 = (k_{11}p_1 + k_{12}p_2 + k_{13}p_3) \bmod 26$$
$$c_2 = (k_{21}p_1 + k_{22}p_2 + k_{23}p_3) \bmod 26$$
$$c_3 = (k_{31}p_1 + k_{32}p_2 + k_{33}p_3) \bmod 26$$

The cipher-text letters are generated by the linear combination of n successive plain-text letters.

Decryption: The multiplicative inverse of matrix K, that is, K^{-1}, is used as the decryption key, and the decryption process is defined as:

$$P = K^{-1} C \bmod 26 \tag{5.4}$$

Since K^{-1} is required for the decryption of the cipher-text at the recipient end, the matrix K is required to be non-singular.

Example 5.4

Let $n = 2$. Suppose the plaintext to be sent is "CD"

$$P = \begin{bmatrix} "C" \\ "D" \end{bmatrix} = \begin{bmatrix} 2 \\ 3 \end{bmatrix}, \text{ put such structures in matrix form,}$$

and $K = \begin{bmatrix} 2 & 3 \\ 3 & 4 \end{bmatrix}$.

Encryption: $C = KP \bmod 26 = \begin{bmatrix} 2 & 3 \\ 3 & 4 \end{bmatrix} \times \begin{bmatrix} 2 \\ 3 \end{bmatrix} \bmod 26$

$$= \begin{bmatrix} 13 \\ 18 \end{bmatrix} = \begin{bmatrix} "N" \\ "S" \end{bmatrix}$$

The "CD" is transmitted as "NS" after encryption.

Decryption: Determine the Decryption Key K^{-1},

$$K^{-1} = \begin{bmatrix} 4 & -3 \\ -3 & 2 \end{bmatrix}^T = \begin{bmatrix} 4 & -3 \\ -3 & 2 \end{bmatrix} = \begin{bmatrix} -4 & 3 \\ 3 & -2 \end{bmatrix}$$

$$(2 \times 4) - (3 \times 3) = -1$$

$$P = K^{-1} C \bmod 26 = \begin{bmatrix} -4 & 3 \\ 3 & -2 \end{bmatrix} \times \begin{bmatrix} 13 \\ 14 \end{bmatrix} \bmod 26$$

$$= \begin{bmatrix} 2 \\ 3 \end{bmatrix} = \begin{bmatrix} "C" \\ "D" \end{bmatrix}$$

Thus, after decryption at the recipient end, the original plaintext "CD" is recovered.

Example 5.5

Let $n = 2$. Suppose the plaintext to be sent is "EB"

$$P = \begin{bmatrix} "E" \\ "B" \end{bmatrix} = \begin{bmatrix} 4 \\ 1 \end{bmatrix}, \text{ put such structures in matrix form, and } K = \begin{bmatrix} 7 & 5 \\ 4 & 3 \end{bmatrix}.$$

Encryption: $C = KP \bmod 26 = \begin{bmatrix} 7 & 5 \\ 4 & 3 \end{bmatrix} \times \begin{bmatrix} 4 \\ 1 \end{bmatrix} \bmod 26$

$$= \begin{bmatrix} 7 \\ 19 \end{bmatrix} = \begin{bmatrix} "H" \\ "T" \end{bmatrix}$$

The "EB" is transmitted as "HT" after encryption.

Decryption: Determine the Decryption Key K^{-1},

$$K^{-1} = \begin{bmatrix} 3 & -4 \\ -5 & 7 \end{bmatrix}^T = \begin{bmatrix} 3 & -5 \\ -4 & 7 \end{bmatrix} = \begin{bmatrix} 3 & -5 \\ -4 & 7 \end{bmatrix}$$

$$(7 \times 3) - (5 \times 4) = 1$$

$$P = K^{-1} C \bmod 26 = \begin{bmatrix} 3 & -5 \\ -4 & 7 \end{bmatrix} \times \begin{bmatrix} 7 \\ 19 \end{bmatrix} \bmod 26$$

$$= \begin{bmatrix} (21 - 95) \bmod 26 \\ (-28 + 133) \bmod 26 \end{bmatrix} = \begin{bmatrix} (-74) \bmod 26 \\ (105) \bmod 26 \end{bmatrix}$$

$$= \begin{bmatrix} 4 \\ 1 \end{bmatrix} = \begin{bmatrix} "E" \\ "B" \end{bmatrix}$$

Thus, after decryption at the recipient end, the original plaintext "EB" is recovered.

5.2.3.1 Strength of the Hill Cipher

Each cipher-text letter is generated by the linear combination of n successive letters of plaintext. Alternately, we can say that each plaintext letter affects many cipher-text letters. Thus, the statistical structure of plaintext is not reflected in the resulting cipher-text; rather it gets diffused into the long-term statistics of the cipher-text. This phenomenon is known as "Diffusion." The larger the size of the key matrix, the more pronounced the diffusion will be. This makes the cipher scheme difficult to cryptanalyze. For a sufficiently large key-matrix size, the scheme will be very hard to break.

5.2.4 Play-Fair Cipher

The Play-Fair Cipher makes use of a 5×5 matrix of letters for encryption/ decryption as illustrated in Table 5.4.

TABLE 5.4 Play-Fair Cipher of a 5×5 Matrix of Letters for Encryption/Decryption

C	O	M	P	U
T	E	R	A	B
D	F	G	H	I/J
K	L	N	Q	S
V	W	X	Y	Z

The Play-Fair Cipher operates as follows:

1. It uses a 5 x 5 matrix of uppercase English letters ("A" . . . "Z").

2. A key is chosen (like COMPUTER in the previous case), which is entered into the matrix, starting from the top-left corner, filling the values in row-major fashion. Any duplicate letters in the key are entered only once.

3. The remaining letters of the alphabet ("A" . . . "Z"), other than the key letters, are entered into the remaining cells of the matrix. The letters "I" and "J" are entered in the same cell.

4. The plaintext letters are encrypted in pairs such that:
   - Any duplicate letters falling in the same pair are separated by inserting a filler letter different from the duplicate letter.
   - If the number of letters in the plaintext is odd, then a dummy letter is appended at the end to make the number even.

Encryption:

- If a pair of letters falls in the same row, then the letters are replaced by the letters immediately on their right, respectively, in the same row, in a cyclic manner. The first letter of a row is taken as the letter to the right of the last letter of that row.

  ELSE

  If a pair of letters falls in the same column, then the letters are replaced by the letters immediately beneath them in the same column, in a cyclic manner. The letter at the top of a column is taken as the letter beneath the last letter of that column.

  ELSE

  Each letter in the pair is replaced by a letter that falls at the intersection of the row of the given letter and column of the other letter in the pair.

Decryption:

The Decryption algorithm is the reverse of the Encryption Algorithm. The cipher-text letters are also divided into pairs for decryption. The decryption is performed according to the following rule:

- If a pair of letters falls in the same row, then the letters are replaced by the respective letters on the left in that row. For this purpose, the last letter of a row is taken as letter to the left of the first letter in that row.

  ELSE

  If a pair of letters falls in the same column, then the letters are replaced by the respective letters just above in that column. For this purpose, the last letter in a column is taken as the letter above the first in that column.

  ELSE

  Each letter in the pair is replaced by a letter that falls at the intersection of the given letter's row and the other letter's column.

Example 5.6

Plaintext: COMING AT SIX

CO MI NGAT SI XP % P is added at end to complete the last pair

Cipher-text: OM UG XN BE ZS YM

5.2.5 Poly-Alphabetic Cipher (Vigenere Cipher)

- The Vigenere Cipher or Poly-Alphabetic Cipher is a substitution cipher that encrypts plaintexts coded in English letters ("A" ... "Z").

- The key is also a string formed from letters drawn from ("A" ... "Z").

- The length of the key is exactly the same as the length of the plaintext to be encrypted.

- The key is generated by repeating some code word that is kept secret between the sender and the intended recipients; for example, if the plaintext length is 20 and the secret key word is "COMPUTER," then the key will be: "COMPUTERCOMPUTERCOMP," which is of length 20.

Encryption:

Let $p[0...n-1]$ be the plaintext string and $k[0...n-1]$ be the key string, both of length n.

- The letters are assigned equivalent integer values "A" = 0, "B" = 1, "C" = 2, ... "Z" = 25.

$$\text{Then } c[i] = (p[i] + k[i]) \bmod 26, \quad \text{for } 0 < i < n \qquad (5.5)$$

where

$p[i]$: ith letter in the plaintext

$k[i]$: ith letter in the key

$c[i]$: ith letter in the cipher-text

Decryption:

The decryption process is the reverse of the encryption process.

$$p[i] = (c[i] - k[i]) \bmod 26, \quad \text{for } 0 < i < n \qquad (5.6)$$

Implementation of the scheme:

The scheme is implemented by generating a 26×26 look-up table as illustrated in Table 5.5, with plaintext letters indicated along the *x-axis* and the key letters indicated along the *y-axis*. For a given plaintext letter and a given key letter, the cipher-text letter would be the one that appears at the cross-section of the column of the plaintext letter and the row of the key letter.

Example 5.7

Plaintext: COMI NGATSE VEN

Key: COM PU TERCO M PU

Cipher-text: e c y x h z e k u s h t h

Hint: The cipher-text has been indicated in lowercase letters just to distinguish it from the plaintext.

Strength of the Vigenere Cipher: If the length of the code word used for key generation is large enough, then the Vigenere Cipher will be highly secure.

5.2.6 One-Time Pad

This cipher is similar to the Vigenere Cipher, but with the following differences:

- It uses an additional character, blank (" "), added to the character set; thus, the encryption and decryption will be mod 27.

- For each message, a new string of characters is chosen as a key, which is exactly of the same length as the plaintext to be encrypted. The key is conveyed to the recipient in a secure manner prior to transmission of the message.

- It makes use of a 27×27 matrix comprising characters from the set ("A" ... "Z" and " ") for encryption/decryption, similar to the Vigenere Cipher.

Let $p[0...n-1]$ be plaintext and $k[0...n-1]$ be the chosen key, each comprising n letters.

Encryption:

$$c[i] = (p[i] + k[i]) \bmod 27, \quad \text{for } 0 \le i < n \tag{5.7}$$

Decryption:

$$p[i] = (c[i] + k[i]) \bmod 27, \quad \text{for } 0 \le i < n \tag{5.8}$$

5.2.6.1 Strength of the One-Time Pad:

Since the key is a random string of the same length as the plaintext to be encrypted and a new key is generated for each message to be sent, the One-Time Pad is considered highly secure, in fact, unbreakable.

TABLE 5.5 Encryption/Decryption Look-Up

Plaintext Letters ------------→

	A	B	C	D	E	F	G	H	I	J	K	L	M	N	O	P	Q	R	S	T	U	V	W	X	Y	Z
A	A	B	C	D	E	F	G	H	I	J	K	L	M	N	O	P	Q	R	S	T	U	V	W	X	Y	Z
B	B	C	D	E	F	G	H	I	J	K	L	M	N	O	P	Q	R	S	T	U	V	W	X	Y	Z	A
C	C	D	E	F	G	H	I	J	K	L	M	N	O	P	Q	R	S	T	U	V	W	X	Y	Z	A	B
D	D	E	F	G	H	I	J	K	L	M	N	O	P	Q	R	S	T	U	V	W	X	Y	Z	A	B	C
E	E	F	G	H	I	J	K	L	M	N	O	P	Q	R	S	T	U	V	W	X	Y	Z	A	B	C	D
F	F	G	H	I	J	K	L	M	N	O	P	Q	R	S	T	U	V	W	X	Y	Z	A	B	C	D	E
G	G	H	I	J	K	L	M	N	O	P	Q	R	S	T	U	V	W	X	Y	Z	A	B	C	D	E	F
H	H	I	J	K	L	M	N	O	P	Q	R	S	T	U	V	W	X	Y	Z	A	B	C	D	E	F	G
I	I	J	K	L	M	N	O	P	Q	R	S	T	U	V	W	X	Y	Z	A	B	C	D	E	F	G	H
J	J	K	L	M	N	O	P	Q	R	S	T	U	V	W	X	Y	Z	A	B	C	D	E	F	G	H	I
K	K	L	M	N	O	P	Q	R	S	T	U	V	W	X	Y	Z	A	B	C	D	E	F	G	H	I	J
L	L	M	N	O	P	Q	R	S	T	U	V	W	X	Y	Z	A	B	C	D	E	F	G	H	I	J	K
M	M	N	O	P	Q	R	S	T	U	V	W	X	Y	Z	A	B	C	D	E	F	G	H	I	J	K	L
N	N	O	P	Q	R	S	T	U	V	W	X	Y	Z	A	B	C	D	E	F	G	H	I	J	K	L	M
O	O	P	Q	R	S	T	U	V	W	X	Y	Z	A	B	C	D	E	F	G	H	I	J	K	L	M	N
P	P	Q	R	S	T	U	V	W	X	Y	Z	A	B	C	D	E	F	G	H	I	J	K	L	M	N	O
Q	Q	R	S	T	U	V	W	X	Y	Z	A	B	C	D	E	F	G	H	I	J	K	L	M	N	O	P
R	R	S	T	U	V	W	X	Y	Z	A	B	C	D	E	F	G	H	I	J	K	L	M	N	O	P	Q
S	S	T	U	V	W	X	Y	Z	A	B	C	D	E	F	G	H	I	J	K	L	M	N	O	P	Q	R
T	T	U	V	W	X	Y	Z	A	B	C	D	E	F	G	H	I	J	K	L	M	N	O	P	Q	R	S
U	U	V	W	X	Y	Z	A	B	C	D	E	F	G	H	I	J	K	L	M	N	O	P	Q	R	S	T
V	V	W	X	Y	Z	A	B	C	D	E	F	G	H	I	J	K	L	M	N	O	P	Q	R	S	T	U
W	W	X	Y	Z	A	B	C	D	E	F	G	H	I	J	K	L	M	N	O	P	Q	R	S	T	U	V
X	X	Y	Z	A	B	C	D	E	F	G	H	I	J	K	L	M	N	O	P	Q	R	S	T	U	V	W
Y	Y	Z	A	B	C	D	E	F	G	H	I	J	K	L	M	N	O	P	Q	R	S	T	U	V	W	X
Z	Z	A	B	C	D	E	F	G	H	I	J	K	L	M	N	O	P	Q	R	S	T	U	V	W	X	Y

---------------→ Key Letters

5.2.6.2 Limitations of the One-Time Pad:

The One-Time Pad Scheme has the following limitations:

1. There is a practical problem of creating a large number of random keys (a new key for each message).

2. For each message, a unique key is required to be exchanged between the sender and the recipient. Secure distribution of such keys becomes a daunting task. Since the key is of the same length as the message to be encrypted, rather than sending the key to the recipient by highly secure means, the plaintext itself may be transmitted by those secure means without encryption. Thus, the scheme is of no practical use. It may only be used as a benchmark to judge the strength of practical schemes.

5.3 TRANSPOSITION CIPHERS

The Transposition Ciphers perform permutations on the plaintext to produce a scrambled cipher-text.

5.3.1 Rail-Fence Cipher

The Rail-Fence Cipher is a form of transposition cipher. The plaintext is written as a sequence of diagonals as shown in the following example, and then read off as a sequence of rows. The depth of the rail fence forms the key that needs to be exchanged between the communicating parties.

Example 5.8

Plaintext: ATTACK TIGER HILL AT SEVEN PM

Encryption: Suppose the depth of the rail fence is chosen to be 3. This parameter is a key which must be communicated to the intended recipient prior to transmission of the encrypted message. Then, for encryption, the plaintext is represented as a set of diagonals as shown in the following:

```
A   A   T   E   I   A   E   N
  T   C   I   R   L   T   V   P
    T   K   G   H   L   S   E   N
```

If the message length is not a whole-number multiple of the fence depth, then some dummy letters are appended at the end.

Now read it off row-wise to generate the cipher-text:

Cipher-text: AATEIAENTCIRLTVPTKGHLSEM

Decryption: Knowing that the depth of the rail fence is 3, the cipher-text is divided into three equal parts and the parts are written row-wise. Then, the resulting message is read column-wise, and that represents the plaintext.

AA TE IAE N

T C I R LTV P

TKG HLSEM

Now, the above text is read off column-wise to form the original plaintext.

Plaintext: ATTACKTIGERHILLATSEVENPM

The dummy letters at the end can be recognized and ignored by the recipient.

5.3.1.1 Strength of the Rail-Fence Cipher

The strength of Rail-Fence Cipher depends on its depth; more the depth more secure will be the resulting cipher.

5.3.2 Rectangular Transposition Cipher

- The scheme uses a key that is communicated to the intended recipients by secure means. Let the length of the key be N.

- The key comprises N digits in the range $1 \ldots N$, with each digit appearing precisely once.

Encryption: For encryption, the plain-text is written row by row in rectangular form, with each row having N elements. Some dummy letters may have to be appended at the end to complete the rectangle formed by the message.

Then, the message is read off, column by column, permuting the order of the columns in accordance with the key. Supposing the key is 4312, column 3 is read off first, followed by column 4, column 2, and finally column 1.

Decryption: For decryption, the received text is divided into N equal groups. Each group is written as a column, in accordance with the key. Then the resulting rectangle is read off row by row, thus forming the original plaintext.

Example 5.9

Let the key be 4231.

The row size will be 4.

Plaintext: ATTACK TIGER HILL AT SEVEN PM

Key: **4 2 3 1**
           A T T A
           C K T I
           G E R H
           I L L A
           T S E V
           E N P M

Cipher-text: AIHAVMTKELSNTTRLEPACGITE

- Since the key is 4231, column 4 is read first, followed by column 2, column 3, and finally column 1.

Decryption: The recipient will know the row-size of the message rectangle used at the sender end from the key-size.

- In Example 5.9, since the key-size is 4, the recipient will know that the row-size of the message rectangle is 4. The received cipher-text is divided into four equal parts. Each part represents a column of the encrypted plaintext. So, the columns are written as per the key to form the message rectangle, which would be exactly the same as it was at the sender end.

- Then, the message is read off from the rectangle row-wise, and that forms the plaintext. The dummy letters (if any) at the end can be made out by the recipient and ignored.

The cipher can be made more secure by performing transpositions repeatedly, by using the same key more than once. The number of transpositions must be known to the intended recipient to enable the deciphering of the received cipher-text.

5.4 STEGANOGRAPHY

- Steganography implies concealment (or hiding) of information.

- One of the common techniques used for steganography is the hiding of information in a digital picture.

- A digital picture is stored in the form of a matrix of pixels with each pixel represented by 24-bits of RGB information. If the Least Significant Bit (LSB) of each pixel is modified, the picture quality remains almost unaffected. This feature is exploited for steganography.

- If user "A" is to send a message to user "B," then "A" will choose a digital picture. Suppose the picture has 2048×3072 pixels.

- Then 2048×3072 bits of binary information (one bit in the LSB of each pixel) can be inserted into the picture by substituting the LSBs with the bits of the information to be sent.

- The modified picture is transmitted to user "B," the recipient.

- The recipient will extract the information from the pixels.

5.4.1 Limitation of Steganography

- If an adversary gets a clue about the scheme, then the adversary can steal the information with as much ease as a valid user.

5.4.2 Steganography Combined with Cryptography

- Steganography can be made secure by combining it with cryptography. The information is first encrypted, and the resulting cipher-text is concealed using steganographic techniques.

5.5 EXERCISES

1. Explain how the Mono-Alphabetic Cipher is prone to statistical analysis attacks. How is this problem eliminated in the Vigenere Cipher?

2. Why is the encryption key matrix of the Hill Cipher required to be a non-singular matrix?

3. Why is the One-Time Pad cipher considered to be unbreakable? Is the scheme practically implementable? Justify your answer.

4. Differentiate between cryptography and steganography.

5. Use the following matrices as a key for the Hill Cipher:

   A. Encrypt the message "STOP MOVE"

   B. $\begin{bmatrix} 2 & 3 \\ 5 & 8 \end{bmatrix}$

   C. $\begin{bmatrix} 3 & 5 \\ 5 & 8 \end{bmatrix}$

   D. $\begin{bmatrix} 3 & 7 \\ 2 & 5 \end{bmatrix}$

   Determine the corresponding decryption keys and decrypt the cipher-text.

6. Use the following keys for the Play-Fair Cipher:

   A. SOFTWARE

   B. BLACK

   C. CAPITAL

       i. Encrypt the messages: "REACHING AT SEVEN"
   "ATTACK TIGER HILC"

       ii. Decrypt the cipher-texts

7. Using the following encryption/decryption table, encrypt the following plain texts:

   A. WAIT FOR FURTHER ORDERS

   B. REPORT PROGRESS

TABLE 5.6 Encryption/Decryption Table for Mono-Alphabetic Cipher

Plaintext Alphabet	Cipher-Text Alphabet	Plaintext Alphabet	Cipher-Text Alphabet
A	J	N	G
B	E	O	D
C	N	P	I
D	A	Q	W
E	C	R	L
F	K	S	Q
G	S	T	O
H	F	U	Z
I	B	V	M
J	H	W	Y
K	U	X	T
L	V	Y	R
M	P	Z	X

8. Using the One-Time Pad Cipher, encrypt the following message:

   A. Message: "MOVE FURTHER"
      KEY: "COMPUTERCOMP"

9. Using the Rail-Fence Cipher with depth = 4, encrypt the following messages:

   A. "CONFIRM OP SUCCESS"

   B. "SEND MORE TROOPS"

CHAPTER 6

MODERN SYMMETRIC CIPHERS

Chapter Outline

6.1   Introduction

6.2   Some Basic Concepts for Symmetric Ciphers

6.3   Claude Shannon's Theory of Diffusion and Confusion

6.4   Feistel Cipher

6.5   Data Encryption Standard (DES)

6.6   Avalanche Effect

6.7   Multiple DES

6.8   International Data Encryption Algorithm (IDEA)

6.9   Advanced Encryption Standard (AES)

6.10 Key Management: Symmetric Encryption

6.11 Pseudo-Random Number Generators

6.12 Exercises

6.1   INTRODUCTION

In this chapter we will study some modern symmetric ciphers like the Data Encryption Standard (DES) and the International Data Encryption Algorithm (IDEA). Though simple DES is no longer considered secure, there are highly secure schemes involving multiple applications of DES like Triple-DES. IDEA is considered highly secure and is in extensive use.

6.2 SOME BASIC CONCEPTS FOR SYMMETRIC CIPHERS

6.2.1 Concept of Binary Block Substitution

A Block Cipher takes a plaintext block of a particular size (say n bits) and produces a cipher-text block of the same size. Figure 6.1 illustrates the logic of a general substitution cipher for $n = 4$.

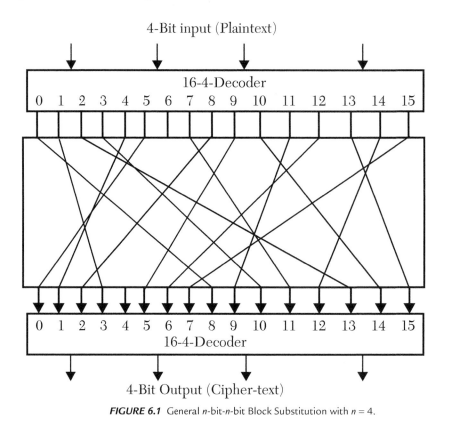

FIGURE 6.1 General n-bit-n-bit Block Substitution with $n = 4$.

- For a block size n, there will be 2^n possible different plaintext blocks.

- For the encryption to be reversible, each distinct plaintext block must map onto a distinct cipher-text block. Thus, there must be 2^n distinct cipher-text blocks, each mapping onto a distinct plaintext block. Such a transformation is called a *reversible* or *non-singular transformation*.

- If n is sufficiently large and an arbitrary reversible substitution is performed between the plaintext and cipher-text, then the statistical characteristics of the plaintext get masked to a great extent, making cryptanalysis difficult to perform.

For example, a 4-bit input produces one of 16 possible input states, which is mapped by the substitution cipher into one of 16 unique possible output states, where each of them is represented by 4 cipher-text bits. Tables 6.1 and 6.2 illustrate the encryption and decryption for the substitution cipher of Figure 6.1.

TABLE 6.1 Encryption Table (for *n* = 4, i.e., 4-Bit Block Size)

Plaintext	Cipher-text
0000	1000
0001	0011
0010	1101
0011	1010
0100	0001
0101	0000
0110	0100
0111	1011
1000	0010
1001	0101
1010	1110
1011	1001
1100	0110
1101	1111
1110	1100
1111	0111

TABLE 6.2 Decryption Table (for *n* = 4, i.e., 4-Bit Block Size)

Plaintext	Cipher-text
0000	0101
0001	0100
0010	1000
0011	0001
0100	0110
0101	1001
0110	1100
0111	1111
1000	0000
1001	1011
1010	0011
1011	0111
1100	1110
1101	0010
1110	1010
1111	1101

6.2.2 Strength of the Substitution Cipher

For $n = 4$, the plaintext can assume $2^4 = 16$ different values.

Similarly, the cipher-text can also have $2^4 = 16$ possible different values.

To determine the number of possible distinct transformations from plaintext to cipher-text, ensuring that the transformations are reversible, the following argument holds:

1. A plaintext value 0 can be mapped to any of the 16 possible cipher-text values (say cipher-text value 5).

2. A plaintext value 1 can be mapped onto any of the remaining 15 cipher-text values (except cipher-text value 5).

3. Similarly, plaintext value 2 can be mapped onto any of the remaining 14 cipher-text values and so on.

Therefore, the number of distinct reversible transformations from plaintext to cipher-text is equal to $16 \times 15 \times 14 \times \ldots \times 2 \times 1 = 16! = 2^4!$

For block size n, the number of distinct reversible transformations is equal to $2^n!$. For a practical block size of 64 or 128 bits, the number of distinct reversible transformations will be extremely high, thus making the substitution cipher highly resistant to brute-force attacks.

6.2.3 Key Size for the Simple Substitution Cipher

The ordered set of entries on the right-hand side of the encryption table forms the key, the first entry representing the cipher-text corresponding to plain-text 0 and the last entry representing the cipher-text corresponding to plaintext $2^n - 1$.

The size of the key (for $n = 4$) = $4 \times 24 = 64$ bits.

In general, for an n-bit block size, the key size = $n \times 2^n$ bits.

For a 64-bit block size, the size of key = $64 \times 2^{64} = 2^{70}$ bits (very large value).

To get an idea for the memory space required to store the key, the memory of a PC with 4GB RAM is 2^{35} bits. Thus, the number of PCs required to store the key of a 64-bit substitution cipher is 2^{35} or 4GB. This makes the simple substitution cipher very difficult to implement.

6.3 CLAUDE SHANNON'S THEORY OF DIFFUSION AND CONFUSION

In cryptographic terms, Diffusion and Confusion are two encryption processes that make the resulting cipher-text very difficult to cryptanalyze.

6.3.1 Diffusion

Diffusion causes each element of the plaintext to affect many elements of the resulting cipher-text. Thus, each element of the resulting cipher-text is influenced by many elements of the plaintext. For example, suppose M = m_1, m_2, … m_n is a plaintext message comprising n letters of the English alphabet.

The encryption algorithm may generate each cipher-text letter c by modular addition of k successive letters of plaintext, that is, $c_n = \sum_{i-1}^{k} m_{n+1} \left(\mathrm{mod}\, 26 \right)$.

Thus, each letter of the cipher-text is influenced by k successive letters of plaintext. This operation dissipates (diffuses) the statistical structure of the plaintext into long-range statistics of the cipher-text, that is, the letter frequencies in the resulting cipher-text will be more nearly equal than the letter frequencies in the plaintext. Another example is the Hill cipher, in which each letter of cipher-text is generated by linear combination of many plain-text letters. In the Binary-Block Cipher, the diffusion is achieved by repeatedly performing some permutation on the plaintext bits and then applying some complex mathematical function to the permuted bit sequence. The mathematical function is applied using a secret key. The effect will be that many bits from different positions in the plaintext will contribute to each bit of the cipher-text, or each cipher-text bit will be affected by many plaintext bits. The main goal is that the statistical relationship between the plaintext and the cipher-text should be made as complex as possible, so as to make the crypt-analysis extremely difficult.

6.3.2 Confusion

Confusion makes the relationship between the key and the statistical structure of the cipher-text as complex as possible, so that it is not possible to deduce the key from the cipher-text statistical structure. This is achieved by making the application of the key complex. In a Binary-Block Cipher, confusion is achieved by using a Complex Substitution Algorithm.

6.4   FEISTEL CIPHER

- Considering the impracticable key size of a simple substitution cipher, Feistel proposed a structure known as a "Feistel Cipher Structure" that represents a practical implementation of Claude Shannon's Diffusion and Confusion concepts.

- It performs transformations of the plaintext by performing substitution and permutation repeatedly. That is why it is also known as a Substitution-Permutation Network (SPN). It makes use of both Diffusion and Confusion very effectively.

Figure 6.2 depicts a general Feistel Cipher Structure for Encryption with n identical rounds of processing. The inputs to the Encryption Algorithm comprise (*i*) a plaintext block of length $2w$ bits and (*ii*) a key K. The plaintext is divided into two halves L_0 and R_0 of w bits each, which are fed to Round 1 of the encryption algorithm. The data passes through n rounds of processing and produces a cipher-text block of size $2w$ bits, same as the size of the input plaintext. Let the inputs to Round i be denoted as L_{i-1} and R_{i-1}, which are derived from the output of the previous round, and a sub-key K_i, which is derived from the overall key K. In general, the sub-keys are different from each other and also different from the overall key K.

All the rounds of processing have the same general structure. A substitution is performed on the left half of the data by taking the XOR (Exclusive OR) of the Left Half input with the output of function F, which has the Right Half Data and Sub-Key K_i as inputs. The function F has the same structure for each round, and it is parameterized by the sub-key K_i, which is different for each round. Following the substitution of the Left Half, a Permutation is performed on the data by switching the two halves. So, each round performs substitution and permutation. Note that each round of the Feistel Cipher maps the right-hand input, without any change, into the left-hand output; and the right-hand output is obtained by XOR in the left-hand Input with the output of function F that operates on the right-hand input acted upon by a 48-bit sub-key. So, in each round, only half of the Input gets transformed, and the other half remains unchanged. In fact, one half of the input data is used to transform the other half, and then the two halves are swapped.

The Decryption Algorithm is exactly the same as the Encryption Algorithm, except that the sub-keys are applied to the decryption rounds in reverse order, that is, key K_n is applied to round 1, and key K_1 is applied to round 16 of decryption.

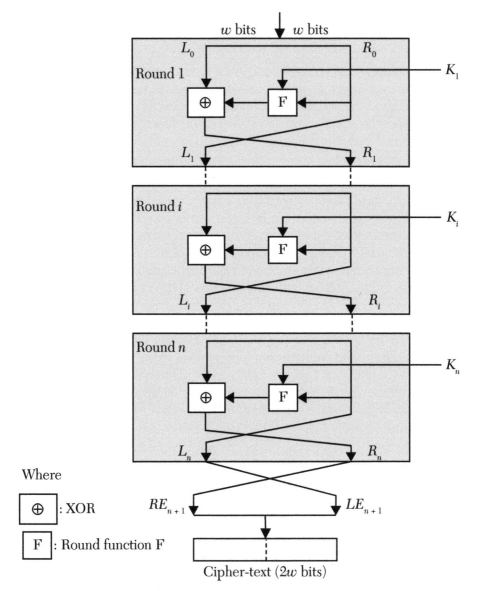

FIGURE 6.2 Feistel Cipher Structure (Encryption).

6.4.1 Strength of the Feistel Cipher

The strength of Feistel Cipher depends on the following factors:

1. **Block Size:** The larger the block size, the more secure the cipher will be. Currently, the typical size is 128 bits.

2. **Key Size:** The larger the key-size, the more secure the cipher. Currently, the typical size is 128 bits.

3. **Number of Rounds:** The higher the number of Rounds, the higher the security. The typical number is 16.

4. **Complexity of Sub-Key Generation Algorithm:** The more complex the algorithm, the more secure the cipher will be.

5. **Complexity of Round Function "F":** The more complex the Round Function "*F*," the more secure the cipher will be.

While the design of a cipher system should be resistant to cryptanalysis, it should also meet the following criteria:

1. **Faster Encryption/Decryption:** It should meet the system throughput requirement.

2. **Easy to Understand:** Though performing complex transformations, the algorithm should be concise and easy to understand, so that it can be easily analyzed for any vulnerability to cryptanalysis.

Increasing the security level of a cipher scheme may result in higher encryption/decryption overheads. A balance has to be struck between the two.

6.5   DATA ENCRYPTION STANDARD (DES)

The Data Encryption Standard (DES) was adopted by the National Bureau of Standards (now called the National Institute of Standards and Technology) as Federal Information Processing Standard 46 (FIPS 46). The algorithm used in DES is called the Data Encryption Algorithm (DEA), which encrypts plaintext data blocks of a size of 64 bits using a 56-bit overall key and outputs 64-bit cipher-text blocks as in Figure 6.3. DES is built around a Feistel Cipher Network with 16 rounds of processing, each round having a 48-bit sub-key drawn from a 56-bit overall key. Figures 6.4 and 6.5 show Feistel encryption and decryption algorithm processes for DES.

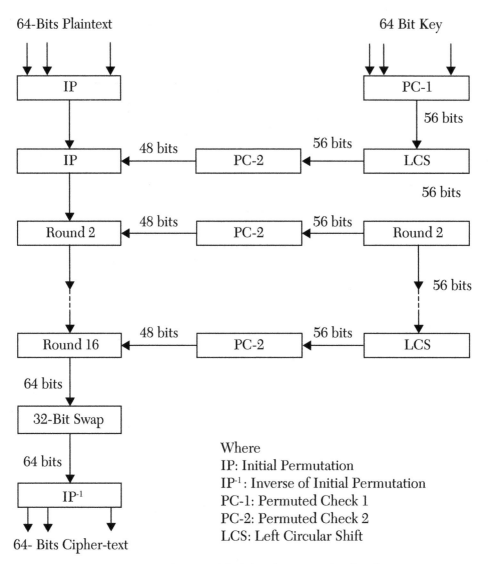

FIGURE 6.3 General depiction of DES encryption algorithm.

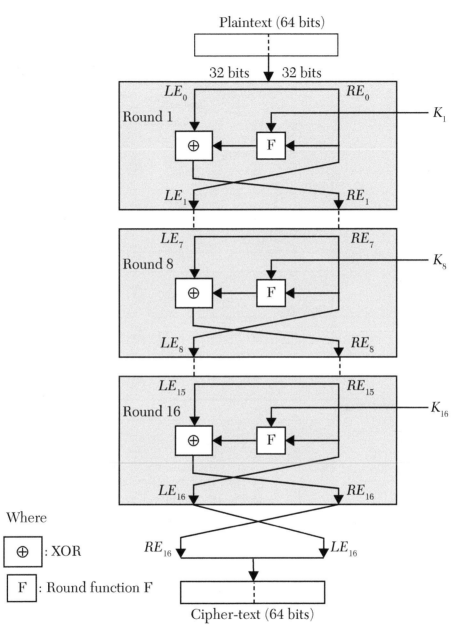

FIGURE 6.4 Feistel encryption algorithm (for DES).

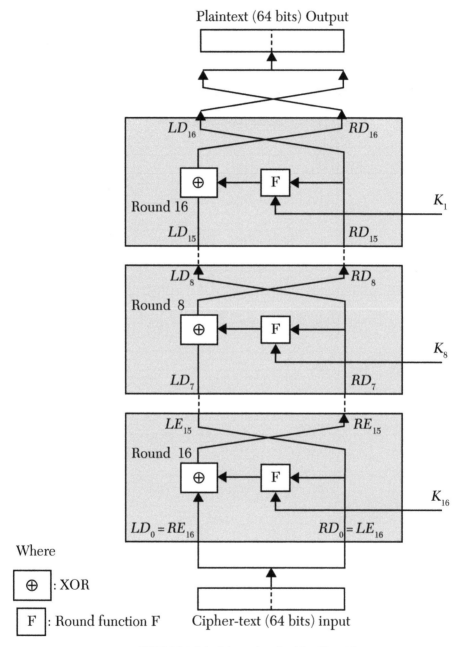

FIGURE 6.5 Feistel decryption algorithm (for DES).

Example 6.1

Prove that decryption is the reverse of encryption.

Solution

Plaintext input to Encryption $LE_0 \parallel RE_0$.

Encryption

Input to Round 1: $LE_0 \parallel RE_0$.

Output of Round 1:

$LE_1 = RE_0$

$RE_1 = LE_0 \oplus F(RE_0, K_1)$

Output of Round i:

$LE_i = RE_{i-1}$

$RE_i = LE_{i-1} \oplus F(RE_{i-1}, K_i)$

Output of Round 16:

$LE_{16} = RE_{15}$

$RE_{16} = LE_{15} \oplus F(RE_{15}, K_{16})$

Decryption

Input of Round 1:

$RD_0 = LE_{16} = RE_{15}$

$LD_0 = RE_{16} = LE_{16} \oplus F(RE_{15}, K_{16})$

Output of Round 1:

$LD_1 = RD_0 = LE_{16} = RE_{15}$

$LD_1 = LD_0 \oplus F(RD_0, K_{16})$

$\quad = LD_0 \oplus F(RE_{15}, K_{16})$

$\quad = LE_{15} \oplus F(RE_{15}, K_{16}) + F(RE_{15}, K_{16})$

$\quad = LE_{15}$

Output of Round i:

$LD_i = RE_{16-i}$

$LD_1 = LE_{16-i}$

Output of Round 16:

$$RD_{16} = LE_0$$

$$LD_{16} = RE_0$$

Therefore, the output of the Decryption Algorithm: $RD_{16} \parallel LD_{16} = LE_0 \parallel RE_0$ (the same as the plaintext input to encryption).

Let the 64-bit plaintext block (input to Encryption) be represented as depicted in Table 6.3. It comprises 8 bytes.

TABLE 6.3 64-Bit Plaintext Block

M_{01}	M_{02}	M_{03}	M_{04}	M_{05}	M_{06}	M_{07}	M_{08}
M_{09}	M_{10}	M_{11}	M_{12}	M_{13}	M_{14}	M_{15}	M_{16}
M_{17}	M_{18}	M_{19}	M_{20}	M_{21}	M_{22}	M_{23}	M_{24}
M_{25}	M_{26}	M_{27}	M_{28}	M_{29}	M_{30}	M_{31}	M_{32}
M_{33}	M_{34}	M_{35}	M_{36}	M_{37}	M_{38}	M_{39}	M_{40}
M_{41}	M_{42}	M_{43}	M_{44}	M_{45}	M_{46}	M_{47}	M_{48}
M_{49}	M_{50}	M_{51}	M_{52}	M_{53}	M_{54}	M_{55}	M_{56}
M_{57}	M_{58}	M_{59}	M_{60}	M_{61}	M_{62}	M_{63}	M_{64}

The transformation of a 64-bit plaintext block into a 64-bit cipher-text block is done in three major steps:

1. **Initial Permutation (IP):** It performs the initial permutation of the 64-bit plaintext block in accordance with the following IP table in Table 6.4:

TABLE 6.4 Initial Permutation (IP)

M_{58}	M_{50}	M_{42}	M_{34}	M_{26}	M_{18}	M_{10}	M_{02}
M_{60}	M_{62}	M_{44}	M_{36}	M_{28}	M_{20}	M_{12}	M_{04}
M_{62}	M_{54}	M_{46}	M_{38}	M_{30}	M_{22}	M_{14}	M_{06}
M_{64}	M_{56}	M_{48}	M_{40}	M_{32}	M_{24}	M_{16}	M_{08}
M_{57}	M_{49}	M_{41}	M_{33}	M_{25}	M_{17}	M_{09}	M_{01}
M_{59}	M_{51}	M_{43}	M_{35}	M_{27}	M_{19}	M_{11}	M_{03}
M_{61}	M_{53}	M_{45}	M_{37}	M_{29}	M_{21}	M_{13}	M_{05}
M_{63}	M_{55}	M_{47}	M_{39}	M_{31}	M_{23}	M_{15}	M_{07}

2. **Feistel Processing:** It comprises 16 identical rounds of the Feistel Network, followed by a 32-bit swap. Each round *i* has a 48-bit sub-key K_i drawn from the overall 56-bit key. The right-side input to a round is not changed and it is output as left-side input to the next round. The left-side input to a round is transformed by taking its XOR with the output of round function *F* that operates on the right-side input acted upon by the round sub-key. A detailed description of the round function is given subsequently. The Decryption algorithm is exactly the same as the Encryption Algorithm, except that the sub-keys are applied in the reverse order; that is, sub-key K_{16} is applied to Round 1, sub-key K_{15} is applied to Round 2, and so on, with sub-key K_{16} applied to Round 16 of decryption.

3. **Inverse of Initial Permutation** (IP^{-1})**:** The inverse of Initial Permutation, that is, IP^{-1}, is a permutation performed as per IP^{-1} Table 6.5. The effect of this permutation is to undo the effect of the Initial Permutation (IP).

TABLE 6.5 Inverse Initial Permutation (IP^{-1})

M_{40}	M_{08}	M_{48}	M_{16}	M_{56}	M_{24}	M_{64}	M_{32}
M_{39}	M_{07}	M_{47}	M_{15}	M_{55}	M_{23}	M_{63}	M_{31}
M_{38}	M_{06}	M_{46}	M_{14}	M_{54}	M_{22}	M_{62}	M_{30}
M_{37}	M_{05}	M_{45}	M_{13}	M_{53}	M_{21}	M_{61}	M_{29}
M_{36}	M_{04}	M_{44}	M_{12}	M_{52}	M_{20}	M_{60}	M_{28}
M_{35}	M_{03}	M_{43}	M_{11}	M_{51}	M_{19}	M_{59}	M_{27}
M_{34}	M_{02}	M_{42}	M_{10}	M_{50}	M_{18}	M_{58}	M_{26}
M_{33}	M_{01}	M_{41}	M_{09}	M_{49}	M_{17}	M_{57}	M_{25}

6.5.1 Description of the Critical Functions of Each Round of DES

Figure 6.6 shows the internal structure of each round of DES.

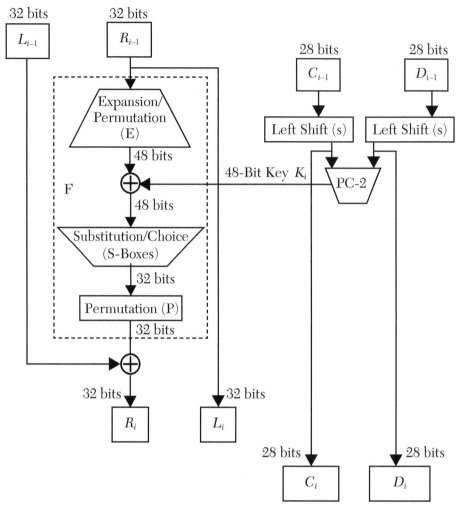

FIGURE 6.6 Schematic diagram of each of DES algorithm.

1. **Expansion Permutation (E):** This performs permutation on the 32-bit input and also expands it to a 48-bit output as follows:

   A. The 32-bit input is divided into 8 groups of 4 bits each.

B. Then each group i is expanded to 6 bits by appending a copy of the last bit of the previous group $i-1$ to the beginning of group i, and appending a copy of the first bit of the next group $i+1$ to the end of group i. For this purpose, the last group is taken as before the first group and the first group is taken as the next to last group. Table 6.6 shows the Expansion Permutation (E):

TABLE 6.6 Expansion Permutation (E)

32	1	2	3	4	5
4	5	6	7	8	9
8	9	10	11	12	13
12	13	14	15	16	17
16	17	18	19	20	21
20	21	22	23	24	25
24	25	26	27	28	29
28	29	30	31	32	1

Example 6.2

Input ... 0010   1010   1100 ....

The middle group (1010) will be expanded to (010101) and so on.

2. **Substitution/ Choice (by Use of S-Boxes):** DES uses 8 specially designed S-Boxes as non-linear components. Each box has 4 rows indexed (0 ... 3) and 16 columns indexed (0 ... 15) of decimal numbers (0 ... 15). The numbers are distributed in each row in a random manner and none of the digits is repeated in a row; that is, each of the 16 digits (0 ... 15) appears precisely once in a row.

A sample S-box is appended in Table 6.7:

TABLE 6.7 A Sample S-Box

10	00	09	14	06	03	15	05	01	13	12	07	11	04	02	08
13	07	00	09	03	04	06	10	02	08	05	14	12	11	15	01
13	06	04	09	08	15	03	00	11	01	02	12	05	10	14	07
01	10	13	00	06	09	08	07	04	15	14	03	11	05	02	12

6.5.2 S-Box Transformation

Suppose the 6-bit input to a S-Box is: $b_5\,b_4\,b_3\,b_2\,b_1\,b_0$.

The substitution/choice by S-Boxes is performed as follows:

- The decimal number formed by two bits $b_5\,b_0$ (0...3) is used to choose the S-Box Row Number n.

- And the decimal number formed by four bits $b_4\,b_3\,b_2\,b_1$ (0...15) is used to choose the S-Box column number m.

- The decimal number stored in the S-Box at the intersection (n, m) forms the 4-bit output.

- The S-Boxes are so designed that if two inputs to an S-Box differ just in one bit, the outputs must differ in at least 2 bits. Also, all transformations are reversible.

Figure 6.7 shows the rule of the S-boxes in the function of F.

48-bit input to S-Boxes

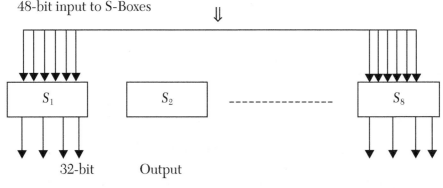

32-bit   Output

FIGURE 6.7 Rule of the S-boxes in the function of F.

Example 6.3

Suppose the 6-bit input to the S-Box as shown in Figure 6.7 is: 011011.

1. Find the 4-bit output of the S-Box.

2. How many bits of output will the concatenation of 4-bit outputs from 8 S-Boxes generate?

Solution

1. Row Number $n = (01) = 1$
   Column Number $m = (1101) = 13$

   The Decimal Number stored at location $(1, 13)$ is 11.

   Therefore, the 4-bit output of the S-Box will be: 1011

2. The concatenation of 4-bit outputs from 8 S-Boxes will generate a 32-bit output.

   Permutation (P): The 32-bit information is permuted in accordance with the Permutation Table P shown in Table 6.8. The bit from the 16th position is shifted to the 1st position; the bit from 07th position is shifted to position 2, and so on.

TABLE 6.8 Permutation Table P

16	07	20	21	29	12	28	17
01	15	23	26	05	18	31	10
02	08	24	14	32	27	03	09
19	13	30	06	22	11	04	25

6.5.3 Generation of Sub-Keys ($K_1 ... K_{16}$)

A total of 16 sub-keys (one per round) are computed starting from key size 64. The generation of 16 sub-keys is achieved through the following steps:

1. First the 64-bit input is compressed to 56 bits by ignoring every 8th bit of the input as shown in Table 6.9. Then, the 56-bit key is permuted according to Table PC-1 (Permuted Choice-I) as shown in Table 6.10.

TABLE 6.9 Input 64-Bit Key

01	02	03	04	05	06	07	08
09	10	11	12	13	14	15	16
17	18	19	20	21	22	23	24
25	26	27	28	29	30	31	32
33	34	35	36	37	38	39	40
41	42	43	44	45	46	47	48
49	50	51	52	53	54	55	56
57	58	59	60	61	62	63	64

Column 8 from the key input is eliminated, and the remaining 56 bits are permuted in accordance with the permutation table in Table 6.10. The bit from position 57 is shifted to bit position 1 and the bit from position 49 is shifted to position 2, and so on.

TABLE 6.10 Permutation for Permuted Choice-1 (PC-1)

57	49	41	33	25	17	09
01	58	50	42	34	26	18
10	02	59	51	43	35	27
19	11	03	60	52	44	36
63	55	47	39	31	23	15
07	62	54	46	38	30	22
14	06	61	53	45	37	29
21	13	05	28	20	12	04

2. The output of PC-1 is divided into two halves of 28 bits each, which are fed to the Left Shifters. The Left Shifters rotate the two halves left by 1 or 2 bits, depending on the round. The rotation left is by 1 bit in rounds 1, 2, and 9, and the rotation left is by 2 bits in the remaining 13 rounds.

3. The outputs of the Two Left-Shifters are concatenated and fed to the Permutation/Concentration Block. This block permutes the input and also reduces it to 48 bits according to Table Permuted Choice-2 (PC-2) as shown in Table 6.11, by ignoring 8 bits of the 56-bits input. The 48-bit output forms the Key K_1 for the first Round. The bit from position 14 is shifted to position 1, the bit from position 17 is shifted to position 2, and so on.

TABLE 6.11 Permutation for Permuted Choice-2 (PC-2)

14	17	11	24	01	05	03	28
15	06	21	10	23	19	12	04
26	08	16	07	27	20	13	02
41	52	31	37	47	55	30	40
51	45	33	48	44	49	39	56
34	53	46	42	50	36	29	32

4. The 28-bit outputs of the two left-shifters form inputs for the key generation of the next round.

6.5.4 DES Decryption Algorithm

The DES decryption uses the same algorithm as for encryption except that the application is in the reverse order. The cipher-text generated by the encryption algorithm is input to round 1 of the decryption algorithm, which gets sub-key K_{16} as input. Any round i of the decryption algorithm gets sub-key K_{16-i+1} as input. Thus, round 16 of the decryption algorithm gets sub-key K_1 as input. The output of round 16 will be the original plaintext that generated the cipher-text.

6.6 AVALANCHE EFFECT

A desirable property of any Encryption Algorithm is that a small change in either the Plaintext or the Key should produce a significant change in the Cipher-text, so that the space of possible plaintexts and Keys that an adversary should need to try for an attempted cipher-break should be very large. In fact, for a one-bit change in the Plaintext or key, many bits should change in the cipher-text. This effect is called the *Avalanche Effect*. In DES, if two inputs to an S-Box differ by exactly one bit, the outputs must differ in at least two bits.

Plaintext – Cipher-Text Transformations in DES

- Plaintext/Cipher-text Block Size in DES = 64 bits

- Therefore, size of Plaintext Space = 2^{64}

- And size of Cipher-text Space = 2^{64}

- Let us denote the Plaintext space by set X and the cipher-text space by set Y.

Consider the situation when different plaintexts are encrypted using same key K:

- For a given key K, the transformation from Plaintext Space to Cipher-text Space will be one-to-one, that is, reversible.

- This implies that for each plaintext pair (P_1, P_2) belonging to set X such that $P_1 \neq P_2$, there will be cipher-texts $C_1 = E_k[P_1]$ and $C_2 = E_k[P_2]$ belonging to set Y that will satisfy $C_1 \neq C_2$; and for each cipher-text pair (C_1, C_2) belonging to set Y such that $C_1 \neq C_2$, there will be plain-texts $P_1 = D_k[C_1]$ and $P_2 = D_k[C_2]$ belonging to set X that will satisfy $P_1 \neq P_2$.

- This implies that the plaintext space X and cipher-text space Y will be equal, that is, Set X = Set Y. In fact, the Plaintext Space and Cipher-text Space are exactly the same, as illustrated in Figure 6.8.

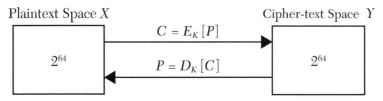

FIGURE 6.8 Plaintext space X and cipher-text space Y are equal.

Now, let us consider the scenario when a given Plaintext P is encrypted using different keys:

- DES Key Size = 56 bits

- Size of DES Key Space = 2^{56}

- Consider encryption of a given plaintext P using all possible keys in the Key Space. This will result in a set of cipher-text Y_1, which will be a subset of Y.

- The set Y will have a size = $|Y_1| \leq 2^{56}$, since two different keys may map the plaintext P to the same cipher-text C, as illustrated in Figure 6.9.

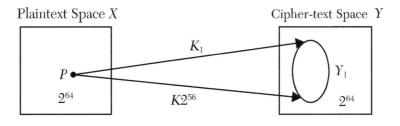

FIGURE 6.9 Plaintext P is encrypted using different keys.

6.6.1 Strength of DES

Key Size: With a 56-bit Key Size, there would 2^{56} possible keys. In a brute force attack, an adversary has to try an average of 2^{55} keys to meet success.

Algorithm and S-Boxes: The Strength of DES lies basically in the design of S-Boxes. The design criteria of S-boxes have never been made public, and no fatal weaknesses have so far been reported in their design.

Resistance to Timing Attacks: Timing attacks exploit the fact that Encryption or Decryption Algorithms take a slightly different amount of time on different inputs. The algorithm for timing attacks yields the Hamming Weight (i.e., number of bits equal to 1) of the Secret Key. DES is fairly resistant to such attacks.

In 1998, DES Encryption was broken in less than three days, using a special purpose "DES Cracker" machine. Thus, a simple DES with a 56-bit key size is virtually useless.

6.6.2 Possible Attacks on DES

DES is claimed to be prone to the following types of Cryptanalysis attacks:

- Differential Cryptanalysis
- Linear Cryptanalysis

6.6.2.1 Differential Cryptanalysis

- A Differential Cryptanalysis Attack is an "Adaptively Chosen Plaintext," wherein the attacker has access to encryption equipment.

- The attacker analyzes the effect of particular differences in plaintext pairs on the differences in resulting cipher-text pairs.

- The attacker chooses certain plaintext pairs with a particular XOR difference (say Δm). The chosen plaintext pairs are made to pass through the encryption process and their XOR differences are observed at the output of each round.

- It will be observed that certain XOR differences in the plaintext pairs have a high probability of causing certain XOR differences in the corresponding cipher-text pairs. Such pairs are of interest to the analysts.

- The transformation of XOR difference at the output of successive rounds is a function of the sub-keys of those rounds. This information is used to predict the sub-keys. This attack requires chosen plaintexts of the order of 2^{47} to break the cipher.

To understand the approach more clearly, we can do the following steps:

- Consider a plaintext pair (m, m')

- XOR difference between m and m' equal to $\Delta m = m \oplus m'$

- Let Δm be split into two equal halves Δm_0 and Δm_1 such chat $\Delta m = \Delta m_0 \| \Delta m_1$

- The plaintexts are passed through various rounds of the encryption algorithm of DES, and their XOR differences are observed at the outputs of various rounds.

- The transformation of the XOR differences at the outputs of various rounds of DES is as indicated in Figure 6.10.

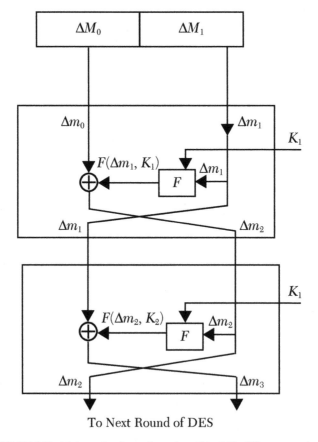

FIGURE 6.10 A Schematic of transformation of the XOR differences at the outputs of various rounds of DES.

- XOR difference at the input co round 1 $= \Delta m_0 \| \Delta m_1$

- XOR difference at the output of round 1 $= \Delta m_1 \| \Delta m_2$

- where $\Delta m_2 = \Delta m_0 \oplus F(\Delta m_1, K_1)$

- Thus, Round 1 transforms the XOR difference from $\Delta m_0 \| \Delta m_1$ to $\Delta m_1 \| \Delta m_2$

- Only one half of the input gets transformed as a function of sub-key K_1 and the other half remains unchanged.

- The XOR difference at the output of Round 1 goes as input to Round 2.

For the transformation at round i $(1 \leq i \leq 16)$ we do the following steps:

- XOR difference at the input of round $i = \Delta m_{i-1} \| \Delta m_i$

- XOR difference at the output of round $i = \Delta m_i \| \Delta m_{i+1}$ where $\Delta m_{i+1} = \Delta m_{i-1} \oplus F(\Delta m_i, K_i)$

- Thus, Round i transforms the XOR difference from $\Delta m_{i-1} \| \Delta m_i$ to $\Delta m_i \| \Delta m_{i+1}$

- The transformation at Round i is a function of sub-key K_i

- The cryptanalyst will study the changes in the XOR differences at the outputs of all rounds.

- Since these XOR changes are a function of the sub-keys used in the successive rounds, this information is used to assign probabilities to the sub-key bits.

- As we analyze more and more plaintext-cipher-text pairs, the most probable values of the sub-keys will emerge. Differential Cryptanalysis needs of the order of 2^{47} chosen plaintexts to break the cipher.

Finally, the Differential Cryptanalysis attack can be summarized as follows:

- The Differential Cryptanalysis Attack is an "Adaptively Chosen Plaintext Attack" wherein the attacker has access to the encryption equipment.

- The attacker chooses certain plaintext pairs with a particular XOR difference (say Δm). The cryptanalyst encrypts those pairs using the same key (which is to be determined) and determines the XOR differences between the resulting cipher-texts. Let the XOR difference between the cipher-texts be Δc

- There will be certain XOR differences in the plaintext pairs that will result in particular XOR differences in the cipher-text pairs with a high probability. Such XOR differences are of interest to the analysts. The plaintext pairs with such XOR differences are made to go through encryption, and transformation of the XOR differences are noted at the outputs of successive rounds.

- This evolution of the XOR differences at the outputs of successive rounds of DES is a function of the sub-keys of those rounds; thus, the information is used to predict the bits of the sub-keys. Analysis of more and more plaintext pairs will enable prediction of the sub-keys completely.

6.6.2.2 Linear Cryptanalysis

This cryptanalysis is based on the finding that if we XOR some of the bits of plaintext and XOR some of the bits of corresponding cipher-text and then have the XOR of the result of the two, then we get a bit that would form the XOR of some of the bits of the key.

- Consider an n-bit plaintext and m-bit key.

- Let the bits of a plaintext block be labeled as $p[1], p[2], ..., p[n]$; the bits of a cipher-text block be labeled as $c[1], c[2], ..., c[n]$; and the key bits be labeled as $k[1], k[2], ..., k[m]$

- Let us denote

$$P[\alpha_1, \alpha_2, ..., \alpha_a] = P[\alpha_1] \oplus P[\alpha_2] \oplus ... \oplus P[\alpha_a] \text{ where } 1 \leq a \leq n$$

$$C[\beta_1, \beta_2, ..., \beta_b] = C[\beta_1] \oplus C[\beta_2] \oplus ... \oplus C[\beta_b] \text{ where } 1 \leq b \leq n$$

$$K[\gamma_1, \gamma_2, ..., \gamma_c] = K[\gamma_1] \oplus K[\gamma_2] \oplus ... \oplus K[\gamma_c] \text{ where } 1 \leq c \leq m$$

- The goal of linear cryptanalysis is to determine linear equations of the form:

$$P[\alpha_1, \alpha_2, ..., \alpha_a] \oplus C[\beta_1, \beta_2, ..., \beta_b] = K[\gamma_1, \gamma_2, ..., \gamma_c]$$

- If the result of the equation is 0 most of the time, then we assume that the value of $K[\gamma_1, \gamma_2, ..., \gamma_c] = 0$; if the result is 1 most of the time, then we assume that the $K[\gamma_1, \gamma_2, ..., \gamma_c] = 1$

- By getting many such equations, we can deduce the bits of all sub-keys.

   For example, suppose the cryptanalyst is able to establish the following:

   $K[3,17,23] = 0$ and $K[3,23] = 1$

   From these equations, it can be deduced that bit-17 is likely to be 1.

- The number of known plaintexts required to break the cipher completely is of the order of 2^{43}

6.6.3 Differential Cryptanalysis vs. Linear Cryptanalysis

- Differential Cryptanalysis requires plaintexts of the order of 2^{47} whereas Linear Cryptanalysis requires plaintexts of the order of 2^{43} to break the cipher. Therefore, Linear Cryptanalysis requires slightly lesser effort than a Differential Cryptanalysis Attack.

- Differential Cryptanalysis requires Chosen Plaintexts whereas Linear Cryptanalysis requires Known Plaintexts. Obtaining Known Plaintexts is considered to be much easier than obtaining Chosen Plaintexts.

6.7 MULTIPLE DES

The Single DES was cracked in 1998 by the use of a special machine known as a "DES Cracker." The attack took just three days to break the cipher. Since then, the single DES became virtually useless, so the designers came out with some solutions involving multiple blocks of DES used for encryption and decryption.

6.7.1 Double DES

The simplest form of multiple encryption/decryption has two encryption/ decryption stages and two keys. Two blocks of DES with two 56-bit keys are used for encryption/decryption as follows:

6.7.1.1 Encryption

Figure 6.11 illustrates the two blocks of DES with two 56-bit keys that are used for encryption.

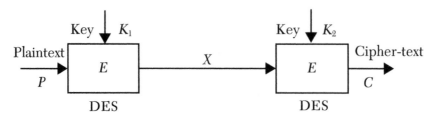

FIGURE 6.11 Two blocks of DES with two 56-bit keys are used for encryption.

Given a plaintext P and two encryption keys K_1 and K_2 cipher-text C is generated as

$$X = E_{K_1}[P] \tag{6.1}$$

$$C = E_{K_2}[X] = E_{K_2}\left[E_{K_1}[P]\right] \tag{6.2}$$

6.7.1.2 Decryption

For decryption, the keys are used in reversed order. Figure 6.12 illustrates the two blocks of DES with two 56-bit keys that are used for decryption.

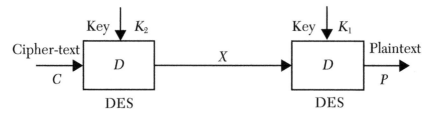

FIGURE 6.12 Two blocks of DES with two 56-bit keys are used for decryption.

Decryption requires that the keys be used in reverse order:

$$X = D_{K_2}[C] = D_{K_2}\left[E_{K_2}[X]\right] \tag{6.3}$$

$$P = D_{K_1}[X] = D_{K_1}\left[E_{K_1}[P]\right] \tag{6.4}$$

6.7.1.3 Strength of Double DES

It uses two keys, each the size of 56 bits. So, the combined key size is 112 bits. Any brute force attack will require an effort of the order of 2^{112} attempts to break the cipher. However, Double DES is prone to a special type of attack known as a "Meet-in-the-Middle" Attack, which can break the cipher with much less effort.

6.7.1.4 "Meet-in-the-Middle" Attack on Double DES

This attack is performed as follows:

- **Step 1:** Take a pair of plaintext and cipher-text, say (P,C)

- **Step 2**: Use all possible values of key K_1 to encrypt the plaintext, and save the output values that comprise the intermediate cipher-text (X) in the following table. The table will have 2^{56} values of X one for each possible value of K_1

- **Step 3:** Sort the table in ascending or descending order of X so that the table can be used for a binary search of X values.

  Now start decrypting C for all possible values of K_2

- **Step 4:** Decrypt C using the next value of K_2 This will produce a value of X

- **Step 5:** Carry out a binary search in the previous table to find a match for the value of X generated in Step 4.

- **Step 6:** If a match is found for X then the value of K_1 (which matches X), along with the value of K_2 selected at Step 4, form the likely key-pair. Now, take another plaintext-cipher-text pair, say (P_1,C_1) and encrypt the plaintext P_1 using the likely key-pair. If the cipher-text generated by the likely key-pair matches with C_1 then (K_1,K_2) is the key-pair with a very high probability. To confirm it more, test with more plaintext-cipher-text pairs. If the test passes with all chosen pairs, then quit as the key-pair is confirmed; if the test fails then go back to Step 4.

If no match is found, then go back to Step 4 and repeat Steps 4 to Step 6 with the next value of key K_2

6.7.1.5 Effort Required for "Meet-in-the-Middle" Attack on Double DES

The effort required for the "Meet-in-the-Middle" attack can be divided into two parts:

1. **Creation of K_1 vs. X Table:** The attacker needs to try all possible values of the 56-bit key K_1, so the effort required will be of the order of 2^{56}

2. **Decryption of cipher-text using K_2 and finding a match with X values stored in the table**: On the average, the attacker may need to try half the possible values of K_2 **T**his requires an effort of the order of $\dfrac{2^{56}}{2} = 2^{55}$

The total effort required will be of the order of $2^{56} + 2^{55}$ that is, of the order of $2 \times 2^{56} = 2^{57}$

This effort is slightly more than the effort required for breaking a Single DES by Brute Force Attack (i.e., 2^{55}). Thus, Double DES is almost as insecure as Single DES.

6.7.2 Triple DES

It makes use of three blocks of DES with two 56-bit keys, K_1 and K_2 It is a relatively popular alternative to DES, and it has been adopted for use in the key management standards.

6.7.2.1 Encryption

For encryption, it makes use of both the Encrypt (E) and Decrypt (D) functions. For the same key value, the function D is the inverse of function E Figure 6.13 illustrates the three blocks of DES with two 56-bit keys K_1 and K_2 used for encryption.

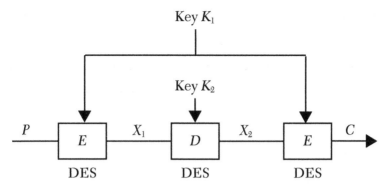

FIGURE 6.13 Three blocks of DES with two 56-bit keys K_1 and K_2 are used for encryption.

Where,

P: Plaintext Block, X_1 X_2: Intermediate Cipher-Text Blocks, C: Final Cipher-Text Block

$$X_1 = E_{K_1}[P] \qquad (6.5)$$

$$X_2 = E_{K_2}[X_1] = D_{K_2}\Big[E_{K_1}[P]\Big] \qquad (6.6)$$

$$C = E_{K_1}[X_2] = E_{K_1}\Big[D_{K_2}\big[E_{K_1}[P]\big]\Big] \qquad (6.7)$$

The plaintext goes through the following steps of processing:

1. Transformation by Encrypt (E) function using key K_1 The output is intermediate cipher-text X_1

2. Transformation by Decrypt (D) function using key K_2 It gets X_1 as input and generates intermediate cipher-text X_2 as output.

3. Transformation by Encrypt (E) function using key K_1 It takes X_2 as input and generates final cipher-text C as output.

6.7.2.2 Decryption

The decryption also makes use of both the Encrypt (E) and Decrypt (D) functions. Figure 6.14 illustrates the three blocks of DES with two 56-bit keys K_1 and K_2 used for decryption.

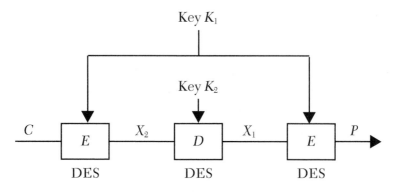

FIGURE 6.14 Three blocks of DES with two 56-bit keys K_1 and K_2 are used for decryption.

Where,

P: Plaintext Block, X_1 X_2: Intermediate Cipher-Text Blocks, C: Final Cipher-Text Block

$$X_2 = D_{K_1}[C] = D_{K_1}\left[E_{K_1}[X_2]\right] \tag{6.8}$$

Where D_{K_1} is inverse of E_{K_1}

$$X_1 = E_{K_2}[X_2] = E_{K_2}\left[D_{K_2}[X_2]\right] \tag{6.9}$$

Where E_{K_2} is inverse of D_{K_2}

$$C = D_{K_1}[X_1] = D_{K_1}\left[E_{K_1}\left[E_{K_1}[P]\right]\right] \tag{6.10}$$

Where D_{K_1} is inverse of E_{K_1}

The cipher-text goes through the following steps of processing:

1. Transformation by Decrypt (D) function using key K_1 The output is intermediate cipher-text X_2

2. Transformation by Encrypt (E) function using key K_2 It gets X_2 as input and generates intermediate cipher-text X_1 as output.

3. Transformation by Decrypt (D) function using key K_1 It takes X_1 as input and generates plaintext P as output.

6.7.2.3 "Meet-in-the-Middle" Attack on Triple DES

- Triple DES is highly secure against a "Meet-in-the-Middle" Attack.

- If an adversary attempts a "Meet-in-the-Middle" Attack against Triple DES, the middle point for the attack can be chosen as intermediate cipher-text X_1 or intermediate cipher-text X_2

- If the point chosen is X_2 then:

  - The attacker will need to create a table that will give values of X_2 for every possible value of key K_1 and every possible value of key K_2 The total number of possibilities will be $2^{56+56} = 2^{112}$

  - Then X_2 will need to be generated by decrypting cipher-text using possible values of K_1 On the average, at least half the possible values will need to be tried. This will need an effort of the order of 2^{55}

  - Thus, the total effort will be of the order of $2^{112} + 2^{55}$ The second term is negligible as compared to the first term. Thus, the effort required will be of the order of 2^{112}

  - This effort is extremely large as compared to the effort required for breaking a single DES using a brute force attack.

- Triple DES, being highly secure, is used for encryption of highly sensitive data.

6.7.3 Block Cipher vs. Stream Cipher

- A Block Cipher divides plaintext into blocks of a fixed size, a normal block size being 64/128 bits. The encryption is performed block-by-block, producing cipher-text blocks of the same size. For encryption to be reversible (or non-singular), each distinct plaintext block must produce a distinct cipher-text block. Now, for block-size n there will be 2^n distinct plain-text blocks and 2^n distinct cipher-text blocks.

- A Stream Cipher encrypts a digital data stream bit-by-bit or byte-by-byte, producing cipher-text of the same denomination as the plain-text. Normally stream ciphers handle one character (8 bits) at a time.

- A Stream Cipher is more suitable for real-time inputs where data is continuously flowing in. The moment a byte is received, it is immediately encrypted and transmitted without any delay at the sender end. Yet in a block cipher, the sender-end has to wait for one block of data to be received; only then can encryption be performed.

6.7.4 Block/Stream Cipher Modes of Operation

There are five modes of operation in the following list that are commonly used. Some of these modes are suitable for both the block and stream cipher, but some modes are suitable only for the block cipher.

- Electronic Code Book (ECB) Mode
- Cipher Block Chaining (CBC) Mode
- Cipher Feedback (CFB) Mode
- Output Feedback (OFB) Mode
- Counter (CTR) Mode

6.7.4.1 Electronic Code Book (ECB) Mode

- ECB is the simplest mode, in which the plaintext is handled 64 bits at a time and each block of plaintext is encrypted using the same key. ECB secures transmission of a single value.
- The plaintext is divided into blocks of, for example, n bits each. If the plaintext length is not a whole number multiple of n the last block is padded with some dummy bits to make its length n
- Each block is encrypted using the "Encrypt" function and secret Key K The secret key is communicated to the intended recipients by secure means.
- At the receiving end the decryption is performed, using the "Decrypt" function and the same key K
- The plaintext consists of a sequence of 64-bit blocks $P_1, P_2, ..., P_N$ corresponding to a sequence of cipher-text blocks $C_1, C_2, ..., C_N$

6.7.4.1.1 Encryption and Decryption of ECB

Encryption of ECB

Figure 6.15 shows the Electronic Code Book (ECB) Mode encryption.

$$C_i = E_K(P_I) \qquad (6.11)$$

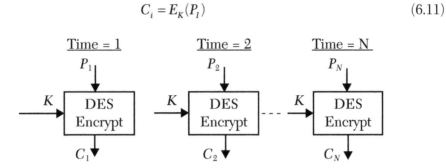

FIGURE 6.15 Electronic Code Book (ECB) Mode encryption.

Decryption of ECB

Decryption is performed one block at a time, always using the same key. Figure 6.16 shows the Electronic Code Book (ECB) Mode decryption.

$$D_K\left(C_I\right) = D_K\left(E_K(P_I)\right) = P_I \qquad (6.12)$$

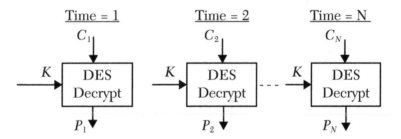

FIGURE 6.16 Electronic Code Book (ECB) Mode decryption.

6.7.4.1.2 Advantages and Limitations of ECB

The advantages of ECB are:

- The scheme is very simple and easy to implement.
- It is most suitable for the sending of small messages like session keys.

    The limitations of ECB are:

- Identical plaintext blocks will result in identical cipher-text blocks; thus, the statistical structure of the plaintext is reflected in the resulting cipher-text. This feature can be exploited by the cryptanalysts. ECB is, therefore, not suitable for the sending of long messages, which are likely to have repetitive plaintext blocks.

6.7.4.2 Cipher Block Chaining (CBC) Mode

- In Cipher Block Chaining (CBC) Mode, the cipher-text produced by a plaintext block is chained to the input of the next encryption block, thus influencing the value of the cipher-text block.

- Since no cipher-text block is available for the encryption of the first plaintext block, an Initial Vector (IV) is input to the first encryption block, which affects the value of the first cipher-text block. The N is communicated to the intended recipients by the same secure means as the secret key K

- The value, resulting from the XOR of the plaintext block and chained cipher-text block, is encrypted using secret key K thus producing a cipher-text block, which is chained to the input of the next encryption block.

- The decryption is the reverse of encryption, wherein the cipher-text block is first decrypted using the "Decrypt" function and key K Then, XOR is performed between the output of the "Decrypt" function and the cipher-text derived from the previous decryption block, thus resulting in the output of the plaintext block.

6.7.4.2.1 Encryption and Decryption of CBC

At the sender side, XOR is done before encryption; at the receiver site, the decryption is done before XOR.

Encryption of CBC

In Cipher Block Chaining (CBC) Mode, the input to the encryption algorithm is the XOR of the next 64 bits of plaintext and proceeding 64 bits of cipher-text. The CBC mode is a general-purpose, block-oriented transmission. Figure 6.17 shows the CBC mode encryption.

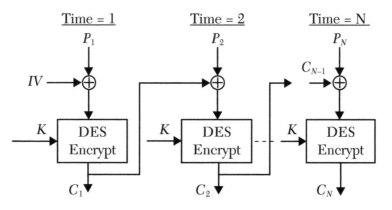

FIGURE 6.17 Electronic Code Book (CBC) Mode encryption.

For the encryption algorithm, we do the following:

For $i = 1$ to n do

$C_i = E_K \left(P_i \oplus C_{I-1} \right)$ with $C_0 = IV$

IV is initial vector (C_0)

P_i is plaintext block i

K is secret key

C_i is cipher-text block i

Decryption of CBC

On decryption, the initial vector (IV) is XOR with the output of the decryption algorithm to recover the first block of plaintext. Each cipher block in decryption is passed through the decryption algorithm. The result is XOR with the proceeding cipher-text block to produce the plaintext block as in the following:

For $i = 1$ to n do

$$
\begin{aligned}
\text{Plaintext} \quad &= D_K \left(C_I \right) \oplus C_{i-1} \quad \text{with} \ \ C_0 = IV \\
&= D_K \left(E_K \left(P_i \oplus C_{i-1} \right) \right) \oplus C_{i-1} \\
&= P_i \oplus C_{i-1} \oplus C_{i-1} \\
&= P_i
\end{aligned}
$$

Figure 6.18 shows the CBC mode decryption.

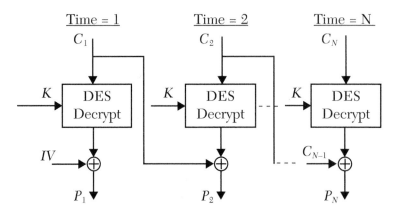

FIGURE 6.18 Electronic Code Book (CBC) Mode decryption.

6.7.4.2.2 Advantages and Limitations of CBC

The advantages of CBC are:

- Like ECB, CBC also uses the same key for the encryption of all plaintext blocks, but identical plaintext blocks still do not result in identical cipher-text blocks. Thus, CBC is more secure as compared to ECB Mode and is suitable for sending long messages.

The limitations of CBC are:

- If a cipher-text block gets corrupted in transit, it will affect the decryption of two cipher-text blocks.

6.7.4.3 Cipher Feedback (CFB) Mode

- The Cipher Feedback Mode makes use of a Shift Register the size of, for example, 64 bits.

- It encrypts plaintext elements of size s bits. Normally, s equals 8, the size of a character. Thus, Cipher Feedback Mode is suitable for a stream cipher.

- This is suitable for real-time applications wherein a data character (normally 8 bits) can be encrypted and sent without waiting for a large block of data to be ready.

- The Shift Register is initialized to a value (IV), which is communicated by secure means to the intended recipient of the message.

- The contents of the Shift Register are encrypted using a secret key K The value of K is also communicated by secure means to the intended recipient of the message.

- Most significant s bits from the encrypted contents of the shift register are XORed with s-bit plaintext block P_1 generating s-bit cipher-text block C_1

- The contents of the shift register are shifted left s-bits and the s-bit cipher-text C1 is placed in the lowest s-bits of the shift register.

- Now, the contents of the shift register are encrypted using the key K, and the encrypted contents are used for generation of cipher-text C_2 for plain-text P_2 This process is repeated for all subsequent plaintext blocks.

6.7.4.3.1 Encryption and Decryption of CFB

A schematic diagram of the CFB Encryption/Decryption is indicated in Figure 6.19.

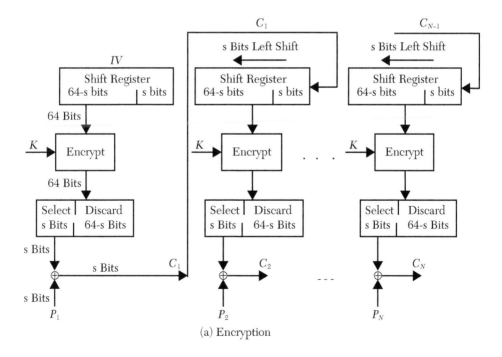

(a) Encryption

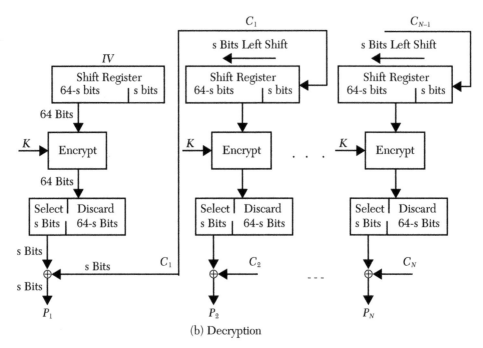

(b) Decryption

FIGURE 6.19 *s*-Bit Cipher Feedback (CFB) Mode encryption/decryption.

Encryption of CFB

$S_s(X)$: Most significant s bits of shift register X

$C_i = P_i \oplus S_s\big(E_k(IV)\big)$

Decryption of CFB

First Step (for Cipher-text C_1)

Plaintext = $C_1 \oplus S_s\big(E_k(IV)\big)$

$\qquad = P_1 \oplus S_s\big(E_k(IV)\big) \oplus S_s\big(E_k(IV)\big) = P_1$

Subsequent Steps (for Cipher-text C_I)

Plaintext = $C_i \oplus S_s\big(E_{I-1}(IV)\big)$

$\qquad = P_i \oplus S_s\big(E_{I-1}(IV)\big) \oplus S_s\big(E_{I-1}(IV)\big) = P_i$

6.7.4.3.2 Advantages and Limitations of CFB

The advantages of CFB are:

- The CFB mode is suitable both for Block and Stream Cipher modes.

- This mode uses same Algorithm, that is, "Encrypt," at both the ends, unlike the ECB and CBC modes, which use the Encrypt and Decrypt algorithms.

- In Stream Cipher Mode, it offers the following advantages:

  - It eliminates the requirement of padding.

  - Each character of plaintext can be encrypted and transmitted when ready. Thus, it is suitable for real-time applications.

The limitations of CFB are:

If a cipher-text block gets corrupted in transit, it would affect the decryption of many subsequent cipher-text blocks, since each cipher-text block affects the contents of the shift-register for many subsequent blocks. For example, if the register size is 64 bits and the plaintext/cipher-text size is 8 bits, then each cipher-text block influences the output of eight subsequent blocks.

6.7.4.4 Output Feedback (OFB) Mode

The Output Feedback (OFB) Mode is similar to the Cipher Feedback (CFB) Mode, except that the feedback in this case is the most significant s bits of the Encrypted contents of the shift register rather than the Cipher output of the previous step.

6.7.4.4.1 Encryption and Decryption of OFB

A schematic diagram of the OFB Encryption/Decryption is indicated in Figure 6.20.

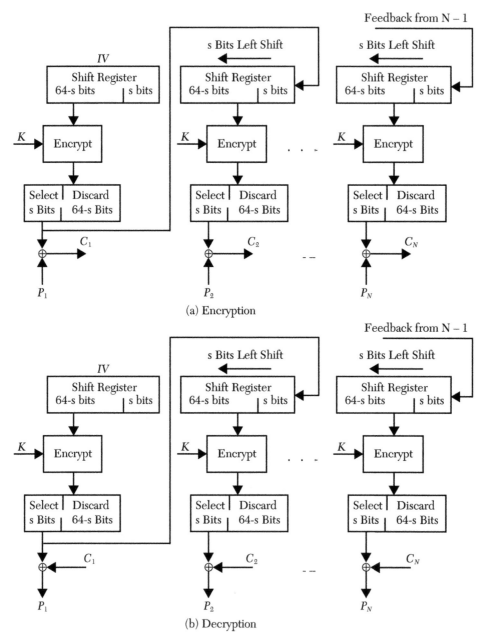

FIGURE 6.20 *s*-Bit Output Feedback (OFB) Mode encryption/decryption.

Encryption of OFB

The Encryption Algorithm is identical to the Cipher Feedback (CFB) Mode:

First Step (for P_1)

Let $S_s(X)$ be defined as the most significant s bits of shift register X

$$C_1 = P_1 \oplus S_s\left(E_k(IV)\right)$$

For Subsequent Steps (for Plaintext Block P_i)

Let X_{I-1} be the contents of the shift Register after Step $i-1$

$$C_i = P_i \oplus S_s\left(E_k(X_{i-1})\right)$$

Decryption of OFB

The decryption algorithm of OFB is exactly the same as the decryption algorithm of the CFB Mode:

First Step (for Cipher-text C_1)

$S_s(X)$: Most significant s Bits of shift register X

Plaintext $= C_1 \oplus S_s\left(E_k(IV)\right)$

$\qquad = P_1 \oplus S_s\left(E_k(IV)\right) \oplus S_s\left(E_k(IV)\right) = P_1$

First Subsequent Steps (for Cipher-text C_I)

Plaintext $= C_i \oplus S_s\left(E_{I-1}(IV)\right)$

$\qquad = P_i \oplus S_s\left(E_{I-1}(IV)\right) \oplus S_s\left(E_{I-1}(IV)\right) = P_i$

6.7.4.4.2 Advantages and Limitations of OFB

The advantages of OFB are:

- Like CFB, OFB mode is also suitable for a stream cipher, and thus has the following advantages of a stream cipher:

  - It eliminates requirement of padding, whereas in the Block Cipher the last block may need padding.

  - Each Character of plaintext can be encrypted and transmitted when ready. On the other end, each character can be decrypted and used immediately on reception. Thus, this mode is suitable for real-time applications.

- Like CFB, it also uses only one algorithm, that is, Encrypt, both at the Sender and the Recipient ends.

- Unlike CFB, if a cipher-text block gets corrupted in transit, it will affect the decryption of only that block of cipher-text and not the subsequent blocks.

- The output feedback for various blocks depends only on the Initial Vector (IV) value and the Secret Key (K) value. It does not depend upon the plaintext or the cipher-text. Thus, the feedback value for subsequent blocks can be pre-processed and kept ready for encryption/decryption. The moment a plaintext or cipher-text block is received, it can be immediately taken up for encryption/decryption. Also, many plaintext blocks may be encrypted, or cipher-text blocks may be decrypted in parallel. Also, a block may be encrypted/decrypted at random out of sequence.

The limitations of OFB are:

- Like the CFB mode, the patterns at the block level are not preserved.

- Any change in the cipher-text affects the plaintext encrypted at the receiver side.

6.7.4.5 Counter (CTR) Mode

The Counter (CTR) Mode is an extremely simple scheme, but it is as secure as other schemes. A Counter, equal in size to the plaintext block-size, is used for Encryption and Decryption. Its value is initialized to the same value on both ends. For each subsequent block of plaintext, the counter value is incremented by one. It uses only the Encrypt Algorithm both at Sender and Receiver ends. CTR mode has no feedback.

6.7.4.5.1 Encryption and Decryption of CTR

Encryption of CTR

CTR uses the encryption function of the underlying block cipher (E_k) for both encipherment and decipherment. The encrypting algorithm needs to wait to get a complete N-bit block of data before encrypting. The relationship between the plaintext and the cipher-text blocks i is given by $C_i = P_i \oplus E_{k_i}$

Figure 6.21 shows the Counter (CTR) Mode encryption.

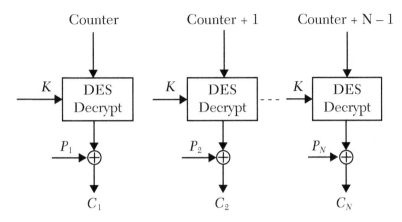

FIGURE 6.21 Counter (CTR) Mode encryption.

Decryption of CTR

The relationship between the plaintext and the cipher-text blocks i is given by the decryption of CTR $P_i = C_i \oplus E_{k_i}$ Figure 6.22 shows the Counter (CTR) Mode decryption.

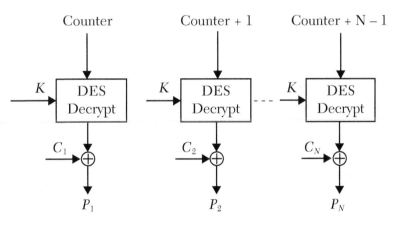

FIGURE 6.22 Counter (CTR) Mode decryption.

6.7.4.5.2 Advantages and Limitations of CTR

The advantages of CTR are:

- *Parallel Processing:*

  In CFB and OFB, the plaintext blocks have to be encrypted sequentially, since feedback from the previous step is required for the encryption/decryption of the next block of plaintext. However, in the counter mode, knowing Block Number (K) of a block, it can be encrypted/decrypted out of sequence by using the Counter Value (Counter $+ K - 1$). This feature enables encryption/decryption of more than one block in parallel. Thus, the processors that support parallel processing can be employed to enhance the encryption/decryption speed tremendously.

- *Pre-processing:*

  The output of Encrypt Algorithms for various values of Counter can be computed in advance and stored in memory (if sufficient memory is available and security of these values can be ensured). These pre-computed values of Encrypt output are then used to encrypt/decrypt a plaintext block much more efficiently.

- *Random Access:*

  Knowing the block number, any block of plaintext can be encrypted and any block of cipher-text can be decrypted randomly.

- *Simplicity:* Unlike the ECB and CBC modes, Counter Mode requires implementation of only the Encrypt Algorithm both for the Encryption and Decryption sides.

- *Provable Security:*

  CTR is at least as secure as the other modes. Due to these advantages, the Counter Mode makes an ideal choice for Asynchronous Transfer Mode (ATM) security and IP Security (IPSec).

The limitations of CTR are:

- The CTR mode, like the ECB mode, cannot be used for real-time processing.

- Like the OFB mode, the patterns at the block level are not preserved.
- Any change in the cipher-text affects the plaintext encrypted at the receiver side.

Comparison of the Block/Stream Cipher Modes of Operation:

Table 6.1 illustrates a comparison of the five different Block/Stream Cipher modes of operations. The size of a block in DES is N and the size of plaintext or a cipher-text block is r.

TABLE 6.1 Comparison of the Five Different Block/Stream Cipher Modes of Operation

Operation Mode	Description	Typical Applications	Type of Result	Data Unit Size
Electronic Code Book (ECB)	Each N-bit block is encrypted independently with the same cipher key	Secure transmission of single values (e.g., encryption key)	Block Cipher	N
Cipher Block Chaining (CBC)	Similar to ECB, except that each block is first XORed with previous cipher-text	General-purpose, block-oriented transmission and for authentication	Block Cipher	N
Cipher Feedback (CFB)	Input is processed s-bit at a time. Proceeding cipher-text is used as input to the encryption algorithm to produce pseudorandom output	General-purpose, block-oriented transmission and for authentication	Stream Cipher	$N \geq r$
Output Feedback (OFB)	Same as CFB, but the input to the encryption algorithm is the preceding DES output	Stream-oriented transmission over noisy channel (e.g., satellite communications)	Stream Cipher	$N \geq r$
Counter (CTR)	Similar to CFB, except that a counter is used instead of a shift register	Parallelizability and obvious correctness	Stream Cipher	N

6.8 INTERNATIONAL DATA ENCRYPTION ALGORITHM (IDEA)

IDEA is a Symmetric Block Cipher developed between 1990–1992. It is now considered as one of the most secure block-cipher algorithms available to the public.

6.8.1 Description of IDEA

IDEA is a Block Cipher, which operates on 64-bit plaintext blocks and uses a 128-bit overall Key.

- The encryption and decryption algorithms are identical, except for the application of sub-keys.

- Each 64-bit plaintext block is divided into 4 sub-blocks X_1, X_2, X_3, and X_4 of 16 bits each. These 4 sub-blocks are input to the first round of the encryption algorithm.

- The 4 sub-blocks of data are repeatedly subjected to the following mathematical operations, which can be easily implemented in hardware as well as software:

  (i)   Modulo $(2^{16} + 1)$ Multiplication

  (ii) Modulo 2^{16} Addition

  (iii) Bit-by-bit XOR

- The encryption/decryption algorithm comprises 8 identical rounds of mathematical operations, followed by one final output-transformation round.

- The algorithm uses a total of 52 sub-keys (16 bits each) generated from the overall 128-bit key. Six sub-keys are used in each of the 8 identical rounds, and the remaining 4 sub-keys are used in the final output-transformation round.

- In each round, the 4 sub-blocks of data are XORed, added, and multiplied with each other and with the 6 sub-keys used in the round. Between the rounds, the middle 2 sub-blocks are swapped with each other.

- Finally, the 4 sub-blocks are subjected to the final output-transformation round, which outputs 4 16-bit sub-blocks of cipher-text.

- The mathematical operations performed in each round are depicted in the schematic diagram in Figure 6.23.

- The following sequence of operations is performed in each round:
  1. Multiply X_1 and the first sub-key
  2. Add X_2 and the second sub-key
  3. Add X_3 and the third sub-key
  4. Multiply X_4 and the fourth sub-key
  5. XOR the results of Steps (1) and (3)
  6. XOR the results of Steps (2) and (4)
  7. Multiply the result of Step (5) with the fifth sub-key
  8. Add the result of Steps (6) and (7)
  9. Multiply the result of Step (8) with the sixth sub-key
  10. Add the results of Steps (7) and (9)
  11. XOR the results of Steps (1) and (9)
  12. XOR the result of Steps (3) and (9)
  13. XOR the result of Steps (2) and (10)
  14. XOR the result of Steps (4) and (10)

- The output of each round comprises the 4 sub-blocks output by steps (11), (12), (13), and (14).

- At the output of each round, the inner 2 blocks are swapped, except in the last round.

- After the last round (Round 8), the 4 sub-blocks go through the final output transformation, with the application of 4 sub-keys Z_1 (9), Z_2 (9), Z_3 (9), and Z_4 (9).

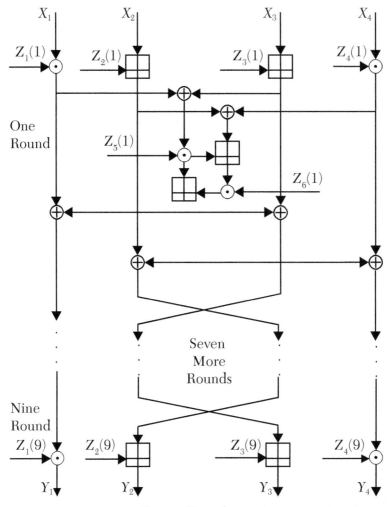

Output Transformation

where X_i: 16-bit plaintext sub-block; Y_i: 16-bit cipher-text sub-block;
Z_i: 16-bit key sub-block

⊕ : Bit-by-bit XOR of two 16-bit sub-blocks

⊞ : Addition modulo 2^{16} of two 16-bit sub-blocks

⊙ : Multiplication modulo $(2^{16} + 1)$ of two 16-bit sub-blocks. All zeroes sub-block is taken as $2^{16} = -1$. Multiplicative Inverse of 0 is taken as 0.

FIGURE 6.23 Mathematical operations performed in each round of the IDEA Encryption process.

6.8.2 Generation of Sub-Keys in IDEA

IDEA encryption/decryption uses 52 sub-keys: Six sub-keys are in each round, and the remaining 4 sub-keys are used in the final output transformation. The sub-keys are generated from the overall 128-bit key as follows:

1. First the 128-bit overall key is divided into 8 16-bit sub-keys. The first six are used in the first round, and the remaining two are used as the first two sub-keys of the second round.

2. Then the 128-bit overall key is rotated left by 25 bits and again divided into 8 16-bit sub-keys. Four are used in the second round, and the remaining 4 are used in the third round.

3. Step (2) is repeated to generate all the remaining sub-keys.

6.8.2.1 Decryption Algorithm in IDEA

The decryption in IDEA is exactly same as encryption, except that the sub-keys are applied as follows:

- The sub-keys applied in decryption are in reverse order vis-à-vis the sub-keys applied in encryption.

- The sub-keys applied to the addition blocks in decryption are the additive inverse of the sub-keys applied to the addition blocks in encryption.

- The sub-keys applied to the multiplication blocks in decryption are multiplicative inverses of the sub-keys applied to the multiplication blocks in encryption.

6.8.2.2 Why is multiplication performed modulo ($2^{16} + 1$)?

- Since the decryption algorithm uses multiplicative inverses of the sub-keys used for multiplication operations in the encryption algorithm, each sub-key must have its multiplicative inverse defined.

- $2^{16} + 1 = 65537$ is a prime number. All integers n $(0 \le n \le 2^{16})$ will have their multiplicative inverses defined except integer value zero.

- To ensure that integer value zero also has its multiplicative inverse defined, this value is taken as $2^{16} = -1$, and $(-1) \mod (2^{16} + 1)$ will be congruent to 2^{16}. Thus, zero will have its multiplicative inverse = $2^{16} = 0$.

- Therefore, all integers n $(0 \leq n \leq 2^{16})$ will have their multiplicative inverses defined, thus making the decryption process feasible.

- Thus, in IDEA, the multiplicative inverse of 0 is 0. (Actually, in Modular Arithmetic, the multiplicative inverse of 0 does not exist.)

6.8.2.3 Speed of IDEA and Strength of IDEA

IDEA implementations are considered to be twice as fast as DES.

IDEA's key size is 128, which is more than twice that of DES. For a Brute Force attack, it would require of the order of 2^{127} encryptions to recover the key. For a chip that can test billions of keys per second, it would take 10^{13} years (longer than the age of universe) to recover the key. An array of 1034 such chips will require a day, but sufficient silicon does not exist on the earth to make 1034 chips. So, brute force is not the way to recover the key.

The designers have done their best to make the algorithm immune to Differential Cryptanalysis. IDEA is claimed to be immune to differential cryptanalysis after the first four rounds.

6.8.3 IDEA Modes of Operation

It can work with any mode of Block Cipher Operation. It is used extensively for encryption of sensitive information such as banking data. It forms part of popular Pretty Good Privacy (PGP) used for the security of e-mails.

6.9 ADVANCED ENCRYPTION STANDARD (AES)

The Advanced Encryption Standard (AES) is a Symmetric Cipher Standard that was adopted by the U.S. Government in 2002 as a replacement for 3-DES.

Major Parameters:

- **Plaintext Block Size**: 128 bits
- **Key Size**: 128 bits (caters to 192-bit and 256-bit key-size also)

- **Number of Rounds**: 10/12/14 (depending on key-size; 10 rounds for 128-bit key-size, 12 rounds for 192-bit key-size, and 14 rounds for 256-bit key-size)

- **Round-Key Size**: 128 bits

6.9.1 Processing of Plaintext

- The processing of input plain text is done in terms of blocks the size of 18 bits.

- A 128-bit (16 bytes) input plaintext is depicted as a 4×4 matrix.

- The input plaintext matrix is copied into a State Matrix the size of 4×4 bytes. The State Matrix is transformed at each round of processing. After the final round of processing, the State Matrix is copied into an Output Matrix of the same size.

- The 128-bit key is also depicted as a matrix the size of 4×4 bytes. The key is expanded into an array of 44 words of 32 bits each. Let the array of 44 expanded keywords be denoted as $W[0], ..., W[43]$.

- The 44 key-words form 11 round keys, each round key comprising 4 words.

- Unlike its predecessor, the Decryption Algorithm in AES is different from the Encryption Algorithm. For each transformation algorithm used in encryption, an inverse algorithm exists that is to be used in decryption to make encryption reversible. Also, the round keys in decryption are input in reverse order vis-à-vis encryption.

- There are 10 rounds of processing in encryption and decryption, as shown in Figure 6.24:

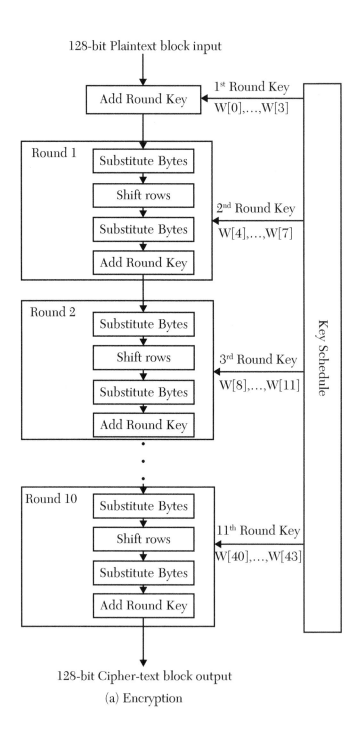

(a) Encryption

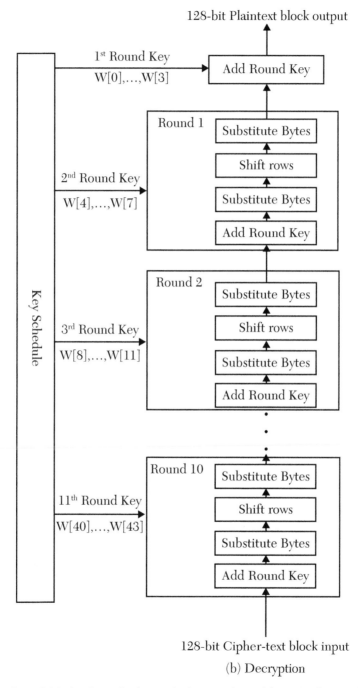

FIGURE 6.24 The 10 rounds of processing in encryption and decryption for AES of 128-bit.

128-Bit Cipher-Text Output

▪ Each round comprises four stages of transformation except Round 10, which comprises only 3 stages of transformation.

▪ Thus, there are four kinds of transformations performed:

- Substitute Bytes

- Shift Rows

- Mix Columns

- Add Round-Key

Each of these four kinds of transformations have two algorithms: Forward and Inverse. The Forward Algorithm is used for encryption and the Inverse Algorithm is used for decryption. Various kinds of transformations are explained as follows:

1. Substitute Bytes:

It uses an S-Box to perform byte substitution. AES defines a 16 × 16 byte S-Box. It contains a permutation of all 256 possible 8-bit values. There are two types of transformations: (a) Forward Substitute Byte Transformation and (b) Inverse Substitute Byte Transformation. The S-Box for Forward Substitute Byte Transformation is constructed as follows:

- Initialize the 256 bytes of the S-Box, with 8-bit values starting from 00, in an ascending sequence row by row. The first row will contain 00, 0l,..., 0F, and the second row will contain 20, 21,..., 2F, and so on. The byte at row x and column y will contain xy.

- Transform the value of each byte to its multiplicative inverse in the finite field GF (2^8) using the irreducible polynomial $m(x) = x^8 + x^4 + x^3 + x + 1$. The byte with value 00 is transformed to 00 itself.

- Let $\{b_0, b_1, b_2, b_3, b_4, b_5, b_6, b_7\}$ denote the 8 bits of a byte. Now, bits of each byte of the S-Box are substituted as follows: $b_i' = b_i \oplus b_{(i+4) \bmod 8} \oplus b_{(i+5) \bmod 8} \oplus b_{(i+6) \bmod 8} \oplus b_{(i+7) \bmod 8} \oplus c_i$ where c_i is the ith bit of byte c with value 63.

- The Foward Substitute Byte Transformation of a byte of data is performed by splitting the data byte into two nibbles. Then the left nibble is used to index into the S-Box rows and the right nibble is used to index into the S-Box columns. The value of the S-Box byte at the intersection of the indexed row and column is used to substitute the data byte. As demonstrated as follows, suppose the data byte before substitution contains value 24. The upper nibble value 2 is used to index into the S-Box rows, and the lower nibble value 4 is used to index into the S-Box columns. The S-Box value at the intersection of row 2 and column 4, that is, 53, is used to substitute the data byte. Thus, the data byte value after substitution becomes 53, as shown in Figure 6.25.

- The Inverse Substitute Byte Transformation is performed by using the Inverse S-Box. The Inverse S-Box is constructed by applying the inverse of the transformation applied in the equation, that is,

$$b_i' = b_{(i+2)\bmod 8} \oplus b_{(i+5)\bmod 8} \oplus b_{(i+7)\bmod 8} \oplus d_i$$

where d_i is the i th bit of byte d with value 05.

- This is followed by taking the multiplicative inverse in the finite field GF (28) using the irreducible polynomial $m(x) = x^8 + x^4 + x^3 + x + 1$. The byte with value 00 is transformed to 00 itself.

2. **"Shift Rows" Transformation**

   - **Forward "Shift Rows" Transformation:** In Forward Shift Row Transformation, the 1st row is not shifted, the 2nd row goes through a one-byte circular left shift, the 3rd row goes through a two-byte circular left shift, and the 4th row goes through a three-byte circular left shift.

   - **Inverse "Shift Rows" Transformation:** In an Inverse Shift Row Transformation, the 1st row is not shifted, the 2nd row goes through a one-byte circular right shift, the 3rd row goes through two bytes circular right shift and the 4th row goes through three bytes circular right shift.

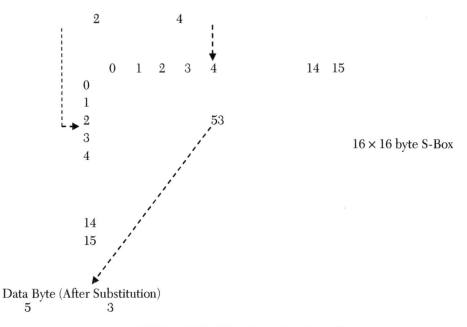

FIGURE 6.25 The AES defines a 16 × 16 byte S-Box.

3. **Forward and Inverse "Mix Columns" Transformations**: Each byte of a column is transformed to a value that is a function of all 4 bytes of that column. This is achieved by Matrix Multiplication on the state. Each element of the product matrix will be the sum of the products of one row and one column. The multiplications and additions are performed in GF (2^8).

4. **Forward and Inverse "Add Round-Key" Transformations:** The Forward and Inverse "Add Round-Key Transformation" is performed by a bit-by-bit XOR of a 128-bit Round-Key with 128-bit data.

Implementation

AES can be efficiently implemented on 8-bit processors for smart cards and on 32-bit processors for PCs. Table 6.2 shows a brief comparison between DES and AES.

TABLE 6.2 Comparison between DES and AES

Parameter	DES	AES
Input Data Size	64-bit	128-bit
Key Size	56-bit	128-bit/192-bit/512-bit
Number of Rounds	16 rounds (Feistel Network)	10/12/14 rounds, depending on key-size (not a Feistel Network)
Round-Key Size	48-bit	128-bit
Number of Round Keys	16	44/52/60; depending on key-size
Symmetry of Encryption and Decryption Algorithms	Yes, only the round keys in decryption are input in reverse order vis-à-vis encryption	No, the encryption and decryption algorithms are different. For each kind of transformation used in encryption, there exists an inverse transformation algorithm to be used in decryption. Also, the round keys in decryption are input in reverse order vis-à-vis encryption

6.10   KEY MANAGEMENT: SYMMETRIC ENCRYPTION

The main issues concerning any Key Management are:

- Secure Distribution of Keys
- Generation of Keys

6.10.1 Secure Distribution of Keys

Key distribution refers to the function of delivering a secret key to two concerned parties without compromising the key. The strength of a cryptographic system lies in a foolproof Key-Distribution Technique. For Symmetric Encryption, two parties exchanging information will share a Secret Key, which must not be known to others. Also, it is advisable to change the keys frequently so as to limit the amount of data that will be compromised in case of a key leak.

The Key distribution to two parties ("A" and "B") can be achieved by any of the following techniques:

- "A" selects a Key and delivers it to "B" physically.
- A trusted third party can select the Key and physically deliver to "A" and "B".

- If "A" and "B" have previously exchanged a master key, a key can be exchanged that is encrypted by the master key. In this case, the issue is "how to exchange the master key securely." Also, if an attacker gets hold of the master key, then all future keys will be compromised.

6.10.2 Key Distribution Schemes

Figure 6.26 illustrates the following key distribution schemes:

- Centralized Key Distribution
- Decentralized Key Distribution

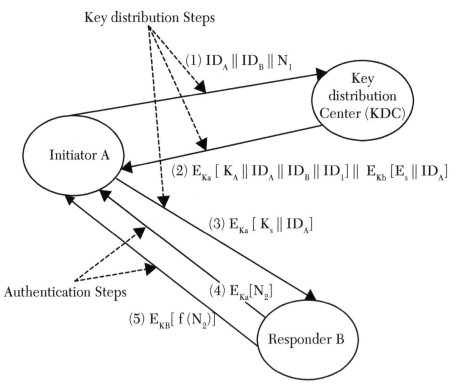

FIGURE 6.26 Key distribution schemes.

There are two kinds of keys:

1. **Master Keys:** A Master Key is shared between a KDC and an end-user. If there are N end-users, then there will be N Master Keys. The

Master Keys are distributed by Non-Cryptographic methods, like physical delivery by secure post.

2. **Session Keys:** Data Communication between end-users is protected using temporary keys called Session Keys. A Session Key for a session between end-user A and end-user B is assigned by the KDC, and its distribution is through cryptographic means. A Session Key, assigned for a session, is used for that session and discarded thereafter.

6.10.2.1 Strength of Encryption Using Master Keys vs. Encryption Using Session Keys

The messages encrypted using master keys are not as safe as the messages encrypted using Session Keys. But since the messages encrypted using Master Keys are normally very short messages, cryptanalysis of such messages is difficult.

The Centralized Key Distribution Scheme operates as follows:

Let us assume that end-user "A" wishes to establish connection with end-user "B" and requires a one-time session key. Let K_a be the Master Key that "A" shares with the KDC. Similarly, let K_b be the Master Key that "B" shares with the KDC. The Distribution of the Session Key would need the following steps:

1. "A" issues a request to the KDC for issue of a Session Key to protect a logical connection to "B." The message includes the identities of "A" and "B" and a unique identifier N_1 called Nonce. The Nonce may be a time-stamp, a counter, or a random number. This message is encrypted using Master Key K_a so that only the KDC can read the message successfully. Also, it verifies that the message has been originated by "A" only.

2. The KDC responds with a message, part of which is encrypted using K_a, the master key shared between KDC and "A." Since it is encrypted using K_a, "A" is the only one who can read it successfully. Also, it verifies that the message has originated at the KDC only. The message includes the following items:

   - **One-time session key K5, assigned for the Session**.

   - **The original Request Message received from "A" and Nonce** N_1. This is echoed back to "A" so as to enable "A" to verify that its original request-message was received by the KDC unaltered. The presence of Nonce in the message provides verification that the message from the KDC is not a replay of some earlier response of the KDC. Thus, it prevents masquerade.

3. The second part of the message is encrypted using K_b, that is, the master key shared between the KDC and "B." It includes the following data items, intended to be delivered to "B." Since it is encrypted K_b, "A" cannot tamper with it.

   • **One-Time Session Key K_s, to be used for the session**

   • **An identifier of W (network address of "A", i.e., ID_A)**

   These data items are to be used by "B" to establish connection with "A."

4. "A" decrypts the portion of the message encrypted with K_a, recovers the session key K_s, and saves it for use in the upcoming session. Since this portion of the message is encrypted using K_a, it is also verified that this message has originated at KDC alone.

5. Also, "A" forwards $E_{kb}[K_s \| ID_A]$ to "B." Because it is encrypted using K_b, only "B" can read it. "B" decrypts the message, recovers the K_s, and saves it for use in next session with "A." Now, "B" has the session key K_s, and also knows the identity of the other party ID_A.

6. Encrypted with session key K_s, "B" sends a Nonce N_2 to "A."

7. "A" responds to "B" $f(N_2)$ encrypted using K_s.

The last two steps are meant to provide mutual authentication between "A" and "B."

Limitations of Centralized Key Control using KDC:

1. The scheme is based on the trust placed by all users in the KDC. The trust may be betrayed.

2. If KDC fails, then the scheme will be rendered non-functional. It is an "all eggs in one basket" situation.

6.10.2.2 Decentralized Key Distribution

The Decentralized Key Control Scheme attempts to obviate the limitations of the Centralized KDC-based Key Distribution Scheme. The

Decentralized Scheme is based on the concept that each end-user must be able to establish secure connection with any other end-user independently. Figure 6.27 illustrates the Decentralized Key distribution schemes.

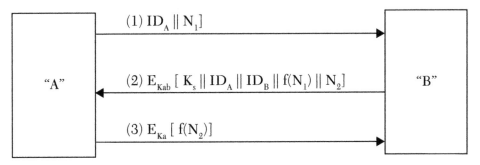

FIGURE 6.27 Decentralized Key distribution schemes.

The steps for a Decentralized Key Distribution Scheme are:

1. "A" issues a Request to "B" for a session key and includes a Nonce N_1. This message is encrypted using Master Key K_{ab} that "A" shares with "B."

2. "B" responds with a message that is encrypted using shared master key K_{ab}. The response includes the following items:
   - Session Key K_s selected by "B"
   - An identifier of "B", that is, "B"'s network address ID_8
   - Value $f(N_1)$
   - Another Nonce N_2

3. Using the new Session Key K_s, "A" returns $f(N_2)$ to "B."

If "A" is the number of End-Users, each Node must maintain $(N-1)$ master keys. Thus, the total number of master keys at any moment would be $\dfrac{N(N-1)}{2}$. So, the total number of Master Keys required in this scheme is much larger as compared to the Centralized Scheme, and their distribution will be a major task.

6.11 PSEUDO-RANDOM NUMBER GENERATORS

A Pseudo-Random Number Generator output must have the following characteristics:

1. **Randomness:** The numbers appearing in the sequence must be random.

2. **Uniform Distribution:** All random numbers in the sequence should have approximately equal frequency of occurrence.

3. **Independence:** It should not be possible to infer a random number from other random numbers in the sequence.

4. **Unpredictability:** It should not be possible to predict the sequence of random numbers.

6.11.1 Pseudo-Random Number Generation (PRNG) Algorithms

- Linear Congruential PRNG (also known as Lehmer's Method)
- Cyclic PRNG
- ANSI X9.17 PRNG
- Blum Blum Shub (BBS) Pseudo-Random Bit Generator
- Output Feedback (OFB) PRNG

i. Lehmer's Algorithm (Linear Congruential Method)

- Choose the following parameters:

    Modulus: q (value determined by range of PRNGs to be generated)

    Multiplier: m ($0 < a < m$)

    Increment: a ($0 \le c < m$)

    Seed: X_0 ($0 \le X_0 < m$)

- The next random numbers are generated as: $X_{n+1} = (mX_n + a) \bmod q$,

    where X_n is the just previous random number generated by the algorithm.

- It will generate random numbers in the range $0...(q-1)$.

- The values of a, m, and q have to be carefully chosen to get a good random number sequence.

  One good choice of values is: $a = 0$, $m = 75$, $q = 2^{31} - 1$.

  Weakness: If an adversary is able to capture a sequence of four consecutive random numbers X_0, X_1, X_2, and X_3, then the adversary can determine the values of a, m, and q by solving the following three equations:

  $$X_1 = (mX_0 + a) \bmod q$$
  $$X_2 = (mX_1 + a) \bmod q$$
  $$X_3 = (mX_2 + a) \bmod q$$

Once these values are known, all future random numbers can be determined.

ii. Cryptographically Generated Random Numbers

A. Cyclic Encryption

This algorithm makes use of a counter which is initialized to C_0 and incremented after generation of each random number.

- If a 56-bit key is to be produced (for DES), a counter period of 2^{56} will need to be used.

- After a random number is produced, the counter is incremented by one. So, the counter value used for each random number generation will be different.

- The counter value is encrypted using a secret master key K. The encrypted value of the counter forms the next Random Number: $X_i = E_k(c + i)$.

- It is not possible for a cryptanalyst to determine the next random number from the knowledge of the previous random number.

Figure 6.28 illustrates the Cryptographically Generated Pseudo-Random Numbers.

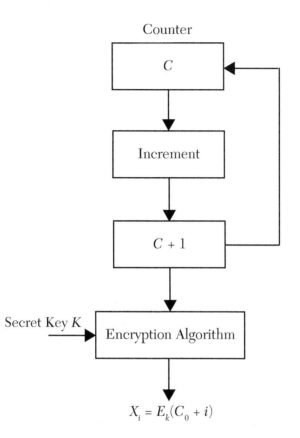

Counter

$$X_i = E_k(C_0 + i)$$

where X_i: i^{th} Pseudo Random Number
C_0: Initial value of counter
K: Secret Encryption Key

FIGURE 6.28 Cryptographically generated pseudo-random numbers.

B. ANSI X9.17 Pseudo-Random Number Generator

This is cryptographically one of the strongest Pseudo-Random Number Generators, which is used in Financial Security applications and in PGP. The ingredients of this algorithm are:

• **Inputs:**

It has two inputs:

– Current date and time DT_i in 64-bit representation. It is updated after each random number generation.

– A 64-bit seed value V_i. It is initialized to some arbitrary value and updated during the generation process.

• **Three Triple-DES Modules EDE**

• **Keys:** It makes use of a pair of 56-bit Secret Keys K_1 and K_2, which are used by all three Triple-DES Modules.

• **Output:** The output comprises 64-bit Pseudo-Random-Number R_i and 64-bit seed value V_{I+1}, to be used for generation of the next random number.

A schematic Diagram of the random number generator is indicated in Figure 6.29 as follows:

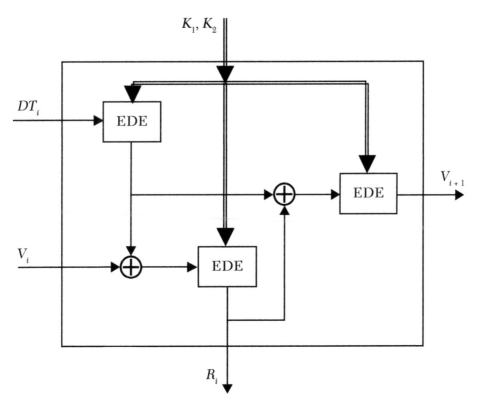

FIGURE 6.29 Schematic diagram of the Random Number Generator.

Strength of ANSI X. 9. 17 PSNG

The value of a pseudo-random number is a function of:

- Secret Keys used in three blocks of 3-DES. As such, 3-DES is considered to be highly secure. The effort required to break a 3-DES cipher is of the order of 2^{112}.

- Current Date-Time value DT_i obtained in real-time from the system. It is extremely difficult to predict its value that existed at the time of generation of a random number.

- A seed V_i, obtained as output during the generation of a previous random number. This number is also difficult to predict.

- Thus, ANSI X.9.17 is considered to be highly secure and used in highly sensitive financial transactions.

iii. Blum Blum Shub (BBS) Pseudo-Random Bit Generator

A Cryptographically Secure Pseudo-Random Bit Generator (CSPRBG), it proceeds as follows:

- Choose two prime numbers p and q such that $p \equiv q \equiv 3 \pmod{4}$. For example, prime numbers 7 and 11 satisfy this condition.

- Compute $n = pq$

- Now choose a random number s, which should be relatively prime to n, that is, s should not have p and q as its factors.

- Then the BBS bit generator produces a series of bits according to the following algorithm:

- $X_0 = s^2 \bmod n$

- For $I = 1$ to μ do

- $X_i = (X_{i-1})^2 \bmod n$

- $B_i = X_i \bmod 2$

- The least significant bit is taken as output at each iteration

- BBS is considered a "Cryptographically Secure Pseudo-Random Bit Generator," since it passes the "Next-Bit Test."

- The "Next-Bit Test" is defined as follows:

A Pseudo-Random Bit Generator algorithm passes the Next-Bit Test if there exists no polynomial time algorithm, that, on the input of the first k bits of its output, can predict the $(K+1)$ st bit with a probability significantly higher than 1/2.

iv. Output Feedback (OFB) Random Number Generator

- The Output Feedback Random Number Generator makes use of a Shift Register the size of, for example, b bits. Normally b equals 64 or 128. Figure 6.30 illustrates the Output Feedback Random Number Generator.

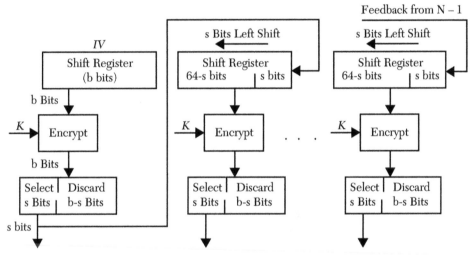

FIGURE 6.30 A Schematic diagram of the Output Feedback Random Number Generator.

- The Shift Register is initialized to a value IV.

- The contents of the Shift Register are encrypted using a secret key K. This encrypted value of the shift register contents forms the next random number.

- After generating a random number, the contents of the shift register are shifted left s bits, and those s bits are filled by copying s bits from the encrypted value of the shift register contents.

- The modified contents of the shift register are used for generating the next random number.

6.12   EXERCISES

1. What is the practical difficulty in the implementation of a simple substitution cipher?

2. Differentiate Confusion and Diffusion as applicable to cryptography. How are they implemented using the Substitution-Permutation Network (SPN) by Feistel Cipher?

3. What are the factors affecting the strength of the Feistel Cipher?

4. What are the non-linear components used in DES encryption/decryption?

5. What is the avalanche effect (as applicable to cipher schemes)? Is it effectively achieved in DES?

6. Differentiate between Differential Cryptanalysis and Linear Cryptanalysis. What is the order of effort required for both?

7. What is the order of effort required to break 2-DES with a "Meet-in-the-Middle" attack?

8. Is 3-DES also prone to a "Meet-in-the-Middle" attack? If so, what is the order of effort required to break 3-DES?

9. What are the merits of Output-Feedback (OFB) as compared to Cipher Feedback (CFB)?

10. What are the characteristics of a good Pseudo-Random Number generator?

11. What makes the ANSI X.9.17 Pseudo-Random Number Generator highly secure? How many blocks of 3-DES are used in this scheme?

12. Why is the BBS Pseudo-Random-Bit-Generator considered Cryptographically Secure?

13. Suppose there are 1 million users in a secure network. What will be the number of Secret Keys required for symmetric encryption in a (i) decentralized key distribution scenario and in a (ii) centralized key distribution scenario?

14. For an 8-bit substitution cipher, determine:

15. Size of the Encryption/Decryption key

16. Number of distinct reversible transformations from plaintext to ciphertext

17. Explain how the effect of Initial Permutation (IP) is undone by the IP-1 function in DES.

18. Using the following S-Box, determine 4-bit outputs for the following 6-bit inputs:

   A. 101101

   B. 110010

   C. 011010

10	00	09	14	06	03	15	05	01	13	12	07	11	04	02	08
13	07	00	09	03	04	06	10	02	08	05	14	12	11	15	01
13	06	04	09	08	15	03	00	11	01	02	12	05	10	14	07
01	10	13	00	06	09	08	07	04	15	14	03	11	05	02	12

19. Explain the arithmetic and logical functions used in IDEA. Compare its strength with DES.

20. Taking the following parameters for Lehmer's Pseudo-Random Number Generator, determine the first 5 Pseudo-Random Numbers:

   A. Send $X_0 = 37$

   B. Multiplier $m = 7$

   C. Increment $a = 13$

   D. Modulus $q = 1023$

21. Taking the following parameters for the Blum Blum Shub (BBS) Pseudo-Random Bit Generator, determine the first 10 bits:

   A. Prime Numbers $(p,q) = (7,11)$

   Seed $s = 31$

   B. Prime Numbers $(p,q) = (11,19)$

   Seed $s = 137$

7

PUBLIC-KEY CRYPTOGRAPHY FOR DATA CONFIDENTIALITY

Chapter Outline

7.1   Introduction

7.2   Requirements of Public-Key Cryptography

7.3   Data Confidentiality Using Public-Key Cryptography

7.4   RSA Algorithm

7.5   Key Management Using Public-Key Cryptography

7.6   El-Gamal Encryption Scheme

7.7   Elliptic Curve Cryptography (ECC)

7.8   Exercises

7.1   INTRODUCTION

Public-Key Cryptography is based on the concept of two keys for each user, that is, a Private Key which is kept secret by the user and a Public Key that is made available to all other users in the cryptosystem. Though both keys belonging to a user are related to each other, one cannot determine the Private Key of another user by knowing its related Public Key.

7.2   REQUIREMENTS OF PUBLIC-KEY CRYPTOGRAPHY

1. Each user generates a pair of keys; for example, a user "N" may generate Public Key "PU_A" and Private Key "PR_A".

2. The Private Key "PR_A" is kept private (secret) by the user "A," and the Public Key "PU_A" is made available to all other users in the cryptosystem.

3. A Public Key "PU_A" can be easily obtained by adversaries. Though the Private Key "PR_A" is related to the Public Key "PU_A," by just knowing the Public Key "PU_A" it is computationally infeasible to generate Private Key "PR_A". Thus, an adversary will not be able to determine the Private Key from the Public Key.

4. The Encryption/Decryption of a message can be performed by using a companion key-pair (PU_A, "PR_A") in any order. This implies that if a message is encrypted using Public Key "PU_A," then it can be decrypted by using Private Key "PR_A; " and if a message is encrypted using Private Key "PR_A," then it can be decrypted using companion Public Key "PU_A."

7.3 DATA CONFIDENTIALITY USING PUBLIC-KEY CRYPTOGRAPHY

1. Any user (say User "B") sending a secure Message "M" to user "X" encrypts the message using N's Public Key and then transmits the resulting cipher-text to user "X."

   $$C = EruA[M]$$

2. At the recipient end, the user "X" can easily decrypt the cipher-text "C" using its Private Key "PR_A."

   $$M = DrRA\left[EruA[M]\right]$$

3. It is computationally infeasible for an adversary, knowing the Cipher-text 1C and Public Key"PU_A," to decrypt "C" (which has been generated using Public Key "PU_A"). Even the sender cannot decrypt "C."

7.4 RSA ALGORITHM

- It is a Public Key Algorithm that was developed in 1997 by a team of three computer scientists from MIT. It is named after its developers, Rivest, Shamir, and Adleman (popularly known as RSA).

- The algorithm can be used for data confidentiality as well as for digitally signing the messages to assure source authentication, data integrity, and source non-repudiation.

- The strength of the algorithm lies in the extent of difficulty encountered in factoring a large composite number into its prime factors.

7.4.1 Main Components

- Determination of Keys

- Encryption Algorithm

- Decryption Algorithm

7.4.1.1 Determination of Keys

A User (Say User "A") computes its Private Key and Public Key as follows:

- Choose two large prime numbers "p" and "q." (The larger the prime numbers, the more difficult it would be to break the cipher.)

- Compute $n = pq$

- Compute $\Phi(n) = (p-1)(q-1)$

- Choose an integer "e" such that e is less than $\Phi(n)$ and relatively prime to $\Phi(n)$, that is, $GCD = (e, \Phi(n)) = 1$. Note that e will always be odd, since $\Phi(n)$ is even.

- Compute integer "d" as the multiplicative inverse of $e \bmod \Phi(n)$:

$$d = e^{-1} \bmod \Phi(n)$$

Thus, "e" and "d" form multiplicative inverses of each other $(\bmod \Phi(n))$.

- The pair (e, n) forms the Public Key of the user "A," which is made public and distributed to other users in the cryptosystem.

- The pair (d, n) forms the Private Key of the user "A," which "A" keeps secret; it is not known to anyone except "A."

7.4.1.2 Encryption Algorithm

If any user in the cryptosystem (say User "B") intends to send a message $M(0 \leq M < n)$ to user "A," then "B" encrypts the message using A's Public Key (e, n) and sends the resulting cipher-text "C" to user "A:"

$$C = M^e \bmod n$$

7.4.1.3 Decryption Algorithm

User "A" receives the cipher-text "C" and recovers the message "M" by decrypting it using its own Private Key (d, n):

$$M = C^d \bmod n$$

Prove that the Decrypted Value of a cipher-text at the recipient end is an exact copy of the plaintext encrypted at the sender end.

Proof

Decrypted Value $= C^d \bmod n$

$$= \left(M^e \bmod n\right)^d \bmod n$$

$$= M^{ed} \bmod n$$

Since, $d \equiv e^{-1} \bmod \Phi(n)$

$\therefore ed = 1 \bmod \Phi(n)$

$\therefore ed = k\Phi(n) + 1$; for some integer "$k$"

$\therefore$ Decrypted Value at the recipient $end = M^{ed} \bmod n$

$$= \left(M^{k\Phi(n)+1}\right) \bmod n$$

Now, we need to prove that $\left(M^{k\Phi(n)+1}\right) \bmod n = M$

The value of "M" has two possibilities:

- Case 1: M relatively prime to n, that is, $GCD(M,n) = 1$
- Case 2: M not relatively prime to n, that is, $GCD(M,n) \neq 1$

Case 1:

$GCD(M,n) = 1$, that is, M is relatively prime to n.

Then, $M^{\Phi(n)} = (1) \bmod n$ (by Euler's Theorem)

Raising both sides of the congruence to power "k":

$\therefore M^{k\Phi(n)} \equiv (1) k \bmod n$

$\qquad \equiv (1) \bmod n$

Multiplying both sides by M:

$\therefore M^{(k\Phi(n)+1)} = M \bmod n = M$

Case 2:

$GCD(M,n) \neq 1$, that is, M is not relatively prime to n.

Under this condition, there are two possibilities:

1. M not relatively prime to p. Since M cannot have both p and q as its factors, M will be relatively prime to q, that is, $GCD(M,q)=1$

2. M not relatively prime to q. Therefore, M will be relatively prime to q, that is, $GCD(M,q)=1$

Case 2(a):

Since M is relatively prime to q

$\therefore M^{\Phi(q)} = (1)\bmod q$ (by Fermat's Theorem)

Raising both sides of the above congruence to power $k\Phi(p)$

$\left[M^{\Phi(q)} \right]^{k\Phi(p)} \equiv (1)^{k\Phi(p)} \bmod q$ (for some integer k)

$M^{\Phi(q)k\Phi(p)} \equiv (1)\bmod q$

$M^{k\Phi(n)} \equiv (1)\bmod q$

For some integer j, we will have

$M^{k\Phi(n)} = jq + 1$

Multiplying both sides of the above congruence by $M = cp$

$M^{(k\Phi(n)+1)} = jcpq + cp = jcn + M$

$\therefore M^{(k\Phi(n)+1)} = M \bmod n = M$

Case 2(b):

q divides M, and $GCD(M,p)=1$

Proof is similar to Case 2(a).

Example 7.1: (RSA)

Let $p = 11$, $q = 23$

$N = p \times q = 11 \times 23 = 253$

$\Phi(n) = (p-1)(q-1) = 10 \times 22 = 220$

Choose $e = 13$ which is less than $\Phi(n)$ and relatively prime to $\Phi(n)$.

Then $d = e^{-1} \bmod \Phi(n)$

$d = 13^{-1} \bmod 220 = 17$

Public Key $= (e,n) = (13,253)$

Private Key $= (d,n) = (17,253)$

Suppose a Message $M = 2$ to be sent by another user to this user.

$C = M^e \bmod n$

$\quad = 2^{13} \bmod 253$

$\quad = 8192 \bmod 253 = 96$

$M = C^d \bmod n$

$\quad = 96^{17} \bmod 253$

$\quad = \left(\left(96^3 \bmod 253 \right) \times \left(96^3 \bmod 253 \right) \times \left(96^3 \bmod 253 \right) \right.$

$\qquad \left. \times \left(96^3 \bmod 253 \right) \times \left(96^3 \bmod 253 \right) \times \left(96^2 \bmod 253 \right) \right) \bmod 253$

Now,

$96^3 \bmod 253 = 884736 \bmod 253 = 248$

$96^2 \bmod 253 = 9216 \bmod 253 = 108$

$\therefore M = \left(248^5 \times 108 \right) \bmod 253 \therefore .$

$\quad = \left(\left(248^2 \bmod 253 \right) \left(248^2 \bmod 253 \right) \times 248 \times 108 \right) \bmod 253$

$\quad = \left(\left(61504 \bmod 253 \right) \left(61504 \bmod 253 \right) \times 248 \times 108 \right) \bmod 253$

$\quad = \left(25 \times 25 \times 248 \times 108 \right) \bmod 253$

$\quad = \left(16740000 \right) \bmod 253 = 2$

We are able to extract the original message $M = 2$.

7.4.2 Strength of RSA

Knowing Public Key (e, n) and plaintext M, it is easy to compute Cipher-text $C = M^e \bmod n$ but knowing C and Public Key (e, n), it is computationally very difficult to determine $M = \log_e C (\bmod n)$. Thus, even if an adversary intercepts a cipher-text, it would be computationally infeasible to extract M without knowledge of the related Public Key (d, n).

To determine the Private Key (d, n) from the knowledge of Public Key (e, n), the adversary has to follow the following approach.

- Factorize modulus n into its prime factors p and q
- Determine $\Phi(n) = (p-1)(q-1)$
- Determine $d \equiv e^{-1} \bmod \Phi(n)$

Since the prime factors of modulus n are chosen to be very high, factorizing n is considered to be computationally infeasible. For n having 1024 bits (or 309 digits), it is considered computationally infeasible to factor it into primes p and q. To make it more robust, the following steps are recommended:

1. The primes p and q should differ in length only by a few digits. Thus, for a 1024-bit (309 digits) key, both p and q should be of the order of 10^{75} to 10^{100}.

2. Both $(p-1)$ and $(q-1)$ should contain a large prime factor.

3. $GCD(p-1, q-1)$ should be small.

7.4.2.1 Different Types of Attacks on RSA

RSA is prone to the following types of attacks:

1. **Attempt to Determine Private Key without Knowledge of Prime Factors p and q of Modulus n**.

   To determine the Private Key of a third party, an adversary may follow any of the following approaches:

   a. – Factoring n into primes p and q

   – Determining $\Phi(n) = (p-1)(q-1)$

   – Computing $d \equiv e^{-1} \bmod \Phi(n)$

   For a large n (typical size of n is 1024 bits or 309 decimal digits), factoring it into p and q is highly time-consuming. For 155 decimal digits, the factoring effort is estimated to be 8000 MIPS-Years.

   b. Determining $\Phi(n)$ directly, without determining p and q, and then determining

   $d \equiv e^{-1} \bmod \Phi(n)$

   c. Attempt to determine directly, without determining $\Phi(n)$.

2. Common Modulus Attack on RSA.

A plaintext M is encrypted using RSA and two Public Keys (n, e) and (n, f) such that $GCD(e, f) = 1$. It produces cipher-texts C_e and C_f.

$$C_e = M^e \bmod n$$

$$C_f = M^f \bmod n$$

The attacker can determine the plaintext without determining $\Phi(n)$.

Solution: This attack is known as a "Common Modulus Attack." Basically, it is a "Cipher-Text-Only" Attack, used to determine the Plaintext without determining $\Phi(n)$, as follows:

Let $re + sf = 1$ (for some integers r and s)   (7.1)

$re = 1 - sf$

$\qquad = 1 + (-s) f$

$\therefore re = (1) \bmod f$

Since $GCD(e, f) = 1$

Therefore, r is the multiplicative inverse of $e \bmod f$.

Determine r using the Extended Euclidean Algorithm.

It is determined by substituting the value of r in (7.1).

Then, determine plaintext $M = \left((C_e)^r (C_f)^s \right) \bmod n$

$\qquad$ Since $\left((C_e)^r (C_f)^s \right) \bmod n = \left(M^{er} \times M^{sf} \right) \bmod n$

$\qquad\qquad\qquad = \left(M^{(er+sf)} \right) \bmod n$

$\qquad\qquad\qquad = M \bmod n = M$

Example 7.2 (Common Modulus Attack on RSA)

Let $p = 7$ and $q = 11$

RSA modulus $n = p \times q = 7 \times 11 = 77$

Let the two RSA exponents be $e = 13$ and $f = 17$

$GCD = (13, 17) = 1$

Let message $M = 2$

$$C_e = M^e \bmod n$$

$$C_e = (2)^{13} \bmod 77 = \left((2)^{10} \times 8\right) \bmod 77 = (1024 \times 8) \bmod 77$$

$$= (8192) \bmod 77 = 30$$

$$C_f = M^f \bmod n$$

$$C_f = (2)^{17} \bmod 77 = \left((2)^{10} \times 128\right) \bmod 77 = (1024 \times 128) \bmod 77$$

$$= (131072) \bmod 77 = 18$$

Let $r \times e + s \times f = 1$

For some integers r and s

$$r \times e = (1) \bmod f$$

$$r \times 13 = (1) \bmod 17)$$

Determine "r," that is, the multiplicative inverse of $(13) \bmod 17$ using the Extended Euclidean Algorithm.

(1, 0, 17)	(0, 1, 13)	(1, −1, 4)	1
(0, 1, 13)	(1, −1, 4)	(−3, 4, 1)	3

$$\therefore r = 4$$

Substituting the value of "r" in (7.1)

$$4 \times 13 + s \times 17 = 1$$

$$\therefore s = \frac{(-51)}{17} = -3$$

Now computing $M = \left((C_e)^r (C_f)^s\right) \bmod n$

$$= \left((30)^4 (18)^{-3}\right) \bmod 77$$

$$= \left((30)^4 \left((18)^{-1}\right)^3\right) \bmod 77$$

Determine $(18)^{-1} \bmod 77$ using the "Extended Euclidean Algorithm."

(1, 0, 77)	(0, 1, 18)	(1, −4, 5)	4
(0, 1, 18)	(1, −4, 5)	(−3, 13, 3)	3
(1, −4, 5)	(−3, 13, 3)	(4, −17, 2)	1
(−3, 13, 3)	(4, −17, 2)	(−7, 30, 1)	1

$$\therefore (18)^{-1} \bmod 77 = 30$$

$$\therefore M = \left((30)^7\right) \bmod 77$$

$$= \left(\left((30)^2\right)^2 \times (30)^2 \times (30)\right) \bmod 77$$

$$= \left((900)^2 \times 900 \times 30\right) \bmod 77$$

$$= (21870000000) \bmod 77$$

$$= 2$$

Thus, it is possible to extract M from C_e and C_f without determining $\Phi(n)$. This attack is called a "Common Modulus Attack." This is possible if same message is encrypted with different Public Keys, relatively prime to each other, and the modulus for both is the same.

3. **Digital Signature (Using the RSA Algorithm)**

   User "A" can Encrypt a message $X(0 < X < n)$ by using its Private Key (d, n).

   $$Y = X^d \bmod n Y$$

   The cipher-text Y can be decrypted by a recipient by using the Public Key (e, n) of "A."

   $$Y \bmod n = \left(X^d \bmod n\right)^e \bmod n$$

   $$= X^{ed} \bmod n$$

   $$= X \bmod n$$

   $$= X \text{ (Original Plaintext message)}$$

7.5 KEY MANAGEMENT USING PUBLIC-KEY CRYPTOGRAPHY

7.5.1 Diffie-Hellman Algorithm for Key Distribution

This algorithm facilitates the exchange of a secret key securely among users. The key can be subsequently used for encryption/decryption of messages using a symmetric cipher.

The effectiveness of the algorithm depends on the difficulty of computing discrete logarithms.

7.5.2 Global Parameters

The Diffie-Hellman Key Exchange Algorithm makes use of two global parameters that are made public among the users:

1. A large prime number p and

2. A primitive root g of p.

If two users "A" and "B" wish to exchange a secret key, they proceed as follows:

User A:

1. Chooses a random number $X_A \left(0 < X_A < \Phi(p) \right)$
2. Computes $Y_A = g^{X_A} \bmod p$
3. Keeps X_A secret and transmits Y_A to User "B."

On receiving the message from "A," User "B" responds as follows:

User B:

4. Chooses a random number $X_B \left(0 < X_B < p-1 \right)$
5. Computes $Y_B = g^{X_B} \bmod p$
6. Keeps X_B secret and transmits Y_B to user "A."

User A:

7. Now user "A" computes the key $K_A = \left(Y_B \right)^{X_A} \bmod p$

User B:

8. Similarly, user "B" computes the key $K_B = \left(Y_A \right)^{X_B} \bmod p$

The Diffie-Hellman Algorithm can be better represented as follows in Figure 7.1.

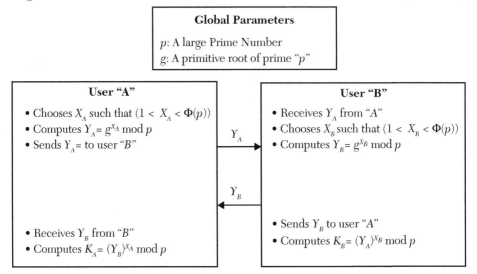

FIGURE 7.1 A schematic diagram of the Diffie-Hellman Algorithm.

Example 7.3

Prove that the keys K_A and K_B computed by users "A" and "B," respectively, are equal.

Solution:

The Proof is as follows:

$$K_A = \left(Y_B\right)^{X_A} \bmod p$$

$$= \left(g^{X_B} \bmod p\right)^{X_A} \bmod p$$

$$= \left(g^{X_B X_A}\right) \bmod p$$

$$= \left(g^{X_A} \bmod p\right)^{X_B} \bmod p$$

$$= \left(Y_A\right)^{X_B} \bmod p$$

$$= K_B$$

7.5.3 Strength of Diffie-Hellman Key-Exchange Scheme

- An adversary will have access to global parameters p and g. Also, it can intercept Y_A and Y_B from the communication media.

- But, for determining K, the previous parameters are not sufficient. The adversary needs either X_A or X_B. But these parameters are kept secret by "A" and "B," respectively. And, if p is sufficiently large, then determining X_A from Y_A or determining X_B from Y_B is considered computationally infeasible.

- Thus, it is considered computationally infeasible for an adversary to compute the common key K without knowledge of either X_A or X_B.

Example 7.4

Let

$$p = 7,\ g = 3 \ \text{(a primitive root of 7)}.$$

Let

$$X_A = 3,\ X_B = 5$$

Now,

$$Y_A = (g)^{X_A} \bmod p$$
$$= (3)^3 \bmod 7$$
$$= 6$$

And

$$Y_B = (g)^{X_B} \bmod p$$
$$= (3)^5 \bmod 7$$
$$= 5$$

$$K_A = (Y_B)^{X_A} \bmod p = (5)^3 \bmod 7 = 125 \bmod 7 = 6$$
$$K_B = (Y_A)^{X_B} \bmod p = (6)^5 \bmod 7 = (7776) \bmod 7 = 6$$

7.5.4 Types of Attacks against Diffie-Hellman

- Clogging Attack
- Man-in-the-Middle Attack

7.5.4.1 Clogging Attack

An adversary may initiate many key-exchange requests, one after another, forcing the victim to perform costly computations. This may computationally clog the victim.

7.5.4.2 Man-in-the-Middle Attack on Diffie-Hellman Key-Exchange Algorithm

- This attack is based on the assumption that the adversary is capable of intercepting the communications.

- Suppose there are two Users "A" and "B" who want to exchange a Secret Key, and "C" is an adversary capable of intercepting the communications between "A" and "B." Here C is the man in the middle.

- Then the adversary can perform the "Man-in-the-Middle Attack" as follows:

  - User "A" computes Y_A and sends it to B with the aim of initiating Key-Exchange with B.

  - Adversary "C" intercepts the value Y_A and responds to A's request masquerading as B, and exchanges a key K_A with User "A". The user "A" wrongly considers that it has exchanged the key K_A with User "B."

  - Also, Adversary "C" sends key-exchange request to User "B" masquerading as User "A."

  - User B responds to the request as if it is responding to a valid request from User "A," and wrongly exchanges a key K_B with "C."

  - At this stage, the Adversary "C" has exchanged key K_A with User "A" and K_B with User "B." The Users "A" and "B" wrongly assume that they have exchanged the keys with each other.

  - Now, when User "A" sends a message M encrypted with key K_A to User "B," C can intercept it, decrypt the cipher-text using key K_A, modify the plaintext message from M to M', encrypt it using key K_B, and send it to User "B" masquerading as User "A." The User "B" will wrongly believe that the message has been sent by User "A."

The scheme can be better explained by the following schematic in Figure 7.2.

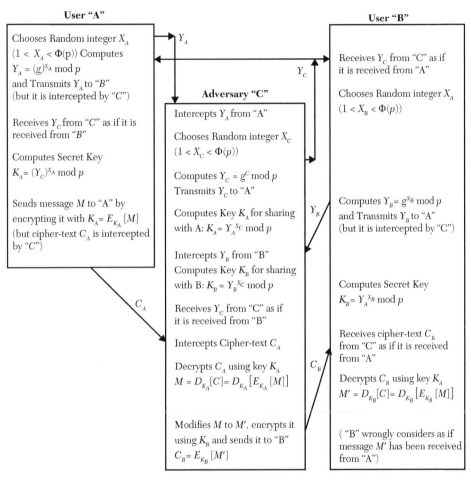

FIGURE 7.2 A schematic diagram of the Man-in-the-Middle Attack.

7.6 EL-GAMAL ENCRYPTION SCHEME

This El-Gama Encryption Scheme depends for its effectiveness on the difficulty of computing discrete logarithms. It is a Public-Key Encryption Scheme, wherein each user has a Public Key, which is distributed to all Users, and a Private Key, which is kept secret.

7.6.1 Determination of Private Key and Public Key (by User "A")

1. Choose a large prime number p such that $\Phi(p)$ has a large prime factor.

2. Choose g: a primitive root of p

3. Choose an integer x such that $1 < x < \Phi(p)$.

4. Compute $y = g^x \bmod p$.

5. The triplet (x, g, p) forms the Private Key and the triplet (y, g, p) forms the Public Key of User "A".

6. User "A" keeps the Private Key (x, g, p) secret and makes the Public Key (y, g, p) available to all those users with whom "A" intends to communicate.

7.6.1.1 Encryption

When any user (User "B") possessing N Public Key (y, g, p) intends to send a message $M\ (0 \le M < p)$ to User "A," User "B" proceeds as follows:

1. Choose a random integer k such that $1 < k < \Phi(p)$.

2. Knowing Public Key (y, g, p) of intended recipient "A," User "B" computes the cipher-text, which comprises a pair of integers:

$$\left(g^k \bmod p, M\left(y^k\right)\bmod p\right)$$

3. User "B" transmits the cipher-text to the intended recipient, User "A."

The first component of the cipher-text, that is, $g^k \bmod p$, is called *Clue*. It contains a clue of the random value k, which is not known to the intended recipient of the cipher-text. The intended recipient will use the clue for the extraction of plaintext from the second component of the cipher-text.

7.6.1.2 Decryption

User "A" receives the cipher-text $\left(g^k \bmod p, M\left(y^k\right)\bmod p\right)$.

"A" proceeds to decrypt the received cipher-text using its Private Key (x, g, p).

1. Compute $(-x)\bmod \Phi(p) = \Phi(p) - x = p - 1 - x$

2. Compute $\left(g^k \bmod p\right)^s \bmod \Phi(p)\bmod p = g^{kx} \bmod p$

3. Compute $M = \left(\left(M\left(y^k\right)\bmod p\right)\times\left(g^{-kx}\bmod p\right)\right)\bmod p$

Example 7.5

Prove that the message received at the recipient end is the same as the message sent.

Solution:

The Proof is as follows:

The message decrypted at

$$\begin{aligned}
\text{the recipient end} &= \left(\left(M\left(y^{k}\right)\bmod p\right)\times\left(g^{-kx}\bmod p\right)\right)\bmod p \\
&= \left(\left(M\left(g^{kx}\right)\bmod p\right)\times\left(g^{-kx}\bmod p\right)\right)\bmod p \\
&= M\left(g^{kx}g^{-kx}\right)\bmod p \\
&= M\bmod p \\
&= M\ (\text{Same as the message sent})
\end{aligned}$$

Thus, the recipient is able to extract the original plaintext message M from the received cipher-text.

Example 7.6 (El-Gamal)

Suppose a user "A" computes its private and Public Keys as follows:

1. Determination of Public Key and Private Key

   Let $p=11$; $g=2$

   Let $x=5$

   $y=g^{x}\bmod p=\left(2\right)^{5}\bmod 11=\left(32\right)\bmod 11=10$

   Thus, "A's" Private Key $=\left(x,g,p\right)=\left(5,2,11\right)$

   And "A's" Public Key $=\left(y,g,p\right)=\left(10,2,11\right)$

2. Encryption

   If a user "B" wants to send message $M=3$ to "A," then "B" will encrypt M as follows and transmit C to "A":

   "B" will select an integer k such that $\left(0<k<\Phi(p)\right)$

   Let $k=7$

   $C=\left(g^{k}\bmod p,M\left(y^{k}\right)\bmod p\right)=\left(\left(2\right)^{7}\bmod 11,3\times\left(10\right)^{7}\bmod 11\right)$

$$= \left(128\,\mathrm{mod}\,11, 3 \times (10)^7 \,\mathrm{mod}\,11\right)$$

$$= \left(128\,\mathrm{mod}\,11, (100 \times 100 \times 100 \times 30)\,\mathrm{mod}\,11\right)$$

$$= (7, 8)$$

3. Decryption

   Knowing (x, g, p), user "A" will decrypt the cipher-text C as follows:

   A. Compute $(-x)\,\mathrm{mod}\,\Phi(p) = (-x)\,\mathrm{mod}\,10 = 10 - x = 10 - 5 = 5$

   B. Compute $\left(g^k\right)^{-x}\,\mathrm{mod}\,p = (7)^5\,\mathrm{mod}\,11 = (49 \times 49 \times 7)\,\mathrm{mod}\,11$

   $$= (5 \times 5 \times 7)\,\mathrm{mod}\,11 = 10$$

   C. Compute $\left(M \times (y)^k \times (g)^{-xk}\right)\mathrm{mod}\,p = (8 \times 10)\,\mathrm{mod}\,11$

   $$= 3 = M \text{ (Original Message)}$$

7.7 ELLIPTIC CURVE CRYPTOGRAPHY (ECC)

Elliptic Curve Cryptography (ECC) makes use of Elliptic Curves that draw values for their variables and coefficients from finite fields. It is a futuristic technology for Public Key Cryptography. The older technologies like RSA require exceedingly large key-sizes to provide desired levels of security. Larger key sizes result in higher overheads for Encryption/Decryption. The ECC promises to provide the same levels of security with much smaller key sizes, thus with much lower overheads. The U.S. National Security Agency has already endorsed the ECC technology for the protection of classified information up to Top Secret, with a key-size of 384 bits.

7.7.1 Elliptic Curves

Mathematically, an Elliptic Curve is expressed by a quadratic equation of the form:

$$y^2 = x^3 + ax + b$$

where "x" and "y" are variables and "a" and "b" are coefficients.

The Elliptic Curve is represented by the set of (x, y) pairs that satisfies the previous quadratic equation. There will be an infinite set of (x, y) pairs satisfying the quadratic equation. The set also includes a point at infinity, called the zero point. The complete set of points forms an abelian group, with the point at infinity forming the identity element.

Letting $a = 1$ and $b = 1$, the Curve described by $y^2 = x^3 + ax + b$ is given in Figure 7.3:

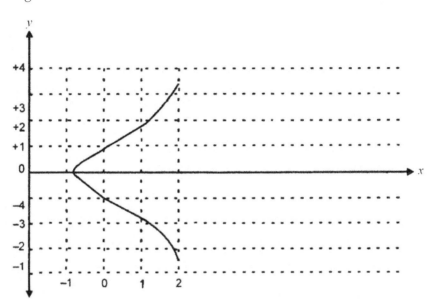

FIGURE 7.3 A schematic diagram of an elliptic curve $y^2 = x^3 + ax + b$.

7.7.2 Elliptic Curves in Cryptography (ECC)

The ECC makes use of Elliptic Curves with finite sets. The ECC quadratic equations draw the values of their variables and coefficients from a finite set of integers.

There are two types of Elliptic Curves used in Cryptography:

1. **Prime Curves**: A prime curve is defined over a prime field $Z_p = \{0, 1, 2,..., (p - 1)\}$ where p is a large prime number.

    A Prime Curve makes use of a quadratic congruence, whose variables and coefficients draw their values from the set of residues (mod p), that is, Z_p where p is a prime number.

2. **Binary Curves**: A Binary Curve is defined over Galois Field (GF) (2^n) where n is an integer. It is a finite field with (2^n) values.

7.7.3 Prime Elliptic Curves

Let $Z_p = \{0, 1, 2,\ldots, (p-1)\}$ where p is a prime number.

A cubic congruence of the following form is used, whose variables x and y and coefficients a and b draw their values from Z_p.

$$y^2 \equiv \left(x^3 + ax + b\right)\bmod p \tag{7.2}$$

7.7.4 Prime Elliptic Curve Set

- A Prime Elliptic Curve Set $E_p\ (a, b)$ is the set of all (x, y) pairs of non-negative integers that satisfy, p, the congruence (7.2).

- The set represents a finite set of points occurring on the Elliptic Curve $E_p\ (a, b)$). It also includes a p point O (point at infinity), called the zero point.

- If $(x^3 + ax + b)$ does not have any repeated factor, then the set $E_p\ (a, b)$ forms an Abelian Group with respect addition (+) operation, with O as an Additive Identity Element.

Example 7.7

Let us consider an elliptic curve defined by the equation:

$$y^2 \equiv \left(x^3 + x + 1\right)\bmod 11$$

y	y^2
0	0
1	1
2	4
3	9
4	5
5	3
6	3
7	5
8	9
9	4
10	1

Here $p = 11$, $a = 1$, $b = 1$.

7.7.5 Computation of Elliptic Curve Set E_{11} (1, 1)

x	y^2	y
0	1	1 10
1	3	5 6
2	0	0
3	9	3 8
4	3	5 6
5	10	–
6	3	5 6
7	10	–
8	4	2 9
9	2	–
10	10	–

$\therefore$ Elliptic Curve Set $E_{11}(1,1)$:

x	y
0	1 10 (−1)
1	5 6 (−5)
2	0
3	3 8 (−3)
4	5 6 (−5)
6	5 6 (−5)
8	2 9 (−2)
O	

The number of points N in $E_p(a, b)$ is bounded by:

$$(p+1) - 2\sqrt{p} \leq N \leq (p+1) + 2\sqrt{p}$$

For a large p, $2\sqrt{p}$ will be insignificant as compared to p.

$$\therefore N\sqrt{p}$$

7.7.6 Rules for Addition (+) Operation over E_p (a, b)

Let P, Q be the points in $E_p(a, b)$), such that $P : (x_P, y_P)$ and $Q : (q_P, q_P)$

The addition operation within $E_p(a, b)$ follows the following rules:

1. O is an additive Identity element.
    $$\therefore P + O = P$$

2. $(-P) = (x_P, -y_P)$ will form the additive inverse of P.
    $$\therefore P + (-P) = O$$

3. $R = (P + Q) = (x_R, y_R)$ will be a point from the Elliptic Cover Set $E_p(a, b)$).
    The (x_R, y_R) coordinates of point R are determined as follows:

    $$x_R = \left(\lambda^2 - x_P - x_Q\right) \bmod p \quad y_R = \left(\lambda\left(x_P - x_R\right) - y_P\right) \bmod p$$

    where $\lambda = \left(\dfrac{\left(y_Q - y_P\right)}{\left(x_Q - x_P\right)}\right) \bmod p$, if $P \neq Q$

    $$\lambda = \left(\dfrac{\left(3x_P^2 + a\right)}{2y_P}\right) \bmod p, \text{ if } P = Q$$

Special Case

Suppose $P = (x_P, 0)$, and $(-P) = (x_P, 0)$.

Then, $2P$ is defined as $2P = P + P = P + (-P) = O$

7.7.7 Multiplication over the Set E_p (a, b)

The multiplication kP (where $P \in E_p(a, b)$ and k is an integer) is defined as the repeated addition of P, k-times:

$$kP = P + P + P + \cdots \text{ (k times)}$$

......

Order of a Point G

- Let G be a point in the set $E_p(a, b)$.
- The order of a point G is defined as the least integer n that satisfies $nG = O$.
- Then set $\{G, 2G, \ldots, nG\}$ represents a set of distinct points from $E_p(a, b)$.

Base Point

- In an ECC-based Crypto Scheme, a point $G \in E_p(a,b)$ is chosen as a Base Point.
- The Base Point is so chosen that its Order should be very high.
- This would make the set of distinct points $\{G, 2G, \ldots, nG\}$ very large; this set forms the cipher-text space of the ECC Scheme.
- The larger the cipher-text space, the more secure the ECC Scheme will be.

Example 7.8

Determine Order of Point $P = (0,6)$ in Elliptic Curve Set $E_7(1,1)$

Solution:

Here $a = 1, b = 1, p = 1$

$E_7(1, 1) = \{(0, 1), (0, 6), (2, 2), (2, 5), O\}\ P = (0, 6)$

To determine $2P = P + P$:

$$\lambda = \left(\frac{(3 \times 0 + 1)}{2 \times 6}\right) \bmod 7 = \left(\frac{1}{12}\right) \bmod 7$$

$$\lambda = (1 \times 12 - 1) \bmod 7 = (1 \times 3) \bmod 7 = 3$$

$$x_R = \left(\lambda^2 - x_P - x_Q\right) \bmod p = (9 - 0 - 0) \bmod 7 = 2$$

$$y_R = \left(\lambda\left(x_P - x_Q\right) - y_P\right) \bmod p = (3(0 - 2) - 6) \bmod 7 = (-12) \bmod 7 = 2.$$

$\therefore 2P = (2,2)$, which belongs to the set $E_7(1,1)$.

Now $3P = P + P + P + Q$ where $P = (0,6)$ and $Q = (2,2)$

$$\lambda = \left(\frac{2}{-4}\right) \bmod 7 = \left(\frac{-1}{2}\right) \bmod 7 = (6 \times 2 - 1) \bmod 7 = (6 \times 4) \bmod 7 = 3$$

$$x_R = \left(\lambda^2 - x_P - x_Q\right)\bmod p = \left(9-0-2\right)\bmod 7 = 0$$

$$y_R = \left(\lambda\left(x_P - x_Q\right) - y_P\right)\bmod p = \left(3\left(0-0\right)-6\right)\bmod 7 = \left(-6\right)\bmod 7 = 1$$

$\therefore 3P = \left(0,1\right)$ also belongs to set $E_7\left(1,1\right)$

Now $P = \left(0,6\right)$ and $3P = \left(0,1\right) = -P$

$\therefore 4P = 3P + P = \left(-P\right) + P = 0$

Since $4P = 0$,

:. The order of point $(0, 6)$ is 4.

Example 7.9

Let $G = \left(1,6\right)$ be the base point for Elliptic Curve Set $E_{11}\left(1,1\right)$. Determine its Order.

Solution:

The Elliptic Curve: $y^2 \equiv \left(x^3 + x + 1\right)\bmod 11$ Elliptic Curve Set $E_{11}\left(1,1\right)$:

x	y
0	1
	10 (−1)
1	5
	6 (−5)
2	0
3	3
	8 (−3)
4	5
	6 (−5)
6	5
	6 (−5)
8	2
	9 (−2)
O	

$\therefore$ Base Point $G = \left(1,6\right)$

Determine 2G:

$$2G = G + G = (1,6) + (1,6)$$

$$\lambda = \left(\frac{\left(3x_P^2 + a\right)}{2y_P}\right) \bmod p = \left(\frac{(3+1)}{12}\right) \bmod 11 = \left(\frac{1}{3}\right) \bmod 11 = 4$$

$$x_R = \left(\lambda^2 - x_P - x_Q\right) \bmod p = (16 - 1 - 1) \bmod 11 = 3$$

$$y_R = \left(\lambda\left(x_P - x_Q\right) - y_P\right) \bmod p = (4(1-3) - 6) \bmod 11 = (-8 - 6) \bmod 11 = 8$$

$$\therefore 2G = (3,8)$$

Determine 3G:

$$3G = G + 2G = (1,6) + (3,8) \quad \lambda = \left(\frac{\left(y_Q - y_P\right)}{\left(x_Q - x_P\right)}\right) \bmod p = \left(\frac{(8-6)}{(3-1)}\right) \bmod 11 = 1$$

$$x_R = \left(\lambda^2 - x_P - x_Q\right) \bmod p = (1 - 1 - 3) \bmod 11 = 8$$

$$y_R = \left(\lambda\left(x_P - x_Q\right) - y_P\right) \bmod p = (1(1-8) - 6) \bmod 11 = 9 \therefore 3G = (8,9)$$

Determine 4G:

$$4G = 2G + 2G = (3,8) + (3,8)$$

$$\lambda = \left(\frac{\left(3x_P^2 + a\right)}{2y_P}\right) \bmod p = \left(\frac{(27+1)}{16}\right) \bmod 11$$

$$= \left(\frac{7}{4}\right) \bmod 11 = (7 \times 3) \bmod 11 = 10$$

$$x_R = \left(\lambda^2 - x_P - x_Q\right) \bmod p = (100 - 3 - 3) \bmod 11 = 94 \bmod 11 = 6$$

$$y_R = \left(\lambda\left(x_P - x_Q\right) - y_P\right) \bmod p = (10(3-6) - 8) \bmod 11 = (-38) \bmod 11 = 6$$

$$\therefore 4G = (6,6)$$

Determine 5G:

$$5G = 2G + 3G = (3,8) + (8,9)$$

$$\lambda = \left(\frac{\left(y_Q - y_P\right)}{\left(x_Q - x_P\right)}\right) \bmod p = \left(\frac{(9-8)}{(8-3)}\right) \bmod 11 = \left(\frac{1}{5}\right) \bmod 11 = 9$$

$$x_R = \left(\lambda^2 - x_P - x_Q\right) \bmod p = (81 - 3 - 8) \bmod 11 = 70 \bmod 11 = 4$$

$$y_R = \left(\lambda\left(x_P - x_Q\right) - y_P\right) \bmod p = \left(9(3-4) - 8\right) \bmod 11 = (-17) \bmod 11 = 5$$

$$\therefore 5G = (4,5)$$

Determine 6G:

$$6G = 3G + 3G = (8,9) + (8,9)$$

$$\lambda = \left(\frac{\left(3x_P^2 + a\right)}{2y_P}\right) \bmod p = \left(\frac{(3 \times 64 + 1)}{18}\right) \bmod 11 = \left(\frac{193}{18}\right) \bmod 11$$

$$= (6 \times 8) \bmod 11 = 4$$

$$x_R = \left(\lambda^2 - x_P - x_Q\right) \bmod p = (16 - 8 - 8) \bmod 11 = 0$$

$$y_R = \left(\lambda\left(x_P - x_Q\right) - y_P\right) \bmod p = \left(4(8 - 0) - 9\right) \bmod 11 = (23) \bmod 11 = 1$$

$$\therefore 6G = (0,1)$$

Determine 7G:

$$7G = 6G + G = (0,1) + (1,6)$$

$$\lambda = \left(\frac{\left(y_Q - y_P\right)}{\left(x_Q - x_P\right)}\right) \bmod p = \left(\frac{(6-1)}{(1-0)}\right) \bmod 11 = (5) \bmod 11 = 5$$

$$x_R = \left(\lambda^2 - x_P - x_Q\right) \bmod p = (25 - 0 - 1) \bmod 11 = 2$$

$$y_R = \left(\lambda\left(x_P - x_Q\right) - y_P\right) \bmod p = \left(5(0 - 2) - 1\right) \bmod 11 = (-11) \bmod 11 = 0$$

$$\therefore 7G = (2,0)$$

Determine 8G:

$$8G = 4G + 4G = (6,6) + (6,6)$$

$$\lambda = \left(\frac{\left(3x_P^2 + a\right)}{2y_P}\right) \bmod p = \left(\frac{(3 \times 36 + 1)}{12}\right) \bmod 11 = \left(\frac{109}{12}\right) \bmod 11 = 10$$

$$x_R = \left(\lambda^2 - x_P - x_Q\right) \bmod p = (100 - 6 - 6) \bmod 11 = 0$$

$$y_R = \left(\lambda\left(x_P - x_Q\right) - y_P\right) \bmod p = \left(10(6 - 0) - 6\right) \bmod 11 = (54) \bmod 11 = 10$$

$$\therefore 8G = (0,10)$$

Determine 9G:

$$9G = 8G + G = (0,10) + (1,6)$$

$$\lambda = \left(\frac{(y_Q - y_P)}{(x_Q - x_P)}\right) \bmod p = \left(\frac{(-4)}{(1)}\right) \bmod 11 = (-4) \bmod 11 = 7$$

$$x_R = \left(\lambda^2 - x_P - x_Q\right) \bmod p = (49 - 0 - 1) \bmod 11 = 4$$

$$y_R = \left(\lambda(x_P - x_Q) - y_P\right) \bmod p = (7(0 - 4) - 10) \bmod 11 = (-38) \bmod 11 = 6$$

$$\therefore 9G = (4,6)$$

Determine 10G:

$$10G = 5G + 5G = (4,5) + (4,5)$$

$$\lambda = \left(\frac{(3x_P^2 + a)}{2y_P}\right) \bmod p = \left(\frac{(3 \times 16 + 1)}{10}\right) \bmod 11$$

$$= \left(\frac{49}{10}\right) \bmod 11 = (5 \times 10) \bmod 11 = 6 =$$

$$x_R = \left(\lambda^2 - x_P - x_Q\right) \bmod p = (36 - 4 - 4) \bmod 11 = (28) \bmod 11 = 6$$

$$y_R = \left(\lambda(x_P - x_Q) - y_P\right) \bmod p = (6(4 - 6) - 5) \bmod 11 = (-17) \bmod 11 = 5$$

$$\therefore 10G = (6,5)$$

Determine 11G:

$$11G = 10G + G = (6,5) + (1,6)$$

$$\lambda = \left(\frac{(y_Q - y_P)}{(x_Q - x_P)}\right) \bmod p = \left(\frac{(-1)}{(5)}\right) \bmod 11 = (10 \times 9) \bmod 11 = 2$$

$$x_R = \left(\lambda^2 - x_P - x_Q\right) \bmod p = (4 - 6 - 1) \bmod 11 = (-3) \bmod 11 = 8$$

$$y_R = \left(\lambda(x_P - x_Q) - y_P\right) \bmod p = (2(6 - 8) - 5) \bmod 11 = (-9) \bmod 11 = 2$$

$$\therefore 11G = (8,2)$$

Determine 12G:

$$12G = 11G + G = (8,2) + (1,6)$$

$$\lambda = \left(\frac{(y_Q - y_P)}{(x_Q - x_P)}\right) \bmod p = \left(\frac{(-4)}{(7)}\right) \bmod 11 = (7 \times 8) \bmod 11 = 1$$

$$x_R = \left(\lambda^2 - x_P - x_Q\right) \bmod p = (1 - 8 - 1) \bmod 11 = (-8) \bmod 11 = 3$$

$$y_R = \left(\lambda(x_P - x_Q) - y_P\right) \bmod p = (1(8-3) - 2) \bmod 11 = (3) \bmod 11 = 3$$

$$\therefore 12G = (3,3)$$

Determine 13G:

$$13G = 12G + G = (3,3) + (1,6)$$

$$\lambda = \left(\frac{(y_Q - y_P)}{(x_Q - x_P)}\right) \bmod p = \left(\frac{(-3)}{(2)}\right) \bmod 11 = (8 \times 6) \bmod 11 = 4$$

$$x_R = \left(\lambda^2 - x_P - x_Q\right) \bmod p = (16 - 3 - 1) \bmod 11 = (12) \bmod 11 = 1$$

$$y_R = \left(\lambda(x_P - x_Q) - y_P\right) \bmod p = (4(3-1) - 3) \bmod 11 = (5) \bmod 11 = 5$$

$$\therefore 13G = (1,5) = -G$$

Determine 14G:

$$14G = 13G + G = (-G) + G = (1,5) + (1,6) = (1,5) + (-(1,5)) = O$$

Since $14G = 0$,

$$\therefore \text{Order of } G = (1,6) = 14$$

Multiples of $G = (1,6)$ in $E_{11}(1,1)$

G	$(1, 6)$
$2G$	$(3, 8)$
$3G$	$(8, 9)$
$4G$	$(6, 6)$
$5G$	$(4, 5)$
$6G$	$(0, 1)$
$7G$	$(2, 0)$
$8G$	$(0, 10)$
$9G$	$(4, 6)$
$10G$	$(6, 5)$
$11G$	$(8, 2)$
$12G$	$(3, 3)$
$13G$	$(1, 5) = -G$
$14G = 13G + G = (-G) + G$	O

7.7.8 Strength of ECC-Based Schemes

- Let $E_p(a, b)$ be an Elliptic Curve Set where p is a large prime number.
- Let $G \in E_p(a,b)$ be the Base Point chosen, and n is the Order of Base Point G. The Base Point G is so chosen that its Order n should be very large.
- Let n_1 be an integer such that $(1 < n_1 < n)$.
- Knowing n_1 and G, it is easy to compute $P_1 = n_1 G$.
- But, knowing P_1 and G, it is very difficult (computationally infeasible) to determine n_1. This is equivalent to taking discrete logarithms. This difficulty provides the strength to ECC-based Schemes.

7.7.9 ECC-Based Key-Exchange Algorithm

1. Suitable Global Parameters are chosen, which are shared among all the users in the crypto-system:

   $E_p(a, b)$: Elliptic Cover Set, where p is a large number and a, b are coefficients of the congruence.

   $$y^2 \equiv (x^3 + ax + b) \bmod p$$

   G: Base Point in $E_p(a, b)$ such that it has large Order.

   n: Order of Base Point G in $E_p(a, b)$

2. A key exchange between two Users "A" and "B" is accomplished by the following steps as in Figure 7.4:

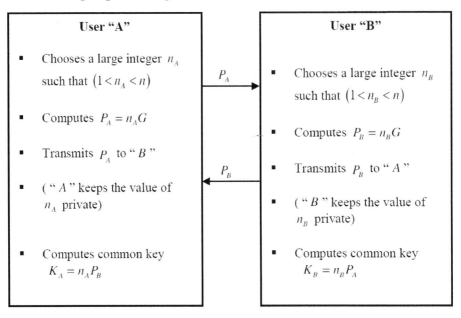

FIGURE 7.4 A schematic diagram of the ECC-Based Key-Exchange Algorithm.

A. User "A" selects a Private Key n_A such chat $(1 < n_A < n)$ and computes a Public Key

$$P_A = n_A \times G.$$

P_A will be a point from $E_p(a, b)$. User "A" keeps n_A secret and sends P_A to User "B."

B. User "B" selects a Private Key n_B such chat $(1 < n_B < n)$ and computes a Public Key

$$P_B = n_B \times G.$$

P_B will be a point from $E_p(a, b)$. User "B" keeps n_B secret and sends P_B to User "A."

C. User "A" computes secret key $K_A = n_A \times P_B$

And user "B" computes secret key $K_B = n_B \times P_A$

It can be verified that the secret keys K_A and K_B computed by "A" and "B," respectively, are same:

$$K_A = n_A \times P_B = n_A \left(n_B \times G \right) = n_B \left(n_A \times G \right) = n_B \times P_A = K_B$$

7.7.10 Strength of ECC Key-Exchange Algorithm

$E_p\,(a, b)$, G, and n are global parameters, known to all users in the system. It is presumed that an adversary will also have access to these parameters. In addition, it is presumed that an adversary can access P_A and P_B also from the communication media. But, to compute the common secret key, adversary needs knowledge of either n_A or n_B, which are known only to User "A" and User "B," respectively. And computing n_A from P_A and computing n_B from P_B are considered very difficult (or infeasible), since n is very large. Thus, an adversary would not be able to determine the common secret key.

7.7.11 ECC-Based Encryption/Decryption Scheme

1. **Selection of Suitable Global Parameters:** Suitable Global Parameters are chosen, which are shared among all the users in the cryptosystem:

   $E_p\,(a, b)$: Elliptic Cover Set, where p is a large number and a, b are coefficients of the congruence.

   $$y^2 \equiv \left(x^3 + ax + b \right) \bmod p$$

   G: Base point in $E_p\,(a, b)$ such that its order will be very high.

   n: Order of Base Point G in $E_p\,(a, b)$

2. **Determination of Keys by the Users:** Each user (User "A") in the cryptosystem determines its Private Key and Public Key as follows:

   - "A" selects a large integer n_A as its Private Key, which "A" keeps private (secret).

   - Then "A" determines its Public Key $P_A = n_A G$ and makes it available to all other users in the cryptosystem.

3. **Encryption of Plaintext by Sender:** Supposing any user in the cryptosystem intends to send a message M to user "A," then it proceeds as follows:

    - First the message M is encoded for mapping it to one of the points (say P_m) in $E_p(a, b)$. This encoding is reversible, that is, for each possible value of plaintext M, there will be a unique point from $E_p(a, b)$.

    - Encryption of P_m by Sender

    - Sender selects a random integer k such that $(1 < k < n)$

    - Using the Public Key P_A of intended recipient "A," the sender encrypts the plain text P_m and creates a cipher-text C_m:

    $$C_m = \{kG, (P_m + kP_A)\}$$

    The cipher-text C_m comprises two components. Both components are the points from $E_p(a, b)$. The first component "kG" is called "clue," since it provides a clue about parameter "k" to the recipient, since "k" is known only to the sender.

    - The Cipher-text C_m is transmitted to the intended recipient "A."

4. **Decryption of C_m by recipient "A":** User "A" receives the cipher-text C_m and decrypts it as follows using its Private Key n_A, which is known only to "A":

    - Multiplies kG by n_A

    - Subtracts the result of step (1) from $P_m + kP_A$

      that is, $P_m + kP_A - n_A kG = P_m + kP_A - kP_A = P_m$ (since $P_A = n_A G$)

    Thus, the recipient "A" is able to extract the encoded plaintext P_m.

    - Then "A" decodes P_m to extract the message m, without having any knowledge of parameter k, which is known only to the sender of the cipher-text.

Figure 7.5 illustrates the ECC-based Encryption/Decryption Chain.

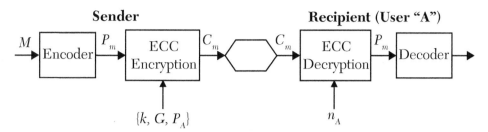

FIGURE 7.5 A schematic diagram of the ECC-based Encryption/Decryption Chain.

7.7.12 Strength of ECC-based Encryption/Decryption Scheme

To break the cipher C_m an adversary would need to follow one of the following two approaches:

1. First Approach

- Attempt to determine n_A from P_A
- Multiply kG by n_A and subtract the result from C_m to determine P_m.
- But for large n, determining n_A from P_A is considered computationally infeasible. It is equivalent to computing Discrete Logarithms.

2. Second Approach

- Attempt to determine k from kG
- Multiply P_A by k and subtract the result from C_m to determine P_m.
- But determining k from kG is also equivalent to computing discrete logarithms, which is considered as difficult as determining n_B from P_B.

Thus, if the value of parameter n is very large, breaking the ECC is considered computationally infeasible.

Example 7.10: (ECC Key Exchange and ECC Encryption/Decryption)

Let the scheme be based on the Elliptic Curve:

$$y^2 \bmod 11 \equiv \left(x^3 + x + 1\right) \bmod 11$$

Elliptic Curve Set E_{11} (1, 1):

x	y
0	1
0	10 (−1)
1	5
1	6 (−5)
2	0
3	3
3	8 (−3)
4	5
4	6 (−5)
6	5
6	6 (−5)
8	2
8	9 (−2)
	O

There are a total of 14 points in the elliptic group $E_{11}(1,1)$, including the point at infinity 0.

Let us choose Base Point: $G = (1,6)$.

Order of the Base Point: $G = (1,6) = 14$

Multiples of $G = (1,6)$:

G	(1, 6)
$2G$	(3, 8)
$3G$	(8, 9)
$4G$	(6, 6)
$5G$	(4, 5)
$6G$	(0, 1)
$7G$	(2, 0)
$8G$	(0, 10)
$9G$	(4, 6)
$10G$	(6, 5)
$11G$	(8, 2)
$12G$	(3, 3)
$13G$	$(1,5) = -G$
$14G$	O

Suppose user "A" chooses $n_A = 7$

Then $P_A = n_A G = 7 \times (1,6) = (2,0)$ (as indicated previously)

User "A" sends $P_A = (2,0)$ to User "B."

Suppose user "B" chooses $n_B = 5$

Then $P_B = n_B G = 5 \times (1,6) = (4,5)$ (as indicated previously)

User "B" sends $P_B = (4,5)$ to User "A".

User "A" computes common secret key, $K = n_A P_B = 7 \times (4,5)$ as follows:

$2P_B = P_B + P_B = (4,5) + (4,5)$

$\lambda = \left(\dfrac{(3 \times 16 + 1)}{10} \right) \bmod 11 = \left(\dfrac{49}{10} \right) \bmod 11 = (5 \times 10) \bmod 11 = 6$

$x_R = \left(\lambda^2 - x_P - x_Q \right) \bmod p = (36 - 4 - 4) \bmod 11 = (28) \bmod 11 = 6$

$y_R = (6(4-6) - 5) \bmod 11 = (-17) \bmod 11 = 5$

$\therefore 2P_B = (2,5)$

$4P_B = 2P_B + 2P_B = (6,5) + (6,5)$

$\lambda = \left(\dfrac{(3 \times 36 + 1)}{10} \right) \bmod 11 = \left(\dfrac{109}{10} \right) \bmod 11 = (10 \times 10) \bmod 11 = 1$

$x_R = (1 - 6 - 6) \bmod 11 = (-11) \bmod 11 = 0$

$y_R = (1(6-0) - 5) \bmod 11 = (1) \bmod 11 = 1$

$\therefore 4P_B = (0,1)$

$6P_B = 4P_B + 2P_B = (0,1) + (6,5)$

$\lambda = \left(\dfrac{2}{3} \right) \bmod 11 = (2 \times 4) \bmod 11 = 8$

$x_R = (64 - 0 - 6) \bmod 11 = (58) \bmod 11 = 3$

$$y_R = \left(8(0-3)-1\right)\bmod 11 = (-25)\bmod 11 = 8$$

$$\therefore 6P_B = (3,8)$$

$$7P_B = 6P_B + P_B = (3,8)+(4,5)$$

$$\lambda = \left(\frac{(5-8)}{(4-3)}\right)\bmod 11 = (-3)\bmod 11 = 8$$

$$x_R = (64-3-4)\bmod 11 = (57)\bmod 11 = 2$$

$$y_R = \left(8(3-2)-8\right)\bmod 11 = (0)\bmod 11 = 0$$

$$\therefore 7P_B = (2,0)$$

$$\therefore \text{Common Secret Key } K = (2,0)$$

User "B" computes common secret key, $K = n_B P_A = 5 \times (2,0)$ as follows:

$$2P_A = P_A + P_A = (2,0)+(2,0) = (2,0)+(-(2,0)) = 0$$

$$4P_A = 2P_A + 2P_A = 0+0 = 0$$

$$5P_A = 4P_A + P_A = 0+(2,0) = (2,0)$$

$$\therefore \text{Common Secret Key } K = (2,0)$$

Thus, the common secret key computed both by "A" and "B" $= (2, 0)$

ECC-based Encryption/Decryption Scheme

Using the Prime Curve $E_{11}(1,1)$ and Base Point $(1, 6)$

Determination of Private Key and Public Key

Suppose user "A" selects Private Key $n_A = 7$

Then "A" computes Public Key $P_A = n_A G = 7 \times (1,6)$

Encryption:

Supposing any user wants to send message m to User "A," then the sender will first encode the message to P_m in $E_{11}(1,1)$.

Let $P_m = (8,9)$

Let the random number chosen by sender $= k = 2$

Then P_m is encrypted as follows:

$$C_m = \{kG, (P_m + kP_A)\}$$
$$= \{2(1,\ 6), (8,\ 9) + 2(2,\ 0)\}$$
$$= \{(3,\ 8), (8,\ 9) + 0\}$$
$$= \{(3,\ 8), (8,\ 9)\}$$

C_m is sent as Cipher-text to User "A."

Decryption by User "A":

User "A" receives the Cipher-text $C_m = \{(3,\ 8), (8,\ 9)\}$ as follows:

1. Compute $n_A(kG) = 7 \times (3,8)$
    This is computed as follows:
    $2(3,8) = (3,8) + (3,8)$

    $$\lambda = \left(\frac{(27+1)}{(16)}\right) \bmod 11 = \left(\frac{7}{4}\right) \bmod 11 = 10$$
    $$x_R = (100 - 3 - 3) \bmod 11 = (94) \bmod 11 = 6$$
    $$y_R = (10(3-6) - 8) \bmod 11 = (-38) \bmod 11 = 6$$
    $$\therefore 2(3,8) = (3,8) + (3,8)$$
    $$4(3,8) = 2(3,8) + 2(3,8) = (6,6) + (6,6)$$
    $$\lambda = \left(\frac{(108+1)}{(12)}\right) \bmod 11 = \left(\frac{109}{12}\right) \bmod 11 = 10$$
    $$x_R = (100 - 6 - 6) \bmod 11 = (88) \bmod 11 = 0$$
    $$y_R = (10(6-0) - 6) \bmod 11 = (54) \bmod 11 = 10$$
    $$\therefore 4(3,\ 8) = (0,\ 10)$$
    $$6(3,\ 8) = 2(3,8) + 4(3,8) = (6,6) + (0,10)$$
    $$\lambda = \left(\frac{(4)}{(-6)}\right) \bmod 11 = \left(\frac{2}{-3}\right) \bmod 11 = 3$$
    $$x_R = (9 - 6 - 0) \bmod 11 = (3) \bmod 11 = 3$$
    $$y_R = (3(6-3) - 6) \bmod 11 = (3) \bmod 11 = 3$$
    $$\therefore 6(3,\ 8) = (3,\ 3)$$

$$7(3,8) = 6(3,8) + (3,8) = (3,3) + (3,8)$$
$$= (3,3) + (-(3,3))$$
$$= 0$$

2. Subtract the result of step (1) from $(P_m + kP_A)$ to get P_m.
$$P_m = (8,9) - 0 = (8,9)$$

Thus, the plaintext (8, 9) is extracted by the user "A."

Example 7.11

Elliptic Cover set of $y^2 \equiv (x^3 + x + 1) \mod 23$ is given as follows:

Elliptic Curve Set E_{23} (1, 1):

(x, y)	(x, y)
(0,1)	(9,7)
(0,22)	(9,16)
(1,7)	(11,3)
(1,16)	(11,20)
(3,10)	(12,4)
(3,13)	(12,9)
(4,0)	(13,7)
(5,4)	(13,16)
(5,19)	(17,3)
(6,4)	(17,20)
(6,19)	(18,3)
(7,11)	(18,20)
(7,12)	(19,5)
	(19,19)
	O

Let $G(6, 4)$ be the Base Point. Determine its Order.

Also, determine a scheme for encoding English Alphabet prior to encryption using $E_{23}(1, 1)$.

Determining Order n of G:
$$2G = G + G = (6,4) + (6,4)$$
$$\lambda = \left(\frac{(108 + 1)}{(8)} \right) \mod 23 = (17 \times 3) \mod 23 = 5$$

$$x_R = (25 - 12) \bmod 23 = (13) \bmod 23 = 13$$

$$y_R = (5(6 - 13) - 4) \bmod 23 = (-39) \bmod 23 = 7$$

$$\therefore 2G = (13, \ 7)$$

$$3G = 2G + G = (13,7) + (6,4)$$

$$\lambda = \left(\frac{3}{7}\right) \bmod 23 = (3 \times 10) \bmod 23 = 7$$

$$x_R = (49 - 19) \bmod 23 = (30) \bmod 23 = 7$$

$$y_R = \left(\lambda\left(x_P - x_Q\right) - y_P\right) \bmod p = (7(13 - 7) - 7) \bmod 23 = (35) \bmod 23 = 12$$

$$\therefore 3G = (7, \ 12)$$

$$4G = 3G + G = (7,12) + (6,4)$$

$$\lambda = \left(\frac{-8}{-1}\right) \bmod 23 = 8$$

$$x_R = (64 - 13) \bmod 23 = 5$$

$$y_R = (8(7 - 5) - 12) \bmod 23 = 4$$

$$\therefore 4G = (5, \ 4)$$

$$5G = 4G + G = (5,4) + (6,4)$$

$$\lambda = 0$$

$$x_R = (-11) \bmod 23 = 12$$

$$y_R = (-4) \bmod 23 = 19$$

$$\therefore 5G = (12, \ 19)$$

$$6G = 4G + 2G = (5,4) + (13,7)$$

$$\lambda = \left(\frac{3}{8}\right) \bmod 23 = (3 \times 3) \bmod 23 = 9$$

$$x_R = (81 - 5 - 13) \bmod 23 = (63) \bmod 23 = 17$$

$$y_R = (9(5 - 17) - 4) \bmod 23 = (-112) \bmod 23 = 3$$

$$\therefore 2G = (17, \ 3)$$

$$7G = 4G + 3G = (5,4) + (7,12)$$

$$\lambda = \left(\frac{8}{2}\right) \mod 23 = 4$$

$$x_R = (16 - 12) \mod 23 = 4$$

$$y_R = (4(5-4) - 4) \mod 23 = 0$$

$$\therefore 7G = (4,\ 0)$$

$$8G = 7G + G = (4,0) + (6,4)$$

$$\lambda = \left(\frac{4}{2}\right) \mod 23 = 2$$

$$x_R = \left(\lambda^2 - x_P - x_Q\right) \mod p = (4-10) \mod 23 = 17$$

$$y_R = \left(\lambda\left(x_P - x_Q\right) - y_P\right) \mod p = (2(4-17) - 0) \mod 23 = (-26) \mod 23 = 20$$

$$\therefore 8G = (17,20)$$

$$9G = 7G + 2G = (4,0) + (13,7)$$

$$\lambda = \left(\frac{7}{9}\right) \mod 23 = (7 \times 18) \mod 23 = 11$$

$$x_R = (121 - 17) \mod 23 = 12$$

$$y_R = (11(4-12) - 0) \mod 23 = (-88) \mod 23 = 4$$

$$\therefore 9G = (12,4)$$

$$10G = 9G + G = (12,4) + (6,4)$$

$$\lambda = 0 \quad x_R = (-18) \mod 23 = 5$$

$$y_R = (-4) \mod 23 = 19$$

$$\therefore 10G = (19,5)$$

$$11G = 4G + 7G = (5,4) + (4,0)$$

$$\lambda = \left(\frac{-4}{-1}\right) \bmod 23 = 4$$

$$x_R = (16 - 9) \bmod 23 = 7$$

$$y_R = (4(5-7) - 4) \bmod 23 = (-12) \bmod 23 = 11$$

$$\therefore 11G = (7,11)$$

$$12G = 9G + 3G = (12,4) + (7,12)$$

$$\lambda = \left(\frac{8}{-5}\right) \bmod 23 = (-8 \times 14) \bmod 23 = (-112) \bmod 23 = 3$$

$$x_R = (9 - 12 - 7) \bmod 23 = 13$$

$$y_R = (3(12 - 13) - 4) \bmod 23 = (-7) \bmod 23 = 16$$

$$\therefore 12G = (13,16)$$

$$13G = 8G + 5G = (17,20) + (12,19)$$

$$\lambda = \left(\frac{-1}{-5}\right) \bmod 23 = 14$$

$$x_R = (196 - 17 - 12) \bmod 23 = (167) \bmod 23 = 6$$

$$y_R = (14(17 - 6) - 20) \bmod 23 = (134) \bmod 23 = 19$$

$$\therefore 13G = (6,19)$$

$$14G = 13G + G = (6,19) + (6,4) = O$$

Since $14G = O$,

$\therefore$ Order of $G = n = 14$

Multiples of $G = (6, 4)$:

G	(6, 4)
2G	(13, 7)
3G	(7, 12)
4G	(5, 4)
5G	(12, 19)
6G	(17, 3)
7G	(4, 0)
8G	(17, 20)
9G	(12, 4)
10G	(5, 19)
11G	(7, 11)
12G	(13, 16)
13G	(6, 19) = −G
14G	O

The below table is for the encoding of English letters prior to encryption:

(x, y)	(x, y)
"A" : (0,1)	"N" : (9,7)
"B" : (0,22)	"O" : (9,16)
"C" : (1,7)	"P" : (11,3)
"D" : (1,16)	"Q" : (11,20)
"E" : (3,10)	"R" : (12,4)
"F" : (3,13)	"S" : (12,9)
"G" : (4,0)	"T" : (13,7)
"H" : (5,4)	"U" : (13,16)
"I" : (5,19)	"V" : (17,3)
"J" : (6,4)	"W" : (17,20)
"K" : (6,19)	"X" : (18,3)
"L" : (7,11)	"Y" : (18,20)
"M": (7,12)	"Z" : (19,5)
	"–" : (19,19)
	O

Supposing the following message is to be transmitted, it will be encoded as follows:

Plaintext: REACHING AT SEVEN TODAY

Encoded Plaintext: (12,4) (3,10) (0,1) (1,7) (5,4) (5,19) (9,7) (4,0) (19,19) (0,1) (13,7) (19,19) (12, 9) (3,10) (17, 3) (3,10) (9,7) (19, 19) (13,7) (9, 16) (1,16) (0, 1) (18, 20)

7.7.13 ECC Encryption/Decryption vs. RSA

ECC requires a smaller key-size for equivalent Security Levels:

- For a given security level, the size of the key required in ECC is much smaller as compared to RSA.

- The largest ECC System broken to date is a 108-bit system, whereas the largest RSA System broken so far is a 512-bit system.

- The computational effort required to break the 108-bit ECC System was roughly 50 times the effort required to break the 512-bit RSA system.

- Comparative key sizes in terms of Computational Effort for Cryptanalysis:

Symmetric Scheme RSA/DSA ECC-Based Scheme (Key Size in Bits)	RSA/DSA (Modulus Size in Bits)	ECC-Based Scheme (Size of n in Bits)
56	512	112
80	1024	160
112	2048	224
128	3072	256
192	7680	384
256	15360	512

7.7.14 Efficient Hardware Implementation

- ECC can be more efficiently implemented than RSA for equivalent Security Levels.

- A 155-bit ECC Processor used about 11000 gates, whereas a 512-bit RSA processor used about 50000 gates. Both have almost the same security level.

7.8 EXERCISES

1. What is the strength of RSA? If the modulus used in RSA has very small prime factors, will the RSA implementation be secure? Justify your answer.

2. What are the different kinds of attacks possible against RSA? Explain the Common Modulus Attack on RSA.

3. In RSA, if repeated encryption using Public Key e results in decryption of the message, what is the likely cause?

4. In RSA, suppose Private Key d is leaked out; is it safe to generate the new keys without changing the modulus n?

5. Suppose more than one block of RSA cipher-text are available to an adversary. Suppose it is known that one of the blocks has a common factor with modulus $n = pq$. Does it help the adversary in breaking the cipher in any way?

6. Given a prime number p, its primitive root g, and integer x $(1 < x < \Phi(p))$, why is it easier to compute $y = g^x \bmod p$, but difficult to compute discrete logarithm $x = \log_g y \pmod{p}$?

7. What is the strength of the Diffie-Hellman Key Exchange Algorithm? If the prime modulus used in the algorithm is very small, will the key exchange be secure?

8. What is a Clogging Attack on a Dillie-Hellman Key Exchange? Suggest a suitable countermeasure.

9. What is the strength of the ECC-based Encryption Scheme? Explain how to increase the security level.

10. What is the major advantage offered by ECC-based cryptography vis-à-vis existing Public Key Schemes?

11. Explain RSA for Data Confidentiality. Perform RSA Encryption/Decryption for the following set of data:

    A. $p = 3; q = 11; e = 7; M = 5$

    B. $p = 5; q = 11; e = 3; M = 9$

    C. $p = 7; q = 11; e = 17; M = 8$

D. $p = 11; q = 13; e = 11; M = 7$

E. $p = 17; q = 31; e = 7; M = 2$

12. In RSA, if cipher-text $C = 10$, $e = 5$, and $n = 35$, determine M.

13. In RSA, if $e = 31$ and $n = 3599$, determine Private Key d.

14. A plaintext is encrypted using (e, n) and (f, n) Public Keys, generating cipher-texts C_e and C_f, respectively, where $GCD(e, f) = 1$. Is it possible to determine plaintext M without determining $\Phi(n)$? If yes, how?

15. Explain the Dillie-Hellman Key-Exchange Algorithm. Let $p = 353$ be the prime number and $a = 3$ be its primitive root. Let the secret keys of A and B be $X_A = 97$ and $X_B = 233$. Compute the following:

A. Public Keys of A and B

B. Common Secret Key

16. Users A and B use a Dillie-Hellman key exchange using prime $q = 71$ and primitive root $a = 7$.

A. User A has Private Key $X_A = 5$; what is A's Public Key Y_A?

B. User B has Private Key $X_B = 12$; what is B's Public Key Y_B?

C. What is the shared secret key?

17. Consider a Dillie-Hellman scheme with a common prime $q = 11$ and a primitive root $a = 2$.

A. Verify that 2 is a primitive root of 11.

B. If user A has Public Key $Y_A = 9$, what is A's Private Key X_A?

C. If user B has Public Key $Y_B = 3$, what is B's Private Key X_B?

D. What is the shared secret key of A and B?

18. Explain the "Man-in-the-Middle Attack" on a Dillie-Hellman Key-Exchange Algorithm.

19. With the following parameters, implement the El-Gamal Encryption/Decryption scheme:

Prime Number = 19

Primitive Root of $p = g = 3$

Suppose user "A" chooses Private Key $= x = 7$

And message to be sent by User "B" to User "A" $= M = 12$

Random number chosen by user "B" for encryption $= k = 5$

Determine:

A. Public Key y of "A"

B. Cipher-text created by the sender "B"

C. Show how the plaintext is extracted from the cipher-text by User "A."

20. What is ECC? Explain Encryption/Decryption in this context.

21. With the following parameters, design an ECC Key Exchange Scheme:
Elliptic Curve Set: $E_{11} = (1,1)$

Base Point: $G = (1,6)$

Order of Base Point: $n = 14$

Suppose user "A" chooses Private Key, $n_A = 3$

And User "B" chooses Private Key, $n_B = 5$

A. Determine the Public Key, P_A of "A" and Public Key P_B of "B"

B. Determine the Common Secret Key computed both by "A" and "B."

22. Within the following parameters, design an ECC Encryption/Decryption scheme:
Elliptic Curve Set: $E_{11} = (1,1)$

Base Point: $G = (1,6)$

Order of Base Point: $n = 14$

Suppose User "A" chooses Private Key, $n_A = 3$

And User "B" wants to send message $P_m = (6,6)$ to user "A" and user chooses random integer $k = 5$ for encryption. Then

A. Determine Public Key, P_A of "A"

B. Determine the cipher-text computed by user "B"

C. Show how User "A" will decrypt the received cipher-text.

CHAPTER **8**

AUTHENTICATION SCHEMES

Chapter Outline

8.1 Introduction

8.2 What Is Message Authentication?

8.3 Types of Authentication Services

8.4 Application Modes of Digital Signatures

8.5 Authentication Protocols

8.6 Message Digest (Hash Function) Algorithms

8.7 Secure Hash Algorithm (SHA-1)

8.8 Digital Signature Schemes

8.9 Exercises

8.1 INTRODUCTION

This chapter covers the concepts and the mechanisms needed to provide Message Authentication, namely, Message Authentication Codes, Hash Functions, and Digital signatures, followed by detailed coverage of popular algorithms for the generation of Message Digests (Hash Values) and Digital Signatures. The chapter also provides in detail the mathematical concepts of the "Birthday Attack" on Digital Signatures.

8.2 WHAT IS MESSAGE AUTHENTICATION?

- Message Authentication is a service that assures the recipients of messages about the identity of senders.

- Digital Signature is an authentication technique that also assures the recipient about the integrity of the received message, that is, that messages are received without any alteration in transit. Integrity also covers the sequencing and timeliness of the received messages.

- Digital Signature also assures the recipient about source non-repudiation, that is, the sender cannot later refute having sent the message.

8.3 TYPES OF AUTHENTICATION SERVICES

There are two kinds of authentication services:

1. **Peer-to-Peer Authentication:** This service is applicable to a connection-oriented environment, like TCP. It provides confidence against masquerade or unauthorized replay of previous connections.

2. **Data Origin Authentication:** This service is applicable to a connectionless communication, for example, UDP. It provides confidence to the recipient that the message received has in fact been sent by the alleged sender.

8.3.1 Different Techniques of Message Authentication

1. **Encryption of Entire Message:** This is the mode used normally in Symmetric Cryptography. The cipher-text of the entire message serves as a value for authentication. In this case, the recipient is assured of the source of the message, since the message is encrypted using a secret key that the recipient shares only with the alleged sender.

   A. Symmetric Encryption

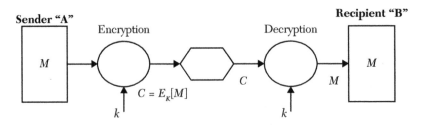

FIGURE 8.1 A schematic diagram of symmetric encryption.

- The Sender encrypts the entire message using symmetric encryption and secret key K.

- The recipient attempts to decrypt the received cipher-text using symmetric decryption and the same key K as used by the alleged sender.

- If the recipient is able to successfully decrypt the cipher-text using key K, then the recipient is assured of the following:

    - The sender's identity, since the message could have been encrypted only using key K, which is known only to User "A" and User "B."

    - Also, the recipient is assured of data integrity of the received message, since no adversary could have modified the message that is encrypted using key K, which is known only to "A" and "B" and no one else.

    - In addition, it also assures data confidentiality, since key K is not known to anyone else except "A" and "B."

    - But this does not ensure source non-repudiation, since the key K is known to "B," and "B" can also create cipher-text C by encrypting M using key K.

B. Public Key Encryption

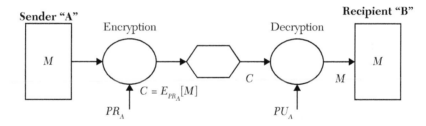

FIGURE 8.2 A schematic diagram of public key encryption.

- The Sender encrypts the entire message using public key encryption and the private key PR_A. The private key PR_A is known only to "A."

- The recipient attempts to decrypt the received cipher-text using public key decryption and public key PU_A from the sender.

- If the recipient is able to successfully decrypt the cipher-text using key PU_A, then the recipient is assured of the following:

- The sender's identity, since the message could have been encrypted only using the key PR_A which is known only to user "A."

- Data integrity of the received message, since no adversary could have modified the message that is encrypted using A's private key.

- It also ensures source non-repudiation, since the key PR_A is known only to user "A" and no one else.

- But it does not ensure data confidentiality, since any one can decrypt it using A's public key.

1. *Message Authentication Code (MAC) Appended to Message*

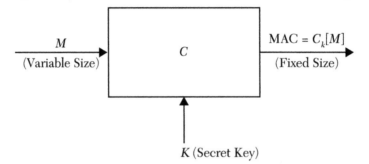

K (Secret Key)

- MAC refers to a small fixed-length code, generated by a public function C, in relation to a message M of any length and a secret key K. MAC is also called Cryptographic Checksum.

- The MAC is appended to the message M prior to its transmission.

i. Encrypted Hash Function Appended to Message

- This method is used in Public-Key Cryptography. It makes use of a public function H, which maps a message M of any length onto a fixed-length hash value b (also called message-digest).

- The hash value is encrypted using the private key of the sender and is appended to the message M prior to its transmission. The encrypted hash value is called a digital signature.

M
$E_{PR}[H(M)]$

▪ At the recipient end, the encrypted hash value is decrypted using the sender's Public Key. Also, another value is generated from the received message M. This hash value is compared with the hash value received from the sender. If the two hash values match, then the message is considered to be authenticated. This also assures integrity of the received message. Since the hash value received from the sender side is encrypted using a key that is known only to the sender, it assures Source Non-Repudiation.

8.3.2 Digital Signatures Using Public-Key Cryptography

1. User "A" can digitally sign a message by encrypting a Hash Value of M using the Private Key PR_A, and then append the digital signature to the message M and send the package to the intended recipient.

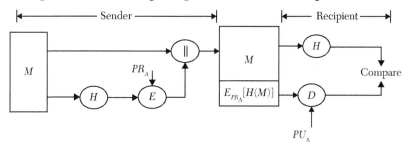

FIGURE 8.3 A schematic diagram of digital signatures using Public-Key Cryptography.

2. At the recipient end, the recipient decrypts the digital signature using the sender's Public Key PU_A and compares the decrypted value with the Hash Value of the Message M. If the two values match, the digital signature is deemed to be verified. A Digital signature provides the following services:

  • **Source Authentication:** Since the recipient is able to decrypt the digital signature using the alleged sender's private key, it implies that the signature was created using the alleged sender's private key; thus, it authenticates the alleged sender's identity.

  • **Data Integrity:** The decrypted value of the signature is the hash value of the message that was computed at the sender end. If it matches with the hash value of the message computed at the recipient end, it implies that the message was not altered in transit.

  • **Source Non-Repudiation:** The recipient will preserve the digital signature along with the message received. If the sender denies having sent the message, the recipient can disprove the sender's claim by verifying the digital signature using the sender's public key. Since it is decrypted using the sender's public key, it implies that it was encrypted using the sender's private key.

8.3.3 Message Authentication Code (MAC)

The sender and the intended recipient share a secret key K. When the sender (User "A") has to send a message M (of any arbitrary length) to the intended recipient (say user "B"), then "A" computes MAC as follows:

$$MAC = C_K(M)$$

The *MAC* is a code of fixed length, which is appended to message M prior to its transmission. At the receiving end, "B" also computes the MAC using global function C and secret key K, and compares this value with the received value of MAC. If the two values match, then:

1. The recipient "B" is assured that the message has been sent by "B" alone, since "A" shares the secret key K only with "B." Thus, it provides authentication of the message source.

2. The recipient is assured that the message has not been altered en route, since an attacker cannot generate MAC without the knowledge of key K. Thus, the integrity of the received data is also assured.

8.3.4 Many-to-One Relationship between Messages and MAC Values

If an m-bit message is mapped onto an n-bit MAC (where m is much larger than n), then the message-space will comprise 2^m distinct messages and the MAC-space will comprise 2^n distinct MAC Codes. The 2^m messages will map onto 2^n MAC Codes, thus making the MAC a many-to-one function, which is not reversible. If the secret key K is k bits long, then there will be 2^k distinct keys and thus 2^k different mappings from the message-space to the MAC-space.

Message-Space
(2^m distinct messages)

Mappings

MAC-Space
(2^m distinct MAC values)

FIGURE 8.4 A schematic diagram of the Many-to-One Relationship between Messages and MAC Values.

Suppose the messages are 1024 bits long and the MACs are 64 bits long, then the message space will have 2^{1024} distinct messages and the MAC space will have 2^{64} distinct MAC Codes. On the average, $2^{1024}/2^{64} = 2^{960}$ messages will map onto each MAC Code. If the secret key is 256 bits long, then there will be 2^{256} different mappings from the message space to the MAC space.

8.3.5 Use of MAC for Message Authentication

1. Message Authentication only

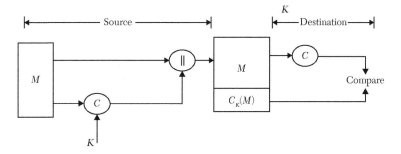

FIGURE 8.5 A schematic diagram of the use of MAC for Message Authentication.

- If the MAC value generated at the recipient end matches exactly with the hash value received from the sender end, the message is considered to be authenticated.

- Also, it assures Data Integrity, since no adversary could have modified the message M, since the adversary cannot generate another MAC without knowledge of key K.

- But it does not assure source non-repudiation since key K is also known to the recipient.

2. Message Authentication and Confidentiality (MAC linked to Plaintext)

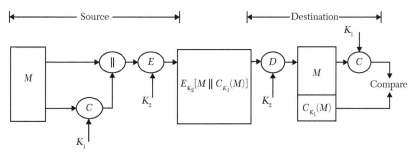

FIGURE 8.6 A schematic diagram of the Message Authentication and Confidentiality (MAC linked to plaintext).

- At the recipient end, MAC is generated as a function of plaintext M and key K_1. The MAC is appended to the plaintext.

- The resulting package, comprising plaintext and MAC, is then encrypted using a secret key K_2, and the resulting cipher-text is transmitted. The outer encryption by K_1 ensures data confidentiality.

3. **Message Authentication and Confidentiality (MAC linked to cipher-text)**

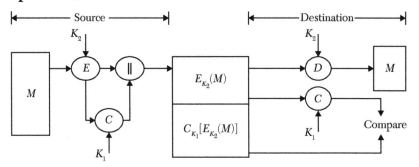

FIGURE 8.7 A schematic diagram of the Message Authentication and Confidentiality (MAC linked to cipher-text).

- The plain text is first encrypted using symmetric encryption and key K_2. MAC is then generated as a function of the cipher-text and key K_1. The MAC is appended to the cipher-text. The MAC is thus linked to the cipher-text.

- The resulting package, comprising cipher-text and MAC, is then transmitted.

- At the recipient end, MAC is generated from the received cipher-text and this MAC is compared with the MAC received from the sender end. If the two match, then the message is considered to be authenticated.

- Then message M is recovered from the cipher-text by decrypting it using symmetric decryption and key K_2.

8.3.6 Chosen Plaintext Attack on MAC

If the message is not encrypted, then an opponent has access to the plaintext messages and their associated MAC values. Suppose k is the size of the secret key and n is the size of MAC and $k > n$. Then, given a known plaintext message M_1 and its $MAC_1 = C_K(M_1)$, a cryptanalyst may apply all possible values of the key to message M_1 and determine corresponding MAC values. At least one of the keys (K_i) will produce a MAC value matching with MAC_1. In fact, a total of 2^k MAC values will be produced. Since $k > n$, we have $2^k > 2^n$; thus, more than one key will produce a match for MAC_1. On the average, $2^k/2^n = 2^{k-n}$ keys will produce a match for MAC_1.

Based on these facts, there is a chosen plaintext attack on MAC, which is summed up as follows:

Round 1

- Randomly choose a message M_1 and its MAC_1
- The adversary will determine the set of keys that satisfy $\text{MAC}_1 = C_K(M_1)$
- The number of keys that will produce a match for $\text{MAC}_1 \approx 2^{(k-n)}$

Round 2

- Now, randomly choose another message M_2 along with its MAC_2
- Now, use $2^{(k-n)}$ keys, determined in the previous round, and determine MAC value of message M_2
- The number of keys that are likely to produce a match for $\text{MAC}_2 \approx 2^{(k-2n)}$
- Continue to iterate till we narrow down to a single key that produces a match for the chosen MAC.

If $k = \alpha\,n$, then on the average, α rounds will be required to determine the exact key. However, if $k \leq n$ then the exact key may be determined in the first round itself. It is possible that more than one key may produce the chosen MAC, but the probability is low.

8.3.7 Hash Function

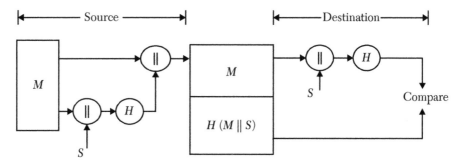

FIGURE 8.8 A schematic diagram of the Hash Function.

- A hash value h is generated by a public function H as $h = H(M)$, where M is a message of variable length and h is the hash value of fixed size.

- The hash value is encrypted using a sender's private key. The encrypted hash value is called a Digital Signature.

- At the sender end, the encrypted hash value is appended to the message prior to its transmission.

- Using the sender's public key, the recipient of the message decrypts the encrypted hash value received from the sender end.

- The recipient re-computes the hash value from the received message and compares it with the hash value received from the sender end. If the two values match exactly, then the message is considered to be authenticated.

8.3.7.1 Symmetric Encryption of a Signed Message

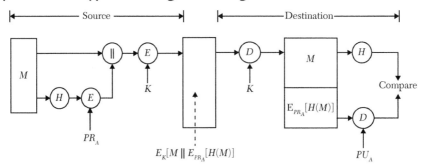

FIGURE 8.8 A schematic diagram of Symmetric Encryption of a signed message.

Here, the bulk encryption of the message is performed after the appending of the signature. This scheme provides data confidentiality along with source authentication.

8.3.7.2 Digital Signature without Encryption Using a Secret Value

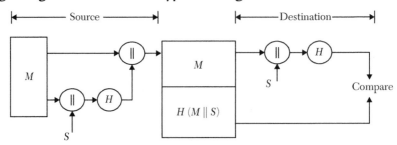

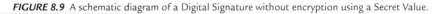

FIGURE 8.9 A schematic diagram of a Digital Signature without encryption using a Secret Value.

The hash value is not encrypted. A secret value, which is shared with the recipient, is appended to the message before hashing it. The recipient also appends the same secret value to the message before hashing at the recipient end as shown here.

8.3.7.3 Symmetric Encryption of a Signed Message (Using a Secret Value to Make the Hash Value Secure)

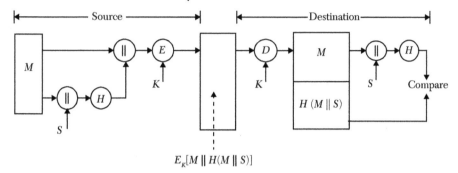

$$E_K[M \parallel H(M \parallel S)]$$

FIGURE 8.10 A schematic diagram of Symmetric Encryption of a Signed Message (using a Secret Value to make the Hash Value secure).

8.3.7.4 Characteristics of a Hash Function

The purpose of a Hash Function is to produce a "fingerprint" of a file or a message or a block of data. To be useful for message authentication, a hash function H must satisfy the following properties:

1. H can be applied to a block of data of any size.

2. H produces a hash value h of fixed size.

3. One-Way Property: For a given x, it should be easy to compute its hash value $h = H(x)$. And for a given hash value h, it should be computationally infeasible to compute $x = H^{-1}(h)$. This is called the One-Way Property.

4. Weak Collision Resistance: For any given x, it should be computationally infeasible to find $y \neq x$ such that $H(y) = H(x)$. This property is called Weak Collision Resistance.

5. Strong Collision Resistance: It should be computationally infeasible to find a pair (x,y) such that $H(y) = H(x)$. This property is called Strong Collision Resistance.

The "One-Way Property" refers to the feature that it is easy to generate the hash value of a given message M, but it is impossible to determine M from being given $h = H(M)$. The property of "Weak Collision Resistance" implies that it should be extremely difficult to determine an alternative message hashing onto the same value as a given message.

The property of "Strong Collision Resistance" implies that it should be extremely difficult to determine a message pair (x, y) having the same hash value, that is, $H(x) = H(y)$.

These properties are necessary to prevent any forgery of the digital signature appended to a message.

8.4 APPLICATION MODES OF DIGITAL SIGNATURES

Mainly there are two modes of application of Digital Signatures:

- Direct Digital Signature
- Arbitrated Digital Signature

8.4.1 Direct Digital Signature

Direct Digital Signature involves only the communicating parties (the Source and the intended Recipient). It is assumed that the intended recipient knows the Public Key of the Source. A digital signature may be formed either by encrypting the entire message or a hash code of the message with the Sender's Private Key. Data Confidentiality can be provided by encrypting the message plus the signature with either the intended recipient's public key (in Public-Key Encryption) or with the secret key that may be shared with the intended recipient (in symmetric encryption), as indicated here:

1. **Direct Signature with Data Confidentiality by Symmetric Encryption**

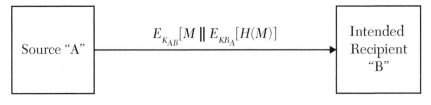

$$E_{K_{AB}}[M \parallel E_{KR_A}[H(M)]$$

Source "A" ——→ Intended Recipient "B"

FIGURE 8.11 A schematic diagram of direct digital signature with data confidentiality by symmetric encryption.

2. Direct Signature with Data Confidentiality by Public Key Encryption

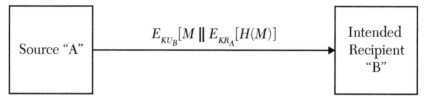

FIGURE 8.12 A schematic diagram of direct digital signature with data confidentiality by public key encryption.

The validity of a direct digital signature depends on the security of the sender's private key. If a sender later wishes to deny the sending of a message, he or she can claim that his or her private key was lost or stolen and that someone else has forged his or her signature. Such ploys can be thwarted to a great extent by including a time stamp (date/time) and by making prompt reporting of compromised private keys to a central authority mandatory.

8.4.2 Arbitrated Digital Signature

This addresses the problems associated with Direct Digital Signatures. Every signed message from a sender X to receiver Y first goes to an arbitrator A. The arbitrator verifies the message and ensures that it is encrypted using a private key which was not compromised at the time of signing the message. Then the arbitrator time-stamps the message and sends it to the intended receiver Y, with an indication that it has been verified to the satisfaction of the arbiter. Various modes of Arbitrated Digital Signature are as follows:

1. Conventional Encryption: Arbitrator can see the Message

A. $X \rightarrow A: M \parallel E_{Kxa} [ID_X \parallel H(M)]$

B. $A \rightarrow Y: E_{Kay} [ID_X \parallel M \parallel E_{Kxa} [ID_X \parallel H(M)] \parallel T]$

It is assumed that the senders X and A share a secret key K_{xa} and A shares a secret key K_{ay} with the receiver Y. The signature comprises ID_x and $H(M)$, encrypted using K_{xa}. A decrypts the signature using K_{xa} and recovers $H(M)$. A re-computes $H(M)$ and compares it with the received value for verification. Then it transmits the message to Y after appending time-stamp T and encrypting the entire message using K_{ay}. Y decrypts the received message to recover M. Y cannot directly check the signature of X; however, it scores the entire signature with itself. In case of any dispute with X, Y transmits the following message to A for verification:

$$E_{Kay} [IDX \| M \| E_{Kxa} [ID_X \| H(M)]]$$

So, the signature is used only to settle a dispute, if any. Y considers the signature verified, since it is received through A. So, both sides must have a high degree of confidence in A, that is,

- X must trust A not to reveal K_{xa} and not to generate false signatures of the form

$$E_{Kxa} [ID_X \| H(M)]$$

- Y must trust A to send $E_{Kay} [ID_X \| M \| E_{Kxa} [ID_X \| H(M)] \| T]$, only if the hash value is correct and the signature was generated by X only

- Both sides must trust A to resolve disputes fairly

So, if A is fully trustworthy, X is assured that its signatures will not be forged, and Y is assured that X cannot disown its signatures. But A is able to read the messages from X to Y. So, confidentiality of the messages is missing.

2. Conventional Encryption; Arbitrator cannot see the Message

This scheme provides signature verification by the Arbiter and also ensures confidentiality of messages. Here, the Arbiter will compare the hashed value of the message encrypted with key K_{xy}. Thus, the Arbiter will not be able to read the message, but will be able to verify the signature of X.

A. $X \rightarrow A$: $ID_X \| E_{Kxy} [M] \| E_{Kxa} [ID_X \| H(E_{Kxy} [M])]$

B. $A \rightarrow Y$: $E_{Kay} [ID_X \rightarrow E_{Kxy} [M] \| E_{Kx}] ID_X \| H(E_{Kxy} [M])] \| T]$

The recipient Y will preserve the encrypted signature, including the time-stamp:

$$E_{Kxa} [ID_x \| H(E_{Kxy}[M]) \| T]$$

In case of a dispute, Y will present this signature along with the encrypted message for verification by the Arbiter. Since the Arbiter has K_{xa}, the secret key shared with X, the Arbiter will be able to verify the signature and resolve the dispute.

3. Public Key Encryption; Arbitrator cannot see the Message

A. $X \rightarrow A$: $ID_X \| E_{KUy} [M]_{Kxa} E_{Kxa} [ID_X \| [E_{KRx} [H(E_{KUy} [M])]]$

B. $A \rightarrow Y$: $E_{Kay} [ID_X \| E_{KUy} [M] \| E_{Kxa} [ID_x \| E_{KRx} [H(E_{KUy} [M]) \| T]$

A can decrypt the outer encryption using the Public Key of X, that is, KU_x, and verify that the message has been received from X only. But the arbiter cannot read the message M. Only Y can decrypt fully using Public Key KU_a of A, its own private key KR_y, and the public key KU_x of X.

This scheme has a distinct advantage over the earlier schemes, that is, there is no shared secret key used. So, it protects the alliances from fraud. Second, no correct-dated message can be sent even if KR_x is compromised, assuming that KR_a is not compromised. Finally, the message from X to Y is kept secret from everyone else, including from A.

8.5 AUTHENTICATION PROTOCOLS

8.5.1 Mutual Authentication

These protocols enable the communicating parties to be mutually satisfied about each other's identity and to exchange session keys. The messages pertaining to the exchange of session keys have to be encrypted. This requires the prior existence of shared secret keys or public/private keys specifically meant for this purpose. The second issue is to prevent message replays. The techniques used to counter the message replays are:

1. **Time-Stamps:** This approach requires synchronization of clocks among the communicating parties. This scheme must allow a sufficiently large window of time to accommodate network delays; at the same time the window should be sufficiently small to prevent attacks.

2. **Nonce Value:** Party A, expecting a fresh message from B, first sends B a Nonce N (random integer value) and requires that the subsequent message from B contains the correct Nonce value N. This scheme is unsuitable for connectionless communication, since it requires a prior "handshake" of the communication parties, which goes against the basic principle of the connectionless approach.

8.5.2 Symmetric Encryption Approaches

This approach involves the use of a trusted Key Distribution Center (KDC). Each party in the network shares a secret key (called a Master Key) with the KDC. The KDC is responsible to issue one-time Session Keys to the parties in the network. A Session Key is meant for a single session use only. Supposing party A wishes to have a session with party B, Needham Schroeder Protocol enables a session key to be issued to A and

B as depicted here. While K is a secret key shared between the KDC and A and K_b is the secret key shared between the KDC and B, N_1 and N_2 are Nonce values used for preventing Replay Attacks. K_s is the session key issued for one session only.

8.5.3 Needham Schroeder Protocol

1. $A \rightarrow KDC: ID_A \parallel ID_B \parallel N_1$
2. $KDC \rightarrow A: E_{Ka} [K_s \parallel ID_B \parallel N_1 \parallel E_{Kb} [K_s \parallel ID_A]]$
3. $A \rightarrow B: E_{Kb} [K_s \parallel ID_A]$
4. $B \rightarrow A: E_{Ks} [N_2]$
5. $A \rightarrow B: E_{Ks} [f(N_2)]$

The protocol has a drawback. If an opponent (X) is able to compromise an old session key, then it can use Step 3, impersonate A, and trick B into using the old session key. Now, if X can intercept the Step 4 message, it can send the response of Step 5. Now, X can send fraudulent messages to B, who in turn will consider the messages as coming from A. Denning proposed the inclusion of a time-stamp in Step 2 and Step 3 to remove this weakness of the Needham Schroeder Protocol.

8.5.4 Denning Protocol

1. $A \rightarrow KDC: ID_A \parallel ID_B \parallel N_1$
2. $KDC \rightarrow A: E_{Ka} [K_s \parallel ID_B \parallel T \parallel E_{Kb} [K_s \parallel ID_A \parallel T]]$
3. $A \rightarrow B: E_{Kb} [K_s \parallel ID_A \parallel T]$
4. $B \rightarrow A: E_{Ks} [N_1]$
5. $A \rightarrow B: E_{Ks} [f(N_1)]$

The Denning Protocol ensures a higher degree of security as compared to the Needham Schroeder Protocol, but it relies on Time-Stamps, the efficacy of which depends on accurate synchronization of clocks. However, in case of the failure of the synchronization of clocks, the scheme would provide ample scope for replay attacks.

Another approach which avoids use of time-stamps and instead uses Nonce only for preventing replay attacks, is depicted as follows:

8.5.5 NEUM Protocol

1. $A \rightarrow KDC: ID_A \| N_a$
2. $B \rightarrow KDC: ID_B \| N_b \| E_{Kb}[ID_A \| N_a \| T_b]$
3. $KDC \rightarrow A: E_{Ka}[ID_B \| N_a \| K_s \| T_b] \| E_{Kb}[ID_A \| K_s \| T_b] \| N_b$
4. $A \rightarrow B: E_{Kb}[ID_A \| K_s \| T_b] \| E_{Ks}[N_b]$

where T_b is the time-limit for which session key K_S is valid. Let us follow this protocol step-by-step:

1. The Nonce N_a, sent unencrypted by A to B, is returned to A along with session key K_S in an encrypted message at Step 2, thus assuring A of the timeliness of the session key K_S.

2. The Nonce N_b sent by B to the KDC is returned back to B along with session key K_S in an encrypted message in Step 3, thus assuring B of the timeliness of the session key K_S.

3. B instructs the KDC about the validation periodicity of the session key to be issued, thus preventing the replay of old session keys.

4. In Step 4, A encrypts the Nonce N_b by the session key K_S, which authenticates at B that the message has been sent by A only and is not a replay message.

This protocol provides secure means for issue of a session key. This session key can be used between A and B for multiple sessions, but within the time-limit T_b, thus avoiding overheads for the issue of a fresh session key. To avoid attacks, T_b should not have too high a value. Since the time specified is with respect to B's clock, its validity is with respect to B's clock only. For the repeat session, A and B will proceed as follows:

1. $A \rightarrow B: E_{Kb}[ID_A \| K_s \| T_b] \| N_a$
2. $B \rightarrow A: N_b \| E_{Ks}[N_a]$
3. $A \rightarrow B: E_{Ks}[N_b]$

8.5.6 Public-Key Encryption Approaches

A protocol using a time-stamp is depicted as follows:

1. $A \rightarrow AS: ID_A \| ID_B$
2. $AS \rightarrow A: E_{Kras}[ID_A \| KU_A \| T] \| E_{Kras}[ID_B \| KU_B \| T]$

3. $A \rightarrow B: E_{Kras}[ID_A \| KU_A \| T] \| E_{Kras}[ID_B \| KU_B \| T] \| E_{Kub}[E_{Kra} \| K_S \| T]$

Here, the Authentication Server only provides the Public Keys; it does not issue Session Keys. The Session Key is determined by A. Thus, *AS* cannot compromise the session keys. The main limitation of this algorithm is that it depends on the synchronization of clocks. The following algorithm is free of this problem:

1. $A \rightarrow KDC: ID_A \| ID_B$

2. $KDC \rightarrow A: E_{KRautb}[ID_B \| KU_b]$

3. $A \rightarrow B: E_{KUb}[N_a \| ID_A]$

4. $B \rightarrow KDC: ID_B \| ID_A \| E_{KUautb}[N_a]$

5. $KDC \rightarrow B: E_{KRautb}[ID_A \| KU_a] \| E_{Kub}[E_{KRautb}[N_a \| K_s \| ID_A]]$

6. $B \rightarrow A: E_{KUa}[E_{KRautb}[N_a \| K_s \| ID_B] \| N_b]$

7. $A \rightarrow B: E_{Ks}[N_b]$

8.5.7 One-Way Authentication

The purpose of one-way authentication is two-fold:

1. For an e-mail type of application, the message is forwarded to the intended receiver's electronic mailbox. En route the message is handled by a store-and-forward protocol such as Simple Mail Transfer Protocol (SMTP) or X.400. However, it is often desirable that the mail transfer protocol should not have access to the plaintext of the message. Accordingly, the e-mail message must be encrypted such that only the intended receiver has the decryption key.

2. The recipient should be able to authenticate the identity of the alleged sender.

8.5.8 Symmetric Encryption Approach

1. $A \rightarrow KDC: ID_A \| ID_B \| N_1$

2. $KDC \rightarrow A: E_{Ka}[K_s \| ID_B \| N_1 \| E_{Kb}[K_s \| ID_A]]$

3. $A \rightarrow B: E_{Kb}[K_s \| ID_A] \| E_{Ks}[M]$

The approach ensures that only the intended recipient will be able to read the message M. It also authenticates to B that the sender is A. However, it provides no protection against replays.

8.5.9 Public Key Encryption Approach

The message is encrypted using the one-time key K_s. Only B will be able to extract the key K_s using its private key KR_b. Then using K_s, B can decrypt the message M.

$$A \rightarrow B: E_{KUb} [K_s] \| E_{Ks} [M]$$

However, if only authentication is the concern, then the following suffice:

$$A \rightarrow B: M \| E_{KRa} [H(M)]$$

This scheme guarantees that A cannot later deny having sent the message M. It does not provide confidentiality. Anyone can read the plaintext and misuse it. To counter this, both the message and signature can be encrypted with receiver's public key.

$$A \rightarrow B: E_{KUb} [M \| E_{KRa} [H(M)]]$$

The above two schemes require that B know A's Public Key KU_a. An effective way of assuring B about A's valid public key is to append a digital certificate issued by the Authentication Authority, as depicted as follows:

$$A \rightarrow B: E_{KUb} [M \| E_{KRa} [H(M)]] \| E_{KRas} [T \| ID_A \| KU_A]$$

The time-stamp T assures the timeliness of Public Key KU_a of sender A.

8.5.10 The Birthday Paradox

The Birthday Paradox can be stated as follows:

"What must be the minimum value of "k" so that the probability of at least two persons having the same birthday among a group of "k" persons is more than 1/2 (assuming that the birthdays' distribution is uniform)?"

Number of persons in the group $= k$.

Number of possible values of birthdays $= n = 365$ (ignoring the leap years)

Let $P(n, k)$ denote the Probability that at least one pair of persons among the k persons have the same birthday.

Let $Q(n, k)$ denote the probability that no pair among the k persons have same birthday.

$\therefore P(n, k) = 1 - Q(n, k)$

If $k > n$ (i.e., the number of persons in the group is more than 365), then it is impossible for each person in the group to have a distinct birthday. $P(n, k)$ will be equal to l and $Q(n, k)$ will be equal to 0.

Here, we assume that $k < n$ (i.e., the number of persons in the group is less than 365).

8.5.10.1 Determining $Q(n, k)$

For $Q(n, k)$ to be non-zero, the k persons can have their birthdays as follows:

The first person can have any of the possible n birthdays.

The second person can have any of the remaining $(n-1)$ birthdays.

Likewise, the kth person can have any of the remaining $(n-(k-1))$ birthdays.

Thus, for $Q(n, k)$ to be non-zero, the number of ways that k persons can have their birthdays $= n \times (n-1) \times (n-2) \times \ldots \times (n-(k-1))$.

As such, any of the k persons can have any of the n birthdays.

$\therefore$ The total number of ways that k persons can have their birthdays $= n^k$

$\therefore Q(n, k) = [n \times (n-1) \times (n-2) \times \ldots \times (n-(k-1))] / n^k$

$\quad = [(n/n) \times (1-1/n) \times (1-2/n) \times \ldots \times (1-(k-1)/n)]$

$\quad = [1 \times (1-1/n) \times (1-2/n) \times \ldots \times (1-(k-1)/n)]$

$\quad = [(1-1/n) \times (1-2/n) \times \ldots \times (1-(k-1)/n)]$

Since $(1-x) < e^{-x}$ for all $x > 0$

$\therefore (1-1/n) < e^{-1/n}$

$\therefore (1-2/n) < e^{-2/n}$

Likewise $(1-(k-1)/n) < e^{-(k-1)/n}$

$\therefore [(1-1/n) \times (1-2/n) \times \ldots \times (1-(k-1)/n)] < [e^{-1/n} \times e^{-2/n} \times \ldots \times e^{-(k-1)/n}]$

$\quad < e^{-1/n \, [1+2+\ldots+(k-1)]}$

$< e^{-k(k-1)/2n}$

Since $1 + 2 + 3 + \ldots + (k-1)\, k\, (k-1)/2$

$\therefore Q\,(n, k) < e^{-k\,(k-1)/2n}$

$P\,(n, k) > e^{-k\,(k-1)/2n}$

For $P\,(n, k) > 0.5$

$e^{-k(k-1)/2n} = 0.5$

$\therefore e^{-k(k-1)/2n} = 2$

$\therefore k\,(k-1)/2n = \log_e 2$

$\therefore k\,(k-1) = 2n \log_e 2$

If k is large then $k\,(k-1) \approx k^2$

$\therefore$ For large k,

$k^2 = 2n \log_e 2$

$\therefore k = \sqrt{2n \log_e 2}$

$\therefore k = 1.18\ \sqrt{n}$

Since $n = 365$

$\therefore k = 1.18\ \sqrt{365}$

$= 22.54 \approx 23$

Thus, if there are 23 persons in a group, then the probability that at least two of them will have the same birthday is greater than 1/2.

8.5.11 Probability of Two Sets Overlapping

The problem can be stated as follows:

- Let V be a random variable having uniform distribution in the range $1 \ldots n$.

- Let there be two sets X and Y, each having k instances of random variable V, where $k < n$.

- What should be the minimum value of k so that the probability of the two sets overlapping is more than 1 /2?

    Let $X = \{x_1, x_2, .., x_k\}$

$$Y = \{y_1, y_2, ..., y_k\}$$

Probability that x_1 matches y_1 = $1/n$

Probability that x_1 does not match $y_1 = 1 - 1/n$

Probability that x_1 does not match any of the y-values = $(1-1/n)^k$

Probability that none of the x-values match with any of the y-values = $((1-1/n)^k)^k$

Let $R(n, k)$ be the Probability that at least one of the x-values matches with one of the y-values (i.e., probability of the two sets overlapping).

$\therefore R(n, k) = 1-((1-1/n)^k)^k$

Using the inequality $e^{-x} > (1-x)$ for all $x > 0$

We have $e^{-1/n} > (1-1/n)$ for all $1/n > 0$

$\therefore R(n, k) > 1- ((e^{-1/n})^k)^k$

For $R(n, k)$ to be greater than 0.5

$1- ((e^{-1/n})^k)^k = 1/2$

$\therefore ((e^{-1/n})^k)^k = 1/2$

$\therefore ((e^{1/n})^k)^k = 2$

$\therefore k^2/n = \log_e 2$

$\therefore k = \sqrt{n \log_e 2} = 0.83\sqrt{n}$

For large n, $k \approx \sqrt{n}$

8.5.12 Mathematical Basis for Birthday Attack

- Consider a Hash Function H producing an m-bit hash value, that is, there can be 2^n possible different hash values.

- We apply the hash function to a set X of k random messages and produce a set of k hash values.

- We again apply the same hash function to set Y of k random messages and produce another set of k hash values.

- The minimum value of k to have at least one message pair $(x \in X, y \in Y)$ satisfying $H(x) = H(y)$ with a probability greater than $1/2$ is given by:

$$k = 0.83\sqrt{2^m} = 0.83 \times 2^{m/2}$$

This forms the mathematical basis for the Birthday Attack on Digital Signatures.

8.5.13 Birthday Attack

- This attack is carried out by an insider ("Eve") who enjoys the confidence of a valid signer ("A"), but Eve does not have access to A's Private Key.

- If user "A" asks Eve to prepare a message M for A's signatures, then Eve can perform the Birthday Attack as follows:

  Let the size of the hash value be m bits.

1. Eve generates $2^{m/2}$ variants of the valid message M, with all these variants conveying the same meaning as M. Let us denote the set of these valid messages by X.

2. Eve also prepares $2^{m/2}$ variants of a fraudulent message M that Eve wants to convey. Let us denote the set of these fraudulent messages by Y.

3. The two sets of messages are processed to determine a pair of messages ($x \in X$, $y \in Y$) that produce the same hash value, that is, $H(x) = H(y)$. The probability of getting this pair, by the Birthday Paradox, is greater than 1/2.

4. If there is no success in step (3), then repeat steps (1) to (3) by generating new variants of the valid message M and fraudulent message M.

5. If there is success in step (3), then Eve offers the valid variant x to A for signatures.

6. "A" will readily sign the message x using its private key, append the digital signature to the message, and hand over the signed message to "Eve" for transmission.

X
$E_{PR}[H(M)]$

7. Eve replaces the message x with message y, leaving the digital signature intact, and transmits the resulting message to the intended recipient.

Y
$E_{PR}[H(M)]$

8.5.14 Verification of the Digital Signature at the Recipient End

Figure 8.13 illustrates the Verification of the Digital Signature at the Recipient End.

Since $H(y) = H(x)$, the intended recipient will not be able to detect that the original message x has been replaced by a fraudulent message y. The recipient will consider the fraudulent message y as a valid message.

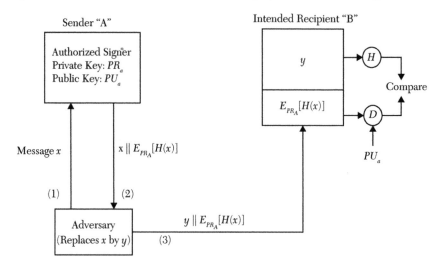

FIGURE 8.13 A schematic diagram of the verification of the digital signature at the recipient end.

8.5.15 How to Create Many Variants of a Message

"Mr. David/Kristy David is arriving/reaching by air/by flight today/on the 19th to discuss/to deliberate on pending problems/Pending issues"

In the above message, we have introduced alternatives at 6 places. This will enable us to generate $2^6 = 64$ variants of the message, all with the same meaning. In this way, we can create a large number of variants from a message of reasonable length.

8.5.16 Weak Collision Resistance

Suppose $X = \{x_1, x_2,..., x_k\}$ is a set of k messages. What must be the minimum size k of the set that for a given message x_i in the set, the probability of at least one more message in the set with same hash value as x_i is greater than 1/2?

Let the number of possible variants of the Hash value = n (assuming that each hash value is equally likely).

The probability that the hash value of x_i matches with the hash value of $x_j = 1/n$.

The probability that the hash value of x_i does not match with hash value of $x_j = 1 - 1/n$.

The probability that the hash value of x_i does not match with the hash values of any of the remaining $(k-1)$ messages = $(1-1/n)^{k-1}$.

Let $R[n, k]$ be the Probability that the hash value of x_i matches with the hash value of at least one of the remaining $(k-1)$ messages.

Then $R[n, k] > 1 - e^{-(k-1)/n}$

For $R[n, k]$ to be greater than 0.5

$1 - e^{-(k-1)/n} = 0.5$

$\therefore e^{-(k-1)/n} = 0.5$

$\therefore e^{(k-1)/n} = 2$

$\therefore (k-1)/n = \log_e 2$

$\therefore k = n \times \log_e 2 + 1$

$\therefore k = 0.693\, n + 1$

Let m be the size of the hash value.

Then $n = 2^m$

$k = 0.693 \times 2^m + 1 \approx 2^m$ for a significantly large value of 2^m.

For Birthday Problem $n = 365$

$k = 0.693 \times 365 + 1 = 253 + 1 = 254$

This implies that there are 254 persons in a group and one person ("A") is chosen from the group. Then the probability of at least one more person in the group having the same birthday as "A" is greater than 1/2.

8.5.17 Strengths of Hash Functions

- The larger the size of the Hash Code, the more secure the system will be against attacks, since the effort required for the birthday attack is of the order of $2^{m/2}$, where m is the size of the hash code.

▪ There are three desirable properties of hash functions:

- **One-Way Function:** For a given hash code h, it is computationally infeasible to find x such that $H(x) = h$.

- **Weak Collision Resistance:** For any given message x, it is computationally infeasible to find $y \neq x$ such that $H(y) = H(x)$.

- **Strong Collision Resistance:** It is computationally infeasible to find a pair
  (x, y) such that $H(x) = H(y)$.

▪ Effort required to break the "Weak Collision Resistance" in Hash Functions. The level of effort required for attacks to break the "Weak Collision Resistance" in hash functions will be of the order of 2^m.

▪ Effort required to break the "Strong Collision Resistance" in Hash Functions. The level of effort required to break the Strong Collision Resistance will be of the order of $2m12$, like in the case of the Birthday Attack.

The strength of a hash function equals the level of effort required to break the strong collision resistance in that function.

A 128-bit Hash Code generated by MD5 was broken in 24 days. However, for a hash code length of 160 bits, the same machine will take more than 4000 years to find a collision. Two most popular hash codes, SHA-1 and RIPEND-160, use 160-bit hash code.

8.6   MESSAGE DIGEST (HASH FUNCTION) ALGORITHMS

8.6.1 MD5 Message Digest Algorithm

MD5 is a Hash Algorithm that takes as input a message of arbitrary length and produces as output a 128-bit Hash Value called a Message Digest. The input message is divided into 512-bit blocks and each block is divided into sixteen 32-bit words for processing. The algorithm makes use of a 128-bit Message Digest Buffer (MD Buffer) that holds the intermediate and final 128-bit Message Digest value.

Figure 8.14 depicts the overall processing of an MD5 Algorithm that consists of the following major steps:

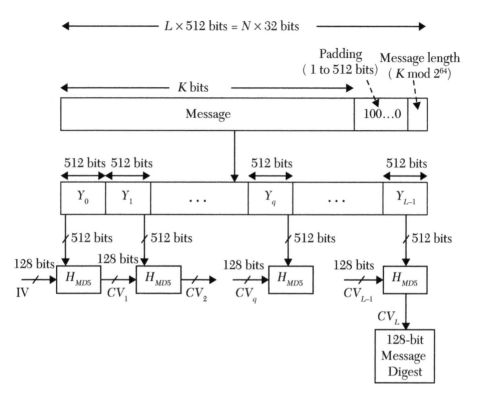

FIGURE 8.14 A schematic diagram of the overall processing of an MD5 algorithm.

1. **Step 1: Append Padding Bits**

    - The input message can be of any arbitrary length (K bits).

    - It is always padded with $1 \ldots 512$ bits such that the message length after padding becomes congruent to 448 mod 512.

    - Even if K is already congruent to 448 mod 512, padding is still added; in that case the padding will be 512 bits.

    - The bit pattern of padding is a "1"-bit, followed by remaining "0"-bits.

2. **Step 2: Append Message Length**

    - After padding, a 64-bit message length equal to ($K \bmod 2^{64}$) is appended to the padded message, where K is the length of the original unpadded message.

    - After adding the message length, the overall length of the message will become an exact multiple of 512.

- The overall message is divided into L blocks of 512-bit blocks each. Let the L blocks be denoted as Y_0, Y_1, ..., Y_{L-1}.

- Each block is further divided into sixteen 32-bit words. Let the overall message M be denoted as M [0 ... N-1], where $N = 16*L$ is the total number of 32-bit words to be processed.

3. **Step 3: Initialize the MD Buffer**

   - The 128-bit MD Buffer is divided into four 32-bit registers designated as A, B, C, and D, which are used to hold the intermediate values and the final result of the message digest (hash value).

   - These four registers are initialized to the following HEX values:

     $A = 67452301$

     $B = EFCDAB89$

     $C = 98BADCFE$

     $D = 10325476$

   - These values are stored in the little-endian format, that is, the least significant byte is stored in the low-address byte position, as shown in the following:

MD Register A:

0	1
2	3
4	5
6	7

MD Register B:

8	9
A	B
C	D
E	F

MD Register C:

F	E
D	C
B	A
9	8

MD Register D:

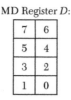

7	6
5	4
3	2
1	0

4. Step 4: Process the Message in terms of 512-bit blocks

- The heart of MD5 processing is a Compression Function H_{M05} that consists of 4 rounds of processing, and each round consists of sixteen steps. Inputs to each Round.

- Current 512-bit message block (S_{ayYq}). The block is divided into sixteen 32-bit words. In each round, each of the sixteen words is used precisely once in one of the sixteen steps; the order in which the words are used depends on the round.

- Current 128-bit MD Buffer value, which is obtained from the processing of previous block of data. For the processing of the first block, MD Buffer will have its value as initialized previously in Step 3.

- Each round also takes as input one fourth of the 64-element Sine-Function Table $T[1...64]$. The 64-element Sine-Function table comprises 32-bit randomized values. The ith element of the table is determined as:

$$T[I] = \text{TRUNC}\ (2^{32} \times ABS\ (\text{Sin}\ (i))),\ 1 < i < 64$$

i is in radians (One radian= 180/Pi deg)

All values are distinct and each of the 64 steps gets a different value of the sine-function, as indicated as follows:

Round	Subset of Sine-Table Used
1	$T\ [\ 1...16]$
2	$T\ [17...32]$
3	$T\ [33...48]$
4	$T\ [49...64]$

- The processing of each round is identical, but it uses a different logical function in each round:

Round 1: Logical Function F

Round 2: Logical Function G

Round 3: Logical Function H

Round 4: Logical Function I

Output

- Each round has a 128-bit output that updates the contents of MD Buffer.

- The first-round input (CV_q) is added to the output of the fourth round. The addition is performed mod 2^{32}, independently for the four registers of the MD Buffer. The 128-bit resulting output CV_{q+1} updates the contents of the MD Buffer. This goes as input for the processing of the next block of data.

- The output resulting from the processing of the last block, that is, CV_L, forms the final 128-bit Message Digest (or Hash Value).

8.6.2 Sequence of Use of Message Words in Various Rounds

- The 512-bit Message Block Y_q is divided into sixteen 32-bit words $X[0...15]$. Let the steps be q numbered as $i = 0...15$.

- Each word is used precisely in one step of each round; the sequence, in which sixteen words are used in the sixteen steps of a round, is explained as follows:

Round 1: Words used in the same sequence as they occur in the message block.

Step	0	1	2	3	4	5	6	7	8	9	10	11	12	13	14	15
Word	$X[0]$	$X[1]$	$X[2]$	$X[3]$	$X[4]$	$X[5]$	$X[6]$	$X[7]$	$X[8]$	$X[9]$	$X[10]$	$X[11]$	$X[12]$	$X[13]$	$X[14]$	$X[15]$

Round 2: Word index $P_{2i} = (1 + 5i) \bmod 16$

Step	0	1	2	3	4	5	6	7	8	9	10	11	12	13	14	15
Word	$X[0]$	$X[6]$	$X[11]$	$X[0]$	$X[4]$	$X[5]$	$X[15]$	$X[4]$	$X[9]$	$X[14]$	$X[3]$	$X[8]$	$X[13]$	$X[2]$	$X[7]$	$X[12]$

Round 3: Word index $P_{3i} = (5 + 3i) \bmod 16$

Step	0	1	2	3	4	5	6	7	8	9	10	11	12	13	14	15
Word	$X[5]$	$X[8]$	$X[11]$	$X[14]$	$X[1]$	$X[4]$	$X[7]$	$X[10]$	$X[13]$	$X[0]$	$X[3]$	$X[6]$	$X[9]$	$X[12]$	$X[15]$	$X[2]$

Round 4: Word index $P_{4i} = (7i) \bmod 16$

Step	0	1	2	3	4	5	6	7	8	9	10	11	12	13	14	15
Word	$X[0]$	$X[7]$	$X[14]$	$X[5]$	$X[12]$	$X[3]$	$X[10]$	$X[1]$	$X[8]$	$X[15]$	$X[6]$	$X[13]$	$X[4]$	$X[11]$	$X[2]$	$X[9]$

8.6.3 Primitive Logical Functions Used in Various Rounds

Round	Function	Logic $g(b, c, d)$
1	F	$(b \wedge c) \vee (\leftarrow b \wedge d)$
2	G	$(b \wedge d) \vee (c \wedge \leftarrow d)$
3	H	$b \oplus c \oplus d$
4	I	$c \oplus (b \vee \leftarrow d)$

Where $\oplus$: *XOR*, $\wedge$: *AND*, $\vee$: *OR*, $\leftarrow$: *NOT*

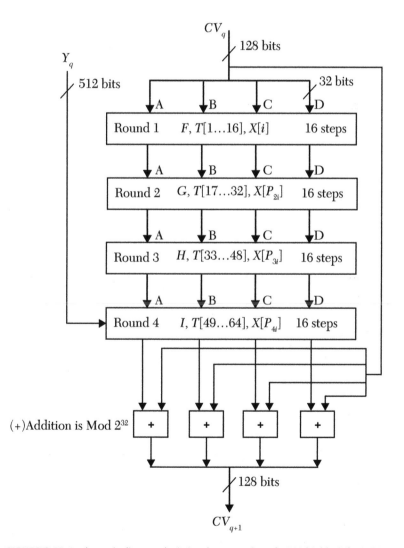

FIGURE 8.15 A schematic diagram depicting the processing of a 512-bit block for MD5.

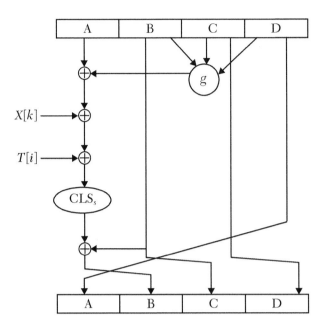

FIGURE 8.16 A schematic diagram depicting the functionality of each step for MD5.

For the first round where the words appear in the 16 steps in the same sequence as they occur in the data block Y_q,

$$X[k] = M[16q + k], \text{ i.e., } k^{\text{th}} \text{ word of } q^{\text{th}} \text{ block}$$

For other rounds, the words get scrambled.

$T[i]$ = 32-bit i^{th} word of Sine Table T.

The *MD* register contents are modified by each step, as follows:

$$a \leftarrow d$$
$$b \leftarrow b + \left[\left(a + g(b,c,d) \right) + X[K] + T[I] <<< s \right]$$
$$c \leftarrow b$$
$$d \leftarrow c$$

8.6.4 Strength of MD5

- It has property that each bit of the 128-bit message digest is a function of every bit of the input message.

- The complex repetition of the logical functions (*F/G/H/I*) produces results that are well mixed; that makes the collision attack highly difficult.

- But a 128-bit Hash Value MD5 was broken in 24 days. However, for a hash value of 160 bits in length, the same machine will take more than 4000 years to break.

8.7   SECURE HASH ALGORITHM (SHA-1)

SHA-1 design is based on the MD4 algorithm. The algorithm takes as input a message of less than 2^{64} bits and produces as output a 160-bit message digest. The input is processed in 512-bit blocks. The overall structure of processing is similar to MD5 as shown earlier. The processing consists of the following steps:

1. **Step 1: Append Padding Bits:** The message is padded with 1...512 bits such that its length after padding is congruent to 448 mod 512. Padding is always added even if the message length is already congruent to 448 mod 512. Padding consists of a single 1-bit followed by the necessary number of 0-bits.

2. **Step 2: Append Message Length:** A 64-bit representation of unpadded message length is appended to the padded message, thus making its overall length an exact multiple of 512. Let the overall length be 512*L* bits and the *L* blocks of 512 bits each be represented by Y_0, Y_1, ..., Y_{L-1}. Equivalently, each 512-bit block can be viewed as 16 32-bit words. The message comprises *N* words, where $N = 16 \times L$. Let the Message *M* be represented as *M*[0 ... *N*-1] words.

3. **Step 3: Initialize the MD Buffer**: A 160-bit Buffer is used to hold the intermediate and final results of the Hash Function. The buffer can be represented as five 32-bit registers (*A*, *B*, *C*, *D*, *E*). These five registers are initialized to the following HEX values:

    A = 67452301

    B = EFCDAB89

    C = 98BADCFE

    D = 10325476

    E = C3D2E1FO

Unlike MD5, the values are stored in big-endian format, that is, the most significant byte of the word in a low-address byte position. The registers after initialization will appear as follows (HEX):

MD Register *A*:

6	7
4	5
2	3
0	1

MD Register *B*:

E	F
C	D
A	B
8	9

MD Register *C*:

9	8
B	A
D	C
F	E

MD Register *D*:

1	0
3	2
5	4
7	6

MD Register *E*:

C	3
D	2
E	1
F	0

4. **Step 4: Process Message in terms of 512-bit (16-word) blocks.** The heart of one algorithm is a Compression Function that consists of 4 rounds of processing of 20 steps each. Each round has an identical structure but uses a different primitive logical function, referred to as f_1, f_2, f_3, and f_4. Each round takes as input the current 512-bit block being processed (Y_q) and 160-bit buffer value ABCD and updates the contents of the buffer.

Each round also makes use of an additive constant K_t, where $0 \leq t \leq 79$ indicates one of the 80 steps across five rounds. In fact, only four distinct constants are used, as indicated in the following:

Round	Hexadecimal	Take Integer part of
I	$K_{t1} = 5A827999$	$2^{10}\,(2)^{1/2}$
II	$K_{t2} = 6ED9EBA1$	$2^{30}\,(3)^{1/2}$
III	$K_{t3} = 8F1BSCDC$	$2^{30}\,(5)^{1/2}$
IV	$K_{t4} = CA62C1D6$	$2^{30}\,(10)^{1/2}$

The 512-bit word is divided into sixteen 32-bit words, which form $W[0] \ldots W[15]$. A word each is used in the first 16 steps of round 1. The remaining words for the remaining 64 steps are derived as follows:

$$W[t] = S^1\,(W[t\text{-}16] \oplus W[t\text{-}14] \oplus W[t\text{-}8] \oplus W[t\text{-}3]) \text{ where } \oplus: XOR.$$

The first-round input, that is, CV_q, is added to the fourth round output, to produce the final output CV_{q1}. The addition is performed modulo 2^{32}, independently for each of the five words (A, B, C, D, E).

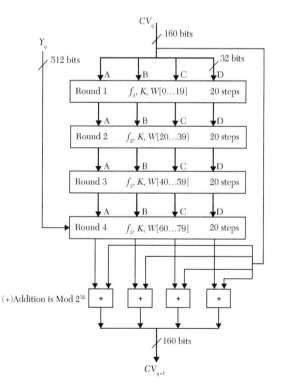

FIGURE 8.17 A schematic diagram depicting the processing of a 512-bit block for SHA-1.

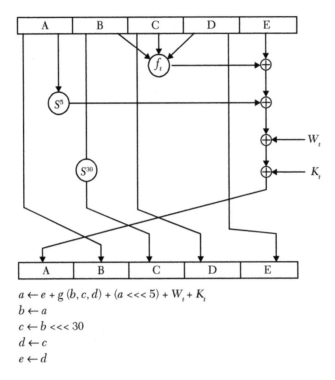

$$a \leftarrow e + g\,(b, c, d) + (a <<< 5) + W_t + K_t$$
$$b \leftarrow a$$
$$c \leftarrow b <<< 30$$
$$d \leftarrow c$$
$$e \leftarrow d$$

FIGURE 8.18 A schematic diagram depicting the functionality of each step for SHA-1.

5. **Step 5: Output:** After the last 512-bit block Y_{L-1} has been processed, the output from the last stage forms the 160-bit Message Digest.

We can summarize the processing as follows:

$$CV_0 = \text{IV}$$
$$CV_{q+1} = \text{SUM}_{32}\,(CV_q,\, ABCDE_q)$$

Final Message Digest Output $= CV_L$

TABLE. 8.1 Primitive Logical Functions Used in Various Rounds of SHA-1

Round	Function	Logic g(b, c, d)
1	f_1	$(b \wedge c) \vee (\leftarrow b \wedge d)$
2	f_2	$b \oplus c \oplus d$
3	f_3	$(b \wedge c) \vee (b \wedge d) \vee (c \wedge d)$
4	f_4	$b \oplus c \oplus d$

Where $\oplus$: *XOR*, $\wedge$: *AND*, $\vee$: *OR*, $\leftarrow$: *NOT*

8.7.1 Difference between MD5 and SHA-1

Though the design of SHA-1 is based on the design of MD5, there are some major differences between the two, which are tabulated here in Table 8. 2.

TABLE 8.2 Some Major Differences between MD5 and SHA-1

Parameter	MD5	SHA-1
Input Message Size	Any Size	< 2^{62} bytes
Message Digest Size	128 bits	160 bits
Number of Processing Steps per round	16	20
Format of Data Storage	Little-Endian	Big-Endian
Additive Used in Step Processing	64 random and distinct Sine Values – one per Step	4 Additive Constants – One per Round

The other parameters like the block size of 512 bits, word size of 32 bits, four steps per processing round, and the set of logical and arithmetic functions used in processing of MD5 and SHA-I are identical. The concept of padding is also similar in both.

8.7.2 Various Upgrades of SHA

SHA has many upgrades with increasing levels of security, like SHA-256, SHA-384, and SHA-512; the numeric part represents the size of the Message Digest output. Though some of the parameters like 4 processing rounds, 20 steps per round, and a Big-endian format of data storage remain the same in all the upgrades, there are some major differences in other parameters. A parameter-wise comparison of the upgrades is tabulated in Table 6.3.

TABLE 8.3 Some Major Differences in Various Upgrades of SHA

Parameter	SHA-1	SHA-256	SHA-384	SHA-512
Input Message Size	< 2^{64} bytes	< 2^{64} bytes	< 2^{128} bytes	< 2^{128} bytes
Message Digest Size	160 bits	256 bits	384 bits	512 bits
Processing Block Size	512 bits	512 bits	1024 bits	1024 bits
Word Size	32 bits	32 bits	64 bits	64 bits

8.8   DIGITAL SIGNATURE SCHEMES

- RSA Digital Signature Scheme
- ElGamal's Digital Signature Scheme
- Digital Signature Algorithm (DSA)

8.8.1 RSA Digital Signature Scheme

The scheme comprises the following components:

- Key Generation
- Signature Algorithm
- Signature Verification Algorithm

8.8.1.1 Generation of Keys

Each user generates its Public Key and Private Key as follows:

- Choose two large prime numbers p and q. (The larger the prime numbers, the harder it would be to break the cipher).
- Compute $n = pq$
- Compute $\Phi(n) = (p\text{-}1)(q\text{-}1)$
- Choose an integer e such that e is less than $\Phi(n)$ and relatively prime to $\Phi(n)$, that is, $GCD(e, \Phi(n)) = 1$.
- Compute integer d as the multiplicative inverse of e modulus $\Phi(n)$: $d \equiv e^{-1} \pmod{\Phi(n)}$ Thus, e and d form multiplicative inverses of each other $(\bmod\ \Phi(n))$.
- The pair (e, n) forms the Public Key and the pair (d, n) forms the Private Key of User "A." The Private Key is kept secret by the owner and the Public Key is made available to all other users in the cryptosystem.

8.8.1.2 Signature Algorithm

The Sender of a message M signs it as follows:

- Generate hash value $H(M)$ of the message using a Hash Function such that $0 < H(M) < n$
- Encrypt the Hash value $H(M)$ using an *RSA* Algorithm and Private Key (d, n) Sign $= (H(M))^d \bmod n$.

▪ The Sign is appended to the message M and transmitted to the intended recipient.

8.8.1.3 Signature Verification

Figure 8.17 illustrates the Signature verification. The recipient of the signed message verifies the Signature as follows:

▪ Computes the Hash Value of the received message M.

▪ Decrypts the Sign using the sender's public key (e, n) and extracts the hash value of the message that was computed at the sender end.

$H(M) = (\text{Sign})^e \bmod n = ((H(M))^d \bmod n) < \bmod n$

▪ Compares the hash value of the message computed at the recipient end with the one computed at the sender end. If both match exactly, the signature is considered to be verified.

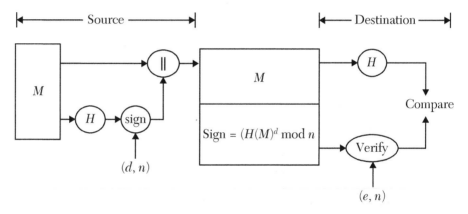

FIGURE 8.19 A schematic diagram of the Signature verification.

Example 8.1: RSA Signature Scheme

Let $p = 11$, $q = 7$

Then $n = p \times q = 77$

$\Phi(n) = 10 \times 6 = 60$

Let public key $e = 13$

Private Key $d \equiv e^{-1} \bmod \Phi(n) \equiv 13^{-1} \bmod 60 = 37$

8.8.1.3.1 Signing

Let $m = H(M) = 2$

Sign $= m^d \bmod n = 2^{37} \bmod 77 = 51$

$$2^{10} \bmod 77 = 1024 \bmod 77 = 23$$

$$2^{30} \bmod 77 = (23)^3 \bmod 77 = (67 \times 23) \bmod 77$$

$$= (-10 \times 23) \bmod 77 = 1$$

$$2^{37} \bmod 77 = (1 \times 128) \bmod 77 = 51$$

8.8.1.3.2 Signature Verification at the Recipient End

$$(\text{Sign})^e \bmod 77 = (51)^{13} \bmod 77 = 2 = m$$

$$(51)^2 \bmod 77 = (2601) \bmod 77 = 60$$

$$(51)^4 \bmod 77 = (60)^2 \bmod 77 = 3600 \bmod 77 = 58$$

$$(51)^8 \bmod 77 = (58)^2 \bmod 77 = (-19)^2 \bmod 77$$

$$= 361 \bmod 77 = 53$$

$$(51)^{13} \bmod 77 = (53 \times 58 \times 51) \bmod 77$$

$$= (-24 \times -19 \times -26) \bmod 77$$

$$= (624 \times -19) \bmod 77$$

$$= (8 \times -19) \bmod 77$$

$$= -152 \bmod 77 = 2$$

Since $(\text{Sign})^e \bmod 77 = m = H(M)$; the signature is verified.

8.8.2 ElGamal's Digital Signature Scheme

Figure 8.20 illustrates ElGamal's Digital Signature Scheme.

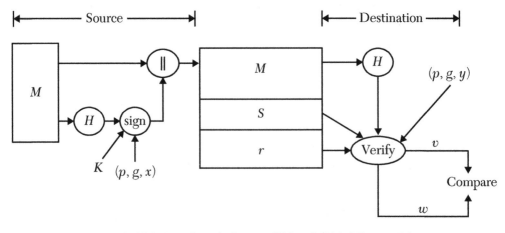

FIGURE 8.20 A schematic diagram of ElGamal's Digital Signature Scheme.

8.8.2.1 Global Parameters

The ElGamal Signature Scheme makes use of two Global Parameters that are made available to all users in the cryptosystem:

p: A large prime number

g: A primitive root of p

The scheme comprises Key Generation, Signature Algorithm, and Signature Verification Algorithm.

8.8.2.2 Key Generation

Each user in the cryptosystem will generate a Private Key and a Public Key, as follows:

- Chooses a random integer x such that $1 < x < \Phi(p)$.

- Computes $y = g^x \bmod p$.

- (p, g, x) forms the private key and (p, g, y) forms the public key of the user.

- The user keeps the private key secret and distributes the public key to all other users in the cryptosystem.

8.8.2.3 Signature Algorithm

Given a message M, the sender signs it as follows:

1. Computes a hash function $m = H(M)$ such that $0 \le m < p$.

2. Selects a random number k such that $1 < k < \Phi(p)$ and $GCD(k, \Phi(p)) = 1$, that is, Integer k must be relatively prime to $\Phi(p)$ so that $k^{-1} \bmod \Phi(p)$ is defined. (It is a time-consuming function to determine k relatively prime to $\Phi(p)$.)

3. Computes $r = g^k \bmod \Phi(p)$.

4. Computes $s = k^{-1}(m - rx) \bmod \Phi(p)$.

5. Now, (r, s) forms the digital signature of the sender, which is appended to the message prior to its transmission.

8.8.2.4 Signature Verification Algorithm

Having the public key (p, g, y) of the signer, the recipient verifies the signature (r, s) as follows:

- Computes Hash Function $m = H(M)$.

- Verifies that $0 < r < \Phi(p)$; else rejects the signature.

- Computes $v = g^m$ mod $\Phi(p)$ and $w = y^r\, r^s\, \Phi(p)$.

- Signature is accepted if $v = w$; else rejected.

Note: Since r is reduced mod $\Phi(p)$ and r is one of the base values for the computation of w, thus w also is to be reduced mod $\Phi(p)$. Since v is compared with w, so v is also to be reduced mod $\Phi(p)$. Thus, both v and w are also to be computed mod $\Phi(p)$; not mod p.

Proof of Correctness:

$w = (y^r \times r^s)$ mod $\Phi(p)$

$y = g^x$ mod p

$r = g^k$ mod $\Phi(p)$

$\therefore\ w = (g^{rx} \times g^{ks})$ mod $\Phi(p)$

$s = k^{-1}\,(m - rx)$

$\therefore\ w = (g^{rx} \times g^{(m-ks)})$ mod $\Phi(p)$

$\therefore\ w = g^m$ mod $\Phi(p) = v$

Thus, the proof.

Example 8.2: (ElGamal Signature Scheme)

Let $p = 11$ and $g = 2$ be global parameters.

8.8.2.5 Determination of Keys

The signer determines its keys as follows:

Let $x = 3$ and $(x, g, p) = (3, 2, 11)$ be the private key of the signer

$y = g^x$ mod $p = 2^3$ mod $11 = 8$

$\therefore$ Public key of the signer $= (y, g, p) = (8, 2, 11)$

8.8.2.6 Signing of the Message

Let $m = H(M) = 5$

Suppose the signer chooses $k = 3$ (which is relatively prime to $\Phi(p) = 10$)

Then $r = g^k$ mod $\Phi(p)$

$\qquad = 2^3$ mod $10 = 8$

$$s = (k^{-1} (m - rx)) \bmod \Phi (p)$$

$$= (3^{-1} (5 - 8 \times 3)) \bmod 10$$

$$= (7 \times (-19)) \bmod 10$$

$$= (7 \times 1) \bmod 10 = 7$$

∴. Digital Signature $= (r, s) = (8, 7)$

8.8.2.7 Signature Verification

$$v = g^m \bmod \Phi (p) = 2\ 5 \bmod 10 = 2$$

$$w = (y^r \times r^s) \bmod \Phi (p) = (8^8 \times 8^7) \bmod 10 = (8^3)^5 \bmod 11$$

$$= (512)^5 \bmod 10 = (2)^5 \bmod 10 = (32) \bmod 10 = 2$$

$$\therefore v = w = 2$$

∴ The Digital Signature stands verified.

Example 8.3: (ElGamal Signature Scheme)

Let $p = 19$, $g = 2$

Let private key $x = 3$

Public Key $y = g^x \bmod p = 2^3 \bmod 19 = 8$

8.8.2.8 Signing of Message by the Sender

Let $m = H(M) = 5$

Let $k = 7$

$$r = g^k \bmod \Phi (p)$$

$$= 2^7 \bmod 18 = 128 \bmod 18 = 20$$

$$s = k^{-1} (m - rx) \bmod \Phi (p)$$

$$= 7^{-1} (5 - 2 \times 3) \bmod 18$$

$$= 13 \times -1 \bmod 18 = 5$$

So, $(M, r, s) = (5, 2, 5)$ is transmitted to the intended recipient.

8.8.2.9 Verification of Signature by the Intended Recipient

$$v = g^m \bmod \Phi (p)$$

$$= 2^5 \bmod 18 = 14$$

$$w = (y^r \times r^s) \bmod \Phi(p)$$
$$= (8^2 \times 2^5) \bmod 18$$
$$= (64 \times 32) \bmod 18$$
$$= (10 \times 14) \bmod 18$$
$$= 14$$

$V = W = 14;$

∴ Signature stands verified.

8.8.3 Digital Signature Algorithm (DSA)

The National Institute of Standards and Technology (NIST) has published a Federal Information Processing Standard (FIPS 186), known as the Digital Signature Standard (DSS). It makes use of the Secure Hash Algorithm (SHA) and incorporates a Digital Signature Algorithm (DSA). The DSA is based on the difficulty of computing Discrete Logarithms and based on the scheme originally presented by ElGamal. The DSS approach is an improvement of the original scheme proposed by ElGamal and Schnorr (explained previously). For its security, it relies on the on the difficulty of computing discrete logarithms.

8.8.3.1 Global Parameters

DSS makes use of three global parameters (p, q, g) that are made available to all the users in the cryptosystem:

1. q: 160-bit prime number

2. p: 512...1024-bit prime number, such that q divides $\Phi(p)$.

3. g: an integer of order q (mod p). The integer g is determined as follows:

   A. $g = (h) \Phi^{(p)/q} \bmod p$, **where** $1 < h < \Phi(p)$ **such that** $g > 1$

   B. If $g = 1$ then choose another value of h and repeat step iii (a).
   If $g = 1$ then y and r will always be equal to 1.

8.8.3.2 Key Generation

A user (say User "A") generates its private key and public key as follows:

1. Chooses an integer x such that $1 < x < q$

2. Computes $y = g^x \bmod p$

3. Now (p, q, g, x) forms the Private Key and (p, q, g, y) forms the Public Key of User "A."

8.8.3.3 Signature Algorithm

Given a message M to be signed, user "A" proceeds as follows:

1. Computes Hash Function $m = H(M)$ such that $0 \leq m < q$.

2. Selects an integer k such that $1 < k < q$. Since $k < q$ and q is a prime number, therefore k will be relatively prime to q. The user does not have to make the extra effort to establish that k and q are co-primes. This is in contrast to the ElGamal Signature Scheme, wherein determining k relatively prime to $\Phi(p)$ involves significant overheads.

3. Computes $r = (g^k \bmod p) \bmod q$.

4. Computes $s = k^{-1}(m + rx) \bmod q$.

5. If $((r = 0)$ or $(s = 0))$ then repeat steps 1 to 4 by choosing another value of k. The parameters have to be non-zero, so that $s^{-1} \bmod q$ is defined.

6. Now, (r, s) forms the digital signature which is sent to the intended recipient along with the message M.

8.8.3.4 Signature Verification Algorithm

Knowing the Public Key (p, q, g, y) of user "A," the recipient will verify the digital signature (r, s) as follows:

1. Compute $m = H(M)$.

2. Verify that $0 < r < q$ and $0 < s < q$; else reject the signature.

3. Compute $t = s^{-1} \bmod q$.

4. Compute $v = ((g^m y^r)^t \bmod p) \bmod q$

5. If $v = r$ then accept the signature; else reject it.

Proof

$$v = ((g^m y^r)^t \bmod p) \bmod q$$
$$= ((g^m y^{xr})^t \bmod p) \bmod q)$$
$$= ((g^{(m+rx)t} \bmod q) \bmod p) \bmod q)$$

Since $s = k^{-1}(m + rx)$

$\therefore (m + rx) = ks$

$\therefore v = ((g^{kst} \bmod q) \bmod p) \bmod q$

Since $t = s^{-1} \bmod q$

$\therefore st \bmod q = 1$

$\therefore v = (g^k \bmod p) \bmod q = r$

Thus, the Proof.

8.8.3.5 Why Are *r* and *v* Computed (mod *p*) and Then (mod *q*) but *s* and *t* Are Computed Directly (mod *q*)?

$r = (g^k \bmod p) \bmod q$

The argument for computation of r is g, which is computed $(\bmod\, p)$. That is why r is first computed $(\bmod\, p)$ and then $(\bmod\, q)$.

Similarly, $v = ((g^m y^r)^t \bmod p) \bmod q$.

The arguments for v are g and y and both have been computed $(\bmod\, p)$. That is why v also is first computed $(\bmod\, p)$ and then $(\bmod\, q)$.

$s = k^{-1}(m + rx) \bmod q$.

All the arguments of s, that is, k, m, r, and x, are integers less than q. That is why s is computed $(\bmod\, q)$.

$T = s^{-1} \bmod q$

This argument that holds for s also holds for t.

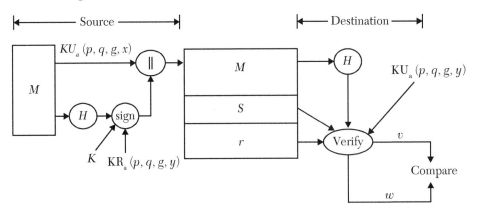

FIGURE 8.21 A schematic diagram depicting DSA.

where

M: Message to be sent

H: Hash Function

$KR_a = (p, q, g, x)$ = Private Key of Sender

p: Prime Number (512 to 1024 bits long)

q: prime (160 bits long) such that q divides $\Phi(p)$

$g = (h) \Phi^{(p)/q} \bmod p$, where $h \in \{0, 1, 2, ..., \Phi(p)\}$ such that $g > 1$

x: a random integer $(1 < x < q)$

Sign: Signature Function

k: a random integer $(1 < k < q)$

$KU_a = (p, q, g, y)$ = Public Key of Sender

$r = (g^k \bmod p) \bmod q$

$s = k^{-1} (m + rx) \bmod q$. $(s \neq 0)$

$y = g^x \bmod p$

$v = ((g^m \, y^r)^t \bmod p) \bmod q$ where $t = s^{-1} \bmod q$.

Example 8.4: (DSA)

Let $p = 23$, $q = 11$ $(q$ divides $\Phi(p))$

$g = (h) \Phi^{(p)/q} \bmod p$

Let $h = 2$

$\therefore g = (2)^{22/11} \bmod 23 = 4$

To verify that $g = 4$ has order 11 (mod 23):

X	g^x mod 23
1	4
2	16
3	18
4	3
5	12
6	2
7	8
8	9
9	13
10	6
11	1

Since all values g^x mod 23 ($1 \leq x \leq 11$) are distinct and less than 23, therefore the order of g mod 23 is 11. Therefore $p = 23$, $q = 11$, and $g = 4$ form global parameters.

8.8.3.6 Determination of Keys by the Authorized Signer

Let private key be $x = 3$

Then Public $y = g^x$ mod $p = 4^3$ mod $23 = 64$ mod $23 = 18$

Signing of A message by the authorized signer

Let the has h value of the message to be signed be $m = 5$ ($0 \leq m < q$)

Let the random integer chosen by the signer be $k = 3$ ($1 < k < q$)

$r = (g^k \bmod p) \bmod q = (4^3 \bmod 23) \bmod 11 = (18) \bmod 11 = 7$

$s = k^{-1} (m + rx) \bmod q = 3^{-1} (5 + 7.3) \bmod 11 = (4 \times 26) \bmod 11$

$\quad = (4 \times 4) \bmod 11 = 5$

Digital Signature $= \{r, s\} = \{7, 5\}$

Verification of the Signature by the authorized Recipient

$t = s^{-1} \bmod q = 5^{-1} \bmod 11 = 9$

$v = ((g^m \times y^r)^t \bmod p) \bmod q$

$\quad = ((4^5 \times 18^7)^9 \bmod 23) \bmod 11$

$\quad = ((12 \times 6)^9 \bmod 23) \bmod 11$

$\quad = ((3)^9 \bmod 23) \bmod 11$

$\quad = ((4 \times 4 \times 4) \bmod 23) \bmod 11$

$\quad = (18) \bmod 11 = 7$

Thus, $v = r = 7$ and signature stands verified.

$(4)^2 \bmod 23 = 16$

$(4)^4 \bmod 23 = (16)^2 \bmod 23 = 3$

$(4)^5 \bmod 23 = 3 \times 4 \bmod 23 = 12$

$(18)2 \bmod 23 = 324 \bmod 23 = 2$

$(18)^4 \bmod 23 = 4$

$(18)^6 \bmod 23 = 8$

$(18)^7 \bmod 23 = (8 \times 18) \bmod 23 = 6$

Example 8.5: (DSA) Construct an element of order 103 in the multiplicative group of residues mod 1237

Here, $p = 1237$

$q = 103;\ q$ divides $q, (p)$

Let $h = 2$

Then the element of order 103 (mod 1237) $= g = (h)\, \Phi^{\,(p)/q} \bmod p$

$= (2)^{1236/103} \bmod 1237$

$= (2)^{12} \bmod 1237$

$= 4096 \bmod 1237$

$= 385$

8.9   EXERCISES

1. Differentiate between Source Authentication and Source Non-Repudiation. Can Source Non-Repudiation be provided by Symmetric Cryptography? Justify your answer.

2. What are the services provided by digital signatures? Does it provide (a) Source Authentication, (b) Data Integrity, and (c) Source Non-Repudiation?

3. Differentiate between Message Authentication Code (MAC) and Hash Value. Which one is encrypted?

4. What is the strength of MAC? Is MAC a reversible function? If no, does it pose any limitation or is designed to be so?

5. What are the characteristics of a good Hash Function?

6. What is a Birthday Attack on Digital Signatures? Can it be performed by an "Outsider"?

7. What is the input message size in MD5 and in SHA-1?

8. What is the Message Digest Size in MD5 and SHA-1?

9. What is the number of rounds and steps per round in MD5 and SHA-1?

10. What are the logical and arithmetic functions used in MD5 and SHA-1?

11. What is the major difference between the ElGamal Signature Algorithm and DSA?

12. What is the strength of MAC? Explain an attack to which MAC is vulnerable. How can MAC be made more secure?

13. Explain the use of MAC to provide source authentication, when MAC is tied to (a) Plaintext, (b) Cipher-text.

14. Explain the characteristics of a good hash function, clearly bringing out the difference between Strong Collision Resistance and Weak Collision Resistance. Which one requires more effort to break?

15. Explain the use of Hash Functions to provide source authentication (a) using public key encryption, (b) without using public key encryption.

16. State and prove the Birthday Paradox. Suppose a Hash Function produces a hash value of m bits. Prove that one needs to create $\sqrt{(2log_e 2)} \times m^{1/2}$ message digests to find two messages having the same hash value with probability more than 1/2.

17. Explain the Birthday Attack on Digital Signatures. Does it involve breaking of strong collision resistance or weak collision resistance? Justify your answer.

18. Explain in detail:

    A. MD5 Message Digest Algorithm

    B. SHA-1 Secure Hash Algorithm

    C. List the differences between MOS and SHA-1

    D. Compare strength of SHA-1 vis-à-vis MD5

19. In MD5, what will be the number of padding bits if the length of original message is:

    A. 960 bits

    B. 1024 bits

    C. 1000 bits

20. Explain the ElGamal Signature Scheme in detail. Provide a proof for the verification algorithm with the following parameters:

    $p = 19$

    Primitive root g of $p = 3$

    Private key of signer $X = 5$

    Random integer $k = 7$ (it is relatively prime to $\Phi(p)$)

    $H(M) = 2$

    Compute:

    i. Public Key of Signer

    ii. Digital signature $\{r, s\}$

    iii. Show verification of the digital signature at the recipient end

21. Explain in detail Digital Signature Standard (DSS) and Digital Signature Algorithm (DSA). Provide a proof for the verification algorithm with the following parameters:

    $p = 23$

    $q = 11$ (q divides $\Phi(p)$)

    $h = 2$

    Private key of signer $x = 5$

    $H(M) = 2$ ($0 \leq H(M) < q$)

    Random integer $k = 7$ ($1 < k < q$)

    Compute:

    i. g that has order q (mod p). Verify.

    ii. Digital Signature $\{r, s\}$

    iii. Show verification 0

CHAPTER 9

CENTRALIZED AUTHENTICATION SERVICE

Chapter Outline

9.1 Introduction

9.2 Centralized Authentication Service

9.3 Motivation for Centralized Authentication Service

9.4 Simple Authentication Exchange in Open Environment

9.5 Architecture of Kerberos V.4

9.6 Exercises

9.1 INTRODUCTION

This chapter covers the concepts of Centralized Authentication Service, motivation for Centralized Authentication Service, Simple Authentication Exchange in Open Environment, Centralized Authentication Service Kerberos Version 4, Inter-Kerberos Authentication Service, and Authentication Service Kerberos Version 5.

9.2 CENTRALIZED AUTHENTICATION SERVICE

In a distributed client-server environment like the Internet, a client can log-on, authenticate itself once, and then access many services without authenticating itself repeatedly. This is made possible by a centralized authentication service provided by KERBEROS. In Greek Mythology, KERBEROS means "Three-Headed Dog."

- KERBEROS is a centralized authentication service, meant for a client-server-based open environment like the Internet.

- Originally, it was conceived with a view to provide three services; namely, Authentication, Accounting, and Auditing. That is why it is named KERBEROS—"Three-headed Dog." But in it its present form, KERBEROS caters only to Authentication; the other two services never took off.

- Its main functions include authentication of registered users (clients) to the registered application servers and authentication of the registered application servers to the registered clients.

- KERBEROS stores the USER-ID and hashed Password of each registered client in a centralized database.

- Whenever any registered client approaches the Authentication Server (AS) of KERBEROS for accessing services provided by any of its registered application servers, the AS performs authentication of the user.

- If the user authenticates successfully, it is granted a Ticket by AS that is used by the user to access services from the application servers. The application servers trust the authentication performed by KERBEROS. In return, the application server also authenticates itself to the authenticated user.

- KERBEROS caters to the secure communication of all message exchanges related to this authentication process.

9.3 MOTIVATION FOR CENTRALIZED AUTHENTICATION SERVICE

For this, we need to understand the authentication process in an open client-server environment. First, we consider a simple authentication exchange in an open environment.

9.4 SIMPLE AUTHENTICATION EXCHANGE IN OPEN ENVIRONMENT

In an open client-server environment, a server is required to authenticate the users requesting services from the server. Then, each application server needs to store information like user-IDs and user passwords, which are required for authentication of users. This places a substantial burden on the server. An elegant alternative is to use a centralized Authentication Server (AS) that has passwords of all the authorized users stored in its database. The AS shares a unique Secret Key with each application server. A simplified authentication exchange using centralized AS in an open environment is appended here:

1. $C \rightarrow AS$: $ID_c \| P_c \| IDV$

2. $AS \rightarrow C$: Ticket

3. $C \rightarrow V$: $ID_c \|$ Ticket

   Ticket $= EK_v [ID_c \| AD_c \| IDV]$

   where C: Client

   AS: Authentication Server

   V: Server

   ID_c: Identifier of user on Client C

   ID_v: Identifier of Server V

   P_c: Password of user on Client C

   AD_c: Network Address of Client C

   K_v: Secret Key shared between AS and server V

In this scenario, a user with identification ID_c logs onto a workstation and requests access to server V. The client module C in the user's work-station requests the user for its password. User enters its password P_c, and then the client module C sends a message to AS. The message comprises user identification ID_c, user password P_c, and requested server identification ID_v. AS checks its database to determine whether the user's password matches or not and whether the user is authorized to access server V or not. If both tests are passed, then AS sends an authentication ticket to C. The ticket is encrypted using secret key K_v that AS shares with server V. Thus,

C cannot access the token. The token contains user ID ID_c, client network address AD_c, and server identification ID_v. Now C sends the Ticket to V, along with its identification ID_c. V decrypts the ticket using secret key K_v and accesses the information contained in the ticket. The server V is assured that the ticket has been created by AS since it is encrypted using K_v and also that C could not have tampered with it. By matching ID_c contained in the ticker with the ID_c appended to the ticket, AS will be assured that the ticket has been forwarded by the authorized user only. This provides authentication of user ID_c making a request from a workstation with network address AD_c to access the services from the server with identification ID_v. Now the user can access the services from server V. ID_v is included in the ticket to assure the server V that the ticket has been decrypted properly. AD_c is included to prevent replay of the ticket from another workstation.

9.4.1 Problems with Simple Authentication Exchange

1. For each request, a user is made to enter its password. Instead, a user should be required to enter its password only once for a single logon session. It should remain valid till the user logs off. For a single logon session, the workstation can save a token issued to the user for accessing V. The token should be reusable for the future accesses of V by the user during its current logon session.

2. For each different service, a user would need a new Token. This is not required. Once a user has been authenticated during a logon session, the same should be valid for different services (being provided by different servers).

3. The user password is transmitted in plaintext. An eavesdropper can capture the password and can access any service authorized for the victim. These problems can be solved by introducing a new server known as a Ticket Granting Server (TGS) and modifying the authentication dialog as follows:

Once per User Logon Session:

1. $C \rightarrow AS$: $ID_c \| ID_{TGS}$

2. $AS \rightarrow C$: E_{Kc} [Ticket$_{tgs}$]
   Ticket$_{TGS}$ = E_{Ktgs} [$ID_c \| AD_c \| ID_{tgs} \|$ Lifetime$_1$]

Once per Type of Service:

3. $C \rightarrow TGS: ID_c \parallel AD_c \parallel \text{Ticket}_{tgs}$

4. $TGS \rightarrow C: \text{Ticket}_v$

$\text{Ticket}_V = E_{Kv} [ID_c \parallel AD_c \parallel ID_v \parallel TS_2 \parallel \text{Lifetime}_2]$

Once per Service Session:

5. $C \rightarrow V: ID_c \parallel \text{Ticket}_v$

The salient features of the modified dialog are:

1. The Client requests a "Ticket-Granting Ticket" from *AS* on behalf of the user, by sending user id-ID_c and Ticket Granting Server id-ID_{tgs}.

2. The user password is not required to be transmitted to *AS*. Instead, *AS* will compute a secret key K_c derived from the user password scored in its database. The Ticket_{TGS} transmitted from *AS* to *C* will be encrypted using K_c. When the response from *AS* is received by *C*, the latter will prompt the user to enter its password. Then the client will derive a key from the password entered by the user and attempt to decrypt the response received from *AS* with this key. The decryption would be successful only if the correct password has been entered by the user. The Ticket_{tgs} recovered from the received message is saved by *C*. Since Ticket_{tgs} is encrypted using the secret key K_{tgs} that *AS* shares with *TGS*, only *TGS* can decrypt it and *C* cannot tamper with it.

3. Since, Ticket_{tgs} is encrypted using the secret key K_{tgs} that *AS* shares with *TGS*, the latter will decrypt it. *TGS* will compare the ID_c sent by *C* with the ID_c contained in the ticket. If both match, then ID_c is considered to be authenticated. AD_c in the ticket will be compared with the source address of the message received. If both match, it assures *TGS* that the message is not being replayed from some other workstation. ID_{tgs} in the ticket assures *TGS* that the ticket has been decrypted properly. TS_1 is the time-stamp indicating the time at which the Ticket was granted, and Lifetime1 indicates the lifetime during which Ticket_{tgs} will remain valid after TS_1. This will enable the probability of a replay attack. Now, user ID_c remains authenticated and will not be required to enter its password again during the current logon session or till the lifetime of Ticket_{tgs} expires, whichever is earlier.

4. *C* will save Ticket_{tgs} for the current logon session of ID_C. Whenever user ID_C requests to access a new service, *C* will forward the Ticket along with ID_C and identification of the server to be accessed, ID_v.

5. The *TGS* will grant Ticket$_v$ for the server to be accessed by user ID_c. This ticket also will be saved by *C*, and it remains reusable for user ID_c for the current logon session or till its life expires, whichever is earlier.

6. Whenever ID_c requests access to server *V*, *C* will send Ticket$_v$ to server *V* along with ID_c, and the user will be enabled to access the service.

7. When the lifetime of a ticket expires, the procedure for its grant again would need to be repeated. The *TS* and Lifetime are meant to reduce the probability of replay attacks.

9.4.2 Full-Service Kerberos Environment (Kerberos Realm)

A Full-Service Kerberos Environment consists of the following:

1. A Kerberos that includes an Authentication Server (AS) and a Ticket-Granting Server (TGS).

2. A set of Users (Clients) registered with the Kerberos. The Kerberos database stores the User-Id and hashed Password of all registered users.

3. A set of Application Servers registered with the Kerberos. The Kerberos shares unique secret keys with the registered Application Server.

Such an environment is called a Full-Service Kerberos Environment, also called a Kerberos Realm. The Kerberos also implements the security policy of the parent organization, by implementing access rights of the registered users for accessing the services provided by the registered servers.

9.4.3 Kerberos Version 4

Kerberos Version 4 is a Full-Service Kerberos. The messages exchanged between clients and servers are made secure by encrypting using DES. The main features of KERBEROS V.4 are as follows:

1. The identity of individual users is assured by their respective workstations, and the servers enforce security policy on the basis of user identification.

2. KERBEROS V.4 requires client workstations to authenticate themselves to the servers and the latter to trust the client workstations concerning the identity of their respective users.

3. It requires the users to prove their identity to the Authentication Server (AS) only once per logon session. If authenticated successfully by AS, the user is granted a ticket to access the Ticket Granting Server (TGS). The *TGS* grants tickets to users for the type of service requested by the user. Every time the user wishes to access this service, the Service-Granting Ticket is to be produced by the user to the application server. This ticket is valid for the current service session. If the user wishes to access another type of service, then it has to approach *TGS* again to obtain a ticket for that type of service.

9.5 ARCHITECTURE OF KERBEROS V.4

Figure 9.1 illustrates the overview of the Kerberos Version 4 Authentication Exchange. The KERBEROS V.4 makes use of the following Servers to perform its assigned functions:

1. **Authentication Server (AS):** The Authentication Server (AS) stores user-id and hashed passwords of all authorized users in a centralized database. Its function is to authenticate the clients requesting access to application servers and issue "Ticket-Granting Tickets" to those clients who are authenticated successfully.

2. **Ticket Granting Server (TGS):** The *TGS* is approached by those clients who have been successfully authenticated by the *AS*. Such clients approach the *TGS* with the "Ticket-Granting Ticket" issued by the *AS*. The *TGS* issues "Service-Granting Tickets" to such clients. The *TGS* shares a secret key with the *AS*, which in turn is used by the *AS* to encrypt the Ticket Granting Tickets. In addition, the *TGS* also shares unique secret keys with all registered application servers. These keys are used by the *TGS* to encrypt the Service-Granting Tickets that are issued by the *TGS* to the authenticated clients to access application servers. The application servers trust the authentication performed by the *AS*. The secret keys shared among different servers are distributed either physically or by some other secure means.

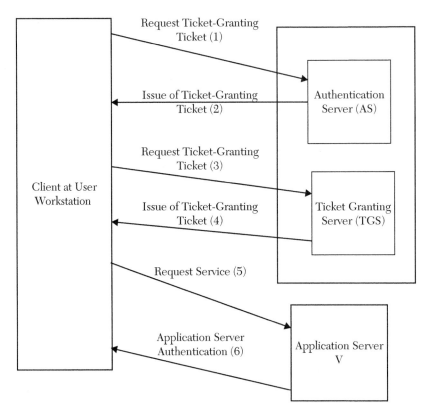

FIGURE 9.1 A schematic diagram of the overview of the Kerberos Version 4 Authentication Exchange.

Whenever a user logs on at a workstation by entering its user ID and requests a service on the Internet, the client module C on the user's workstation performs the following sequence of authentication dialogue with the Kerberos Servers:

Message (1): Request Ticket-Granting Ticket: This message is sent by the Client Module C to the Authentication Server (AS). By this message, the Client Module C requests AS on behalf of the User, for granting a "Ticket-Granting-Ticket." The "Ticket" is required to authenticate the user to the server TGS.

$C \rightarrow AS: ID_C \parallel ID_{tgs} \parallel TS_1$

The Message (1) contains:

1. User Id: ID_C

2. Identification of Ticket Granting Server: ID_{tgs}

3. Time Stamp containing current date & time: TS_1

Time-stamp TS_1 is included in the message to indicate its timeliness.

On receipt of this message, the *AS* will look into its User Database and determine whether ID_c is a valid Registered User or not. If YES, then *AS* will access the hashed password P_c of the User from the database and create an encryption key K_c as a function of P_C.

$$K_c = f(P_c)$$

Then the *AS* will create a session key k_{Ctgs} that is used for communication between *C* and *TGS*. Also, *AS* will create Ticket_{tgs}, which is to be used for authentication of *C* to *TGS*. The Ticket_{tgs} is encrypted using key K_{tgs} that is shared between *AS* and *TGS*.

Message (2): Issue of Ticket-Granting Ticket: This message is sent by *AS* to the Client Module *C* in response to the request for the granting of a Ticket-Granting Ticket (Message (1)). The message is encrypted using K_C (derived as a function of the user's hashed password P_c).

$AS \rightarrow C$: $E_{Kc} [K_{c,tgs} \| ID_{tgs} \| TS_2 \| \text{Lifetime}_2 \| \text{Ticket}_{tgs}$

$\text{Ticket}_{TGS} = E_{Ktgs} [K_{c,tgs} \| ID_c \| AD_c \| ID_{tgs} \| TS_2 \| \text{Lifetime}_2$

On receiving this message, the client module *C* will prompt the user to enter its password. Then the client module *C* will create Key K_C as a function of P_C and use this key to decrypt the received message. *C* will be able to decrypt the received message successfully only if the password entered by the user matches with the user password stored at the *AS*. The message contains:

1. $K_{c,tgs}$: A session key to be used between Client *C* and *TGS*.

2. ID_{tgs}: Identification of *TGS*.

3. TS_2: Time-stamp chat indicates the start time of ticket validity.

4. Lifetime_2: Lifetime of Ticket_{tgs} starting from TS_2.

5. Ticket_{tgs}: The ticket issued by *TS* to enable client *C* to approach server *TGS*. It is encrypted using key K_{tgs}, which is shared between *AS* and *TGS* so that the client cannot alter the ticket; only *TGS* can decrypt it successfully. The ticket is reusable during a session or till its life expires, whichever is earlier; thus, *C* will save the ticket. Now *C* can use the ticket repeatedly for obtaining permission from *TGS* to access the required application servers.

The ticket Ticket$_{tgs}$ contains the following information:

1. $K_{c,tgs}$: The session key to be shared between Client C and TGS.

2. ID_c: Identification of Client C.

3. AD_c: Network Address (IP Address) of Client workstation, from where message 1 was received.

4. ID_c: Identification of TGS itself, to assure TGS that the token has been decrypted successfully.

5. TS_2: Time stamp to assure TGS that it is not a replay Ticket.

6. Lifetime$_2$: Ticket's Lifetime.

After successful decryption of this message, C will recover and save the Ticket$_{tgs}$ and the session key $K_{c,tgs}$. Now, AS will send the following message to TGS for obtaining a Ticket from TGS for accessing an application server (say V):

Message (3): Request Service-Granting Ticket: This message is sent by the Client Module to the Ticket Granting Server for obtaining a Ticket-Granting-Ticket. The Ticket-Granting-Ticket is to be used for obtaining a service from Application Server V.

$$C \rightarrow TGS: ID_v \| \text{Ticket}_{tgs} \| \text{Authenticator}_c$$

where

ID_v = Identification of application server V

Ticket$_{tgs}$: Ticket issued by AS for authentication of C to TGS

Authenticator$_{c1}$ = $E_{Kc,tgs}$ [$ID_c \| AD_c \| TS_3$]

The Authenticator$_{c1}$ comprises User Id ID_c, AD_c (the network address of the user workstation), and Time stamp TS_3 to prevent replays. Since the Authenticator is encrypted using $K_{C,TGS}$, it assures TGS that the message is from C alone. After decrypting the Ticket and the Authenticator, TGS compares the values of ID_c and AD_c specified in the Ticket$_{TGS}$ and in the Authenticator$_{c1}$. Also, it compares the network address AD_c with the source network address of the received message. If all match, then TGS is assured of the User's authentication.

Message (4): Issue of Service-Granting Ticket: This message is sent by the TGS to C in response to the request for a Service-Granting-Ticket

(Message (3)). The message contains $Ticket_v$ (to be used by C for its authentication to server V) and a session key $K_{c,v}$ (to be shared between C and V). The message will be encrypted using K so that only C can decrypt it.

where

$K_{c,v}$: Session key to be shared between C and V.

ID_v: Identification of target application server V.

TS_4: Time Stamp.

$Lifetime_4$: Lifetime of $Ticket_v$.

$Ticket_v = E_{Kv} [K_{c,v} \| ID_c \| AD_c \| ID_v \| TS_3 \| Lifetime_4]$

The $Ticket_v$ is encrypted using key K_v that is shared between TGS and V so that only V can decrypt it successfully.

The ticket Ticket$v$ contains the following information:

A. $K_{c,v}$: The session key to be used between Client C and V

B. ID_c: User Identification on Client C

C. AD_c: Network Address of Client workstation

D. ID_v: Identification of V itself

E. TS_4: Time stamp

F. $Lifetime_4$: Ticket's Lifetime

After successful decryption of the received message, C will recover and save the Ticket and session key $K_{c,v}$. During the current log on session, C can use the $Ticket_v$ repeatedly to access V. Now, C will send the following message to application server V to obtain the required services:

Message (5): Request Service: This message is sent by C to application Server V for obtaining the required service.

$C \rightarrow V$: $Ticket_v \| Authenticator_{c2}$

$Authenticator_{C2} = E_{Kc,v} [ID_C \| AD_c \| TS_5]$

The $Authenticator_{c2}$ is encrypted using $K_{c,v}$ that is shared between C and V. This will assure V that the message has been obtained from C only. V compares the values of ID and AD specified in the $Ticket_{cv}$ and in $Authenticator_{C2}$. If both match, it authenticates the user to V. Now, V sends a message to C

echoing back $(TS_5 + 1)$ where TS_5 is time-stamp received from C in message 5. This is for mutual authentication of C and V.

Message (6): Application Sever Authentication to Client: This message is sent by the Application Server to C in response to the request for service.

$$V \rightarrow C: E_{Kc,v}[TS_5 + 1]$$

9.5.1 Inter-Kerberos Authentication

Different organizations have their own Kerberos Realms catering to their registered clients and servers.

But Clients in one realm may like to access servers in other realms. Also, servers in a realm may be willing to provide service to clients in other realms provided the clients are authenticated by their own parent Kerberos. If a user logging on at Client Workstation C in Realm "A" intends to access a Remote Server V in Realm "B," the user request is processed as follows:

1. The client workstation sends a request to the local AS for the issue of a Ticket to access the local TGS. The request comprises the ID of the user logged on the Client Workstation C, ID_{tgs} of the local TGS, and Time Stamp TS_1.

2. The local AS issues Ticket$_{tgs}$ and a session key $K_{c,tgs}$ for communication between C and the local TGS. The ticket Ticket$_{tgs}$ is encrypted using secret key K_{tgs} that is shared between the AS and the local TGS. So, Ticket$_{tgs}$ can be opened only by the local TGS. The session key $K_{c,tgs}$ is to be used for communication between C and the local TGS.

3. Now, the client workstation sends a request to the local TGS for issue of a Ticket for accessing Remote TGS in Realm "B." The request comprises ID_{tgsrem}, Ticket$_{tgs}$, and Authenticator$_{c1}$.

4. The local TGS issues Ticket$_{tgsrem}$ and session key $K_{c,gsrem}$. The ticket is encrypted using secret key K_{tgsrem} that the local TGS shares with the remote TGS so that only the remote TGS can open the ticket. The session key $K_{c,tgsrem}$ is to be used for communication between C and a remote TGS, that is, TGS_{rem}.

Figure 9.2 illustrates the Authentication Sequence (Kerberos Version 4). Messages (1) and (2) are exchanged once per logon session, while messages (3) and (4) are exchanged per "Type of Service," and messages (5) and (6) are exchanged per Service Session.

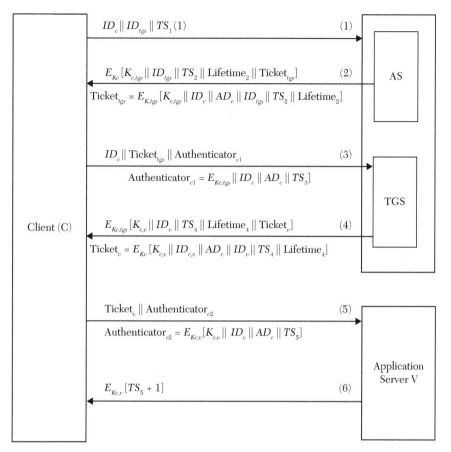

FIGURE 9.2 A schematic diagram of the Authentication Sequence (Kerberos Version 4).

5. Now, the client workstation sends a request to TGS_{rem} for issue of a Ticket to access Remote server V_{rem} in Realm "B." The request comprises ID_{vrem}, Ticket$_{tgsrem}$, and Authenticacor$_{c2}$.

6. The TGS_{rem} issues Ticket$_{vrem}$ and session key $K_{c,vrem}$. The ticket is encrypted using secret key K_{vrem} that is shared between TGS and V. The session key K is to be used for communication between C and remote application server V_{rem}.

7. The client workstation sends a request to V_{rem} in Realm "B" for providing the required service. The request comprises Ticket$_{vrem}$ and Authemicacor$_{c3}$. The Authenticator contains Time Stamp TS_7.

8. Finally, V_{rem} also authenticates itself to client C by sending $(TS_7 + 1)$ to C. This message is encrypted using $K_{c,vrem}$.

Figure 9.3 illustrates the Inner-Kerber Authentication Sequence.

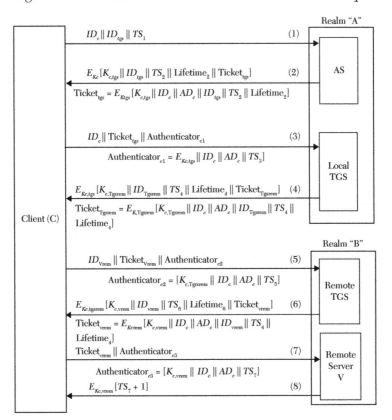

FIGURE 9.3 A schematic diagram of the Inner-Kerber Authentication Sequence.

9.5.2 Kerberos Version 5 Authentication Sequence

Message 1 Authentication Service Request (KRB AS_REQ) from Client C to Authentication Server (AS)

$C \rightarrow AS$: Options $\|\ ID_c\ \|$ Realm$_c\ \|\ ID_{tgs}\ \|$ Times $\|$ Nounce$_1$

Where

Options: Client specified options for the Ticket Granting Ticket (TGT) requested from *AS* like:

FORWARDABLE: The Ticket to be forwardable

PROXIABLE: The ticket to be proxy-able, etc.

The Authentication Server's response to the Options' request will be reflected in a Flag.

ID_c: User ID on the Client

$Realm_c$: Realm of the Client

ID_{tgs}: *TGS* Identification tgs

TIMES: It includes validation period (From ... To)

$Nounce_i$: A random integer value to prevent replay attacks

Message 2 Authentication Service Reply (KRB_AS_REP) from *AS* to *C*, for obtaining Ticket Granting Ticket (TGT) $Ticket_{tgs}$ and a Session Key $K_{c,tgs}$ for communication between *C* and *TGS*.

$AS \rightarrow C$: $Realm_c \parallel ID_c \parallel Ticket_{tgs} \parallel E_{Kc} [K_{c,tgs} \parallel Times \parallel Nounce_1 \parallel Realm_{tgs} \parallel ID_{tgs}]$

$Ticket_{tgs} \parallel E_{Ktgs} [Flags \parallel K_{c,tgs} \parallel Realm_c \parallel ID_c \parallel AD_c \parallel Times]$

The Flag will contain the options made available for the use of $Ticket_{tgs}$, like Forward-able, Proxy-able, and so on. Times will indicate the validity period. Its start-time can even be post-dated, and this fact can be indicated in the Flag.

Message 3 Ticket Granting Service Request (KRB_ TGS_REQ) from *C* to *TGS*, for obtaining Service Ticket $Ticket_v$ and a Session Key $K_{c,v}$ for communication between *C* and Application Server *V*.

$AS \rightarrow C$: $Options \parallel ID_v \parallel Times \parallel Nounce_2 \parallel Ticket_{tgs} \parallel Authenticator_{c1}$

$Authenticator_{c1} = E_{Kc,tgs} [ID_c \parallel Realm_c \parallel TS_1]$

Message 4 Ticket Granting Service Reply (KRB_TGS_REP) from *TGS* to *C*, for conveying of Service Ticket $Ticket_v$ and a Session Key $K_{c,v}$ for communication between *C* and *V*.

$AS \rightarrow C$: $Realm_c \parallel ID_c \parallel Ticket_v \parallel E_{Kc,tgs} [K_{c,v} \parallel Times \parallel Nounce_2 \parallel Realm_v \parallel ID_v]$

$Ticket_v \parallel E_{Kv} [Flags \parallel K_{c,v} \parallel Realm_c \parallel ID_c \parallel AD_c \parallel Times]$

The Flag will contain the options made available for the use of Ticket$_v$, like Forward-able, Proxy-able, and so on.

Times will indicate the validity period. Its start-time can even be post-dated, and this fact can be indicated in the Flag.

Message 5 Service Request (KRB_AP REQ) from C to Application Server for obtaining Service.

$AS{\rightarrow}C$: Options $\|$ Ticket$_v$ $\|$ Authenticator$_{c2}$

Authenticator$_{c2} = E_{Kc,v}$ [$ID_c \|$ Realm$_c \|$ $TS_2 \|$ Sub-Key $\|$ Seq#]

Message 6 Service Reply (KRB_AP REP) from Application Server to C, for mutual authentication.

$AS{\rightarrow}C$: $E_{Kc,v}$ [$TS_2 \|$ Sub-Key $\|$ Seq#]

9.5.3 Differences between Kerberos V.4 and Kerberos V.5

The Kerberos V.4 has the following environmental and technical limitations, which have been successfully overcome in Kerberos V.5:

1. **Encryption Algorithm:** Kerberos V.4 permits use of only DES for encryption. But, Kerberos V.5 permits use of other encryption algorithms also; a tag attached to the cipher-text indicates the *ID* of the algorithm used.

2. **Communication Protocol:** The Kerberos V.4 uses only IP addressing for communication; but Kerberos V.5 permits use of any other network addressing protocols also; a tag indicates the *ID* of the network addressing used.

3. **Protocol for Message Byte Ordering:** Kerberos V.4 uses a little-endian or big-endian format for byte ordering, and the type of formatting used is tagged to the message; but in Kerberos V.5, the message structures are defined using Abstract Syntax Notation (ASN .1) and Basic Encoding Rules (BER), which provide unambiguous byte ordering.

4. **Ticket Lifetime:** In Kerberos V.4, the maximum lifetime for a ticket is restricted to 1280 minutes, which may be insufficient for some applications. Kerberos V.5 permits any start-time and any end-time of the validation period of a ticket. If the validation period is unduly large then the system becomes prone to replay attacks, which are prevented by including Nounce in the ticket requests.

5. **Authentication Forwarding:** Suppose a client sends a request to a Print Server to print a requested file and the file may be stored on a different server, that is, File Server. This requires the Print Server to fetch the requested file from the File Server. In V.5, the Print Server can forward the authentication credentials of the Client to the File Server and obtain the required file for printing. This mechanism of Authentication Forwarding is not supported in V.4.

6. **Double Encryption of Tickets:** In Kerberos V.4, the tickets have double encryption—one inner encryption using the key shared between the issuing server and the target servers, and the other outer encryption using the key shared between the issuing server and the client. The outer encryption is not necessary; it only increases the encryption/decryption overheads. In Kerberos V.5, the tickets have only inner encryption, thus reducing the overheads.

7. **Renegotiation of Session Keys within a Session:** Kerberos V.5 permits re-negotiation of session keys within a session, which is not available in Kerberos V.4. Thus, V.5 is more secure.

8. **Inter-Realm Authentication:** In Kerberos V.4, for Inter-Realm Authentication the client has to go through the local TGS; whereas in V.5, the AS issues a ticket directly for the remote TGS, thus making it faster.

9.6 EXERCISES

1. What are the three services which Kerberos was originally conceived to provide? And which is the service currently provided by it?

2. What are the main features of Kerberos?

3. What are the problems of simple authentication exchange (not Centralized)?

4. What are the limitations of Kerberos V.4?

5. What is Authentication Forwarding?

6. Explain the Full-Service Kerberos Environment. Explain the roles of the Authentication Server (AS) and the Ticket Granting Server (TGS).

7. Explain the architecture of Kerberos V.4. Explain all the messages forming its authentication sequence. What is the problem of Double Encryption in Kerberos V.4?

8. Explain the message sequence of an inter-Kerberos authentication sequence.

9. Explain the message sequence of Kerberos V.5. Also explain its upgrades vis-à-vis Kerberos V.4.

10

PUBLIC KEY INFRASTRUCTURE (PKI)

Chapter Outline

10.1 Introduction

10.2 Format of X.509 Certificate

10.3 Hierarchical Organization of Certification Authorities (CAs)

10.4 Creation of Certificates' Chain for CA's Signature Verification

10.5 Revocation of X.509 Certificates

10.6 Authentication Procedures Defined in X.509

10.7 Exercises

10.1   INTRODUCTION

A Public Key, as the name suggests, is to be made available to all users in the cryptosystem.

The **Public Key Infrastructure (PKI)** is the infrastructure that is necessary for making the public keys available to all users in a convenient, secure, and efficient manner.

RFC 2822 defines **PKI** as the hardware, software, people, policies, and procedures required to create, store, manage, distribute, and revoke Public Key Certificates. ITU-T Recommendations X.500 defines a Directory Service for management of public key certificates.

X.509, which forms part of X.500, defines the formats for Public Key Certificates. The certificates are issued under the digital signatures of designated Certification Authorities (CAs).

There are many companies that provide CA service, like VeriSign and the U.S. Postal Services. VeriSign is the most popular CA service.

Registration with CA: To get a Public Key Certificate issued, a user has to first register with a designated CA by furnishing some information.

Issue of Public Key Certificate: When a user furnishes a Public Key to a CA for issue of a certificate, the CA will issue a certificate digitally signed using its private key. The certificate binds the public key with the user name. A copy of the certificate is returned to the user's workstation, and a copy is stored in the repository available on the Internet. A CA's public key is available to the user for verifying the CA's digital signature on the certificate. Any user can fetch the certificate from the repository.

Certificate Revocation: X.509 also defines a set of authentication protocols and standards for the Certificate Revocation List (CRL). The CRL lists the certificates that have been revoked due to various reasons.

Suppose a user (user "A") intends to send encrypted data to another user (user "B"), then user

"A" would need user "B"'s public key certificate. User A can fetch the certificate from the repository. After verifying the signature on the certificate, "A" can extract "B"'s public key from that certificate and use it to encrypt the message intended for user "B." "B" can decrypt the encrypted message using its private key.

Similarly, if user "A" receives a document digitally signed by user "B." Then user "A" would fetch user "B"'s Public Key Certificate for verification of the digital signature on the document.

10.2 FORMAT OF X.509 CERTIFICATE

Figure 10.1 illustrates a schematic diagram of the format of the X.509 Certificate.

Version No.: This indicates the certificate format Version (1/2/3). Some fields have been added in Version 2 and Version 3.

Certificate Serial Number: This number has to be unique within the Certification Authority (CA). A certificate is uniquely identified by this serial number.

Signature Algorithm and Parameters: This indicates the algorithm and related parameters of CA's signature on the Certificate.

Issuer Name: Name of the CA. In Version 1, it was required to be unique. But in Versions 2 and 3, another field called "Issuer's Unique Identifier" has been added; thus, the issuer name need not be unique.

"Not Before" and "Not After": These two fields indicate the validity period of the certificate.

Subject Name: Name of the user to whom the certificate is being issued.

Public Key Algorithm Parameters and Key: It comprises the subject's public key information, that is, the Algorithm for which the key is to be used, Parameters of the algorithm, and the Public key value.

Issuer's Unique Identifier: This field, included in Versions 2 and 3, has to be unique for each CA.

Subject's Unique Identifiers: This field is to be unique for each subject (user) to whom the certificate is being issued. This field exists in Versions 2 and 3.

Extensions: These fields contain some information considered necessary for proper function of PKI. The fields are explained on the next page.

CA Signature: It comprises the Algorithm used for the CA's signature. Parameters of the Algorithm and encrypted value of the message digest: The message digest is generated by hashing the certificate, minus the signature fields. The CA's signature obviously forms part of all the three versions.

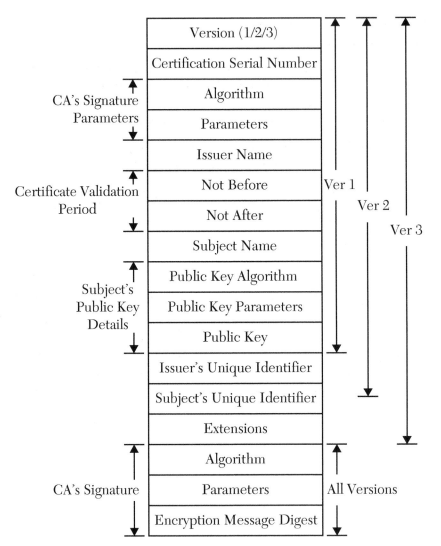

FIGURE 10.1 A schematic diagram of the format of the X.509 Certificate.

10.2.1 Version.3 Extensions

Authority Key Identifier: Identifies the CA's Public Key that is to be used for signature verification.

Subject Key Identifier: Identifies the subject's public key that is being certified. A subject may have multiple keys.

Key Usage: Indicates restrictions imposed on the key; likely to be used only for Digital Signatures, and so on.

Private Key Validity Period: Indicates the validity period of the corresponding private key; for example, for a public key to be used only for signature verification, the corresponding private key will have shorter life, since signatures on the documents created in the past need verification.

Certificate Policies: In a multiple policy environment, this extension lists those security policies that this certificate supports.

Policy Mapping: This extension is used only in a certificate that certifies the public key of a CA by another CA. This maps policies from the issuer CA's domain to the policies in the subject CA's domain. More than one policy together may map onto a single policy.

10.3 HIERARCHICAL ORGANIZATION OF CERTIFICATION AUTHORITIES (CAS)

It is not possible for one centralized Certification Authority to issue Public Key Certificates to all the users across the globe. With this in view, the Certification Authority is decentralized in a hierarchical fashion as indicated in Figure 10.2.

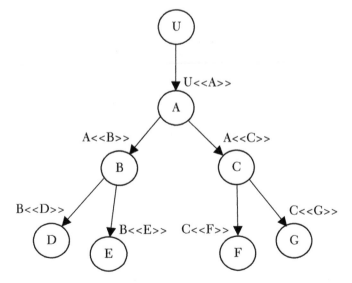

FIGURE 10.2 Hierarchical organization of Certification Authorities.

The standard notation for representation of a certificate is **C<<A>>**, which implies a certificate issued to user "A" and signed by certification agency "C."

The users act as CAs for each other. For example, User "A" issues Certificate **A<<B>>** to User "B" and User "B" issues Certificate **B<<A>>** to User "A." User "D" has been issued Certificate **B<<D>>** by user "B." So, User D will have access to the Public Key of User "B" so that "D" can verify "B"'s signature on its certificate.

10.4 CREATION OF CERTIFICATES' CHAIN FOR CA's SIGNATURE VERIFICATION

Suppose User "D" has to communicate with User "F." Then User "D" will obtain F's Public Key Certificate **C<<F>>.** Now, how will "D" verify C's signature on this certificate, since "D" does not have access to "C"'s Public Key? For this, "D" will obtain the following additional certificates and create a certificate chain:

B<<A>> A<<C>> C<<F>>

Now, user "D" will obtain user C's Public Key from certificate **A«C»** and use that Public Key to verify user "C"'s signature on certificate **C<<F>>.** Then user "D" will obtain user A's Public Key from certificate **B<<A>>** and use that key to verify user "A"'s signature on certificate **A<<C>>.** Regarding verification of user B's signature on certificate **B<<A>>,** the user "D" has direct access to user B's Public Key. Thus, by creating a chain, user "D" is able to verify the digital signature on certificate **C<<F>>.**

Similarly, "F" will obtain certificate **B<<D>>** and verify user "B"'s digital signature on that certificate by creating the following certificate chain:

C<<A>> A<<B>> B<<D>>

Now, both user "D" and user "F" have successfully verified the digital signatures on the certificates required for their communication. Thus, they can communicate with each other by using each other's Public Key.

10.5 REVOCATION OF X.509 CERTIFICATES

An X.509 Certificate can be revoked by the Issuer Certification Agency (CA) by listing the X.509 Certificate in a "Certificate Revocation List" (CRL), which is periodically issued by the CA. The CRL is signed by the concerned CA.

The format of the CRL is as follows in Figure 10.3:

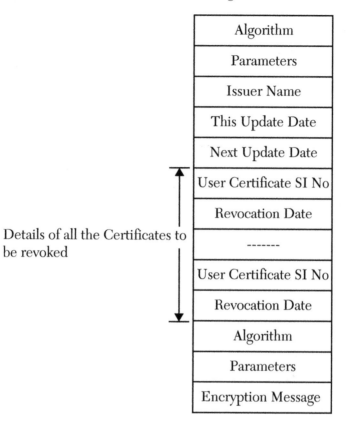

FIGURE 10.3 A schematic diagram of the format of the Certificate Revocation List.

10.5.1 Rules for Revocation

An X.509 Certificate can be revoked under any one of the following conditions:

1. When the corresponding Private Key of the certificate holder has been compromised.

2. When the CA's private key used to sign the certificate has been compromised.

3. When the CA is no longer a certification authority for the certificate holder.

10.6 AUTHENTICATION PROCEDURES DEFINED IN X.509

Notation used: A {I}: Where I is set of data signed by user "A."

One-Way Authentication:

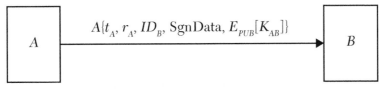

FIGURE 10.4 A schematic diagram of the One-Way Authentication Procedure.

where

t_A: Time Stamp

r_A: Nounce

ID_B: B's Identification

SgnData: Signed Data

PU_B: B's Public Key

K_{AB}: Session Key to be used from A to B

Two-Way Authentication

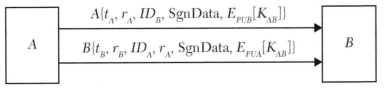

FIGURE 10.5 A schematic diagram of a Two-Way Authentication Procedure.

The Nounce r_A is bounced back by B to A to indicate that B has responded to A's message.

where t_A, t_B: Time Stamps

r_A, r_B: Nounces

ID_A: A's Identification

ID_B: B's Identification

SgnData: Signed Data

PU_A: A's Public Key

PU_B: B's Public Key

K_{AB}: Session Key to be used from A to B

K_{BA}: Session Key to be used from B to A

Three-Way Authentication

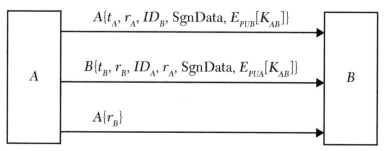

FIGURE 10.6 A schematic diagram of a Three-Way Authentication Procedure.

The additional message from A to B simply bounces back the Nounce r_B received from user B to indicate that A has responded to B's message.

10.7 EXERCISES

1. What is Public Key Infrastructure (PKI)? Why do we need it for Public Key Cryptography?

2. What are the conditions under which X.509 certificates can be revoked? What is the format of the Certification Revocation List (CRL)?

3. Explain the format of Public Key Certificate Version X.509, bringing out the purpose of each field. Name some of the organizations designated as Certification Agencies (CAs) for X.509 Certificates.

4. Explain the concept of hierarchical organization of Certification Agencies for the issue of X.509 certificates. Also explain the concept of a "Certificate Chain" for verification of digital signatures on X.509 certificates.

5. Explain the Authentication Procedures defined in Version X.509.

CHAPTER 11

PRETTY GOOD PRIVACY

Chapter Outline

11.1 Introduction

11.2 Services Supported by Pretty Good Privacy (PGP)

11.3 Radix-64 (R64) Transformation

11.4 Concept of Public Key Ring and Private Key Ring in PGP

11.5 S/MIME (Secure/Multipurpose Internet Mail Extension)

11.6 Exercises

11.1 INTRODUCTION

Pretty Good Privacy (*PGP*) is a freely downloadable open-source software that provides Confidentiality and Authentication Services to emails and file storage applications. It is not controlled by any government organization.

11.2 SERVICES SUPPORTED BY PRETTY GOOD PRIVACY (PGP)

1. **Data confidentiality:** It provides data confidentiality by symmetric encryption using 3-DES or IDEA or CAST-128. It makes use of a "one-time" session key for the symmetric encryption/decryption. The session keys are generated using the Pseudo Random Number Generation

Algorithm specified by ANSI X-12.17. The key is conveyed to the recipient along with cipher-text by encrypting the key with the recipient's Public Key Encryption Algorithm (*RSA* or ElGamal).

2. **Authentication:** The Authentication Service is provided by pre-pending the message with the sender's digital signature at the sender end. The Message Digest for the signature is generated by SHA, and the Message Digest is encrypted by using DSS/DSA or RSA.

3. **Data Compression:** Data Compression is performed using ZIP at the sender end after signing the message but prior to encryption for data confidentiality. At the recipient end the compression is undone using ZIP.

4. **Radix-64 Transformation:** Most of the email services process only printable character information, but cipher-text does not fall in this category. So, PGP performs RADIX-64 Transformation (also called Base-64 Transformation) prior to the transmission of the message at the sender end. The RADIX-64 transformed data comprises only printable characters ("A" . . . "Z," "a" . . . "z," "0" . . . "9," "+," "/"). This feature makes the PGP compatible with all email services. At the recipient end, reverse transformation is performed to undo the RADIX-64 transformation. With Radix-64 transformation, the length of data is increased by 33 percent.

5. **Segmentation and Reassembly:** Most of the email services handle a max message size of only 50,000 bytes. So, if the message length exceeds 50,000 bytes (octets), then the message is segmented such that the length of each segment is within 50,000 bytes. At the recipient end, the segments are reassembled.

11.2.1 Implementation of the Security Services in PGP

- Authentication Only
- Confidentiality Only
- Authentication and Confidentiality

i. *Authentication Only:*
Figure 11.1 illustrates the diagram depicting the "Authentication Only" service.

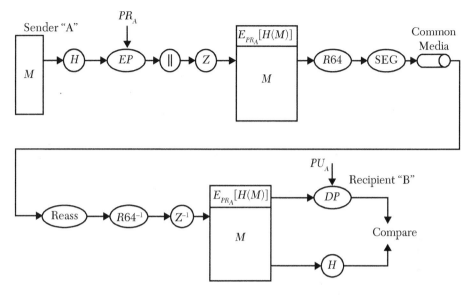

FIGURE 11.1 A schematic diagram depicting "Authentication Only" service.

Where

PR_a: Public Key of the sender "A"

H: Hash function using SHA that generates 160-bit message digest

EP: Public key encryption using *DSS* or *RSA*

Ⓤ: Pre-pending of Digital Signature $E_{PRa}[H(M)]$ to message M

Z: Zip compression

$R64$: Radix-64 Transformation

SEG: Segmentation to segments of length $\leq 50,000$ bytes

Reass: Reassembly of message segments

$R64^{-1}$: Inverse of $R64$ Transformation

Z^{-1}: ZIP Decompression

DP: Decryption of signature using public key PU_a of the sender

11.2.2 Functions at the Sender End and at the Recipient End

1. The sender prepares message M for transmission.

2. A 160-bit message-digest of the message is generate using SHA-1.

3. The sender's digital signature is generated by encrypting the message digest $H(M)$ by using algorithm DSA or RSA and private key PR_a of the sender. The encrypted message digest $E_{PRa}[H(M)]$ is pre-pended to the plain message M.

4. The resulting message is compressed using zip. It is followed by R64 transformation, segmentation, and then transmission of the segments to the recipient.

5. At the receiving end the received message is first reassembled and then the inverse of $R64$ is performed. The resulting message is decompressed.

6. Then the recipient decrypts the digital signature using the sender's public key PU_a. This result is compared with the hash value of the message generated at the recipient end. If the two match then the signature is considered to be verified and the message source is authenticated.

ii. *Confidentiality Only:*

Figure 1.2 illustrates the schematic diagram depicting "Confidentiality Only" service.

Functions at Sender End

1. At the sender end, first the message M is compressed using ZIP.

2. Then the sender generates a 128-bit session key K_s using Random Number Generator (RNG).

3. The compressed message $Z(M)$ is encrypted using a symmetric encryption algorithm (CAST-128 or IDEA or 3DES) and the session key K_s.

4. The session key K_s is also encrypted using a Public Key Algorithm (RSA or ElGamal) and the recipient's Public Key KU_b. The encrypted session key is pre-appended to the encrypted message M.

5. Then the resulting package is $R64$ transformed, segmented, and transmitted.

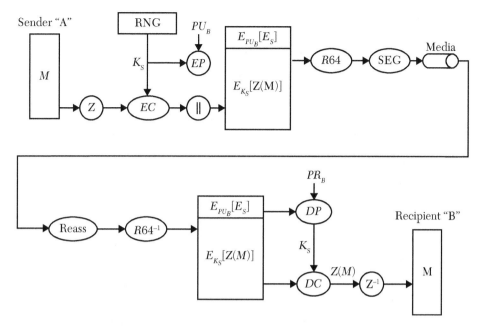

FIGURE 11.2 A schematic diagram depicting "Confidentiality Only" service.

Functions at the Receiving End

1. At the receiving end, first the segments are reassembled. Then the reassembled message is processed to remove $R64$ transformation.

2. Then the recipient end uses its private key PR_b and RSA to decrypt the encrypted session key K_s.

3. The recipient subsequently uses the session key K_s to decrypt the compressed message $Z(M)$.

4. Finally, the recipient decompresses the received message.

iii. *Authentication and Confidentiality:*

Radix-64 Transformation and Segmentation/Reassembly are not included in Figure 11.3 just to avoid complexity, though these functions are provided by *PGP*.

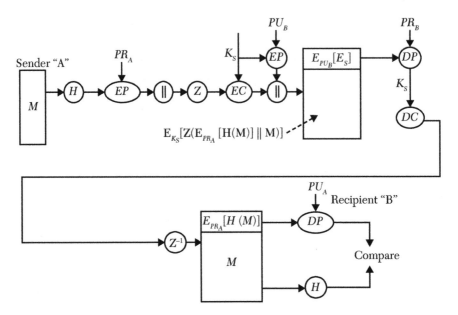

FIGURE 11.3 A schematic diagram depicting the Authentication and Confidentiality function.

11.2.3 Placement of Compression/Decompression Functions in PGP

The compression algorithm used is ZIP. The message is compressed after applying the signature but before encryption, for the following reasons:

1. The signature is applied before compression, since only the uncompressed message will need to be saved along with the signature at the receiving end; this can be used later for signature verification. Otherwise, either the compressed message would need to be saved or the message would need to be compressed for subsequent signature verification, and a compatible ZIP version may not be readily available for compression.

2. Bulk encryption is performed after compression since it reduces the size of the plaintext to be encrypted, thus saving the encrypted overheads.

11.3 RADIX-64 (R64) TRANSFORMATION

Many email services permit the use of only printable ASCII characters. To comply with this requirement, the *PGP* performs *R*64 that converts the input binary data to printable ASCII Characters. Each group of 3 octets of input binary data is divided into four blocks of 6 bits each. Each 6-bit block is mapped onto an 8-bit printable ASCII character, using the following transformation:

0	"A"		26	"a"		52	"0"		62	"+"
1	"B"		27	"b"		53	"1"		63	"/"
2	"C"									
---	---	---	---	---	---	---	---	---	---	---
---	---	---	---	---	---	---	---	---	---	---
25	"Z"		51	"z"		61	"9"			

One more character "=" is used for padding.

The format also appends *CRC* to detect errors in transmission. With Radix-64 the size of the message gets increased by 33 percent. This is the price paid to make the info comprising all printable characters to make the *PGP* email-compatible.

Suppose original size, prior to $R64$ Transformation = X

Size after $R64$ Transformation = $1.33X$

Size after ZIP Compression (assuming 1:2 ratio) = $0.665X$

Overall size reduction = $0.335X$

% Age Reduction = 33.5 %

11.3.1 Segmentation and Reassembly

Almost all email facilities put a max limit on the message size. To accommodate this restriction, *PGP* automatically fragments a message after applying the $R64$ conversion. At the other end the segments are assembled prior to processing.

11.4   CONCEPT OF THE PUBLIC KEY RING AND PRIVATE KEY RING IN PGP

In *PGP*, an email user can have any number of private keys and corresponding public keys. The private keys owned by a user are kept in its private key ring. The corresponding public keys are sent to other users, which are kept on their public key ring. Thus, each *PGP* user has a private Key ring and a Public Key ring.

11.4.1 Fields of the Private Key Ring

The private key ring is a table stored as a file on the disc. Figure 11.4 illustrates the fields of pretty good privacy of the private key ring. Each row in the table comprises the following fields:

1. **Time-Stamp:** This is Date/Time when the private key entry is made on the ring.

2. **Key-Id:** the key id comprises 64 least significant bits of the corresponding public key.

3. **Public Key:** Public key corresponding to the private key.

4. **Encrypted Private Key:** Encrypted value of the private key. This encryption is performed using the hash value of a pass phrase known only to the owner of the private key.

5. **User-Id:** The user id comprises the email address of the private key owner.

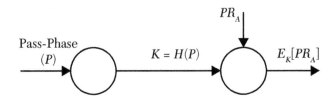

FIGURE 11.4 A schematic diagram of the fields of pretty good privacy of the private key ring.

After encryption of the private key, *PGP* discards the pass-phrase and hash value of the pass-phrase. The owner must remember the pass phrase for subsequent decryption of the private key.

To decrypt the private key, the owner is prompted to enter its pass phrase. The hashed value of the entered pass phrase is used as the decryption key. *PGP* will be able to decrypt and recover the private key only if the user has entered the correct pass phrase.

11.4.2 Generation of Session Keys

The session keys are generated by a true random number generator that generates random numbers as a function of the key-strokes/mouse movements made by the user and the current clock value. Such random numbers are true random numbers. The session keys are used for symmetric bulk encryption of info to achieve data confidentiality.

11.4.3 Use of Key Rings in Authentication

Figure 11.5 shows the sender side for using the key rings in authentications.

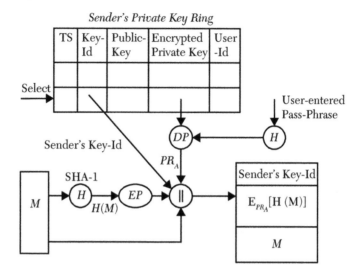

FIGURE 11.5 A schematic diagram of the sender side for using the key rings in authentications.

Figure 11.6 shows the recipient side for using the key rings in authentications.

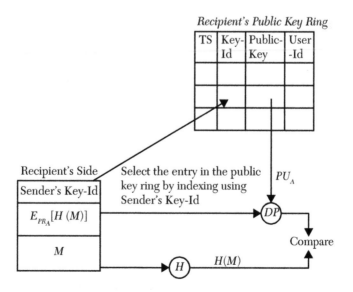

FIGURE 11.6 A schematic diagram of the recipient side for using the key rings in authentications.

11.4.4 Use of Key Rings in Data Confidentiality

Figure 11.7 shows the sender side for using the key rings in data confidentiality.

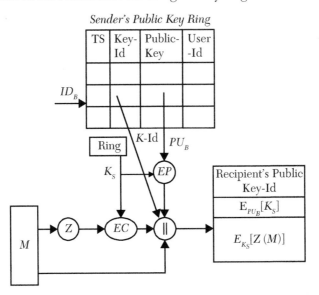

FIGURE 11.7 A schematic diagram of the sender side for using the key rings in data confidentiality.

Figure 11.8 shows the recipient's side for using the key rings in data confidentiality.

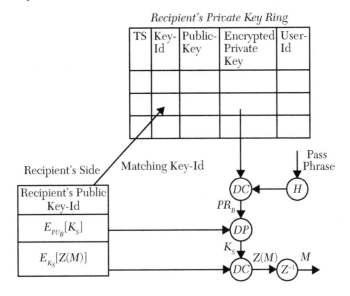

FIGURE 11.8 A schematic diagram of the recipient's side for using the key rings in data confidentiality.

11.4.5 The Trust Model for Management of Public Keys in PGP

- In *PGP*, any user can have any number of Public Key-Private Key Pairs.

- Each user has a Private Key Ring, where it stores its private keys in encrypted form.

- Also, each user has a Public Key Ring, where it stores the public key certificates of other users.

- There are no designated certification agencies for the signing of public key certificates.

- The users themselves act as certification agencies for each other. Whenever a user creates a public key certificate, it obtains digital signatures on the certificate from some users.

- The main issue here is the trust that *PGP* should have in the ownership of public key certificates, that is, whether a public key certificate claimed to be owned by a user "A" is really owned by user "A."

- *PGP* makes use of a "Trust Model" to determine the trust it can have in the binding between a public key and its claimed owner (User-Id), as reflected in a public key certificate. For this, the *PGP* makes use of the following fields that make part of the Public Key Certificate:

  1. **Owner Trust Field:** This indicates the extent of trust in the owner of the Public Key Certificate for signing others' public key certificates.

  2. **Signature Trust Field:** Each Signature on Public Certificate will have an associated Signature Trust Field. The value of this field indicates the extent of trust that *PGP* has in the Signatory for the signing of public key certificates. Its value equals the value of the Owner Trust Field in the Signatory's Public Key Certificate.

  3. **Key Legitimacy Field:** This indicates the extent of trust that *PGP* has in the binding between the associated User-Id and the Public Key in the Certificate. A value of 1 indicates "Complete Trust." Its value is computed as a weighted sum of the Signature Trust Fields on the subject Public Key Certificate.

The owner trust field and Signature Trust Field will assume any of the following six values:

1. Undefined Trust (the field is initialized to this value)

2. Unknown User

3. Usually not trusted to sign others' keys

4. Usually trusted to sign others' keys

5. Always trusted to sign others' keys

6. Ultimate Trust

Whenever a public key certificate is inserted into the public key ring of some user, trust values are assigned to the trust fields as follows:

i. **Assigning value to Owner trust field:** The *PGP* looks into the private key ring of user A. If the Public Key indicated in the subject Public Key Certificate also appears in the Private Key Ring of user "A," then it indicates that user "A" itself is the owner of the subject Public Key Certificate. Then, the "Complete Trust" value is assigned to the "Owner Trust Field" of the subject Public Key Certificate. Otherwise, the PGP will inquire "A" (the owner of the subject Public Key Ring) about the extent of trust "A" has in "B" for signing of other public keys, and "A" will indicate one of the following trust values that is assigned to the "Owner Trust Field":

1. Unknown user

2. Usually not trusted to sign others' keys

3. Usually trusted to sign others' keys

4. Always trusted to sign others' keys

ii. **Assigning values to "Signature Trust Fields":** When a public key certificate is inserted on a public key ring, it will have some signatures by other users. More signatures may be obtained on the certificate subsequently. If a Signatory has a Public Key Certificate, then the value of the "Owner Trust Field" from the signatory's public key certificate is copied into the subject Signature Trust Field; otherwise, a value of "Unknown User" is assigned to the subject Signature Trust Field.

iii. **Determining the value of the Key Legitimacy Field:** The value of the Key Legitimacy Field is determined from the signature trust fields in the certificate. If any of the Signature Trust Field values has the value "Ultimate Trust," then it is taken as weight "one" and the Key Legitimacy Field is set to the value of "Complete Trust"; otherwise, it is computed as a weighted sum of the associated Signature Trust Field values. The weights assigned may be as follows:

1. Unknown user   0

2. Usually not trusted to sign other keys 0

3. Usually trusted to sign other keys $1/Y$

4. Always trusted to sign other keys $1/X$
   Here, $i/X > 1/Y$

Depending upon the weighted sum, the Key Legitimacy Field is assigned one of the following values:

■ Key ownership not trusted (when weighted sum is low)

■ Key ownership marginally trusted (when weighted sum is high but < 1)

■ Complete trust in key ownership (when weighted sum = 1)

Thus, when the value of the weighted sum reaches one, the binding between the public key and its owner is considered to be complete and trustworthy.

11.5 S/MIME (SECURE/MULTIPURPOSE INTERNET MAIL EXTENSION)

S/MIME is an extension of the RFC822 framework that addresses some of the limitations and problem areas of SMTP (Simple Mail Transfer Protocol).

11.5.1 S/MIME Functionality

The following are the S/MIME functionalities:

1. **Enveloped Data:** this caters for symmetric encryption of message contents using a session key. The session key encrypted using the recipient's public key is appended to the encrypted contents of the message. The overall package is called Enveloped Data. The steps required to prepare an Enveloped Data are:

   a. Generate Pseudo random session key for the chosen symmetric encryption algorithm (3DES or RC2/40).

b. For each recipient, encrypt the session key with the recipient's Public Key using the chosen public encryption algorithm.

c. For each recipient, prepare a Recipient-Info block that contains:

Recipient-Info block:

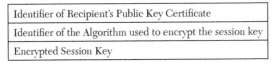

Identifier of Recipient's Public Key Certificate
Identifier of the Algorithm used to encrypt the session key
Encrypted Session Key

d. Encrypt the message contents with the session key, using the chosen symmetric Encryption algorithm.

e. The Recipient-Info block, followed by the encrypted message contents, constitute the Enveloped Data as follows:

Enveloped Data:

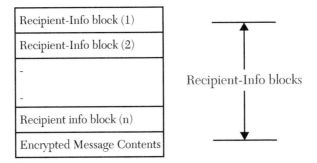

f. The Enveloped-Data block is encoded using base 64 (R64) encoding.

2. Signed-Data: The Signed-Data block caters for multiple signatures. A Digital Signature is formed by taking a message digest of the message contents using the chosen message digest algorithm and then signing the message digest with the signer's private key using the chosen signature algorithm. The message contents plus signature are then encoded using base64 transformation. A Signed-Data message can only be accessed by a recipient with S/MIME capability. The steps required to prepare a Signed-Data are:

a. Select a message digest algorithm (SHA or MD5) and compute a message digest of the message contents.

b. Encrypt the message digest with the signer's private key, using the chosen signing algorithm.

c. Prepare a Signer-Info block that contains:

Signer-Info block:

Signer's Public Key Certificate
Identifier of the Algorithm used to generate the Message Digest
Identifier of the Algorithm used to encrypt the Message Digest
Encrypted Message Digest

d. Prepare the Signed-Data entity that consists of:

Signed-Data block:

Message-Digest Algorithm Identifier
Message Contents
SignerInfo

The Signed-Data entity may also include a set of public-key certificates, sufficient to constitute a chain for the recipient to verify a signature on the signer's public-key certificate.

e. The Signed-Data entity is then encoded using Base64 transformation and then sent to the intended recipients.

To recover the signed message the recipient will reverse the Base64 transformation, obtain the signer's public key from the signer's public key certificate, use the signer's public key to decrypt the message digest (m_1), and compute the message digest of the received message contents (m_2). If $m_1 = m_2$ then the signature is deemed to be verified.

3. **Clear Signed Data:** It is similar to Signed Data with the difference that the message contents are not Base64 transformed, so that the message contents can be viewed by a recipient not having S/MIME capability. But such recipients will not be able to verify the digital signature.

4. **Signed and Enveloped Data:** This functionality combines the basic primitives of Encrypted Data and Signed Data to achieve the following:

   a. The Encrypted Data may be Signed, or

   b. The Signed Data or Clear Signed Data may be encrypted.

Table 11.1 shows the Cryptographic Algorithms supported by S/MIME.

TABLE 11.1 Cryptographic Algorithms Supported by S/MIME

Function	Mandatory Support	Referred Support
Message Digest Generation	SHA-I	MD-5
Message Digest encryption to form a Digital Signature	DSS/DSA	RSA with key-size 512–1024 bits
Session Key encryption using recipient's Public Key	Diffie-Hellman Key Exchange Algorithm	RSA with key-size 512–1024 bits
Encrypt message contents with one-time session key	3DES	RC2/40

11.6   EXERCISES

1. What are the services provided by Pretty Good Privacy (*PGP*)?

2. For Data Confidentiality, what are the Symmetric Encryption schemes supported by *PGP*?

3. What is Radix-64 Transformation? Why is it required in *PGP*?

4. What are the functionalities supported by S/MIME?

5. What is the difference between Signed Data Mode and Clear Signed Data Mode of S/MIME?

6. Explain the use of a Public Key Ring and a Private Key Ring in *PGP*.

7. Explain the Trust Model for Management of Public Keys in *PGP*. If the user itself is the owner of a Public Key Certificate, then what is the value is assigned to the "Owner Trust Field" of that Public Key Certificate? What are the possible values of "Owner Trust Field" and "Signature Trust Field"?

8. How is the value of "Key Legitimacy Field" computed?

9. Explain Enveloped Data and Signed Data formats of S/MIME.

CHAPTER 12

INTERNET SECURITY SERVICES

Chapter Outline

12.1 Introduction

12.2 Internet Protocol Security (IPSec)

12.3 Services Provided by IPSec

12.4 Security Association (SA)

12.5 Security Policies

12.6 ISAKMP

12.7 Secure Socket Layer/Transport Layer Security (SSL/TLS)

12.8 Secure Electronic Transaction

12.9 Key Features of SET

12.10 Exercises

12.1 INTRODUCTION

Today's security threats leave little margin for error. To consistently preempt online attackers that are smart and destructive, enterprise security must incorporate a constantly evolving array of technologies and technical disciplines. Internet Security Services give a complete protection against viruses, spyware, and other threats. In addition, Internet Security Services automatically prevent access to malicious websites and allow selecting and blocking access to web pages that are deemed inappropriate for the place of business.

12.2   INTERNET PROTOCOL SECURITY (IPSEC)

The Internet Protocol Security (IPSec) is an end-to-end Internet security protocol that enables enterprises to set up secure, virtual, private networks over the Internet. Mainly, it covers Data Confidentiality, Data Origin Authentication, and Key Management related to network security.

IPSec operates between the Network Layer and Transport Layer (Layer 3 and Layer 4 of the OSI Model), and is thus completely transparent to the upper layers (TCP/UDP upward).

It is implemented at the routers and the firewalls available at the LAN boundaries, and it provides security only to the traffic that leaves the LAN and enters the WAN; the traffic within the LAN boundaries remains free of security-related overheads.

12.3   SERVICES PROVIDED BY IPSEC

- Access Control
- Connectionless Integrity
- Data Origin Authentication
- Data Confidentiality
- Anti-Replay service (Rejection of Replay Packets)
- Limited Traffic Flow Confidentiality

12.3.1 IPSec Headers

IPSec provides security services through two special headers that are included in the IP packets:

- **Authentication Header (AH):** The AH supports Data Origin Authentication and Connectionless Data Integrity of packets.

- **Encapsulating Security Payload (ESO) -** The ESP provides data confidentiality to packets through symmetric encryption of payload. It also provides limited traffic flow confidentiality through padding. Optionally, it also provides Data Origin Authentication and Data Integrity of packets.

12.3.2 Authentication Header (AH)

The Authentication Header supports a connectionless data integrity and data origin authentication of IP packets, using Integrity Check Value (ICV). IPSec also supports protection against replay attacks by using a sliding window protocol at the recipient end. The ICV covers all the fields of the packet except the mutable fields (the fields that are likely to be altered in transit). One of the mutable fields in the IP Header is the TTL (Time to Live) field. The format of AH is depicted here as in Figure 12.1:

IP Header	TCP Header	Data

(IP-V4 Packet without AH)

IP Header	AH	TCP Header	Data

(IP-V4 Packet with AH)

FIGURE 12.1 Placement of AH in IP-V 4 Packet.

12.3.3 AH Fields

Next Header: It indicates the type of the next payload after the Authentication Header.

Payload length: This indicates length of the AH Header in a 32-bit field that in combination with the Destination IP Address identifies the Security Association (SA) parameters. A Security Association is a one-way relationship between a sender and a recipient that defines the security services to be provided to the traffic flowing from the sender to the recipient. For a two-way peer-to-peer interaction, it needs two SAs to be defined.

Sequence Number: A monotonically increasing sequence number assigned to the packets in the order packets are sent on the SA.

Integrity Check Value (ICV): The ICV is a 96-bit Hashed Mac (HMAC) generated by the following:

- Computing Message Authentication Code (MAC) of Payload M and a secret key K.

- Hashing the MAC value using an embedded Hash function (MD-5 or SHA-1).

- Truncating the HMAC output by selecting the lowest 96 bits.

There are some mutable fields in the IP Header that change during transit from source to destination, like Time to Live (TTL). Their value is set to 0 for computation of ICV at the sender end and at the recipient end. Figure 12.2 illustrates the schematic of AH Fields.

Bits 0…7	Bits 8…15	Bits 16…31
Next Header	Payload Length	Reserved
Security Parameters Index (SPI)		
Sequence Number		
ICV (Variable Size)		

FIGURE 12.2 Schematic of AH fields.

12.3.4 Algorithm for Generation of Integrity Check Value (ICV)

- ICV supports MD5 and SHA-1 as an embedded and Hashing function.

- A secret key K, shared between the sender and the recipient, is used for generating ICV, so that no adversary can modify the message en route. The secret key K is chosen to be of size > n bits, where n is the output message-digest size of function H. For MD5, n equals 128 bits and for SHA-1, it is 160 bits.

- Depending upon the Hashing function H used, the ICV-generating algorithm is designated as:

HMAC-MD5-96: Hashed MAC using embedded Hash Functions MD5 and selecting lowest 96 bits of the output.

or

> HMAC-SHA-1-96: Hashed MAC using embedded Hash Function SHA-1 and selecting lowest 96 bits of the output.

- Let b bits be the input block size of embedded function H. For both MD5 and SHA-1, the input block size $b = 512$ bits.

- The Payload M is divided into K blocks of size b bits each, with the last block suitably padded as per the algorithm. Let the L blocks be denoted as $X_0, X_1, \ldots, X_{k-1}$.

- An additional b-bit block, generated as an XOR of K^+ and ipad, is appended to the payload blocks and then hashed using H.

  where K^+: Secret Key K is padded with zeros on the left side to get the resulting size of b bits (equal to the input block size of H)

  ipad: HEX value 36 (00110110) repeated b/8 times so that the resulting size is b bits

- The n-bit output of H is expanded to b-bits by appending zeros on its left side and it is appended with a b-bit block generated as XOR of K^+ and o-pad, where K^+ is the same as previously and o-pad is HEX value 5C (01011100) repeated b/8 times. The resulting value is again hashed using H.

- The lowest 96 bits are selected from the n-bit message digest output, and that forms the 96-bit Integrity Check Value (ICV).

12.3.5 Encapsulating Security Payload (ESP)

The ESP supports confidentiality of payload through symmetric encryption and limited protection against traffic analysis through padding. Optionally, it also provides data-origin authentication and data-integrity through Integrity Check Value as in the case of AH. Figure 12.3 illustrates the schematic diagram of the ICV-Generating Algorithm.

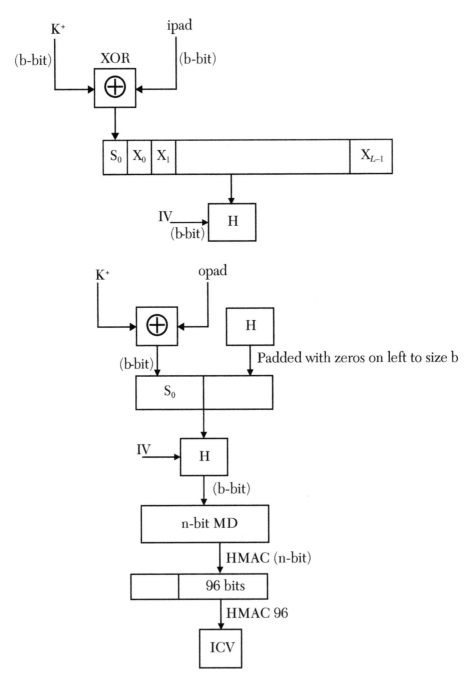

FIGURE 12.3 A schematic diagram of an ICV-generating algorithm.

The fields SPI, Sequence Number, and Next Header are the same as that for AH.

Padding: The Padding is used to prevent Traffic Analysis Attacks.

Pad Length: Number of Padding Bytes.

Authentication data: It compromises ICV as in AH.

The ESP Header compromising SPI and Sequence Number is not encrypted, since information in the ESP Header (like SPI) is required at the recipient end for selection of the Security Association to decrypt the encrypted fields. Figure 12.4 shows the schematic diagram of the ESP Packet Format.

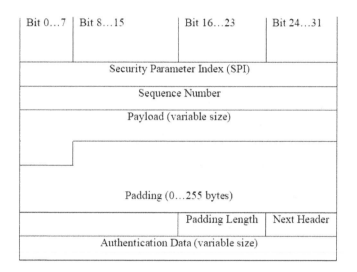

FIGURE 12.4 A schematic diagram of the ESP packet format.

The IP Header is also left clear (free of encryption) as the information in the IP Header (like the Destination IP Address) is required to be accessed by the routers in the Internet for routing of the packet to its final destination. Figure 12.5 shows the schematic diagram of the Format ESP Packet in IP-V4. Table 12.1 illustrates the services supported by AH and/or ESP.

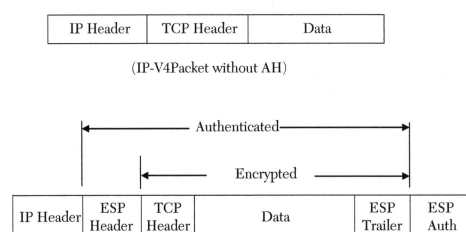

FIGURE 12.5 A schematic diagram of the Format ESP Packet in IP-V4.

TABLE 12.1 Services Supported by AH and/or ESP

Service	AH	ESP (Only Data Confidentiality)	ESP (Auth & Data Confidentiality)
Access Control	Yes	Yes	Yes
Data Integrity	Yes	No	Yes
Data Origin Authentication	Yes	No	Yes
Rejection of Replay Packets	Yes	Yes	Yes
Data Confidentiality	No	Yes	Yes
Traffic Flow Confidentiality	No	Yes	Yes

12.4 SECURITY ASSOCIATION (SA)

It is a concept supported in IPSec. A security Association (SA) is a one-way relationship between a sender and a recipient that affords security services to the traffic flowing from the sender to the recipient. Alternately, it can be viewed as a bundle of algorithms and parameters (such as keys) that are being used to encrypt and authenticate the flow of traffic in one direction. For a two-way secure communication, we need to provide two Security Associations. The choice of encryption and authentication algorithms (from the defined list) is left to the IPSec administrator. An SA will permit either AH or ESP, but not both. Depending upon the type of protection required to be provided for an outgoing packet, the IPSec will specify the following three parameters in the packet header, that together form the Security Association:

- **A Security Parameter Index (SPI):** it is a 32-bit string that points to the parameters associated with the SA. It enables the recipient to select the SA under which the packet is to be processed.

- **Protocol Identifier:** it indicates whether the SA protocol is AH or ESP. It can be either AH or ESP, but not both.

- **IP Destination Address:** It indicates the Destination IP Address of the SA end-point.

12.4.1 SA Parameters

Each implementation of IPSec has a Security Association Database (SAD) that defines the parameters associated with each SA. The parameters that define an SA are:

i. **Sequence Number Counter:** It is a 32-bit monotonically increasing counter value associated with the SA, which is included in the ESP/AH header. The sender initializes the counter to ZERO value. Whenever a new packet is to be sent, the counter is incremented by ONE and the value after incrementing is assigned to the Sequence Number Field in the AH/ESP Header of the new packet.

ii. **Sequence Counter Overflow Flags:** It is a flag that indicates whether the overflow of the Sequence Number Counter should raise an auditable event and prevent further transmission of packets on the associated SA.

iii. **Anti-Replay Window:** It is a sliding-window protocol implemented at the recipient end for rejection of replay packets. The default width of the window is 64 slots.

iv. **AH Information**: It specifies the Authentication Algorithms, associated keys, key life-times, and other related parameters for AH. The hashing algorithms that are supported for HMAC are MD5 and SHA-1.

v.   ESP Information: It specifies the Encryption and Authentication Algorithms, associated keys, key life-times, Initialization Values, and other related parameters for ESP. The Symmetric Encryption Algorithms supported by IPSec are:

- Three-key 3-DES
- IDEA
- Three-key IDEA
- RC5
- CAST
- Blowfish

vi.   SA Lifetime: It specifies the SA Lifetime in terms of period or in terms of byte-count. It also specifies that, after the life-time, whether the SA is to be replaced by a new SA or is to be terminated.

vii.   IPSec Protocol Mode: It specifies whether the SA supports Transport Mode, Tunnel Mode, or Wildcard Mode.

viii.   Path Max Transmission Unit (MTU): It specifies the maximum size of packet that can be transmitted without fragmentation.

12.5   SECURITY POLICIES

Security Policies are a set of rules programmed into an IPSec implementation that dictate the way received packets are to be processed.

12.5.1 Security Policy Database (SPD)

Each IPSec implementation will have a Security Policy Database (SPD). Each entry in SPD defines a subset of IP traffic and points to an SA under which the subset of IP traffic is to be processed.

12.5.2 Security Association Selectors (SA Selectors)

The SA selectors are used to filter the outgoing traffic to map onto a particular Security Association (SA). The security parameters in an outgoing packet are compared against the security parameters defined in SPD entries to determine a matching SPD entry. The matching SPD entry will have a pointer to an SA; this pointer is included in the IPSec header of the outgoing packet. The pointer forms the Security Parameter Index (SPI). At the receiving end, the SPI will enable the recipient to select the SA under which the packet is to be processed.

12.5.3 Combining of Security Associations

An SA supports either AG or Sep, but not both. But consider a situation wherein a sender needs services from both AH and ESP. In that case, more than one SA can be combined as a bundle of SAs. The corresponding SPD entry will have pointers to multiple SA definitions under which the IP traffic, covered by the SA-bundle, is to be processed. The SAs in a bundle may have the same end-point or different end-points.

12.5.4 IPSec Protocol Modes

IPSec supports the following modes of operation:

- Transport Mode
- Tunnel Mode
- Wildcard Mode

Transport Mode

In Transport Mode, protection is provided only to the layers above the Internet Layer (i.e., Transport Layer and above). The original IP Header of the packet is left clear (not encrypted) so that the routers en route can access the destination IP address for the purpose of routing. But the packet remains vulnerable to traffic analysis.

The transport mode formats of IP-V.4 Packets with AH or ESP are shown in Figure 12.6:

- In ESP mode, the payload and the TCP Header SPI require the recipient to select the appropriate SA for performing decryption of the packet.

- Also, the ESP Header contains a sequence number that is to be used by sliding window protocol for rejection of replay packets.

- The main disadvantage of Transport Mode is that the packets are prone to traffic-analysis attack by which an adversary can determine the source and destination IP addresses.

- Since the mode provides protection only to the layers of transport and above, it is called Transport Mode.

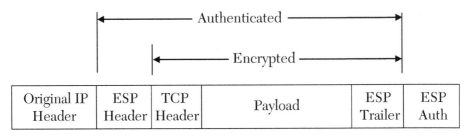

Original IP Header	ESP Header	TCP Header	Payload	ESP Trailer	ESP Auth

(Transport Mode IP-V4 Packet with ESP)

FIGURE 12.6 Transport Mode formats of IP-V.4 Packets.

12.5.5 Tunnel Mode

1. The Tunnel Mode provides protection to the entire packet, including the IP-Header.

2. This mode is used when the communicating nodes are protected by firewalls. The tunnel Mode facilitates creation of a Virtual Private Network (VPN) between the source Firewall and the destination Firewall.

3. All incoming/outgoing packets are routed through firewalls.

4. In ESP, the entire outgoing packet, including the original IP Header, is encrypted at the outgoing firewall and a new IP-Header is pre-appended to the encrypted packet.

5. The new IP-Header contains the IP addresses of the source firewall and the destination firewall. The new IP-Header and the ESP Header are left clear. Using the information in the new IP-Header, the packet is routed to the destination firewall.

6. At the destination firewall, using the information in the ESP Header, the encryption and the new IP-Header are stripped off. Then using the information in the original IP-Header, the packet is routed to the destination end-point.

7. Since the original IP-Header is encrypted between the source and destination firewalls, an adversary cannot determine the Source and Destination IP Addresses. The only information the adversaries can get is the source firewall IP Address and destination firewall IP Address. Thus, the packets

are less prone to traffic analysis attacks. The original packet, including the original IP Header, tunnels through the Internet without exposing itself to adversaries.

8. This mode is used to create Secure Private Networks (SVPNs) over the Internet. Thus, if an organization has many geographically dispersed sites, it can link those sites using SVPNs.

9. The format of a Tunnel Mode IPV.4 Packet, with AH or ESP, is shown in Figure 12.7:

Original IP Header	TCP Header	Payload

(IP-V4 Packet)

New IP Header	AH	Original IP Header	TCP Header	Payload

(Transport Mode IP-V4 Packet with AH)

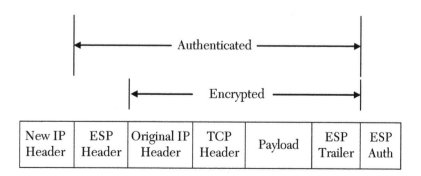

(Transport Mode IP-V4 Packet with ESP)

FIGURE 12.7 Tunnel Mode IPV.4 Packet Formats

Wildcard Mode: Wildcard Mode implies that SA can be used in Transport Mode or Tunnel Mode. The information regarding mode selection is obtained from the associated sockets.

12.5.6 Anti-Replay Window

It is a sliding window protocol used at the recipient end. Let the window size be W and suppose at any time, the right edge of the window is aligned with slot number N as shown in Figure 12.8. Initially, all slots are unmarked.

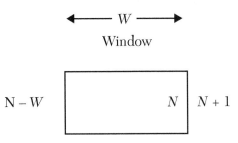

FIGURE 12.8 Anti-Replay Window.

The received packets are processed as follows:

1. If the packet sequential number falls within the window and the packet is a new packet (i.e., the slot in the window is unmarked), then its ICV is checked. If the packet passes the ICV verification, then the packet is accepted and the corresponding slot in the window is marked, indicating that a valid packet has been received.

2. If the sequence number falls within the window but the corresponding slot has already been marked, then it indicates that the valid packet with the same sequence number has already been received; then the new packet is taken as a replay packet and is rejected. Also, if the sequence number falls within the window, but it fails authentication, the packet is rejected. These are Auditable events.

3. If the packet sequence number falls to the left of the window, then the packet is taken as a Replay Packet and is discarded. This is also an auditable event.

4. If packet sequence number falls to the right of the window and the packet passes ICV verification, then the window is slid to the right such that the

sequence number of the new packet is aligned with the right edge of the window. The packet is accepted as a valid packet and its slot is marked.

12.5.7 IPSec Key Management

The automated Key Management Protocol for IPsec is known as the "ISAKMP/Oakley Key Management Protocol," where ISAKMP stands for Internet Security Association Key Management Protocol. It compromises two components:

- **Oakley Key Exchange Protocol:** It is a key exchange protocol, a variant of the Diffie-Hellman Key-Exchange Protocol, with added security features for thwarting Man-in-the-Middle Attacks and Clogging Attacks.

- **Internet Security Association Key Management Protocol (ISAKMP):** It defines the procedures and formats to negotiate, establish, modify, and delete Security Associations.

12.5.8 Features of Oakley Key-Exchange Protocol

The bare Diffie-Hellman Key-Exchange Protocol suffers from the following limitations:

- The key-exchanging entities are not provided with each other's identity.

- It is prone to Man-in-the-Middle Attacks.

- It is prone to Clogging Attacks, where an adversary (Say "E") captures the authentication exchanges of some valid user (say "A"). Then "E" impersonates (masquerades) as user "A" and sends a large number of key-exchange requests to another user (Say "B"). This forces user "B" to perform many computations related to key determination, preventing it from doing other useful work. This is called a clogging attack on user "B."

    The Oakley Key-Exchange Protocol supports the following security features to thwart attacks:

- Use of nounces to thwart replay attacks.

- **Use of Data-Origin Authentication to thwart Man-in-the-Middle Attacks:** Oakley key Determination supports the following techniques for Data-Origin Authentication:

    • Digital Signatures of the sender.

- Encryption of some critical fields in the messages like User-Id and Nounces using the sender's Private Key (Public-Key Cryptography).

- Encryption of some critical fields in the messages by using a secret key that is shared exclusively between the sender and the recipient (Symmetric Cryptography).

■ **Use of Cookies to Thwart Clogging Attacks:** A Cookie is a 64-bit pseudo random number that is generated at the sender end by hashing a string comprising the Source IP address, Destination IP Address, Source Port Number, Destination Port Number, and a secret value. The Key-Exchange messages must be preceded by exchange of cookies between the sender and the recipient. The sequence of messages exchanged between the initiator of the key exchange and the responder is as follows:

There are two global parameters shared among the users:

q : A large prime number

g : A primitive root of q

Figure 12.9 shows the schematic for use of Cookies to thwart Clogging Attacks.

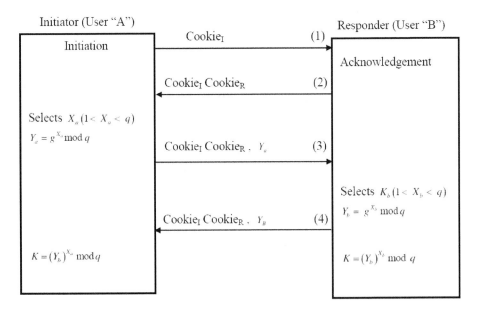

FIGURE 12.9 Schematic for use of Cookies to thwart Clogging Attacks.

- The user "A" (Initiator) sends Cookie$_I$ to user "B" (Responder).

- The user "B" acknowledges to user "A" by sending Cookie$_R$ (generated by "B") along with the Cookie$_I$ that was received from "A." This acknowledgement will be received by User "A" only if user "A" has not impersonated another user while sending Cookie$_I$. If user "A" has impersonated another user, then the acknowledgement will go to the other user. So, user "A" will be able to proceed with key-exchange messages only if "A" does not masquerade as another user.

- If the cookies have been exchanged successfully, then the initiator and the responder will exchange the key-determination messages (3) and (4). The key-determination messages (3) and (4) include both the cookies. The two parties will be able to exchange these messages only if both of them possess both of the cookies generated by each other. This thwarts the clogging attacks.

- **Support of Multiple Groups in Oakley Key Exchange**

  Oakley supports the following Groups for the Diffie-Hellman Key Exchange:

  - Modular exponentiation with 768-bit modulus

    Prime Number $q = 2^{768} - 2^{704} - 1 + 2^{64} + ((2^{638} \times \pi) + 149686)$

    $g = 2$ (*primitive Root of q*)

  - Modular exponentiation with 1024-bit

    Prime Number $q = 2^{1024} - 2^{960} - 1 + 2^{64} + ((2^{894} \times \pi) + 129093)$

    $g = 2$ (primitive Root of q)

  - In addition, it also supports the group with modular exponentiation using 1536-bit modulus and Elliptic Curve Groups over 2^{155} and 2^{185}

12.6   ISAKMP

ISAKMP defines procedures and formats to negotiate, establish, modify, and delete Security Associations (SAs) needed for IPSec message exchanges. As part of the SA establishment, ISAKMP also defines payloads for exchanging key generation messages and authentication data. Figure 12.10 shows the ISAKMP Header Format, and Figure 12.11 shows the ISAKMP Payload Header Format.

Initiator Cookie				
Responder Cookie				
Next Payload	Major Ver.	Minor Ver.	Exchange Type	Flags
Message ID				
Length				

FIGURE 12.10 ISAKMP header format.

Next Payload	Reserved	Payload Length

FIGURE12.11 ISAKMP Payload header format.

Initiator Cookie (64-bit): Cookie generated by the entity that initiated SA negotiation or SA establishment or SA modification or SA deletion.

Responder Cookie (64-bit): Cookie generated by the Responder entity in response to receipt of Initiator Cookie.

Next Payload (8-bit): Indicates the type of the first payload in the message.

Maj Ver (4-bit): Indicates Major Version Number of ISAKMP in use.

Min Ver (4-bit): Indicates Minor Version Number of ISAKMP in use.

Exchange Type (8-bit): Indicates the Type of Message Exchange

Flags: Indicate the specific options chosen. For example, Encryption Bit is set if all payloads following the header are encrypted.

12.6.1 Payload Types

ISAKMP supports the following types of payloads:

- **Proposal Payload:** It contains information required for SA negotiation like Protocol Identifier (AH or ESP) and Security Protocol Index (SPI). It also contains the number of Transforms (security options) that are offered for SA being negotiated with the peer. Each Transform (security option) will be contained in a separate Transform Payload.

- **Transform Payload:** The Transform Payload contains a security option, for example, Three Key 3-DES for ESP and HMAC-SHA-1-96 for AH. The recipient can accept any Transform (security option).

- **Key Exchange Payload:** This contains information pertaining to key exchanges using, for example, the Oakley Key-Exchange Protocol.

- **Identification Payload:** This contains the sender's identification in terms of IP Address.

- **Certificate Payload:** This contains a Public Key Certificate being transferred by the sender to the recipient.

- **Hash Payload:** Contains a message Digest (Hash Value).

- **Signature Payload:** Contains the sender's Digital Signatures.

- **Nounce Payload:** Contains a Nounce to ensure timeliness of the message.

- **Notification Payload:** Contains either an error message or status information.

12.6.2 Important IPSec Documents

IPSec was officially specified by the Internet Engineering Task Force (IETF) in a series of Request for comments (RFC) documents like:

- **RFC 2401:** An overview of security architecture

- **RFC 2402:** Description AH in IPv4 and IPv6

- **RFC 2406:** Description of ESP in IPv4 and IPv6

- **RFC 2403:** Use of HMAC-MD5-96 in AH and ESP

- **RFC 2404:** Use of HMAC-SHA-1-96 in AH and ESP

- **RFC 2405:** DES-CBC Cipher Algorithm for ESP

- **RFC 2408:** Specifications of key management in IPSec

12.7 SECURE SOCKET LAYER/TRANSPORT LAYER SECURITY (SSL/TLS)

Secure Socket Layer (SSL) operates above layer 4 (TCP Layer) and provides confidentiality and authentication services to the TCP Layer. Transport Layer Security (TLS) is an Internet Engineering Task Force (IETF) which is an Internet standard for SSL.

12.7.1 Components of SSL

- SSL Handshake Protocol
- SSL Change Cipher Specs Protocol
- SSL Alerts Protocol
- SSL Record Protocol

Figure 12.12 illustrates the components of SSL.

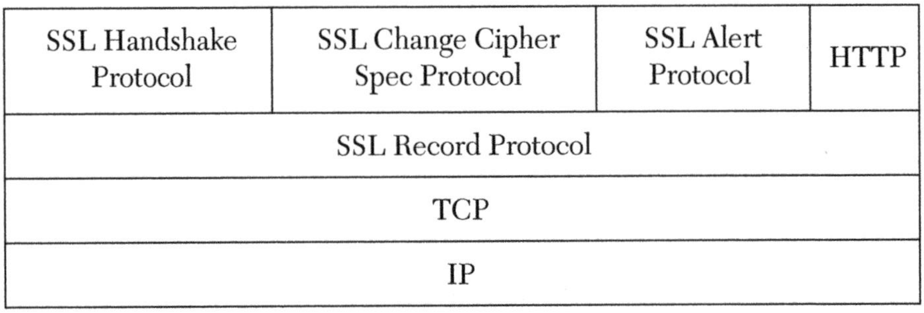

SSL Handshake Protocol	SSL Change Cipher Spec Protocol	SSL Alert Protocol	HTTP
SSL Record Protocol			
TCP			
IP			

FIGURE 12.12 Components of SSL.

12.7.2 SSL Handshake Protocol

This protocol enables clients and servers to validate each other over the Internet and to negotiate Encryption and MAC Algorithms, along with their cryptographic keys, for use in the SSL Record Protocol. It consists of a series of messages exchanged between the clients and servers. This protocol is used prior to transmission of any application data.

12.7.3 SSL Change Specs Protocol

This protocol causes a pending state to be copied into a current state, thus causing a change of service cipher specs.

12.7.4 SSL Alerts Protocol

This protocol is used for conveying SSL-related alerts to peer entities.

12.7.5 SSL Record Protocol

The SSL Record Protocol provides two services for SSL connections:

1. Confidentiality: The Handshake Protocol defines a shared secret key that is used for Conventional encryption of SSL payloads.

2. Message Integrity: The Handshake Protocol also defines a shared secret key that is used to form a MAC. It is similar to HMAC.

Figure 12.13 indicates the overall operation of the SSL Record Protocol.

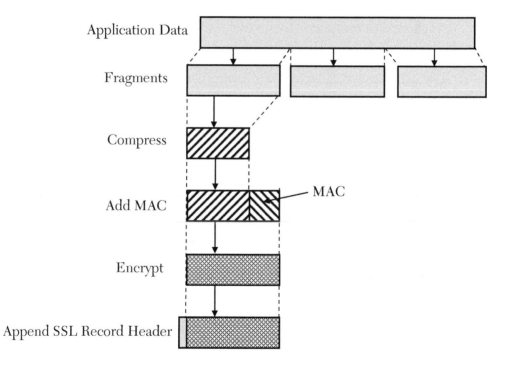

FIGURE 12.13 Overall operation of SSL Record Protocol.

The message received from the upper layers is fragmented such that the size of each fragment is within 2^{14} bytes (16384 bytes). Then each fragment is compressed (optional) and MAC is computed over the compressed fragment, which is appended to the compressed fragment. The HASH Value for the MAC is computed using MD5 or SHA-1, and the Hash Value is encrypted using a shared key. The resulting block is encrypted using symmetric encryption.

12.7.6 Some Terms Related to SSL

SSL Session:

An SSL Session is an association between a client and a server. The sessions are created by Handshake Protocol by defining a set of cryptographic security parameters, which can be shared among many connections under the session. Sessions are used to avoid expensive negotiations of new security parameters for each connection.

SSL Connection:

A connection is a transport for providing service. The connections are transient, and each connection is associated with one session.

Session State:

A session state is defined by the following parameters:

i. **Session Identifier:** An arbitrary byte sequence chosen by the server.

ii. **Peer Certificate:** An X.509.V3 Certificate of the peer.

iii. **Compression Method:** The algorithm used to compress data prior to encryption.

iv. **Cipher Spec:** A Symmetric Encryption Algorithm like AES for providing data confidentiality and a MAC algorithm using a secret key and an embedded Hash algorithm (like MD5 or SHA-1) used for MAC calculation.

v. **Master Secret:** A 48-byte secret, shared between the client and the server.

vi. **Resumable:** It indicates whether the session can be used to initiate new connections.

Connection State: A connection state is defined by the following parameters:

i. **Server and Client Random:** Byte sequences chosen by the server and the client for each connection.

ii. Server Write MAC Secret: The secret key used in the MAC operation on the data sent by the server.

iii. Client Write MAC Secret: The secret key used in the MAC operation on the data sent by the client.

iv. Server Write Key: The convention encryption key for data encrypted by the client and decrypted by the client.

v. Client Write Key: The convention encryption key for data encrypted by the client and decrypted by the server.

vi. Initialization Vectors(IV): IV for CBC Mode. It is initialized by the SSL Handshake Protocol.

vii. Sequence Numbers: Each party maintains a sequence number for its transmitted messages for each connection. When a party sends or receives a change cipher spec message, the sequence number is set to zero.

12.7.7 Transport Layer Security (TLS)

TLS is a Transport Layer protocol defined in RFC 2246. The protocol is quite similar to SSLV.3, with some minor differences. The protocol is based on the Secure Socket Layer (SSL) protocol that was originally created by Netscape. One advantage of TLS is that it is application-independent. It runs above TCP/IP and below the application protocols like HTTP or IMAP. The HTTP running on top of TLS or SSL is often called HTTPS. The choice of how to initiate the TLS handshaking and how to interpret the authentication certificates exchanged is left to the designers of application protocols that run on top of TLS. TLS provides data confidentiality and data integrity between two communicating entities.

Basically, the TLS comprises two layers:

1. TLS Record Protocol
2. TLS Handshake Protocol

12.7.8 TLS Record Protocol

The TLS Record Protocol is used for encapsulation of various higher-level protocols. It operates on top of the TCP layer and provides connection security, with the following features:

1. *Confidentiality:* Confidentiality is assured by using Symmetric Cryptography (DES, RC4, etc.). The Record Protocol can also be used without encryption. The keys for Symmetric Encryption are generated for each connection and are based on a secret value negotiated by the TLS Handshake Protocol.

2. *Data Integrity:* It provides a message integrity check using MAC. Secure hash algorithms (like SHA, MD5, etc.) are used for MAC computations. The Record Protocol can also operate without MAC.

The Record Protocol takes messages to be transmitted, fragments the messages into blocks of manageable size, compresses the data (optional), computes MAC for each fragment and appends to the fragment, encrypts the resulting block, and transmits it. At the recipient end, the data is decrypted, decompressed, verified, and reassembled and then delivered to the highest-level clients.

12.7.9 TLS Handshake Protocol

The TLS Handshake Protocol enables the server and the client to authenticate each other and to negotiate encryption algorithms and cryptographic keys before the application protocol begins to transmit or receive any data. The TLS Handshake Protocol provides connection security with the following features:

1. The peer identity is authenticated using RSA or DSS.

2. Negotiation of a shared secret is made secure. It is made resistant to Man-in-the-Middle Attack.

3. No attacker can modify the handshake sequence without being detected.
   The TLS Handshake Protocol comprises a suite of three sub-protocols:

   a. Change cipher spec protocol

   b. Alert protocol

   c. Handshake protocol

12.8 SECURE ELECTRONIC TRANSACTION

Secure Electronic Transaction (SET) is a protocol for securing Credit Card transactions over the Internet. It was jointly developed by VISA and Mastercard, with the involvement of some other companies like IBM, Microsoft, Netscape, VeriSign, and so forth. The protocol provides privacy to online transactions over the Internet. Also, it provides mutual authentication to the consumers and the merchants involved in electronic commerce. It makes use of both Symmetric and Public-Key Cryptography for the communications over the Internet. Figure 12.14 displays participants involved in Secure Electronic Transaction (SET).

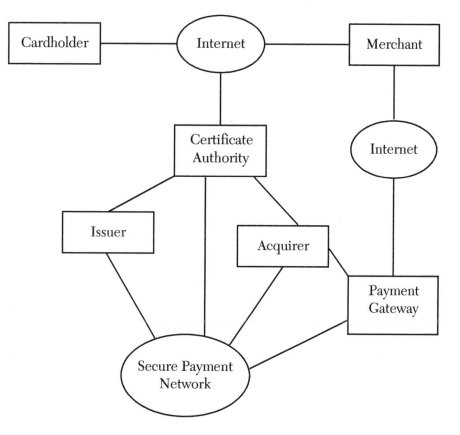

FIGURE 12.14 Participants in Secure Electronic Transaction (SET).

1. **Customer (Cardholder):** A customer (known as Cardholder) is an authorized holder of a Credit Card of some brand, say MasterCard or Visa, and so on, issued by a bank (known as Issuer). Each Cardholder will have an account linked to the credit card, opened in the Issuer Bank. The cardholder is also issued an X.509 V3 Public Key certificate, signed by the issuer bank. The certificate is to be used by the other participants for verification of the cardholder's RSA signatures.

2. **Merchant:** A merchant is a person or an organization that sells goods or provides online services over the Internet. The merchant accepts its payments through specified brands of credit cards. A merchant has a relationship with a bank called the Acquirer. Each merchant is issued two public key certificates—one for the verification of its signatures and the other for the exchange of session keys.

3. **Issuer:** The Issuer is a financial institution (such as a bank) that issues credit cards (like MasterCard or Visa, etc.) to customers, after due verification. Each card will have an account opened in the issuer bank, which is linked to the credit card. The issuer bank is fully responsible for the clearing of all debts of its cardholders.

4. **Acquirer:** The Acquirer is also a financial institution (bank) that establishes relationships with merchants. Each merchant will have an account opened at its acquirer bank, and the acquirer is responsible for the following:

   a. Processing of the Merchant's "payment authorization," which amounts to the confirmation that the cardholder making the related purchases is a valid cardholder and that the related purchases are within the credit limits of the cardholder.

   b. Processing of "Payment Capture," which results in the transfer of funds from the cardholder's account at the Issuer Bank to the Merchant's account at the Acquirer Bank. The "Payment Capture" is *affected* only after the Merchant has delivered the ordered items/provided the ordered services.

5. **Payment Gateway:** This is a function performed by the acquirer bank or by a designated trusted third-party that processes merchant payment messages. The merchant exchanges the SET messages with the payment gateway over the Internet, while the payment gateway communicates with the acquirer over a direct secure link or secure payment network.

12.8.1 Business Requirements of SET

1. Ensure integrity of all transmitted data.

2. Provide authentication that a cardholder is a legitimate user of a credit card account.

3. Provide authentication that a merchant can accept credit card transactions through its relationship with a financial institution (called an acquirer bank).

4. The order Information should be shared only between the cardholder and the merchant (not to be shared with the payment gateway).

5. The payment information (that includes credit card details) should be shared only between the cardholder and the payment gateway (not to be shared with the merchant).

6. Develop a mechanism to link the payment information with the order information, and this linkage should be made available to all the participants. This is to avoid tampering with order-and payment-information by any participant without being detected by other participants. If any of the participants tampers with this information, then the other parties should be able to prove that information has been tampered with.

7. Ensure the use of best security practices and system design techniques to protect all legitimate parties in online transactions.

8. Create protocols that neither depend on the transport security mechanisms nor prevents their use.

9. Facilitate and encourage interoperability among software and network providers.

12.9   KEY FEATURES OF SET

1. **Confidentiality of Information:** The Cardholder account and payment information is secured as it travels across the network, and this information is not provided to the merchant. Credit card information is provided only to the issuing bank. Symmetric encryption by DES is used to provide confidentiality. DES uses one-time session-key encryption. The session key, encrypted by the recipient's public key using RSA, is also sent to the intended recipient along with the message. The encrypted session key is called the "Digital Envelope." At the recipient end, the session is first extracted from the digital envelope by decrypting it using the recipient's private key. Then the session key is used to decrypt the encrypted message. The schematic is shown in Figure 12.15.

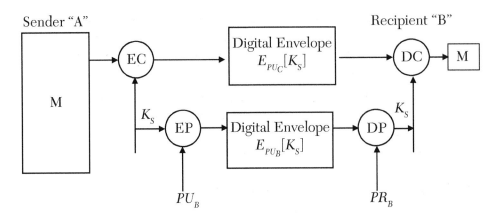

FIGURE 12.15 A schematic diagram displaying confidentiality of information in SET.

2. **Integrity of Data:** SET guarantees that message contents are not altered in transit. RSA digital signatures using SHA-1 hash codes provide message integrity. The signer's public key certificate is sent to the recipient along with the signed message. The recipient will extract the signer's public key from the received certificate and use it for verification of the signature on the received message as in Figure 10.16.

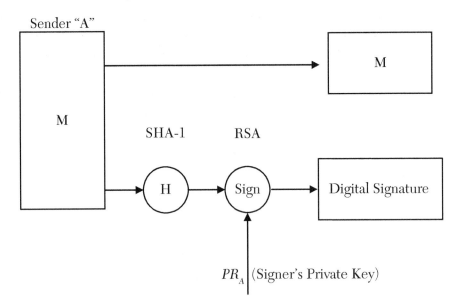

FIGURE 10.16 A schematic diagram showing integrity of data.

3. **Cardholder Account Authentication:** SET enables a merchant to verify that a cardholder is a legitimate user of a valid credit card account. SET uses X.509.V3 digital certificates and RSA signatures for this authentication.

4. Merchant Authentication: SET enables cardholders to verify that a merchant has a relationship with a financial institution allowing it to accept credit card payments. SET uses X.509.V3 digital certificates and RSA signatures for this authentication.

12.9.1 Use of Public Key Certificates in SET

SET makes use of X.809 V.3 certificates of two categories:

1. X.509 V3 certificates for Signature Verification

2. X.509 V3 certificates for exchange of session keys

12.9.2 Sequence of Events in SET

1. The Customer opens a Credit Card Account with an Issuer Bank and obtains a Credit Card of some brand.

2. The Customer receives an X.509V3 digital certificate, signed by the issuer bank. The certificate contains the cardholder's public key (PU), to be used by others for verification of the cardholder's signatures, created using RSA with the cardholder's private key(PR).

3. Merchants have their own certificates, one for signatures using RSA and the other for the exchange of session keys. The merchant also needs a copy of the Payment Gateway's Public Key Certificate.

4. Purchase Request by the Customer

5. Payment Authorization by the Acquirer

6. Payment Capture

The Cardholder and the Merchant first finalize the list of items to be purchased and then perform SET protocols, which comprises the following sequence of messages:

Purchase Request: It comprises four messages:

1. Initiate Request (Cardholder Merchant)

2. Initiate Response (Merchant Cardholder)

3. Purchase Request (Cardholder Merchant)

4. Purchase Response (Merchant Cardholder)

a. **Initiate Request:** The Initiate Request Message from the Cardholder to the Merchant comprises:

   - Brand of the Credit Card used by the Cardholder

   - ID assigned to this Request

   - Nounce N1 (This is to be echoed back by the Merchant)

b. **Initiate Response:** In response, the Merchant generates an Initiate Response Message, signs it with its private key, and sends it to the requesting cardholder. The Initiate Response Message comprises:

   - **Nounce N1** (Echoed back by the Merchant)

   - **Nounce N2** (For the Cardholder to echo back) Message (M)

   - **Transaction ID** (ID assigned to this Transaction)

   - **Signed Message Digest of Message M**

   - **Merchant's Public Key Certificate** (for Merchant's Signature verification)

   - **Payment Gateway's Public Key Certificate** (For Key-Exchange)

c. **Purchase Request:** The cardholder performs the following actions:

   - Verifies signatures on the certificates

   - Verifies Nounce N_1 (echoed back by the Merchant).

   - Verifies Merchant's Signature on the Message Digest by decrypting it using the Merchant's Public key.

   - Prepares **Purchase Request** Message as shown in Figure 12.17 and sends it to the Merchant.

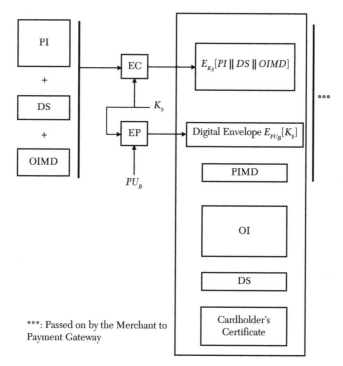

FIGURE 12.17 A schematic diagram of a Purchase Request Message.

Dual Signature (DS): The dual signature is generated by the cardholder as follows in Figure 12.18:

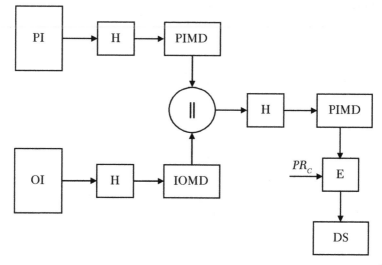

FIGURE 12.18 A schematic diagram of a Verification of dual Signature.

H: Hash Algorithm SHA-1

||: Concatenation (OIMD II PIMD)

OI: Order Information

PI: Payment Information

OIMD: Order Information Message Digest = H(OI)

PIMD: Payment Information Message Digest = H(PI)

POMD: Combined Order & Payment Message Digest = H(PIMD ||OIMD)

E: Public Key Encryption Algorithm (RSA)

PRC: Cardholder's Private Key (for signing of messages)

DS: Dual Signature

$$DS = E_{PR_C}\left[H\left(H(PI)\|H(OI)\right)\right]$$

The purpose of the dual signature is to link two messages that are intended for two different recipients. For obvious reasons, the Cardholder (customer) intends to send the Payment Information (PI) only to the issuer bank, through the Payment Gateway; and the Order Information only to the Merchant. This is because the credit card information, being sensitive, should not be disclosed to anyone other than the issuer bank, and the bank need not know the Order Information. However, both PI and OI must be linked in a way that it can be used to resolve disputes, if any, in future. So, the customer creates a link between the OI and PI through the Dual Signature, which the customer can prove later on to both the Merchant and the Issuer Bank.

Finally, the customer will be in possession of the PI, OI, and Dual Signature.

The Merchant received the OI, PIMD, and Dual Signature.

And the issuer bank received the PI, OIMD, and Dual Signature.

None of the three parties (Customer, Merchant, and Bank) can alter the information it possesses since the other parties will be able to verify and prove any such alteration with the information they possess.

Processing Purchase Request (by the Merchant's Software)

- Verifies the Customer's Public Key Certificate by verifying its CA Signature

- Verifies the Dual Signature as indicated in Figure 12.19 diagrammatically. This ensures that the message has not been tampered with in transit and that the message has been signed by the alleged Customer.

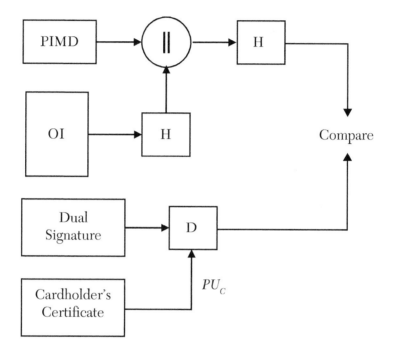

FIGURE 12.19 Verification of Dual Signature.

- Processes the order and sends a purchase response to the customer.

- Forwards the Payment Information to the Payment Gateway for Authorization of Payment.

d. **Purchase Response:** The Purchase Response message from the Merchant to the Customer comprises the following:

- **Response Block** that acknowledges the Order and references the corresponding **Transaction ID.**

- **Signed Message Digest of the message** signed using the Merchant's Private Key.

- **Merchant's Signature Certificate.**

When the Cardholder Software receives the purchase response message, it performs the following actions:

- Verifies Merchant's Certificate
- Verifies the Merchant's signature on the response block
- Displays the appropriate message to the customer

Payment Authorization: The Payment Authorization is meant to get the Issuer Bank's approval (through the Payment Gateway) for the proposed Transaction. This will guarantee that the Merchant will receive the payment. The Payment Authorization exchange comprises two Messages:

i. Payment Authorization Request (Merchant→Payment Gateway)

ii. Payment Authorization Response (Payment Gateway→Merchant)

i. **Payment Authorization Request:** This Message comprises the following components:

- The Purchase-Related Information, encrypted using a **Session Key KS** generated by the Customer as received from the Customer. It includes

  – **PI**

  – **Dual Signature**

  – **OIMD**

- The Digital Envelope, containing Session Key KS (encrypted using the Payment Gateway's Public Key

- Authorization-Related Information, encrypted using a one-time session key (say KSM) generated by the merchant. This information includes:

  – **Authorization Block** (that includes the Transaction ID)

  – **Message Digest,** signed using the Merchant's Private Key

  – **Digital Envelope,** containing session key KSM, encrypted using the Payment Gateways' Public Key

- Certificates: It includes the following:

  - **Customer's Signature Certificate** to be used to verify the Dual Signature

  - **Merchant's Signature Key Certificate** to be used to verify Merchant's Signatures on the Authorization Request Block

  - **Merchant's Key Exchange Certificate** needed for Payment Authorization Response, to be sent by the Payment Gateway

On receipt of the Payment Authorization Request, the Payment Gateway performs the following actions as shown in Figure 12.20:

- Verifies the certificates by the CA's Signatures.

- Decrypts the Digital Envelope of the Authorization Block to obtain the symmetric Key KSM, decrypts the Authorization Block, and verifies the Merchant's Signature on the Authorization Block.

- Decrypts the Digital Envelope of the Payment Information Block to obtain Session Key KS, decrypts the Payment Information Block, and verifies the Dual Signatures of the Customer.

- Verifies that the Transaction ID referred to in the Authorization Block (prepared by the Merchant) matches with the Transaction ID in the Payment Information Block (prepared by the Customer).

- Requests and receives the Payment Authorization from the Issuer Bank.

- Having received the Payment Authorization from the Issuer Bank, the Payment Gateway prepares and sends the Authorization Response to the Merchant. The Authorization Response assures the Merchant that the Cardholder's account is currently active and that the proposed payment is within the Customer's Credit Limit.

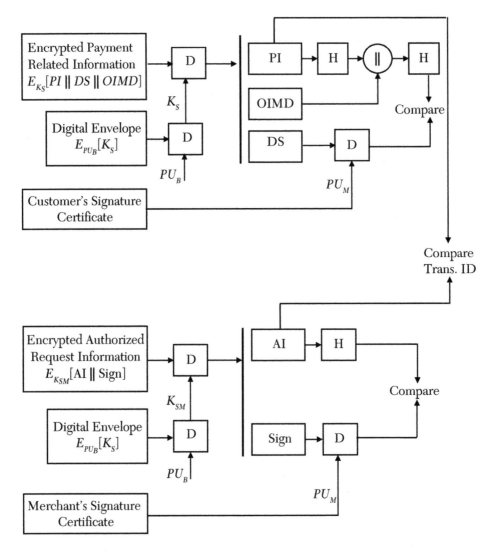

FIGURE 12.20 A schematic diagram of the Payment Authorization Request Message.

i. **Payment Authorization Response:** It includes the following:

- **Authorization-Related Information:** This includes the Authorization Block, signed by the Payment Gateway's Private Signature Key and Encrypted by a one-time session key generated by the Payment Gateway. Also, it includes a digital envelope containing the one-time session key, encrypted using the Merchant's Key-Exchange Public Key.

- **Capture Token Information:** This information will be used later by the Merchant to receive payment. The token is signed by the Payment Gateway, encrypted using a one-time session key, and is also accompanied by a digital envelope. The capture Token is preserved as such by the merchant and returned later to the Payment Gateway, for receiving payment.

- **Certificates:** Contains the Gateway's Signature Certificate.

With the Payment Authorization now received from the Issuer Bank through the Payment Gateway, the Merchant will supply the goods/services as per the Order Information (OI).

12.9.3 Payment Capture

After supplying the goods/services as per the OI, the Merchant will proceed to Capture (receive) the Payment. The Payment Capture comprises two messages:

i. Payment Capture Request (Merchant→Payment Gateway)

ii. Payment Capture Response (Payment Gateway→Merchant)

i. **Payment Capture Request:** This message generated by the Merchant comprises:

- **Capture Request Block** that includes the **Transaction ID** and **Payment Amount.** This message is signed and encrypted. Thus, it is accompanied by the digital envelope.

- **Encrypted Capture Token,** received earlier from the Payment Gateway.

- **Merchant's Signature Key and Key-Exchange Key Certificates.**

- When the Payment Gateway receives the Payment Capture Request, it performs the following actions:

- Decrypts and verifies the Capture Request

- Decrypts and verifies the Capture Token Block

- Verifies the consistency between the Capture Request and Capture Token

- If verified, the Payment Gateway creates a Clearing Request, which is sent to the Issuer Bank on the secure payment network.

- The Clearing Request causes funds to be transferred to the Merchant's Account.

ii. **Capture Response:** This message is sent from the Payment Gateway to notify the Merchant About the Payment. This message includes a Capture Response Block signed by the Public Gateway and encrypted. The message also includes a digital envelope and the Payment Gateway's Signature Key Certificate. The Merchant will decrypt the message, verify it, and store it. The Capture Response is used by the merchant for reconciliation with the payment received from the acquirer bank.

This concludes the transaction.

12.10   EXERCISES

1. What are the services provided by IPSec?

2. What are the Headers through which IPSec provides security services?

3. What are the formats of Authentication Header (AH) and Encapsulating Security Payload (ESP)?

4. What are the services supported by AH and by ESP?

5. What are the Symmetric Encryption Algorithms supported by ESP?

6. What Hashing Algorithms are supported by Integrity Check value (ICV)?

7. What is the size (in bits) of HMAC-SHA-1-96?

8. Are mutable fields in the IP Header considered while computing ICV?

9. What is the purpose of including the Sequence Number in AH and ESP?

10. What is the purpose of padding in ESP?

11. What is Security Association (SA) in IPSec?

12. What are the parameters associated with each Security Association?

13. What do you understand by the combining of Security Associations?

14. What are IPSec Protocol Modes?

15. What is the major difference between Transport Mode and Tunnel Mode?

16. How are Replay Packets rejected in IPSec?

17. What are the security features of the Oakley Key-Exchange Protocol?

18. What is the format of the ISAKMP Header?

19. How are cookies used to thwart clogging attacks?

20. What are the Payload Types supported by ISAKMP?

21. What are the components of a Secure Socket Layer (SSL) Protocol?

22. What is the function of an SSL Handshake Protocol?

23. What are the steps of an SSL Record Protocol?

24. What is the difference between an SSL Session and an SSL Connection?

25. What is the Transport Layer Security (TLS) Protocol? What are its layers?

26. What are the functions of the TLS Record Protocol and the TLS Handshake Protocol?

27. Who are the participants in the Secure Electronic Transaction (SET) Protocol?

28. What are the business requirements of SET?

29. What are the key features of SET?

30. What is the sequence of events in SET?

31. What is a Dual Signature? How does it assure the confidentiality of information between Cardholder and Merchant and between Cardholder and Payment Gateway, while at the same time permitting an Integrity Check by all participants of the complete information?

32. What is the difference between Payment Authorization and Payment Capture?

CHAPTER 13

SYSTEM SECURITY

Chapter Outline

13.1 Introduction

13.2 Intruders

13.3 Intrusion Detection

13.4 Password Management

13.5 Malicious Programs

13.6 Anti-Virus Scanners

13.7 Worms

13.8 Firewall

13.9 Types of Firewalls

13.10 Trusted Systems

13.11 Exercises

13.1   INTRODUCTION

In an open networked environment, System Security deals with the protection of vital information that is made available to authorized users on the NET against security attacks by intruders. This chapter will give an overview of system security.

13.2   INTRUDERS

An intruder (also called a hacker) is an individual who performs security attacks on others' domains in a networked computing environment. The intruder may attempt to read privileged data (like password cracking), perform unauthorized modification of data, or disrupt normal functioning of a system. There are three classes of intruder:

1. **Masquerader:** An individual who is not an authorized user of a system, but who penetrates the access control mechanism of the system to exploit the access rights of an authorized user. The Masquerader is likely to be an outsider.

2. **Misfeasor:** A legitimate user who exceeds access rights by increasing the range of his or her privileges. Obviously, a Misfeasor is an insider.

3. **Clandestine User:** An individual who seizes supervisory control of a system and uses this control to evade auditing or to bypass access control or to suppress audit collection.

13.3   INTRUSION DETECTION

Intrusion detection refers to determining whether some unauthorized entity (called an intruder) has attempted to gain access or has gained access to a protected system. The Intrusion Detection relies on the assumption that the behavior of an intruder differs from that of a legitimate user, in parameters that can be quantified. A fundamental tool for intrusion detection is audit records, that is, records of ongoing activities of the users that form a vital input for intrusion detection. But there will be some overlap between the behavior of legitimate users and intruders. So, an intrusion detection system is likely to generate some false alarms; at the same time, it may fail to detect some actual intrusions.

13.3.1 Intrusion Detection Techniques

1. **Statistical Anomaly Detection involves the following:**
   - Collection of data relating to the behavior of users over a period of time.
   - Application of statistical tests to the observed behavior of users, to determine with a high level of confidence whether that behavior is of a legitimate user or of an intruder. Mainly, there are two approaches for statistical anomaly detection:
     - **Threshold Detection:** This involves the defining of thresholds (independent of user) for the frequency of occurrence of various events. Detection involves counting the number of any of such

occurrences over an interval of time, and if the count exceeds the threshold then an intrusion is assumed.

- **Profile-Based Detection:** This technique is based on developing the activity profile of each legitimate user. The intrusion detection is performed on the basis of "sudden and significant change in the behavior" of a user.

2. **Rule-Based Detection:** This involves defining a set of rules that can be used to decide whether a given behavior is that of a legitimate user or of an intruder. This has two approaches:

- **Anomaly Detection:** It attempts to detect deviations from the previous established usage pattern.

- **Penetration Identification:** It refers to use of an expert system to detect suspicious users.

13.4   PASSWORD MANAGEMENT

A password is the biggest defense against intruders. Each user in a multi-user environment will be assigned a User ID and a Password. A user can change the password anytime. A fundamental principle of Password Management is that it should be known only to its owner. When a user changes a password, the password is transformed using a one-way function, and the transformed value only is saved in the system along with the corresponding User ID. Whenever a user enters passwords to gain access into the system, the password entered by the user is transformed using the same one-way function, and the transformed value is compared with the one saved in the system. If both values match, the user authentication is considered to be verified.

13.5   MALICIOUS PROGRAMS

These are malicious programs used by intruders to attack system security. There are two classes of these programs:

1. **Virus:** Fragment of a program that attaches itself to another program and executes secretly when the host program is run. Once a virus is running, it can perform any function like the erasing of files, and so on.

2. **Worm:** A self-contained program that when executed may produce more copies of itself, to be activated later on in the same or another system.

13.5.1 Different Phases in the Lifetime of a Virus

During its lifetime, a virus goes through the following four phases:

1. **Dormant Phase:** A virus initially hibernates, till it is activated by an event like a date, presence of another file, or disk exceeding some limit, and so on. A virus may not have this state.

2. **Propagation Phase:** A virus places an identical copy of itself into another program or into some system areas on the disk. Each infected program will now contain a copy of the virus that will further enter a propagation phase, thus multiplying exponentially.

3. **Triggering Phase:** The virus is triggered to perform the intended function. This triggering may be caused by an event like the number of clones created by the virus.

4. **Execution Phase:** The intended function is performed.

Types of Virus:

1. **Parasitic Virus:** It attaches itself to executable files and replicates when the infected program is executing.

2. **Memory-Resident Virus:** It lodges itself in RAM as part of a resident system program. Then it infects every program that is being executed.

3. **Boot Sector Virus:** It infects a master boot record or boot record and then spreads when the system is booted from the infected disk.

4. **Stealth Virus:** Designed to hide itself from anti-virus software.

5. **Polymorphic Virus:** A virus that mutates (undergoes change) with every infection, making detection by its signature difficult.

6. **Macro Virus:** The Macro Virus takes advantage of the "Macro" feature of MS applications like MS Word and MS Excel. A Macro is an executable code segment embedded in a word processing document used to perform a repetitive task. Using this feature, an auto-executing Macro Virus will be auto-executing repeatedly without any user input. This is the most common virus occurring today.

7. **Email Virus:** The email virus makes use of an MS Word Macro embedded in an attachment of email. It gets activated when a recipient opens the attachment. Then the virus sends itself to everyone on the mailing list in the users address directory. Also, the virus may cause local harm.

13.6   ANTI-VIRUS SCANNERS

The best option is to prevent entry of the virus from the Internet into the Local Area Network, but it is not possible to completely block the entry virus. So, a practical approach is to "detect, identify, and remove." This needs anti-virus scanner software to be installed on the system to be protected.

13.6.1 Different Generations of Anti-Virus Scanners

- **First Generation Scanner:** It requires a virus signature to identify a virus. Such scanners can tackle only known viruses.

- **Second Generation Scanner:** It uses heuristic rules to search for probable virus infection. It may attempt to identify fragments of code which are often associated with a virus, or it may perform some integrity check like checksum verification.

- **Third Generation Scanner:** These are memory resident and identify a virus by its actions, like mass deletion of files, and so on.

- **Fourth Generation Scanner:** Packages that implement variety of anti-virus techniques.

13.7   WORMS

A worm infects networked machines in quick succession, and each infected machine acts as an automated launching pad for attacks on other machines. A network worm exhibits the characteristics of a virus. To replicate itself, a network worm uses some sort of network transport:

1. **Email Worm:** Worm mails a copy of itself to other systems.

2. **Remote Execution Capability:** A worm remotely executes a copy of itself on another system.

3. **Remote Login Capability:** A worm logs onto a remote source system and then uses commands to copy itself from one system to another.

An email virus has some characteristics of a Worm, as it propagates itself from one system to another.

- **Trap Door:** It is a secret entry point into a program that allows someone to gain access, bypassing all security procedures. The trap doors are normally used for debugging programs during their development. The trap doors are free OS controls and become big threats when exploited by intruders.

- **Logic Bomb:** It refers to code embedded in a legitimate program that is set to be triggered when a certain specific condition occurs. Once triggered, it may alter or delete some files.

- **Trojan Horse:** This refers to a program that is apparently useful, containing some hidden code which when invoked, performs some unwanted action.

- **Zombie:** It is a program that secretly takes over an inter-attached computer and then uses that computer to launch security attacks that are difficult to trace back to the zombie's creator. Zombies are used for "Denial of Service" attacks.

13.8   FIREWALL

A Firewall is a mechanism that protects a local system or a Local Area Network (LAN) from network-based security threats, while at the same time permitting access to the outside world through the network.

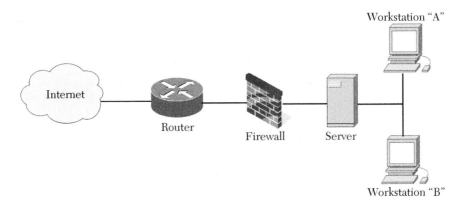

FIGURE 13.1 A Firewall.

13.8.1 Firewall Characteristics

1. All inbound and outbound traffic at a Local Area Network must pass through the firewall.

2. Only authorized traffic as per the local security policy should be permitted to enter the LAN.

3. The firewall must use a Trusted System with a Secure Operating System so as to achieve immunity against penetration of unwanted traffic.

13.8.2 Firewall Techniques to Control Access

1. **Service Control:** It determines the type of services that can be accessed on the Internet. It may filter traffic on the basis of IP Address and TCP Port Number. It may use a Proxy Software to interpret each service request.

2. **Direction Control:** It determines the direction in which particular service requests may be initiated and allowed to pass through the Firewall.

3. **User Control:** It permits particular local users (within the LAN) to access only particular services on the Internet. It may also be applied to external users for the access of local services.

4. **Behavior Control:** It controls how particular services are used; for example, filtering emails to eliminate spam.

13.9   TYPES OF FIREWALLS

1. **Packet Filtering Router:** It applies a set of rules to each incoming IP Packet and decides whether to forward it or discard it. The filtering rules are based on the information contained in the packet, such as Source IP Address, Destination IP Address, Source Port number, Destination Port Number, IP Protocol Field, Router Port Number, and so on.

2. **State-Full Inspection Firewalls:** It tightens up the rules for TCP traffic by creating a directory of outbound TCP connections. The filtering is performed on the inbound traffic on the basis of destination port numbers.

3. **Application-Level Gateway:** The Application Level Gateway is also called a proxy server. A proxy server can be configured to support only specific features of an application, while denying all other features.

4. **Circuit-Level Gateway:** It can be a stand-alone system or a specialized function performed by an Application-Level Gateway. It does not permit an end-to-end TCP connection; rather it splits an end-to-end TCP connection into two parts—one between itself and a TCP user inside and other between itself and a TCP user outside. The security function decides which connections to allow and which connections to deny.

5. **Bastion Host:** A Bastion host serves as a platform for an Application-level or Circuit-level Gateway.

The characteristics of a Bastion Host are:

- It executes a secure version of OS, making it a trusted system.

- Only essential services like Telnet, SMTP, DNS, and FTP are installed.

- A user has to authenticate itself prior to access of proxy services through the Bastion Host.

- Each proxy supports only a subset of a standard application command set, and each proxy allows access only to specific host systems. It runs as a non-privileged user in a secure private directory on the bastion host.

- Each proxy maintains an audit log of network operations. It acts as a tool for detection and termination of intruders' attacks.

- The proxy modules are less complex and easy to debug. Also, each proxy module is independent of other proxy modules on the Bastion Host. Thus, failure of one proxy module does not affect others. If any additional functionality is required, it can be provided by including another proxy module.

- A proxy module normally does not perform any disk access, except initially reading its configuration file. Thus, it is not vulnerable to attacks like Trojan Horse Sniffing.

13.9.1 Firewall Configurations

1. **Simple Configurations:** A simple configuration consists of a single packet-filtering router or a single gateway, but it does not provide sufficient flexibility in defining security policy.

2. **Screened Host Firewall, Single-Homed Bastion:** It consists of two systems:(a) packet-filtering router and (b) bastion host. The router is configured such that only IP Packets destined for the bastion host are allowed out. The bastion host performs authentication and proxy functions. Thus, this configuration is more secure than simple configurations, as it provides both packet-level and application-level filtering, and it provides more flexibility identifying security policy.

However, in a single-homed configuration, if the packet-filtering router is completely compromised, traffic could flow directly through the router between the Internet and other hosts in the private network.

3. **Screened Host Firewall, Dual-Homed Bastion:** This configuration physically prevents direct flow of information between the Internet and other hosts in the private network.

4. **Screened Subnet Firewall:** This is the most secure configuration. In this configuration, two packet-filtering routers are used—one between the bastion host and the internal private network and the other between the bastion host and the Internet. This creates an isolated but more secure sub-network. It offers the following advantages:

   A. There are now three levels of defense – outside packet-filtering router, bastion host, and inside packet-filtering router.

   B. The outside router only advertises the existence of the screened sub-network to the internal systems; therefore, the systems inside the network cannot directly access the Internet.

13.10   TRUSTED SYSTEMS

- A **trusted system** is a system that can be relied upon to a specified extent to enforce a specified security policy.

- Its failure may break the specified policy that it implements.

- According to the concept followed in the U.S. Department of Defense, a Trusted System is implemented as a "Reference Monitor" that is responsible for all access-control decisions.

- The most important design goal of a trusted system is to minimize the size of the "Trusted Computing Base" (TCB). The TCB is a combination of hardware, software, and firmware that enforces the desired system security policy. Because the failure of TCB breaks the implanted security policy, a smaller TCB provides higher assurance.

- Security Labels are attached to Data "Objects," indicating their levels of sensitivity. Also, labels are attached to "Subjects," that is, users indicating their trustworthiness.

- The Subjects are permitted to access the Objects using two security properties: (i) Simple Security Property, and (ii) Confinement Property.

  - **Simple Security Property:** A Subject can only read from an Object if the Subjects' Trustworthiness exceeds the Object's sensitivity. This is also called the "No Read Up" property. In layman's language, it implies that information at a higher sensitivity level should not be permitted to be accessed by a user having lower trustworthiness.

  - **Confinement Property:** It is also called "Property." A Subject can only write to an Object if the Object's sensitivity exceeds the Subject's Trustworthiness. This is also called the "No Write Down" Property. This implies that information should flow uphill and not downhill.

- The reference monitor has access to a file called the "Security Kernel Database." The Security Kernel Database lists the access rights of all Subjects and the security classifications of all Objects. The reference monitor enforces the security rules of "No Read Up" and "No Write Down." A Reference Monitor must have the following properties:

  - **Complete Mediation:** The security rules are enforced on every access of objects.

  - **Isolation:** The reference monitor and the security kernel database are protected from unauthorized modification.

  - **Verifiability:** It must be possible to prove correctness of the Reference Monitor Algorithm, that is, it must be possible to demonstrate that security rules are enforced on every access and the property of isolation is satisfied. A system that can provide this verification is called a Trusted System.

13.11   EXERCISES

1. What are the different classes of Intruders?

2. What are the different Intrusion Detection Techniques?

3. What are the different approaches for Rule-based Intrusion Detection?

4. What are the different phases in the lifetime of a virus?

5. What are the different kinds of virus?

6. What are the different generations of anti-virus scanners?

7. What are the characteristics of a Firewall?

8. What are the Firewall Techniques to control access?

9. What are the different types of Firewall?

10. What are the characteristics of a Bastion host?

11. What are the different configurations of a Firewall?

12. What are the properties of a Reference Monitor?

13. What are "No Read Up" and "No Write Down" properties of Trusted Systems?

CHAPTER 14

SECURITY OF EMERGING TECHNOLOGY

Chapter Outline

14.1 Introduction

14.2 Security of Big Data Analytics

14.3 Security of Cloud Computing

14.4 Security of Internet of Things (IoT)

14.5 Security of Smart Grids

14.6 Security of SCADA Control Systems

14.7 Security of Wireless Sensor Networks (WSNs)

14.8 Security of Smart City

14.9 Security of Blockchain

14.10 Exercises

14.1 INTRODUCTION

This chapter will cover the security of recent emerging technologies including Big Data Analytics, Cloud Computing, the Internet of Things (IoT), Smart Grids, Supervisory control and data acquisition (SCADA) Control Systems, the Wireless Sensor Network (WSN), Smart City, and Blockchain.

14.2   SECURITY OF BIG DATA ANALYTICS

Big Data is large-scale information management and analysis technologies that exceed the capability of traditional data processing technologies.

FIGURE 14.1 A Big data

Big data can be defined by two or more characteristics of the following:

- **Volume:** A system is gathering large amounts of data
- **Variety:** The data being gathered and analyzed varies in structure and format
- **Velocity:** Data is gathered at a high speed
- **Value:** Significant value is derived from the analysis of data
- **Visibility:** Data is accessed or visible from disparate or multiple geographic regions
- **Variability:** Data flows can be highly inconsistent with periodic peaks
- **Complexity:** Complexity of data when it is coming from multiple sources. The data must be linked, matched, cleansed, and transformed into required formats before actual processing.

Big Data can be divided into two groups of processing:

- ***Batch processing:*** the analytics on data at rest (Hadoop for data volumes of desk)

■ ***Stream processing***: the analytics on data in motion (Storm for data volumes of memory)

Big Data analytics is the process of analyzing and mining Big Data. It can produce operational and products knowledge at an unprecedented scale and specificity. The technological advances in storage, processing, and analysis of Big Data can include the following:

1. Rapidly decreasing cost of storage and CPU power in recent years;

2. Flexibility and cost-effectiveness of datacenters and cloud computing for elastic computation and storage;

3. Development of new frameworks such as *Hadoop,* which allow users to take advantage of these distributed computing systems storing large quantities of data through flexible parallel processing.

14.2.1 Big data analysis can transform security analytics in the following ways:

1. Accumulate data from various internal organizational sources as well as external sources to make a consolidated view of the required data into something called a vulnerability database.

2. Perform in-depth analytics on the data using security intelligence, hence uncovering unique patterns that could be the source of many security issues.

3. One-dimensional view of all the related information.

4. Real-time analysis of streaming data and uses previous results as feedback to the system as a whole.

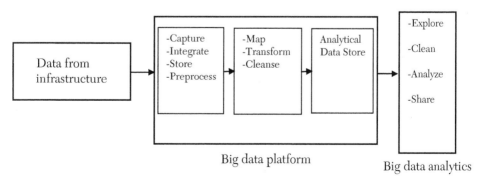

Big data platform

Big data analytics

FIGURE 14.2 Big data flow.

14.2.2 Big data analytics for security issues and privacy challenges:

- **Protected database storage and transaction log file:** availability and scalability have required auto tiering for big data management. Auto tiering solutions do not keep track of where the database is actually stored, which acts as a new demand on protecting database storage.

- **Secure computations in distributed frameworks:** Parallelism is used in computations and physical storage to process very large data. MapReduce framework is an example. Protecting the mappers and protecting the data in the presence of an untrusted mapper are two major attack prevention measures.

- **Privacy issues for non-relational data stores:** NoSQL database embedded protection in the middleware. It does not provide any type of support for enforcing it explicitly in the database. However, gathering aspect of No SQL databases imposes additional demands on the strength of such privacy practices.

- **End-point input validation/filtering:** This method is used to identify the trusted data and to verify that source of data input details is not spiteful.

- **Privacy preserving data mining and analysis:** This method is used to troubling manifestation by the possibly enabling appropriation of security, forward marketing, reducing civil freedoms, and increasing state and corporate control. Anonymizing data for analysis is not sufficient to manage user security.

- **Real-time security and compliance monitoring:** This method gives the number of alerts generated by privacy devices. These alerts lead to many false positives, which are mostly ignored. It is used to provide real-time problem detection based on scalable privacy analysis.

- **Granular audits:** This method is used for compliance, regulation, and forensics reasons. It is used to deal with the data objects, which probably are allocated.

- **Cryptographically enforced access control and secure communication:** This method is used to ensure fairness, authentication, and agreement among the distributed entities.

- **Granulated access control:** Secrecy secures access to data by people that should not have access. Granulated access control gives a data manager the ability to share data as much as possible without agreeing to privacy.

▪ **Information security:** How to tackle big data from a security point of view is a hard task. Thus, information security is one of the big data issues.

▪ **Metadata provenance:** Data will increase in complexity due to large provenance graphs generated from provenance-enabled programming environments in big data applications. Analysis of such large provenance graphs to detect metadata dependencies for security and confidentiality purposes is computationally intensive.

14.3   SECURITY OF CLOUD COMPUTING

▪ Cloud Computing is a type of computing in which services are delivered through the Internet which depend on sharing of computing resources rather than having local servers or personal devices handle the applications.

▪ Cloud Computing makes use of increasing computing power to execute millions of instructions per second.

▪ Cloud Computing uses networks of a large group of servers with specialized connections to distribute data processing among the servers. Instead of installing a software suite for each computer, this technology requires installing a single software program in each computer that allows users to log into a Web-based service and which also hosts all the programs required by the user.

▪ Local computers no longer have to take the entire burden when it comes to running applications.

▪ Cloud computing technology is being used to minimize the usage cost of computing resources.

▪ The cloud network, consisting of a network of computers, handles the load instead. The cost of software and hardware on the user end decreases. The only thing that must be done at the user's end is to run the cloud interface software to connect to the cloud.

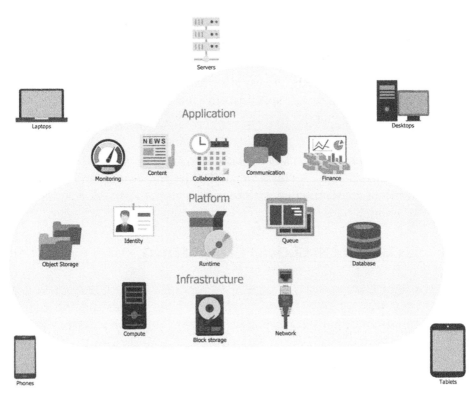

FIGURE 14.3 A cloud computing Architecture

Cloud Computing consists of two ends:

- **Front end:** It includes the user's computer and the software required to access the cloud network.

- **Back end:** It consists of various computers, servers, and database systems that create the cloud.

   The user can access applications in the cloud network from anywhere by connecting to the cloud using the Internet. Some of the real-time applications which use Cloud Computing are Gmail, Google Calendar, and Dropbox, and so on.

14.3.1 Cloud Deployment models:

- **Public Cloud:** the cloud infrastructure is typically owned by an organization selling cloud services known as a cloud service provider (CSP), and it is delivered to the general public on a subscription basis.

- **Private Cloud:** the cloud infrastructure is operated only for an individual organization. The infrastructure may be managed by the organization itself or by a third party, and it may be located either on-premises or off.

- **Community Cloud:** The cloud infrastructure is shared by several organizations and supports a specific community that has shared concerns. The infrastructure may be managed by the organizations or by a third party and may be located on-premise or off-premise.

- **Hybrid Cloud:** the cloud infrastructure is a combination of both private and public cloud instances that remain unique entities but are bound together by standardized or proprietary technology that enables data and application portability.

14.3.2 The three layers of the Cloud computing services model (Software, Platform or Infrastructure (SPI) Model):

- **Software as a Service (SaaS):** provides a way of delivering centrally hosted applications over the Internet as a service. The user consumes a software application across the Internet. The user has no infrastructure or applications to manage and update, no setup or hardware costs, and application accessibility from any Internet connection. It is a user interface. It is a Network-hosted application. An example is IBM Lotus Live.

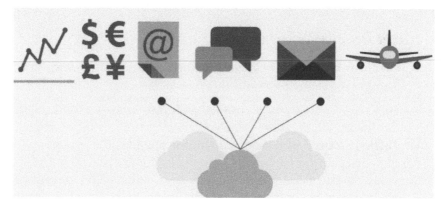

FIGURE 14.4 A SaaS

- **Platform as a Service (PaaS):** provides the service and management that is similar to the operating system. The CSP provides an additional layer on top of the infrastructure. Services include the operating system, network access, storage, database management systems, hosting, server-side scripting, and support. The user can use this environment and the tools provided to create software applications. It is a Network-hosted software development platform. Examples are Google App Engine (GAE) and Microsoft Azure.

FIGURE 14.5 A PaaS

- **Infrastructure as a Service (IaaS):** provides the cloud services of the basic hardware, such as CPU, Network, storage, and so on. The CSP provides the virtualized computing infrastructure. This generally includes virtual computer instances, network connectivity, IP infrastructure, bandwidth, load balancers, and firewalls. The user is responsible for installing and maintaining everything above the hypervisor (from the operating system upward). The provider hosts customer Virtual Machines (VMs) or provides network storage. An example is Amazon Web Service (AWS).

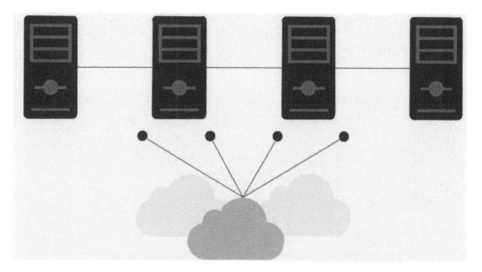

FIGURE 14.6 A IaaS

14.3.3 Security concerns and challenges of Cloud computing:

- **Authentication:** Applications and data are accessed over the Internet, which increases the complexity of the authentication procedures.

- **Authorization:** It is a computing environment that requires the use of the cloud service and providers' services for identifying the access policies.

- **Data Integrity:** Appropriate mechanics are required for detecting accidental and intentional changes in the data.

- **Security of data while at rest:** Appropriate separation procedures are required to ensure the isolation between applications and data from different organizations.

- **Security of data while in motion:** Appropriate security procedures are required to ensure the security of data while in motion.

- **Auditing:** Appropriate auditing procedures are required to get visibility into the application, data accesses, and actions performed by the application users.

14.3.4 Cloud Security as Consumer Service:

- Identity Services and Access Management Services
- Data Loss Prevention (DLP)

- Web Security

- Email Security

- Security Assessments

- Intrusion Management, Detection, and Prevention (IDS/IPS)

- Security Information and Event Management (SIEM)

- Encryption

- Business Continuity and Disaster Recovery

- Network Security

14.4   SECURITY OF INTERNET OF THINGS (IoT)

- The Internet of Things (IoT) is the concept of things, users, and cloud services getting connected via the Internet to enable and provide intelligent services for users. Figure 14.7 shows the IoT concept topology.

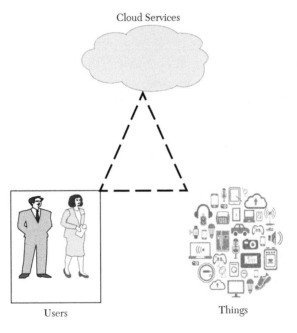

FIGURE 14.7 IoT concept topology.

14.4.1 Evolution of IoT

- Internet service providers (ISPs)

- Radio frequency identification (RFID)

- Application service providers (ASPs)

- Software as a Service (SaaS)

14.4.2 Building Blocks of the Internet of Things (IoT):

- **Sensors/Actuators:** Sensors and actuators are the tools that allow us to monitor and collect data and control the THINGS in the IoT.

- **Devices:** Simply put, devices are the THINGS. Using sensors and actuators, these devices will be more intuitive and efficient than we ever thought possible.

- **Gateways:** IoT gateways will help devices intelligently communicate for greater efficiency, intuitive data management/classification, and increased security.

- **Master of Devices and Service Providers:** For every device or service in the IoT, there must be a master. This could be the device manufacturer, a cloud service provider, and or an IoT solution provider. The master's role is to issue and manage devices as well as facilitate data analysis.

14.4.3 Difference between IoT and Machine-to-Machine (M2M):

M2M	IoT
It focused on connecting machines (or devices) for use in remote mentoring and control and data exchange—mainly proprietary closed systems	It is about corresponding the way humans and machines connect using common public services
Uses either proprietary or non-IP based communication protocols for communication within its area network such as ZigBee, Bluetooth, Z-Wave, ModBus, Power Line Communication (PLC), 6LoWPAN, IEEE 802.15.4, and so on. It focuses on the protocols below the network layer	It focuses on the protocols above the network layer such as HTTP, CoAP, DDS, XMPP, and so on.
Data is collected in point solutions and can be accessed by on-site applications and storage infrastructure	Data is collected in the cloud and can be accessed by cloud applications
Focused on hardware with embedded modules	Focused on software

14.4.4 IoT Layer Models:

14.4.4.1 Three-Layer Model:

- **Application layer:** Information availability, user authentication, information privacy, data integrity, IoT platform stability, middleware security, management platform. For example, remote medical services, cloud computing, smart grids, smart traffic, smart home, and environment monitoring.

- **Transport layer:** DOS/DDOS attacks, forgery/middle attack, heterogeneous network attacks, WLAN application conflicts, capacity and connectivity issues, and so on. For example, LAN, Ad hoc, GPRS, WiFi, and 3G/4G.

- **Sensing layer:** collect and process the data from the physical world. Interruption, interception, modification, fabrication, uniform coding for RFID, conflict collision for RFID, and so on. For example, WSN, RFID, RSN, MEMS, and GPS.

14.4.4.2 Four-Layer Model:

- **Service layer:** provides the interface and communicates with the users. For example, health care, smart home, safety, and smart industry. It uses lightweight security solutions for security of IoT.

- **Platform layer:** supports the IoT applications and services. For example, interface, context awareness, operating system, and cloud services. It uses privacy preserving for security.

- **Network layer:** serves to transmit the data among devices, contents, services, and users. It processes, controls, and manages enormous amounts of network traffic. For example, Context connection, context-based network, group mobility, and gateway PnP. It uses Authentication for security.

- **Device layer:** perceives the environment with various sensing devices, processes it to send it to the sink node or gateway, and responds to it if necessary. For example, actuator, sensor, resource management, and automatic control. It uses sensor data integrity for security.

14.4.4.3 Seven-Layer Model:

- **Physical Devices and Controllers (Layer 1):** It controls multiple devices. These are the "things" in the IoT, and they include a wide range of endpoint devices (computing nodes) that send and receive information, for example, smart controllers, sensors, RFID readers, and so on, and different versions of RFID tags. Data confidentiality and integrity must be taken into account from this level upward. Secure content (silicon).

- **Connectivity (Layer 2):** Communication and processing unit. Reliable and timely information transmission. Secure network access (hardware & protocols).

- **Edge (Fog) Computing (Layer 3):** Data element analysis and transformation. Secure communications (protocols and encryption).

- **Data Accumulation (Layer 4):** Storage and making network data usable by applications. Tamper resistant (software).

- **Data Abstraction (Layer 5):** Aggregation and Access. Also, abstracting the data interface for applications. Secure storage (hardware & software).

- **Application (Layer 6):** Reporting, analytics, and control. Authentication/Authorization (software).

- **Collaboration and Processes (Layer 7):** Involving people and business processes. Identity Management (software).

14.4.5 Applications of IoT:

1. **Wearable**
   - Entertainment
   - Fitness
   - Smart watch
   - Location and tracking

2. **Health Care**
   - Remote monitoring
   - Ambulance telemetry
   - Drugs tracking
   - Hospital asset tracking
   - Access control
   - Predictive maintenance

3. **Building & Home Automation**
   - Access control
   - Light and temperature control
   - Energy optimization
   - Predictive maintenance
   - Connected appliances

4. **Smart Cities**
   - Residential E-meters
   - Smart street lights
   - Pipeline leak detection
   - Traffic control
   - Surveillance cameras
   - Centralized and integrated system control

5. **Automotive**
   - Infotainment
   - Wire replacement
   - Telemetry
   - Predictive maintenance
   - Car to Car (C2C) and Car to Infrastructure (C2I)

6. **Smart Manufacturing**
   - Flow optimization
   - Real-time inventory
   - Asset tracking
   - Employee safety
   - Predictive maintenance
   - Firmware updates

Every connected device creates opportunities for attackers. These vulnerabilities are broad, even for a single small device. The risks posed include data transfer, device access, malfunctioning devices, and always-on/always-connected devices. The main challenges in security remain the security limitations associated with producing low-cost devices, and the growing number of devices, which creates more opportunities for attacks.

14.4.6 New Challenges Created by the IoT:

- **Security:** Prevent attackers and hackers from accessing the IoT

- **Privacy:** protect identity and privacy data from attackers and hacker access of the IoT

- **Interoperability and standards:** ensure that devices communicate securely by IoT manufacturers and ASP developers

- **Legal and regulatory compliance:** contribute toward legal, tax, and regulatory requirements regarding IoT-related business transactions that involve payment for goods and services by the international, federal, and state levels

- **E-commerce and economic development issues:** connectivity and information sharing to be deployed globally by IoT and the economic rules of engagement for conducting business on the World Wide Web.

14.4.7 Security Requirements of the IoT:

- **Confidentiality:** Ensuring that only authorized users access the data and information

- **Integrity:** Ensuring completeness, accuracy, and absence of unauthorized data manipulation

- **Availability:** Ensuring that all system services are available, when requested by an authorized user

- **Accountability:** An ability of a system to hold users responsible for their actions and operations

- **Auditability:** An ability of a system to conduct persistent monitoring of all actions and operations

- **Trustworthiness:** An ability of a system to verify an accurate identity and establish trust in a third party

- **Non-repudiation:** An ability of a system to confirm occurrence/non-occurrence of an action and an operation

- **Privacy:** Ensuring that the system obeys privacy policies and enabling individuals to control their personal data and information

14.4.8 Three Primary Targets of Attack against the IoT:

- **Attacks against a device:**

  An attacker takes advantage of IoT devices because many of the devices will have an inherent value by the simple nature of their function.

  As devices will be trusted with the ability to control and manage things, they also present a value for their ability to impact things. The devices have a value based on what is entrusted to those devices.

- **Attacks against the communication between devices and masters:**

  An attack involves monitoring and altering messages as they are communicated. The volume and sensitivity of data traversing the IoT environment makes these types of attacks especially dangerous, as messages and data could be intercepted, captured, or manipulated while in transit. All of these threats endanger the trust in the information and data being transmitted, and the ultimate confidence in the overall infrastructure.

- **Attacks against the masters:**

  Attacks against manufacturers, cloud service providers, and IoT solution providers have the potential to inflict the most amount of harm. These masters will be entrusted with large amounts of data, some of it highly sensitive in nature. This data also has value to the IoT providers because of the analytics, which represent a core, strategic business asset—and a significant competitive vulnerability if exposed. Disrupting services to devices also poses a threat as many of the devices will depend on the ability to communicate with the masters in order to function. Attacking a master also presents the opportunity to manipulate many devices at once, some of which may already be deployed in the field.

14.4.9 Hybrid Encryption Technique:

Hybrid encryption technique is for information integrity, confidentiality, and non-repudiation in data exchange for IoT.

A. *Creating a Key*

- Key production process in AES is used to create a key

- Two 4x4 matrices (stay and key) are used to produce a key for encryption

- Choose a place from the state matrix and a key from the key matrix randomly and produce a public key of H by the sender in an *XOR* operation

- Produced key of h is on the basis of a hexadecimal. Then the public key h is produced.

B. *Encryption*

- A message sent from the sender to the receiver is in a multinomial called message. After making a multinomial message, the sender randomly chooses a multinomial like r from the collection like L_r.

- We can have a message by multinomial r, therefore, it should not be revealed by the sender.

$$Encryption = p_r \cdot h + message \qquad (14.1)$$

This message will be transmitted to the receiver as an encryption message with security capability.

C. Decryption

- When the message is encrypted, the receiver tries to open the message by its private key or encrypt the message.

- For message decryption, the receiver has both private keys: f and f_p. Where, f_p is conversed with a multinomial of f.

$$a = f \cdot encryption \qquad (14.2)$$

$$a = f(p_r \cdot h + message) \qquad (14.3)$$

$$a = f \cdot p_r \cdot h + f \cdot message \qquad (14.4)$$

– To choose a correct parameter, coefficients of the polynominal formula between $\dfrac{-q}{2}$ and $\dfrac{p}{2}$ are selected.

– As $p = 3$, then it drastically reduces and does not have any effect on the process:

$$p_r \cdot h = 0 \tag{14.5}$$

$$a = f \cdot message \tag{14.6}$$

– Parameter b will be calculated. Just multiply private key f in the initial message which has been sent by the sender:

$$a = b = f \cdot message \tag{14.7}$$

$$Decryption = \frac{(f_p \times b)}{x^2} \tag{14.8}$$

– Whenever $Decryption = Message$, we will be sure that the message will reach security to the recipient without any disorder.

D. *Digital signature*

– Digital signature is used for message validity and proof of identity and security.

– We must go from the sender to the receiver, so the receiver of the former step acts as the sender now and the sender of the former step acts as the receiver.

$$Encryption\ sign = \frac{(message \times f)}{x^2} \tag{14.9}$$

$$Decryption = \left(\frac{\left(\dfrac{h}{2} \times f_p\ Encryption\ sign \right)}{2} \right) \times h \tag{14.10}$$

14.4.10 Hybrid Encryption Algorithm Based on DES and DSA:

■ Regroup 64-bit data according to blocks and put the output into L_0, R_0 two parts, each of 32 bits, and its replacement rule is to exchange the 58th bit with the first, the 50th bit with the second, . . ., and so on; the last one is the original No. 7.

▨ L_0 and R_0 are the two parts after the transposition output; L_0 is the left 32 bits of the output, and R_0 is the right 32 bits.

▨ Sub-key generation algorithm: The 8th, 16th . . . 64th bit is a parity bit according to the DES algorithm rule, and is not involved in the DES operation. The Key actual uses 56 bits; this 56 is Divided into two parts C_0 and D_0, each of 28 bits, and cycle left for the first time, to obtain C_1 and D_1, then the C_1 (28 bits), D_1 (28 bits) obtained are combined to form a 56-bit date, and then selection transposition 2 through the narrow, so as to get a key K_0 (48 bits). And so on, K_1, K_2... K_{15} can be gotten.

▨ Calculated date hash value of the encrypted cipher text using the secure hash algorithm SHA-1. Parameters used in the DSA signature are:

- p : primes of L bits long. L is a multiple of 64 bits; the range is 512~1024 bits;

- q : prime factors of 160bits of $p-1$;

- g : $g = h^{((p-1)/q)} \bmod p$, h satisfy $h < p-1$, $h^{((p-1)/q)} \bmod p > 1$;

- x : $x < q$, x is the private key;

- y : $y = g^x \bmod p$, (p, q, g, y) are public keys;

  Signature process is:

  P : generates a random number k, $k < q$;

  P : compute $r = (g^k \bmod p) \bmod q$ and $s = (k^{(-1)}(H(m) + xr)) \bmod q$

  The result of the signature is (m, r, s).

Where $H(m)$ is the Hash value of m, m is plaintext to be signed or Hash value of the plaintext. The final signature is integers (r, s), which is sent to the authenticator.

▨ To calculate the encrypted digital signature use the SHA-1 algorithm after the reader receives the cipher text; if the signatures are consistent with that provided by the sender, then decrypt the cipher-text with the sub-key generated by the DES algorithm to generate plaintext.

14.4.11 Advanced Encryption Standard (AES):

AES is based on a design principle known as a substitution-permutation network, a combination of both substitution and permutation, and is fast in both software and hardware. Unlike its predecessor DES, AES does not use a Feistel network. AES uses a Rijndael cipher, which has a fixed block size of 128 bits, and a key size of 128, 192, or 256 bits, and is defined in three versions, 10, 12, and 14 rounds respectively.

There are three steps performed in AES:

– encryption

– decryption

– key generation

AES encryption:

Step 1: Get the plaintext and the key

Step 2: Perform the pre-round transformation using the plaintext

Step 3: With "n" key length, perform transformation for "n" rounds

Step 4: cipher-text achieved

AES decryption:

Repeat the steps followed in encryption in reverse order:

Step 1: cipher-text achieved

Step 2: With "n" key length, perform transformation for "n" rounds

Step 3: Perform the pre-round transformation using the plaintext

Step 4: Get the plaintext and the key

Key Generation:

Step 1: Get the key

Step 2: based upon number of round, calculate required number of words

Step 3: In an array of 4 bytes, the first four words are made from the key

Step 4: Get the next word

Step 5: Repeat step 4 until the required number of words are reached

14.4.12 Requirements for Lightweight Cryptography:

- **Size (circuit size, ROM/RAM sizes):** determines the possibility of implementation in a device.

- **Power:** especially important with the RFID and energy-harvesting devices.

- **Power consumption:** It is important with battery-driven devices.

■ **Processing speed (throughput, delay):** A high throughput is necessary for devices with large data transmissions, while a low delay is important for the real-time control processing.

14.4.13 Lightweight Cryptography in the IoT:

■ **Efficiency of end-to-end communication:** Application of the lightweight symmetric key algorithm allows lower energy consumption for end devices.

■ **Applicability to lower resource devices:** The lightweight cryptographic primitives would open possibilities of more network connections with lower resource devices.

14.4.14 Prevention of Attacks on IoT:

Cyber attackers are exploiting vulnerabilities on IoT devices in an increasing number of distributed denials of service (DDoS) attacks. The Prevention of attacks on IoT can be summarized in five steps as follows:

■ **Changing the default credentials of IoT devices:** Devices with weak or default credentials are vulnerable to compromise. IoT devices should be secured with strong authentication to avoid brute force attacks.

■ **Disabling universal plug and play (UPnP) on gateway routers:** UPnP allows ports inside a network to be opened easily. Using UPnP, external computers are able to communicate to devices inside the network. To prevent this, we should disable UPnP on gateway routers. Some applications may be affected by disabling UPnP, so reconfiguration could be necessary.

■ **Update IoT devices frequently:** Update IoT devices with the latest firmware and patches as soon as possible to ensure that the known vulnerabilities are addressed.

■ **Ensure proper firewall configuration and identify malicious traffic:** Configure the firewall to block incoming User Datagram Protocol (UDP) packets because they are used to exploit IoT devices.

■ **Review reliance on easily identified internet connections:** Examine the level of reliance on public-facing web servers that are easy to identify externally and that are used for critical operations. It is important to review incident response procedures as well so that operations are not halted due to a cyberattack. In addition, IoT devices that are on public-facing servers should be secured to prevent unauthorized access.

14.5   SECURITY OF SMART GRIDS

▪ Smart grids utilize communication technology and information to optimally transmit and distribute electricity from suppliers to consumers. It is the next-generation power system.

▪ The grid environment requires security mechanisms that have the following characteristics:

   • cross multiple administrative domains

   • have high scalability in terms of a large and dynamic user population

   • support a large and dynamic pool of resources each probably with different authentication and authorization policies

   • have the ability of grid applications to acquire and release resources dynamically during execution

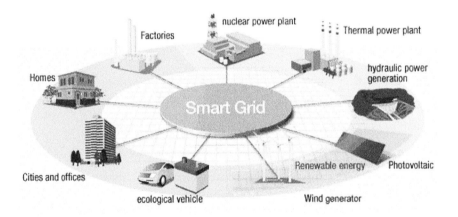

FIGURE 14.8   Smart grid concept topology.

14.5.1 Smart Grid Challenges:

▪ the network congestion and safety related factors;

▪ the lack of pervasive and effective communications, monitoring, fault diagnostics, and automation; and

▪ power grid integration, system stability, and energy storage, which are introduced by the adaptation of renewable and alternative energy sources.

14.5.2 Smart Grid Layers:

- Master station system Layer
- Remote communication network Layer
- Terminal Layer
- Cross (Life cycle of information systems) Layer
- Security management Layer

14.5.3 Information Security Risks and Demands of a Smart Grid

- **Master station system Layer:**
  - Physical layer attacks and protection
  - Network layer attacks and protection
  - Host layer attacks and protection
  - Application layer attacks and protection
  - Data leaks and prevention; Backup and recovery
  - Cloud computing application and its risks
  - Intercept and anti-intercept
- **Remote communication network Layer:**
  - Monitor and anti-monitor
  - Tamper and anti-tamper
  - Encrypted communication channel
  - Fake terminal
  - Fake master station
  - Terminal integrity
  - Terminal network security
- **Terminal Layer:**
  - Lack of computing, storage, and process resources to implement security schemes

- Internet of Things application and its risks
- Lack of security consideration in system planning and system analysis stages
- Lack of security design in system design stage

- **Cross (Life cycle of information systems) Layer:**
  - Code security and secure system development in system implementation stage
  - Security management in system running and maintenance stage
  - Sensitive information processing in system obsolescence stage
  - Social engineering attacks
  - How to build effective Information

- **Security management Layer:**
  - Security Management Systems for smart grids

14.5.4 Smart Grid Security Objectives:

- **Availability:** Ensuring timely and reliable access to and use of information is of the most importance in the Smart Grid.

- **Integrity:** Guarding against improper information modification or destruction is to ensure information non-repudiation and authenticity.

- **Confidentiality:** Preserving authorized restrictions on information access and disclosure is mainly to protect personal privacy and proprietary information.

14.5.5 The Smart Grid System Can Be Divided into Three Major Systems:

- Smart Infrastructure System
- Smart Management System
- Smart Protection System

These major systems are also subdivided into other subsystems, applications, or objectives, as shown in Figure 14.9.

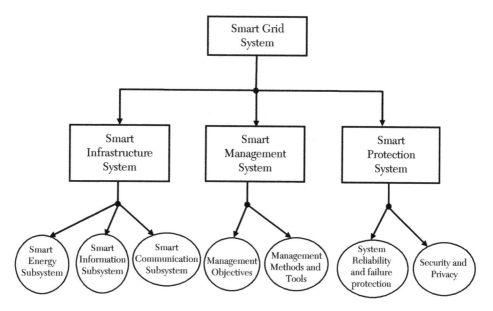

FIGURE 14.9 Smart Grid system classifications.

14.5.6 Types of Security Attacks That Can Compromise the Smart Grid Security:

- **Passive Attacks:** They aim to learn and use the system information without affecting the system resources. The attack target is only transmitted information in order to learn the system configuration, architecture, and normal operation behavior.

- **Active Attacks:** They are planned to affect the system operation through data modification or introducing false information into the system.

14.5.7 Cybersecurity Attacks in a Smart Grid:

- **Eavesdropping:** This is a passive attack described as an unauthorized interception of an on-going communication without the consent of the communication parties.

- **Traffic Analysis:** This is similar to an eavesdropping attack, but the attacker monitors the traffic patterns in order to infer useful information from it.

▪ **Replay:** This attack consists of capture-transmitted messages and their retransmission in order to cause an unauthorized effect. The retransmitted messages are normally valid except the timestamp field.

▪ **Message Modification:** This is similar to a replay attack, but the message is modified to cause unwanted behavior in the system. This attack can also involve message delay and reordering a message stream.

▪ **Impersonation:** This is when the intruder pretends to be an authorized entity or device.

▪ **Denial of Service:** It aims to suspend or interrupt the system communications. To accomplish this effect, the attacker can flood the communication network with messages to disable the physical components' access, inhibiting the system's normal operation.

▪ **Malware:** It aims to exploit internal weaknesses of the system with the goal of stealing, modifying, and destroying information or physical components of the system. It can also obtain unauthorized access to the system.

14.6   SECURITY OF SCADA CONTROL SYSTEMS

▪ A Supervisory Control and Data Acquisition (SCADA) system is a common process automation system which is used to gather data from sensors and instruments located at remote sites and to transmit data at a central site for either control or monitoring purposes.

▪ SCADA systems evolved from hardware and software that include standard PCs and operating systems, TCP/IP communications, and Internet access. SCADA systems can monitor and control hundreds to hundreds of thousands of I/O points.

▪ SCADA systems differ from Distributed Control Systems (DCSs). DCSs cover plant sites, while SCADA systems cover much larger geographic areas.

▪ SCADA architecture supports TCP/IP, UDP, or other IP-based communications protocols as well as strictly industrial protocols such as Modbus TCP, Modbus over TCP, or Modbus over UDP, all working over private radio, cellular, or satellite networks.

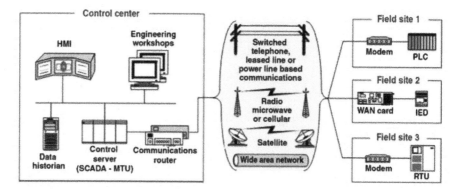

FIGURE 14.10 SCADA concept topology

14.6.1 Components of SCADA Systems:

- Instruments that sense process variables

- Operating equipment connected to instruments

- Local processors that collect data and communicate with the site's instruments and operating equipment; Programmable Logic Controller (PLC), Remote Terminal Unit (RTU), Intelligent Electronic Device (IED), or Process Automation Controller (PAC)

- Short range communications between local processors, instruments, and operating equipment

- Host computers as central point of human monitoring and control of the processes, storing databases, and display of statistical control charts and reports. Host computers are also known as a Master Terminal Unit (MTU), the SCADA server, or a PC with Human Machine Interface (HMI)

- Long range communications between local processors and host computers using wired or wireless network connections.

14.6.2 SCADA System Layers:

- **Supervisory Control Layer:** The supervisory control layer (the control center) is responsible for monitoring the operation of SCADA systems by gathering data from field devices, performing control and supervisory tasks, and sending control commands to field controllers through the communication network. The supervisory control layer of the SCADA system consists of the following elements:

- SCADA server

- builder server

- communication server

- database server

- diagnostic server

- application server

- human–machine interface

- system operators

■ **Automatic Control Layer:** The automatic control layer (regulatory control layer) is in charge of regulating the operation of physical processes based on control commands from the control center and sensor measurements from field devices. The control signals are then transmitted to field devices through the communication network. Various system variables, including control commands, sensor measurements, and control signals, are gathered within the control center for supervisory and management purposes. The automatic control layer of the SCADA system consists of the following elements:

- master terminal units (MTUs)

- remote terminal units (RTUs)

- programmable logic controllers (PLCs)

- intelligent electronic devices

■ **Physical Layer:** The physical processes (e.g., electric power grids, gas pipelines, and water networks) are equipped with actuators (e.g., motors, compressors, pumps, and valves), sensors (e.g., temperature sensors, pressure sensors, flow sensors, level sensors, and speed sensors), and protection devices (e.g., circuit breakers and protective relays) to realize technological goals. The physical elements are controlled and monitored by the control center through the automatic control layer and the communication network.

14.6.3 Requirements and Features for the Security of Control Systems:

■ Critical path protection

■ Strong safety policies and procedures

- Knowledge management

- System development skills

- Enhanced security for device

- Sensor network solutions

- Operating system based on microkernel architecture

- Increasing quality of software with security features

- Security requirements early in the software development cycle

- Compliance to standards for software development

- Integration of different technologies

- Vulnerability analysis based on proactive, discovery, and adaptation solutions

- Innovative risk management approaches

- Ensure authentication, confidentiality, integrity, availability, and non-repudiation

- Calculate risk as impact to security and safety

14.6.4 Categories for Security Threats to Modern SCADA Systems:

- Insiders

- Hackers

- Hidden criminal groups

- Nation-states

14.7   SECURITY OF WIRELESS SENSOR NETWORKS (WSNs)

- A Wireless Sensor Network (WSN) is an infrastructure-less network composed of a large number of sensor nodes. These cooperatively sense and control the environment to enable its interaction with people or devices.

- Wireless Sensor Networks (WSNs) are considered as one of the core technologies in implementing Cyber Physical Systems (CPSs).

- WSNs include sensor nodes, actuator nodes, gateways, and clients. A large number of sensor nodes deployed randomly inside of or near the monitoring area form networks through self-organization.

- The data is captured at the level of the sensor node, compressed and transmitted to the gateway. Through the gateway connection, data is then passed by the base station to a server.

- Sensor nodes monitor the collected data to transmit along to other sensor nodes by hopping. During the process of transmission, the monitored data may be handled by multiple nodes to get to the gateway node after multi-hop routing, and finally reach the management node through the Internet or satellite.

- It is the user who configures and manages the Wireless Sensor Network with the management node, publish monitoring missions and collection of the monitored data.

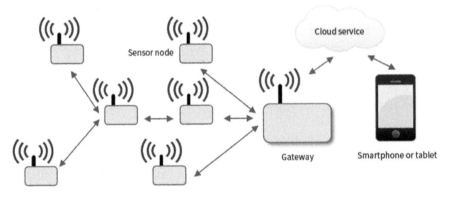

FIGURE 14.11 WSN concept topology

14.7.1 WSN Layers:

- **Transport Layer:** Responsible for managing end-to-end connections. Reliable transport of data.

- **Network and Routing Layer:** Responsible for routing of sensors based on addressing and location awareness, sensor networking, power efficiency, and topology management. It provides more effective routing of the data. From "Node to node, node to sink, node to base station, and node to Cluster head & vice versa." Due to the broadcast method every node works as a router.

- **Data Link Layer:** Responsible for the multiplexing of data streams, data frame detection, medium access, and error control.

- **Physical Layer:** Responsible for frequency selection, carrier frequency generation, signal detection, modulation, and data encryption.

14.7.2 Security Requirements in WSNs:

- **Data Confidentiality:** To provide the data confidentiality, encrypted data is used so that only recipient decrypts the data to its original form. Only the authorized sensor nodes can get the content of the messages.

- **Data Integrity:** Data received by the receiver should not be altered or modified. Original data is changed by an intruder or due to a harsh environment. The intruder may change the data according to its need and sends this new data to the receiver.

- **Data Authentication:** It is the procedure of confirmation that the communicating node is the one that it claims to be. The receiver node needs to make verification that the data is received from an authenticated node.

- **Data Availability:** The services are available all the time whenever necessary.

- **Source Localization:** For data transmission some applications use location information of the sink node. It is essential to give security to the location information. Non-secured data can be controlled by a malicious node.

- **Self-Organization:** In WSN no fixed infrastructure exists, hence, every node is independent, having properties of adaptation to the different situations, and maintains self-organizing and self-healing properties.

- **Data Freshness:** Each message transmitted over the channel is new and fresh. It guarantees that the old messages cannot be replayed by any node. This can be solved by adding some time-related counter to check the freshness of the data.

14.7.3 The Attack Categories in WSNs:

- **Outsider vs. Insider attacks:** Outsider attacks are external attacks and the insider attacks are internal attacks. An outsider attack comes from outside the WSN. With the help of an Outsider attack the bad data is inserted in the network for the services interruption. An insider attack is also known as the internal attack; these attacks come from the inside of the WSN.

- **Passive vs. Active Attacks:** Passive attacks include eavesdropping on or monitoring packets exchanged within the WSN; in active attacks, an attacker has the capability to remove or modify the messages during the transmission on the network.

- **Mote-Class versus Laptop-Class attacks:** In Monte-class attacks, an adversary attacks a WSN by utilizing a few nodes with similar capabilities to the network nodes; in laptop-class attacks, an adversary can use more powerful devices to attack a WSN. These devices have greater transmission range, processing power, and energy reserves than the network nodes.

14.7.4 Attacks and Defense in WSNs at Different Layers:

Layer	Possible Type of Attacks	Defense
Transport	Flooding Desynchronization	Client puzzles Authentication
Network and Routing	Spoofed, altered, or replayed routing information Selective forwarding Sinkhole Sybil Wormholes Hello flood attacks Acknowledgment spoofing	Egress filtering, authentication, monitoring Redundancy, probing Authentication, monitoring, redundancy Authentication, probing Authentication, packet leashes by using geographic and temporal information Authentication, verify the bidirectional link Authentication
Data Link	Collision Exhaustion Unfairness	Error-correcting code Rate limitation Small frames
Physical	Jamming Tampering	Spread-spectrum, priority messages, lower duty cycle, region mapping, mode change Tamper-proofing, hiding

14.7.5 Security Protocols in WSNs:

- **Sensor Protocols for Information via Negotiation (SPINs):**

  · SPIN is an adaptive routing protocol, which transmits the information first by negotiating.

  · The SPIN transmission is data-centric; it is only transmitted to the nodes that have interest in the data. This process continues until the data reaches the sink node. SPIN reduces both the network overhead and the energy consumption in the transmission. There will not be duplicate messages in the network since nodes negotiate before transmitting the data.

- SPIN makes use of metadata of the actual data to be sent. Metadata will contain the description of the message that the node wants to send. The actual data will be transmitted only if the node wishes to receive it. SPIN makes use of 3 messages, namely,

  1. ADV: Before sending a message, a node first generates the descriptor of the message to be sent. This metadata is exchanged by making use of the ADV message. ADV message informs the size, contents, and requirements of the message. This helps the receiving node on deciding transmission of the message.

  2. REQUEST: After receiving the ADV message, the receiver node verifies the descriptor whether the message is a duplicate and whether the receiver node's battery capabilities are enough to transmit the data. If the node is interested in the data, it replies with a REQUEST message to the sender node.

  3. DATA: If the sender node receives a REQUEST message, it starts the actual transmission of data by making use of the DATA message. This is the actual data transfer phase.

▨ Localized Encryption and Authentication Protocol (LEAP)

- LEAP is a protocol with key management scheme that is very efficient with its security mechanisms used for large scale distributed sensor networks. It is designed to support in-network processing such as data aggregation. In-network processing results in reduction of the energy consumption in network. To provide the confidentiality and authentication to the data packet, LEAP uses a multiple keys mechanism. For each node four symmetric keys are used as follows:

  Individual Key: Used for the communication between source node and the sink node.

  Pair wise Key: Shared with another sensor node.

  Cluster Key: Used for locally broadcast messages and is shared between the node and all its neighboring nodes.

  Group Key: Used by all of the network Nodes.

- **TINYSEC**

  - TINYSEC is a lightweight protocol and link layer security architecture for WSNs.

  - It supports integrity, confidentiality, and authentication. To achieve confidentiality, encryption is done by using CBC (Cipher-block chaining) mode with cipher text stealing, and authentication is done using CBC-MAC. No counters are used in TINYSEC. Hence, it doesn't check the data freshness. Authorized senders and receivers share a secret key to compute a MAC.

  - TINYSEC has two different security options. One is for authenticated and encrypted messages (TinySec-AE) and another is for authenticated messages (TinySec-Auth).

  - In TinySec-AE, the data payload is encrypted and the received data packet is authenticated with a MAC.

  - In TinySec-Auth mode, the entire packet is authenticated with a MAC, but on the other hand the data payload is not encrypted.

  - In CBC, Initialization Vector (IV) is used to achieve semantic security. Some of the messages are the same with only little variation. In that case IV adds the variation to the encrypted process. To decrypt the message the receiver must use the IV. IVs are not secret and are included in the same packet with the encrypted data.

- **ZIGBEE**

  - ZIGBEE is a worldwide open standard for wireless radio networks in the monitoring and control fields.

  - IEEE 802.15.4 is a standard used for ZIGBEE. The IEEE 802.15.4 standard defines the characteristics of the physical and MAC layers for Low-Rate Wireless Personal Area Networks (LR-WPAN).

  - To implement the security mechanism, ZIGBEE uses 128-bit keys. A trust center is used in ZIGBEE which authenticates and allows other devices/nodes to join the network and also distribute the keys.

  - Three different roles in ZIGBEE are:

    Trust Manager: It authenticates the devices which are requesting to join the network.

Network Manager: It manages the network keys and helps to maintain and distribute the network keys.

Configuration Manager: It configures the security mechanism and enables end-to-end security between devices.

- A ZigBee network can adopt one of the three topologies: Star, Tree, and Mesh.

14.8 SECURITY OF SMART CITY

- A smart city is a high-tech urban area that connects people, information and technologies in order to increase life quality. A smart city integrates information and communication technology (ICT) in a secure manner so as to manage the city's assets. A smart city uses technology to manage its resources, improve the way it delivers services, reduce costs and generate growth opportunities.

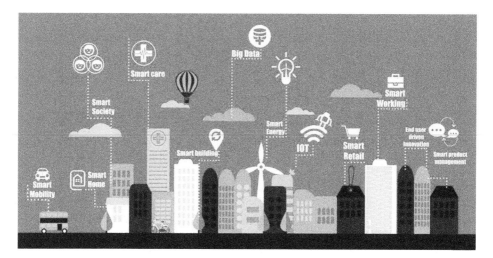

FIGURE 14.12 Smart city concept topology

- Smart cities are those communities that pursue sustainable economic development through investments in human and social capital and manage natural resources through participatory policies.

- A smart city monitors the conditions and integrates critical infrastructures such as bridges, tunnels, roads, subways, airports, seaports, and buildings. Components of a smart city include smart people, smart governance, smart homes, smart infrastructure, smart technology, smart economy, smart mobility, smart living, smart parking, and smart environment as in Figure 14.13.

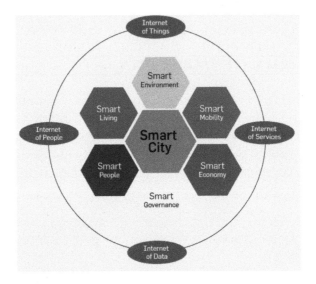

FIGURE 14.13 The main component model for Smart city

- The intelligent city has a wide range of electronic and digital technologies that enable its devices to communicate. Two closely related technologies, the Internet of Things (IoT) and big data (BD), enable the transformation of traditional cities into smart cities.

- Smart cities have been equipped with heterogeneous electronic devices based on the Internet of things (IoT), which is a worldwide network of physical objects using the Internet as a communication network.

- The IoT is the technical backbone of smart cities. The IoT is the network of interconnected devices (called Things) including computers, smartphones, sensors, buildings, structures, vehicles, actuators, and wearable devices. It has four components: the "things," the local area network, the Internet, and the cloud.

14.8.1 Challenges and Benefits of Smart City

- Several initiatives all over the world have been launched to transform towns or cities from scratch to smart cities.

- Smart cities around the world are diverse in their characteristics. Standards (such as established by ISO and IEEE) can play a crucial role in the development of smart cities.

- Ensure that the information is secure and the people are secure. Since networks are believed to be the least secure parts of the system, cities must ensure that the networks are safe before embarking on smart city initiatives.

- Everyone is needed online and needs to be able to access services in order to realize the full benefits of IoT.

- Smart cities act as magnets for highly educated individuals and skilled workforces.

- Smart city initiatives have lofty goals of improving governance and enhancing quality of life for citizens. Smart cities offer untold benefits for government and citizens—service provision, quality of life, and security.

- Improving management of private and public transportation and efficient mobility

- Environmental sustainability by monitoring and reducing waste through informed management of resources.

- Increased citizen participation through e-governance and participatory governance platforms.

- Coordinated emergency services and law enforcement responses

- Fostering economic growth and improving quality and convenience of everyday life.

14.8.2 The security and privacy of information in a smart city

- The information security must be fool proof to ensure the continuity of critical services like health care, governance and energy/utility issues in a smart city.

- The issues in information security in a smart city have several factors that can be taken under consideration as following:

- Technical Factors –IoT Technologies:

  - RFID, WSN M2M communication, samrtphones, and smart grid

- Governance Factors:

  - Utility, critical infrastructure, smart mobility, management

- Socioeconomic Factors:

  -Smart communication, Banking, individual privacy, e-commerce

These factors influence and identify the information security issues in a smart city

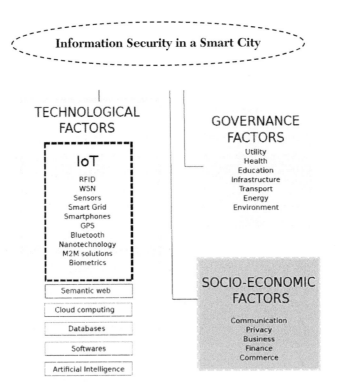

FIGURE 14.14 Factors of Influencing for Information Security in a smart city

- There are some of the key privacy and data protection considerations for smart cities. With each challenge there are a number of ways in which negative effects can be reduced, resulting in smart city initiatives that enhance both privacy and information security.

Data collection: The information communications technology (ICT) used to enable smart cities has the ability to gather unprecedented amounts of data about citizens. Properly managing and protecting this data is integral to mitigating privacy and security risks. Limiting the collection of personal information to that which is necessary to achieve the desired outcome of an initiative is a critical step.

Human error: Intentional or accidental human error can elevate risk of privacy and security breaches. This is often the result of lack of training, oversight practices and access controls. Those with access to personal information need to understand their responsibilities and act in accordance with policies and procedures.

Information sharing: Smart cities are based on connectivity, requiring increased information sharing both within the public sector and with external entities. Many large datasets will be linked or released through open data platforms. Ongoing information sharing agreements combined with techniques such as de-identification are useful to enhance citizens' privacy.

Chilling effect: Where individuals feel they are being monitored, there is potential for change of behavior known as the *"chilling effect."* This is largely due to a lack of trust that collected information will be used appropriately. There are several avenues to alleviate this concern including obtaining consent, giving notice of data collection, and providing the option of anonymity or opting-out.

Security risk management: Technical solutions such as encryption, digital signature and server reliability are important, as are defined document policies, procedures, incident and risk management protocols, physical security, and personnel training and awareness.

Governance: Strong leadership, clear policies, procedures and guidance, accountability, transparency, and a commitment to privacy and security by design will be fundamental regardless if smart cities are lead by the public or private sector.

Malicious attacks: If an entire city is connected and has an "operating system" containing vast amounts of personal information and with control of critical infrastructure, there may be incentive for a malicious intruder to seek unauthorized access.

14.9   SECURITY OF BLOCKCHAIN

- Blockchain (BC) technology is a type of distributed digital ledger that uses encryption to make entries permanent and tamper-proof and can be programmed to record financial transactions. It is used for secure transfer of money, assets, and information via a computer network such as the Internet without requiring a third-party intermediary. Blockchain promises to solve this problem.

- Blockchain, also known as *"distributed ledger technology"* is a peer-to-peer network that sits on top of the Internet. *Bitcoin* is the first application of Blockchain technology.

- Bitcoin is a cryptographic electronic payment system that purports to be the world's first cryptocurrency. It has become the most talked about cryptocurrency. The software is completely open source so that any developer can download it, modify it, and create his own version of the software.

- The Blockchain could bring everything that is good about Bitcoin and translate it into decentralized applications. Blockchain refers to new applications of a distributed database technology that builds on a tamper-proof records of time-stamped transactions. By decentralizing it, Blockchain makes data transparent to everyone involved and this eliminates the risks that come with data being held centrally. A Blockchain facilitates secure online transactions.

- Blockchain refers to the way Blockchain stores transaction data – in "blocks" that are linked together to form a "chain." The chain grows as the number of transactions increases. A block is created whenever a transaction is made. A block is the "current" part of a Blockchain, which records some or all of the recent transactions. The block is broadcasted to all nodes for validation. Once completed, a block goes into the Blockchain as a permanent database. Each time a block gets completed, a new one is generated. Each data item in a BC has a timestamp. A BC is an ordered chain of blocks. All data of a transaction are traceable based on the chain structure of BC. The Blockchain was designed so these transactions are immutable, i.e. they cannot be deleted. Thus, Blockchains are secure and meddle-free by design. Data can be distributed, but not copied. When it comes to digital assets and transactions, you can put almost anything on a Blockchain. Different scenarios call for different Blockchains.

FIGURE 14.15 Blockchain concept

14.9.1 Features of Blockchain Technology

Peer-to-Peer (P2P) network: The first requirement of BC is a network, an infrastructure shared by multiple parties. This can be a LAN at a small scale or the Internet at a large scale. Communication occurs directly between peers instead of through a central node. All nodes participating in a BC are connected in a decentralized P2P network. Transactions are broadcast to the P2P network. Due to some limitations of P2P networks, some vendors have provided cloud-based BCs.

Cascaded encryption: A BC uses encryption to protect transaction data. Blocks are encrypted in a cascaded manner, i.e. the encryption result of the previous block is used in encrypting the current block. The BC is secured by public key cryptography, with each peer generating its own public-private key pairs.

Distributed Database: A BC is digitally distributed across a number of computers. Each party on a BC has access to the entire database and no single party controls the data or the information. Since BC is decentralized, there is no need for central authorizes such as banks.

Transparency with pseudonymity: Each node or participant on a blockchain has a unique 30-plus-character alphanumeric address that identifies it. Users can choose to remain anonymous or provide proof of their identity to others.

Irreversibility of records: Once a transaction is entered in the database and the accounts are updated, the records cannot be altered. Records on the database is permanent, chronologically ordered, and available to all others on the network.

- There are two types of Blochains: public and private.

  - Public Blockchains are cryptocurrencies such as Bitcoin, enabling peer-to-peer transactions.

  - Private Blockchains use Blockchain-based platforms such as Ethereum or Blockchain-as-a-service (BaaS) platforms running on private cloud infrastructure. They limit access to the predefined list of known individuals. A private BC is an intranet, while a public BC is the Internet. Companies will be disrupted the most by public Blockchains.

- BCs may be permissioned or permissionless.

  - In Permissioned BC, each participant has a unique identity.

  - Permissionless BCs allow anyone to join, participate or leave the protocol execution without seeking permission from a centralized or distributed authority.

14.9.2 Benefits and Challenges of Blockchain

- BC is a great solution to the age-old human problem of trust. It enables trustless networks by allowing parties to conduct transactions even though they do not trust each other. The absence of a trusted middleman results in faster reconciliation between parties. BC removes the intermediary and moves towards democratization and decentralization.

- By allowing digital information to be distributed but not copied, BC technology has created the backbone of a new form of Internet. There is no single point of failure from which digital assets can be hacked or corrupted.

- The decentralized nature of BCs makes them an equality technology that can be used to expand freedom, actualization, and realization of all entities, both human and machine. The potential benefits of BC extend into business, political, humanitarian, social, technological, and scientific realms.

These benefits make some to believe that BC has become the fifth disruptive computing paradigm after mainframes, PCs, the Internet, and mobile/social networking.

- A major challenge of BC is security. Companies need to have a security standards and systems to protect them from attackers or bad actors.

- Managing the Blockchains requires substantial computational power in order to maintain security.

- Regulating and standardizing digital currency and money transmission is difficult. There are legal challenges surrounding Blockchain. Blockchain will disrupt all kinds of legal work, notary publics, contracts, lawyers, and judges.

- Other real challenges include complexity, politics, regulatory approval, security of online transactions, and consumer privacy.

- The ever-growing size of the Blockchain is considered by some to be a problem, creating issues of storage and complexity.

14.9.3 Advantages of Blockchain for Security

- **Tamper-proofing:**

   The advantage of tamper-proofing is achieved by the unique date structure and data writing mechanism of blockchain. Once a record, which is known as a transaction, is being created in the chained data structure of blockchain, a new timestamp will be recorded at the same time, as in Figure 14.16. Also, any modification of data created before that timestamp will not be allowed any more.

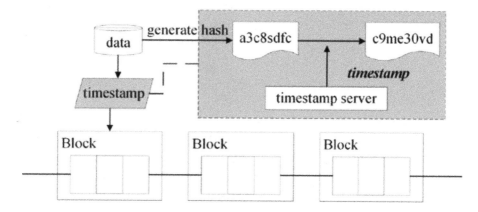

FIGURE 14.16. Tamper-proofing mechanism of blockchain

■ **Disaster Recovery:** Blockchain performs data recording and storing synchronously at all users' side by constructing open source sharing protocols. Unlike the traditional centralized database which stores data in one or several centers. In an application built on blockchain, every user has the right to generate data and keep a full copy of data.

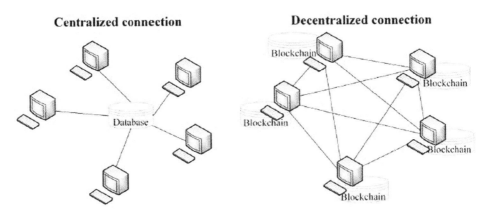

FIGURE 14.17. Decentralized and distributed storage of blockchain

■ **Privacy Protection:** Blockchain adopts asymmetric encryption mechanism to enable users to encrypt data with their own private key. In addition, the hash value of a user's public key is calculated and perform as the ID indicator of the user. On one hand, the hash value has no relation with the real identity of user, thus keeping user's personal privacy information safe. Indeed, the process of calculating hash value is invertible, which means an adversary can't figure out a user's public key from the public user address, and calculating the private key from the public key is impossible. Therefore, blockchain achieves the goal of preserving user anonymity and privacy.

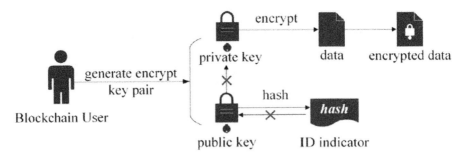

FIGURE 14.18. Privacy protection of blockchain

14.9.4 Security Issues of Blockchain

▣ **Technical Limitations:**

- Limitation of block capacity can limit the wide application of blockchain to a large degree. The capacity of a single block was set to 1MB originally to resist possible DDoS attacks. Bigger block can store more records which will meet the requirement of development. However, bigger blocks may cause difficulty in running and managing blockchain nodes. In additon, while smaller blocks are easy to manage and more reliable to a third-party payment solution, the available space is extremely limited especially in complex big data environments.

- Distributed storage mechanism creates a boarder attack surface in blockchain. A blockchain system chooses to store a complete copy of all data in every user's side. Although content in blockchain is not allowed to tamper, attackers can utilize other techniques such as data mining and correlation analysis to retrieve valuable information related to blockchain applications, users, network structure, etc.

- Consensus mechanism may trigger a cooperative attack. The consensus mechanism of blockchain is based on an assumption that the majority of nodes is honest to run and maintain the system.

▣ **Potential Risk of Cryptography Application:**

- The issue of private key management is not solved in blockchain. Existing blockchain applications usually use private key to confirm a user's identity and complete a payment transaction. Therefore, the precondition that information can't be falsified is the security of private key. Blockchain users are responsible for their own private keys, which mean that a private key is generated and taken care of by user instead of a third-party. If a user loses his private key, it will be impossible to get access to his digital assets on blockchain.

- Wide application of cryptographic algorithm may introduce unknown backdoors or vulnerabilities. There is an extensive adoption of cryptographic algorithms in blockchain, such as ECC and RSA. Backdoors and security vulnerabilities may emerge in the algorithms themselves or the implementation processes. In addition, the new computing technologies such as quantum computer can increase the chance of cracking the asymmetric encryption algorithms.

- **Opensource Blockchain Platforms Attract Intensive Attacks:**
  - Blockchain platform supports interoperation of different applications and users of the upper layer applications. The vast economic benefit motivates hackers flocking to digging the security vulnerabilities of open source blockchain platform.

- **Security Management of Self-organization and Anonymity:**
  - Distributed data storage may cause autonomous and frequent data cross border in blockchain use cases. Once a new transaction is being added to a block, all the data copies should update synchronously.

  - Blockchain calculates the hash value of a user's public key to identify a unique user. However, this privacy preserving operation make it impossible verify and trace a user's true identity in network attack backtrack and cybersecurity regulation.

14.10   EXERCISES

1. Define big data and big data analytics

2. What are the big data characteristics?

3. What are the big data processing groups?

4. Draw the Big data flow.

5. What are the big data analytics for security issues and privacy challenges?

6. Define cloud computing.

7. What are the two ends of cloud computing?

8. What are the cloud computing deployment models?

9. What are the three layers of Cloud computing services model and their services?

10. What are the security concerns and challenges of cloud computing?

11. Define Internet of Things and draw its concept topology.

12. What are the building blocks of the IoT?

13. Make map comparison between IoT and M2M.

14. What are the layered models of IoT?

15. What are the applications of IoT for automation, health care, smart manufacturing, and smart cities?

16. What are the new challenges created by IoT?

17. What are the security requirements of IoT?

18. What are the requirements for lightweight cryptography?

19. What are the three primary targets of attack against IoT?

20. What are the five steps for the prevention of attacks on IoT?

21. Define smart grids.

22. What are the requirements of security mechanism characteristics of the grid environment?

23. What are the challenges of smart grids?

24. What are the smart grid's layers?

25. What are the information security risks and demands of smart grids?

26. Draw the smart grid system classifications.

27. List the possible Cybersecurity attacks in a smart grid.

28. Define SCADA.

29. What are the components of SCADA systems?

30. What are the SCADA system Layers?

31. What are the categories for security threats to modern SCADA systems?

32. Define WSN.

33. What are the WSN Layers?

34. What are the security requirements in WSNs?

35. What are the attack categories in WSNs?

36. List the attacks and defense in WSNs at different layers.

37. What are the security protocols in WSNs?

38. Define ZIGBEE protocol.

39. What are the Challenges and Benefits of Smart City?

40. What are some of the key privacy and data protection considerations for smart cities.

41. What is Blockchain?

42. What are the features of BC technology?

43. What are the security issues of BC and discuss each of its issues?

CHAPTER 15

ARTIFICIAL INTELLIGENCE SECURITY

Chapter Outline

15.1 Introduction

15.2 Machine Learning

15.3 Types of Machine Learning

15.4 Deep Learning

15.5 Types of Deep Learning

15.6 AI for Intrusion Detection system

15.7 Exercises

15.1   INTRODUCTION

As we observed in previous chapters, network security has come to involve a vast range of threats and domains such as intrusion detection, Web application security, malware analysis, social network security, and applied cryptography. This chapter attempts to provide an overview of perspective and ideas on Artificial Intelligence (AI) security. AI can be described as cutting-edge technology with emerging applications in the cybersecurity industry. AI security solutions are essential for industries facing a landscape of increasingly advanced determined attackers and a shortage of security ability. Cyber threats today are one of the key problems every organization faces. This chapter will help readers to implement intelligent solutions to existing cybersecurity challenges and build cutting-edge implementations that cater to increasingly complex organizational needs.

Today's security threats leave little margin for error. To consistently preempt online attackers that are smart and destructive, enterprise security must incorporate a constantly evolving array of technologies and technical disciplines. Internet Security Services give complete protection against viruses, spyware, and other threats. In addition, Internet Security Services automatically prevent access to malicious Websites and allow selecting and blocking access to Web pages that are deemed inappropriate for the place of business. Furthermore, in an open networked environment, System Security deals with the protection of vital information that is made available to authorized users on the NET against security attacks by intruders. Now, the world of cybersecurity has changed. Now, attackers have learned to automate malicious code and vary it to flood an organization until a breach occurs. For decades, traditional antivirus technologies operated using detect and respond model. However, AI can be applied to pinpoint bad actors in the network, prevent malware and other threats, and protect against both known and unknown attacks. In addition, AI improves efficacy and makes cybersecurity implementation and operation a seamless, smooth process, and AI does not employ incremental storage, scanning machines, and reimaging machines. Recently, AI has helped to use minimal system resources (1%–2% CPU usage and 40–50 MB of memory), prevents attacks with superior speed (in milliseconds), and achieves efficacy rates of greater than 99% compared to 50%–60% with antiquated signature-based traditional antivirus. Thus, AI techniques are robust and more flexible as a result of expanding security execution and better defense system from an increasing number of advanced cyber threats.

15.2 MACHINE LEARNING

AI is a subset of data science. AI algorithms are driven by mathematics and statistics. These algorithms find patterns, correlations, and variances in complex data. The purpose of AI is to build machines which are capable of thinking like human. Machine learning (ML) refers to statistical learning algorithms that can create generalizable abstractions (models) by seeing and dissecting a data set. The purpose of ML is to make machines learn through data so that they can solve problems. Furthermore, ML is a subset of AI, which enables the machine to automatically learn from data, improve performance from past experiences, and make predictions. Also, ML contains a set of algorithms that work on a huge amount of data set. Data is fed to these algorithms to train them, and based on training, they build the model and perform a specific task.

Deep learning (DL) is a strict subset of ML referring to a specific class of multilayered models that use layers of simpler statistical components to learn representations of data. The purpose of DL is to build neural networks that automatically discover patterns for feature detection. Figure 15.1 illustrates the AI as it relates to ML and DL. Table 15.1 shows the common difference between the AI, ML, and DL.

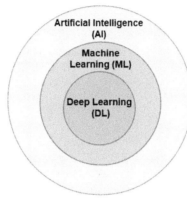

FIGURE 15.1 Artificial intelligence as it relates to machine learning and deep learning.

TABLE 15.1 Common Difference between the AI, ML, and DL

Technique	Description
AI	Any technique that enables machines to mimic human intelligence
ML	Statistical techniques that enable machine to learn tasks from data without explicitly programming
DL	Neural network techniques with many layers that learn representations and tasks directly from data

Because ML uses a continual approach to learn from data, the learning can be easily automated. Table 15.2 shows the common difference between the ML and statistical model.

TABLE 15.2 Difference between the ML and statistical model

Machine Learning	Statistical Model
Label	Dependent variable
Feature	Variable
Feature Creation	Transformation

15.3 TYPES OF MACHINE LEARNING

ML algorithms continue to grow and evolve. In most cases, however, based on the methods and way of learning, ML is divided into mainly four types, supervised learning, unsupervised learning, semi-supervised learning, and reinforcement learning (RL) as shown in Figure 15.2.

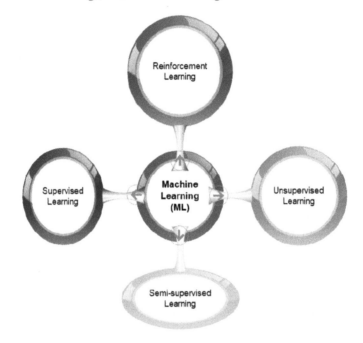

FIGURE 15.2 Machine learning types.

15.3.1 Supervised Learning

Supervised learning is based on supervision. The supervised learning technique trains the machines using the labelled dataset, and based on the training, the machine predicts the output. Here, the labelled data specifies that some of the inputs are already mapped to the output.

The definition of the supervised learning is shown in Figure 15.3. We may consider the two kinds of output value in the supervised learning; the target output which is initially assigned to each training example and the computed output which is computed by the learning algorithm.

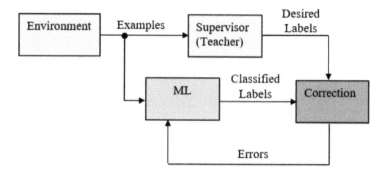

FIGURE 15.3 Supervised learning.

In other word, supervised learning technique train the machine with the input and corresponding output, and then the machine predicts the output using the test dataset. Thus, supervised learning requires labeled data for training. The algorithm training is conducted using an input dataset, from which the type of output to obtain is already known. A training instance is called a *data point* and consists of an input and output pair such as (x, y), where (y) is the output for input (x). That is, the learning aims to relate the labels (y) with the data (x) as $y = f(x)$, where (x) is a sample, and (y) is the label.

Indeed, the algorithms must be trained to identify the relationships between the variables being trained, in order to optimize the learning parameters on the basis of the target variables (labels) that are already known. Now, whatever the model wanted to predict is called as Dependent Variable (x), while variables that are used to predict are called as Independent Variables(y). Therefore, this type of ML method uses labeled datasets to train machines and, based on these datasets, machines predict the output. It needs supervision to train models and predict outputs. Fraud detection and spam filtering and detection are some important applications of supervised ML. In a supervised learning, a data set includes its desired outputs (or *labels*) such that a function can calculate an error for a given prediction. The supervision comes when a prediction is made, and an error produced (actual vs. desired) to alter the function and learn the mapping as illustrated in Figure 15.4. Thus, supervised learning involves feedback to indicate when a prediction is right or wrong.

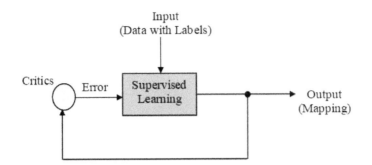

FIGURE 15.4 Supervised learning model for algorithm.

Since supervised learning works with the labelled dataset, so it can have an exact idea about the classes of objects. These algorithms are helpful in predicting the output on the basis of prior experience.

Supervised learning classification algorithms are used for identifying fraud transactions, fraud customers, etc. It is done by using historic data to identify the patterns that can lead to possible fraud. Also, supervised learning classification algorithms are used in spam detection and filtering, classification algorithms are used. These algorithms classify an email as spam or not spam. The spam emails are sent to the spam folder. In addition, supervised learning algorithms are also used in speech recognition. The algorithm is trained with voice data, and various identifications can be done using the same, such as voice-activated passwords, voice commands, etc.

Examples of supervised learning algorithms are linear regression, nearest neighbor, Gaussian naive Bayes, decision trees, support vector machine (SVM), and random forest.

15.3.1.1 Types of Supervised Learning

Supervised learning algorithm has two types: classification and regression. If the label (y) is a discrete value, then the process is termed as classification. If the label (y) is a real value, then it is called regression.

1. Classification: This is the process of assigning one or some among the predefined categories to each item. In classification supervised learning, the model is trained to classify using different models for discrete data. This means that classification essentially means placing the given sample into one of the predefined categories as illustrated in Figure 15.5. Classification supervised learning takes an input value and mapping it to a discrete value.

The output typically consists of classes or categories.

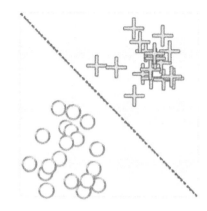

FIGURE 15.5 Classification supervised learning.

For example, spam filtering (classification), it classifies whether an email is spam or not spam. A spam filter is in fact trained by submitting an input dataset to the algorithm containing many examples of emails that have already been previously classified as spam (the emails were malicious or unwanted) or ham (the emails were genuine and harmless). The classification algorithm of the spam filter must therefore learn to classify the new emails it will receive in the future, referring to the spam or ham classes based on the training previously performed on the input dataset of the already classified emails.

The most popular classification algorithms are random forest, decision tree, logistic regression, and SVM.

2. Regression: This is the process of estimating an output value based on multiple factors. In the classification, the output value is discrete, whereas in the regression, the output value is continuous. There are two types of regression:

A. Univariate regression where only one output value is estimated and

B. Multivariate regression where more than one output value is done.

Regression supervised learning is a task where the model is used to predict values for continuous data rather than discrete as shown in Figure 15.6. For example, predicting the price of house or stocks, predicting temperature, etc. Typical regression instances are the nonlinear function approximation and the time series prediction.

FIGURE 15.6 Regression supervised learning

The most popular regression algorithms are simple linear, multivariate, decision tree, and Lasso.

15.3.2 Unsupervised Learning

Unsupervised learning models can perform more complex tasks than supervised learning models, but they are also more unpredictable. Unsupervised learning uses input Data (X) but no labels. The learning aims to learn about the data by grouping the like samples or by deducing the associations, where you only have input data (X) and no corresponding output variables. The training examples which are given for the unsupervised learning are unlabeled, and the clustering prototypes are initialized at random. The unsupervised learning can be defined as the process of optimizing the cluster prototypes, depending on the similarities among the training examples as illustrated in Figure 15.7

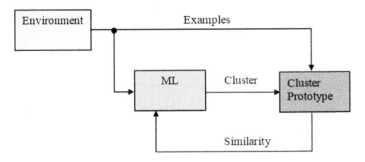

FIGURE 15.7 Unsupervised learning.

In unsupervised learning, a data set doesn't include a desired output; therefore, there's no way to supervise the function. Instead, the function attempts to segment the data set into classes so that each class contains a portion of the data set with common features. Thus, in unsupervised learning, the algorithms must try to classify the data independently, without the aid of a previous classification provided by the analyst. Unsupervised learning involves no response: The algorithm simply tries to categorize data based on its hidden structure as illustrated in Figure 15.8.

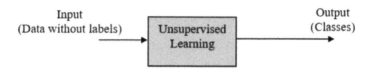

FIGURE 15.8 Unsupervised learning models for algorithm.

The goal for unsupervised learning is to model the underlying structure or distribution in the data in order to learn more about the data. In the context of cybersecurity, unsupervised learning algorithms are important for identifying new (not previously detected) forms of malware attacks, frauds, and email spamming campaigns.

15.3.2.1 Types of Unsupervised Learning

Unsupervised learning algorithm has two types: clustering and association.

1. Clustering: Segmenting data into groups based on data similarity which uncovers the groupings in the data. This technique is used when we want to find the inherent groups from the data. It is a way to group the objects into a cluster such that the objects with the most similarities remain in one group and have fewer or no similarities with the objects of other groups. An example of the clustering algorithm is grouping the customers by their purchasing behavior. The most popular clustering algorithms are K-means clustering algorithm, mean-shift algorithm, density-based spatial clustering of applications with noise Algorithm, affinity propagation, and spectral clustering.

2. Association: This uncovers the rules which associate the events. It finds interesting relations among variables within a large dataset. The main aim of this learning algorithm is to find the dependency of one data item on another data item and map those variables accordingly so that it can generate maximum profit. Example of the association algorithm is market basket analysis (which items are bought together) and customer clustering in retail (which stores people tend to visit together).

15.3.3 Semi-supervised Learning

Semi-supervised lies between supervised and unsupervised ML methods. It represents the intermediate ground between supervised (with labeled training data) and unsupervised learning (with no labeled training data) algorithms and uses the combination of labeled and unlabeled datasets during the training period.

Although semi-supervised learning is the middle ground between supervised and unsupervised learning and operates on the data that consists of a few labels, it mostly consists of unlabeled data.

The semi-supervised learning is illustrated in Figure 15.9. It is intended to utilize unlabeled examples which are very cheap to obtain as well as the labeled examples for training the learning algorithms. The ML learns the labeled examples by minimizing the error between their target label and the computed one and the unlabeled examples, depending on their similarities, as the mixture of the supervised learning and the unsupervised learning. By adding the unlabeled examples, the semi-supervised learning is applied to the classification tasks and the regression tasks.

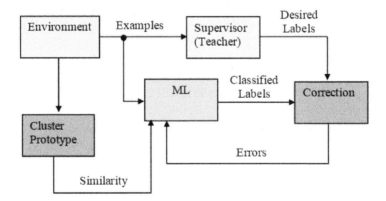

FIGURE 15.9 Semi-supervised learning.

The main aim of semi-supervised learning is to effectively use all the available data, rather than only labeled data like in supervised learning. Initially, similar data is clustered along with an unsupervised learning algorithm, and further, it helps to label the unlabeled data into labeled data. It is because labeled data is a comparatively more expensive acquisition than unlabeled data. For example, identifying a person's face on a Webcam is a semi-supervised learning.

15.3.4 Reinforcement Learning

In the case of RL, a different learning strategy is followed, which emulates the trial and error approach. Thus, drawing information from the feedback obtained during the learning path, with the aim of maximizing the reward finally obtained based on the number of correct decisions that the algorithm has selected as shown in Figure 15.10 .

In practice, the learning process takes place in an unsupervised manner, with the particularity that a positive reward is assigned to each correct decision (and a negative reward for incorrect decisions) taken at each step of the learning path. At the end of the learning process, the decisions of the algorithm are reassessed based on the final reward achieved.

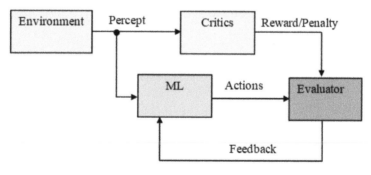

FIGURE 15.10 Reinforcement learning.

Given its dynamic nature, it is no coincidence that RL is more similar to the general approach adopted by AI than to the common algorithms developed in ML.

In reinforcement learning, the algorithm attempts to learn actions for a given set of states that lead to a goal state. An error is provided not after each example, but instead on receipt of a reinforcement signal. This behavior is similar to human learning, where feedback isn't necessarily provided for all actions but when a reward is warranted as illustrated in Figure 15.11.

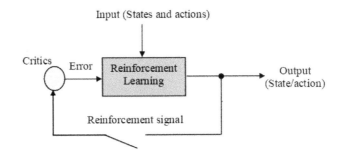

FIGURE 15.11 Reinforcement learning models for algorithm.

Some examples of RL algorithms are Markov process, Q-learning, temporal difference methods, and Monte Carlo methods. In particular, Hidden Markov Models are extremely important in the detection of polymorphic malware threats.

15.4 DEEP LEARNING

DL is a subset of ML in which the model being trained has more than one *hidden layer* between the input and the output. It often refers to neural networks with more than one layer of nodes called *deep neural network (DNN)*. Therefore, DL is a large multilayer neural network. When we have to capture complex and non-linear patterns in the data that would not be possible by simpler shallow learning models, we need models with many layers called *DL models*. DL models learn in stages, or layers, with each layer extracting some pattern that is fed into the next layer.

DL algorithms can be regarded as an evolution of ML algorithms. Thus, DL, or also known as DNN, refers to a set of ML techniques that utilize neural networks with many hidden layers for tasks, where the goal of each layer is to learn to transform input data into a non-linear and more abstract representation. It has become an analytical tool that has attracted more and more attention from researchers in different areas of research in recent years.

DL algorithms use neural networking to process massive data sets in order to execute a specified task. They have been used to predict the quality attribute (output) with the process parameters (input). Data is the key in DL's effectiveness. DL techniques can automatically learn complex high-level data features from a large amount of data. Traditionally, a DL model has to be retrained every time a new rule is included. DL has advantages as following:

- Ability to generate new features from limited available training data sets.

- Ability to work on unsupervised learning techniques helps in generating actionable and reliable task outcomes.

- Ability to reduce the time required for feature engineering, one of the tasks that requires major time in practicing ML.

- With continuous training, its architecture has become adaptive to change and is able to work on diverse problems.

15.4.1 Deep Learning Applications: A Brief Overview

Many fields of research have used DL tools to facilitate the processing of massive data. Applications of DL are almost limitless, with different applications employing different DL models. DL has matured from being a special purpose ML technique to a general-purpose ML tool. It has enjoyed success in various applications such as automatic speech recognition, image recognition, computer vision, object detection, bioinformatics, drug discovery and information retrieval, industrial machines, and manufacturing. DL has the following applications:

1. Smart manufacturing: This refers to using advanced data analytics to complement physical science for improving system performance and decision making. It is a fully integrated collaborative system that uses sensors, Internet connected machines, and big data to monitor the production process and to improve manufacturing efficiencies. Smart manufacturing envisions systems that provide us with insightful information about every step of a product lifecycle.

Information-system-enabled smart manufacturing has increased productivity and quality of industrial organizations. Smart manufacturing will enrich the lives of consumers by providing goods and services with high quality and at an affordable cost. DL is applied in the predictive analytics for defect prognosis, that is, maintenance and service prediction. DL provides advanced analytics tools for processing and analyzing big data in manufacturing and make manufacturing smarter.

2. Automotive industry: The automotive industry covers a wide range of vehicles. DL has many potential applications in the automotive industry during development, manufacturing, and sales. It is also useful in advanced driving assistance systems, autonomous driving, and advanced detection controls.

3. Predictive Maintenance: In predictive maintenance, data is collected over time to monitor and find patterns to predict failures. Although predictive maintenance is applied in many industries, it thrives in manufacturing. AI in manufacturing has come a long way with technologies like predictive maintenance. The adoption of ML and DL in manufacturing will only improve predictive maintenance. DL can aid in the predictive maintenance of complex machinery and connected systems.

4. Automation: In the hope of decreasing costs and increasing quality and the push for higher volumes of output with lower investments, manufacturing industry is making efforts to achieve a higher degree of automation. For years, machine builders in the automation field of assembly equipment have been focusing on the mechanics of machines.

5. Robotics: DL architectures enable robots to learn on their own. Companies use industrial robots to handle complicated and dangerous processes. A robot can train itself for new tasks by object and pattern recognition capabilities of DL models. DL models have proven to be compelling in areas such as financial aspects, time setting data management, and money related.

6. Targeting: Figuring out what you want. DL collects information on what the person likes and decides what he would be most interested in.

7. Speech Recognition: DL has revolutionized speech recognition. Large-scale automatic speech recognition is the first and most persuasive case of DL recently. All major commercial speech recognition systems, such as Google Now, Skype Translator, and Microsoft Cortana, are based on DL algorithms. DL has improved voice search on smart phones.

8. Image Recognition: DL algorithms have shown excellent learning in image recognition problem, such as handwritten classification. They develop advanced pattern recognition systems modeled after human perception.

9. Medical Informatics: DL has been applied in the health domain such as in predicting sleep quality and predicting health complications. DL has been used to detect toxic effects of environmental chemicals in nutrients and drugs.

15.4.2 DL Network Layers

Figure 15.12 illustrates a DL model architecture. DL networks have a total of five or more layers as following:

1. A single input layer: Reserved for the data being fed into the network.

2. Three or more hidden layers: Learn representations from the input data. In dense type hidden layer, all the nodes in a given layer can receive information from each of the nodes in the previous layer

3. A single output layer: Reserved for the values (predictions) that the network yields.

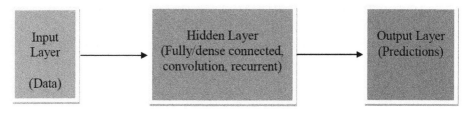

FIGURE 15.12 A DL model architecture.

The DL algorithm determines parameters (weights and biases), using forward and backward propagation. The process of passing data through the DL layers is called forward propagation.

15.4.2.1 Forward Propagation

Each node in hidden or output layer, forward propagation can occur in two stages: preactivation (Summation) and activations. Figure 15.13 illustrates a simple model with one hidden layer.

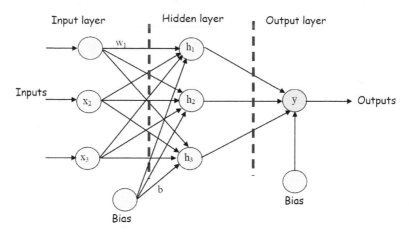

FIGURE 15.13 The forward propagation model.

Preactivation (net inputs) is a weighted sum of the input data and the bias (offset). Preactivation provides the strength of the connection between nodes and the influence of the inputs on the final results (output). If the weight (w_i) has a higher value than the weight (w_j), then the input (x_i) will have a larger impact on the result (output). The bias is required to move the activation function to right/left to generate the required output values.

Let, the vector of inputs is $\mathbf{x} = [x_1, x_2, \ldots, x_n]$, the vector of weights $\mathbf{w} = [w_1, w_2, \ldots, w_n]$, and the bias is b, then the preactivation function is given by $z = \mathbf{x} \cdot \mathbf{w} + b$, where the dot product of the inputs and the weights is given by

$$\mathbf{x} \cdot \mathbf{w} = (x_1 \times w_1) + (x_1 \times w_1) + \cdots + (x_n \times w_n)$$

Now, the next step is the activation function (transfer function) which is based on the calculated net inputs. Activation function is used to modify (transfer) the activation level of an incoming node into an output signal. It is required to add nonlinearity to the outputs of the nodes to provide flexibility to DL through complex functions and significantly affects the speed in the learning process. Table 15.3 shows some popular activation functions.

TABLE 15.3 Activation Functions

Function name	Definition
Sigmoid	$\sigma(z_{sigmoid}) = \dfrac{1}{1 + e^{-z}}$
Hyperbolic tangent (tanh)	$\sigma(z_{tanh}) = \dfrac{e^z - e^{-z}}{e^z + e^{-z}}$
Rectified linear unit (ReLU)	$ReLU(z) = \begin{cases} z, & z > 0 \\ 0, & otherwise \end{cases}$
Softmax	$softmax(z) = \dfrac{e^z}{\sum_i e^{z_i}}$

15.4.2.2 Backward Propagation

Backward propagation (backpropagation) algorithm is used to navigate the space of possible sets of weights and biases that the model can use to make accurate predications. In other words, it used to minimize the cost function with respect to the weights and bias. A loss function is used to understand the model has achieved the desired predicted value. Some most popular loss functions are below:

1. Mean Squared Error (MSE): This is most commonly used in regression loss function.

$$L_{MSE} = (y - \hat{y})^2, \tag{15.1}$$

where y is the actual value, $\hat{y}$ is predicted value

2. Huber loss function: This is used in robust regression and is less sensitive to outliers.

$$L_\delta = \begin{cases} \dfrac{1}{2}(y - \hat{y})^2, & |y - \hat{y}| \le \delta \\ \delta |y - \hat{y}| - \dfrac{1}{2}\delta^2, & otherwise \end{cases} \tag{15.2}$$

where δ is a hyperparameter.

3. Binary Cross Entropy (BCE): This is used for binary classifiers.

$$L_{CE} = -\frac{1}{n}\sum_{i=1}^{n}\left(y_i \log \hat{y}_i + (1 - y_i)\log(1 - \hat{y}_i)\right) \tag{15.3}$$

$$L_{CE} = -\frac{1}{n}\sum_{i=1}^{n}\log(1 - \hat{y}_i), \text{ when } y = 0 \tag{15.4}$$

$$L_{CE} = -\frac{1}{n}\sum_{i=1}^{n}y_i \log \hat{y}_i, \text{ when } y = 1 \tag{15.5}$$

4. Categorical Cross Entropy (CCE): This is used for multiclassification problems.

$$L_{CCE} = \sum_{i=1}^{c}y_{ri} \log(\hat{y}_{ri}), \tag{15.6}$$

where i is the number of categories, r is the number of rows.

While the loss function is defined as an error at one data point, the cost error function is the sum of all errors in the entire data set.

The cost function of MSE is given by:

$$C_{MSE} = \frac{1}{n}\sum_{i=1}^{n}(y - \hat{y})^2 \longrightarrow \min \tag{15.7}$$

Now, to find the optimal weights and bias for DL, the gradient (∇) of the cost function will be used. The gradient of function C at the point a is given by

$$\frac{\partial C}{\partial a} = \left[\frac{\partial C}{\partial a_1}, \frac{\partial C}{\partial a_2}, \ldots, \frac{\partial C}{\partial a_n}\right] \tag{15.8}$$

where $a = [a_1, a_2, \ldots, a_n]$

$\dfrac{\partial C}{\partial a}$ shows the rate of cost function change with respect to the change in its argument (a).

Thus, the gradient shows how much the input parameters (weights and bias) need to be changed to minimize the lost function (C).

For example,

$$\frac{\partial z}{\partial w} = \frac{\partial}{\partial w_i} \sum_{i=1}^{n} (z_i \cdot w_i + b) = x_i \tag{15.9}$$

$$\frac{\partial \hat{y}}{\partial z} = \sigma(z) \times (1 - \sigma(z)) \tag{15.10}$$

$$\frac{\partial C}{\partial \hat{y}} = \frac{2}{n} \times \sum (y - \hat{y}) \tag{15.11}$$

The algorithm steps for gradient descent flow are

(a) Calculate the gradient at the current data point x_1

(b) Take a small step, α (learning rate) in the direction of the gradient to reach the point x_2. The parameter α is used to control how much the weights and bias are changed. Therefore, the new (updated) weights and bias are

$$w_{new} = w - \left(a \times \frac{\partial C}{\partial w}\right) \tag{15.12}$$

$$b_{new} = b - \left(a \times \frac{\partial C}{\partial b}\right) \tag{15.13}$$

(c) Repeat the entire process until the model convergence.

15.5 TYPES OF DEEP LEARNING

15.5.1 Multilayer Neural Network

Multilayer neural networks have input nodes, multilayers of hidden nodes, and output nodes. Different activation (transfer) functions can be used for different layers in the network. Different layers in the network may be functionally different such as being a convolution, dropout, fully/dense connected, or pooling layer. Multilayer neural networks solve classification problem for nonlinear sets by employing hidden layers. The additional hidden layers used to enhance the separation capacity of the network. Figure 15.14 shows typical multilayer network architecture.

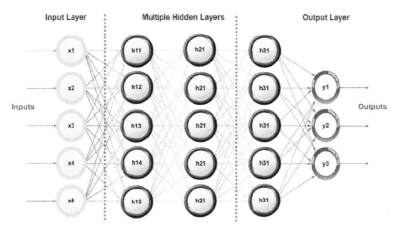

FIGURE 15.14 A typical DL multilayer network architecture.

Example 15.1

In the three layers AI network below, the activation function is sigmoid for the hidden and output nodes.

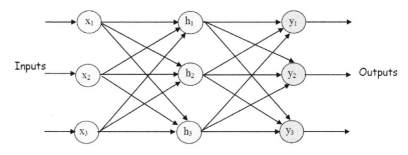

FIGURE 15.15 Example 15.1.

Given: $\vec{I} = \begin{bmatrix} 0.9 \\ 0.1 \\ 0.8 \end{bmatrix}$, $\vec{W}_{input-hidden} = \begin{bmatrix} 0.9 & 0.3 & 0.4 \\ 0.2 & 0.8 & 0.2 \\ 0.1 & 0.5 & 0.6 \end{bmatrix}$, and $\vec{W}_{hidden-output} = \begin{bmatrix} 0.3 & 0.7 & 0.5 \\ 0.6 & 0.5 & 0.2 \\ 0.8 & 0.1 & 0.9 \end{bmatrix}$

1. the input nets to hidden layer, $\vec{X}_{hidden} = \vec{W} \bullet \vec{I}$

$$\vec{X}_{hidden} = \begin{bmatrix} 0.9 & 0.3 & 0.4 \\ 0.2 & 0.8 & 0.2 \\ 0.1 & 0.5 & 0.6 \end{bmatrix} \bullet \begin{bmatrix} 0.9 \\ 0.1 \\ 0.8 \end{bmatrix} = \begin{bmatrix} 1.16 \\ 0.42 \\ 0.62 \end{bmatrix}$$

2. the outputs of the hidden layer, $\vec{O}_{hidden} = sigmoid\left(\vec{X}_{hidden}\right)$

$$\vec{O}_{hidden} = sigmoid \begin{bmatrix} 1.16 \\ 0.42 \\ 0.62 \end{bmatrix} = \begin{bmatrix} 0.761 \\ 0.603 \\ 0.650 \end{bmatrix}$$

3. the input nets to output layer, $\vec{X}_{output} = \vec{W}_{hidden-output} \bullet \vec{O}_{hidden}$

$$\vec{X}_{output} = \begin{bmatrix} 0.3 & 0.7 & 0.5 \\ 0.6 & 0.5 & 0.2 \\ 0.8 & 0.1 & 0.9 \end{bmatrix} \begin{bmatrix} 0.761 \\ 0.603 \\ 0.650 \end{bmatrix} = \begin{bmatrix} 0.975 \\ 0.888 \\ 1.254 \end{bmatrix}$$

4. the outputs of the AI network, $\vec{O}_{output} = sigmoid\left(\vec{X}_{output}\right)$

$$\vec{O}_{output} = sigmoid \begin{bmatrix} 0.975 \\ 0.888 \\ 1.254 \end{bmatrix} = \begin{bmatrix} 0.726 \\ 0.708 \\ 0.778 \end{bmatrix}$$

15.5.2 Convolutional Neural Networks (CNN)

A convolutional neural network (CNN) has convolutional layers in which it works as feedforward neural network that uses convolution, reduces the quantity of weights in the network, and reduces the complexity of calculation. It convolves a feature with the input matrix so that the output emphasizes that feature which effectively finds patterns. Figure 15.16 shows a typical CNN architecture.

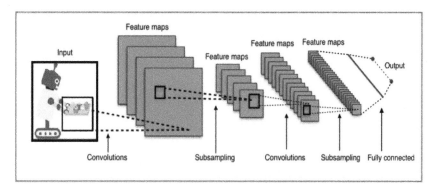

FIGURE 15.16 A typical CNN architecture.

The CNN has a convolution layer to convert inputs into a set of convoluted features by going through a filter of a fixed size. The convoluted features go through activation function and then subsampled by pooling (subsampling) to reduce their dimensionality.

The basic idea of convolution between a function $f(x)$ and a filter h is defined as

$$f(x*h) = \int_{-\infty}^{\infty} f(x-\tau) h(\tau) d\tau = \int_{-\infty}^{\infty} f(\tau) h(x-\tau) d\tau \qquad (15.14)$$

where h is a simple unit slot sliding along a function $f(x)$, the convolution value at any x is the overlapped shaded area in Figure 15.17.

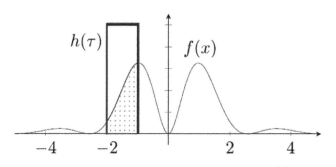

FIGURE 15.17 Simple convolution of $f(x)$ and filter $h(\tau)$.

A color image that is 2 pixels by 2 pixels by 3 colors could be represented with random data using *rand*.

```
>> x = rand(2,2,3)
```

x(:,:,2) =

| 0.5472 | 0.1493 |
| 0.1386 | 0.2575 |

x(:,:,3) =

| 0.8407 | 0.8143 |
| 0.2543 | 0.2435 |

The same number of points could be organized into a single vector using *reshape*.

```
>> reshape(x,12,1)
```
ans =

0.9293

0.3500

0.1966

0.2511

0.6160

0.4733

0.3517

0.8308

0.5853

0.5497

0.9172

0.2858

The numbers are organized differently. CNNs are often used for image structured data. We might also have a vector:

```
>> s = rand(2,1)
```

s =

0.0119
0.3371

To learn a temporal or time sequence, if each column is a time sample, we might have:

>> rand(2,4)

ans =

$$\begin{matrix} 0.1524 & 0.5383 & 0.0782 & 0.1067 \\ 0.8258 & 0.9961 & 0.4427 & 0.9619 \end{matrix}$$

Example 15.2

Consider an image of size 5×5 and a filter of size 3×3. To provide a single value for the feature cell, perform an element wise multiplication between the image pixel values that match the size of the filter and the filter itself and then sum them up.

Convolution operation Step 1

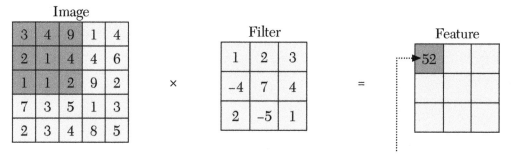

$$(3 \times 1) + (4 \times 2) + (9 \times 3) + (2 \times -4) + (1 \times 7) + (4 \times 4) + (1 \times 2) + (1 \times -5) + (2 \times 1) = 52$$

Convolution operation Step 2

$$(4 \times 1) + (9 \times 2) + (1 \times 3) + (1 \times -4) + (4 \times 7) + (4 \times 4) + (1 \times 2) + (2 \times -5) + (9 \times 1) = 66$$

Convolution operation Step 3

Image

3	4	9	1	4
2	1	4	4	6
1	1	2	9	2
7	3	5	1	3
2	3	4	8	5

×

Filter

1	2	3
–4	7	4
2	–5	1

=

Feature

52	66	20

Convolution operation Step 4

Image

3	4	9	1	4
2	1	4	4	6
1	1	2	9	2
7	3	5	1	3
2	3	4	8	5

×

Filter

1	2	3
–4	7	4
2	–5	1

=

Feature

52	66	20
31		

Convolution operation Step 5

Image

3	4	9	1	4
2	1	4	4	6
1	1	2	9	2
7	3	5	1	3
2	3	4	8	5

×

Filter

1	2	3
–4	7	4
2	–5	1

=

Feature

52	66	20
31	49	

Convolution operation Step 6

Image

3	4	9	1	4
2	1	4	4	6
1	1	2	9	2
7	3	5	1	3
2	3	4	8	5

×

Filter

1	2	3
–4	7	4
2	–5	1

=

Feature

52	66	20
31	49	101

Convolution operation Step 7

Image

3	4	9	1	4
2	1	4	4	6
1	1	2	9	2
7	3	5	1	3
2	3	4	8	5

×

Filter

1	2	3
-4	7	4
2	-5	1

=

Feature

52	66	20
31	49	101
15		

Convolution operation Step 8

Image

3	4	9	1	4
2	1	4	4	6
1	1	2	9	2
7	3	5	1	3
2	3	4	8	5

×

Filter

1	2	3
-4	7	4
2	-5	1

=

Feature

52	66	20
31	49	101
15	53	

Convolution operation Step 9

Image

3	4	9	1	4
2	1	4	4	6
1	1	2	9	2
7	3	5	1	3
2	3	4	8	5

×

Filter

1	2	3
-4	7	4
2	-5	1

=

Feature

52	66	20
31	49	101
15	53	-2

As we see above here that we slide the filter by 1 pixel. This is called *stride*. However, we can have the filter move by different stride values to extract different kinds of features. Also the amount of stride we choose affects the size of the feature extracted. So with a stride of 2, the filter of size 3×3 on a image of size 5×5 would only be able to extract a feature of size 2. To calculate the feature size, we use the below equation:

$$\text{Fearture size} = \left[\frac{\text{Image size} - \text{Filter size}}{\text{Stride}} \right] + 1 \qquad (15.15)$$

Therefore, feature size is

$$\text{Fearture size} = \left[\frac{5-3}{1} \right] + 1 = 3$$

15.5.3 Recurrent Neural Networks (RNNs)

Recurrent neural networks (RNNs) are dynamically driven, with a feedback loop between two (or more) layers, which makes such networks ideal for learning from sequence data. RNNs are a type of recursive neural network, and they are used for time-dependent problems. They combine the last time step's data with the data from the hidden (or intermediate) layer, to produce a representation of the current time step. A RNN has a loop. RNNs use their internal memory to process arbitrary sequences of inputs.

When an RNN processes a sequence of data, the previous output will feedback as part of the input data as shown in Figure 15.18. The RNN must remember the previous output for calculating the current output iteratively. There exist connections between the nodes of hidden layers in the network structure. The input of the hidden layer needs to use the output of the input layer and the output of itself iteratively.

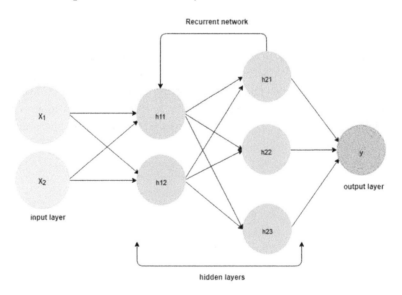

FIGURE 15.18 Basic recurrent neural network (RNN) architecture.

Therefore, an RNN can be seen as short-term memory units that include the input layer, hidden layer, and output layer. RNNs either produce an output for every entity in the input sequence or produce a single output for the entire sequence. RNNs are network design for sequential data and widely used in natural language processing which will be discussed in Chapter 13. RNNs are used in speech recognition, and language translation. The unfolding structure of a RNN in time of the computation involved in its forward computation can be presented in Figure 15.19.

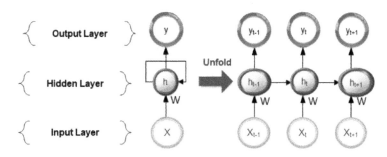

FIGURE 15.19 The unfolding structure of RNN.

15.5.4 Long Short-Term Memory Networks (LSTMs)

Long short-term memory networks (LSTMs) are designed to avoid the dependency on old information. A standard RNN has a repeating structure. An LSTM also has a repeating structure, but each element has four layers. The LSTM layers decide what old information to pass on to the next layer. There are many variants on LSTM, but they all include the fundamental ability to forget things. In neural network, each layer is having same structure and same activation (transfer) function except from output layer. In the other hand, if different layers have different structures, then in LSTM network a choice can be used. Figure 15.20 illustrates the basic structure of LSTM. LSTM can be used for weather forecasting.

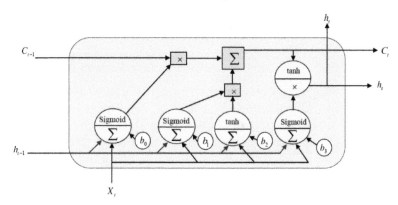

FIGURE 15.20 The structure of LSTM.

15.5.5 Recursive Neural Network (RvNNs)

This is often confused with recursive neural networks (RvNNs), which are a type of recursive neural network. RvNNs operate on structured data. They've been used successfully on language processing as language is structured as opposed to images which are not, recursive autoencoding, and generative modeling of 3D shape structures in the form of cuboid abstractions.

RvNNs simple architecture, nodes are combined into parents using a weight matrix that is shared across the whole network, and a nonlinearity as shown in Figure 15.21. If c_1 and c_2 are n-dimensional vector representation of nodes, their parent will also be an n-dimensional vector, defined as

$$p_{1,2} = \tanh\left(W[c_1;c_2]\right) \tag{15.16}$$

where W is a learned $n\times2n$ weight matrix.

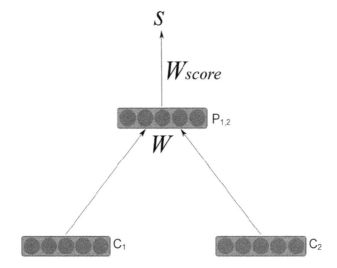

FIGURE 15.21 The basic architecture of RvNN.

The same set of neural node weight is applied recursively over a structured input. This means that, not all of the inputs are processed in batch. Thus, recursion is a standard method used in general estimation when data is coming in at different times and you want the best estimate at the current time without having to process all available data at once.

15.5.6 Stacked Autoencoders

A stacked autoencoder is a neural network made up of a series of sparse autoencoders. An autoencoder is a kind of unsupervised learning algorithm using backpropagation. The structure has three layers: input layer, hidden layer, and output layer as shown in Figure 15.22. The process of an autoencoder training consists of two parts:

(a) encoder: is used for mapping the input data into hidden representation

(b) decoder: is referred to reconstructing input data from the hidden representation

For given the unlabeled input dataset $\{x_n\}, n = 1,...,N$, where $x_n \in R^{m \times 1}$, h_n is the hidden encoder vector calculated from x_n, and $\overline{x}_n$, $\overline{x}_n$ is the decoder vector of the output layer. Therefore, the encoding process is defined as:

$$h_n = f_1\left(W_1 x_n + b_1\right) \tag{15.17}$$

where f_1 is the encoding function, W_1 is the weight matrix of the encoder, and b_1 is the bias vector.

The decoder process is defined as:

$$\overline{x}_n = f_2\left(W_2 h_n + b_2\right) \tag{15.18}$$

where f_2 is the decoding function, W_2 is the weight matrix of the decoder, and b_2 is the bias vector.

The parameter sets of the autoencoder are optimized to minimize the reconstruction error as follows:

$$\phi\left(\Theta\right) = \arg\min_{\theta, \theta'} \frac{1}{n} \sum_{i=1}^{n} L\left(x^i, \overline{x}^i\right) \tag{15.19}$$

where L is a loss function $L\left(x^i, \overline{x}^i\right) = \|x - \overline{x}\|^2$.

Figure 15.23 illustrates the structure of stacked autoencoders is stacking n autoencoders into n hidden layers by an unsupervised layer-wise learning algorithm and then finetuned by a supervised method. So the stacked autoencoders-based method can be divided into the following steps:

1. Train the first autoencoder by input data and obtain the learned feature vector

2. The feature vector of the former layer is used as the input for the next layer, and this procedure is repeated until the training completes

3. After all the hidden layers are trained, backpropagation algorithm is used to minimize the cost function and update the weights with labeled training set to achieve fine-tuning.

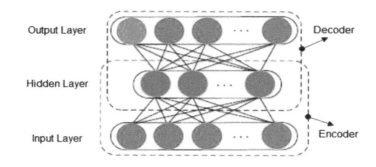

FIGURE 15.22 Structure of autoencoder.

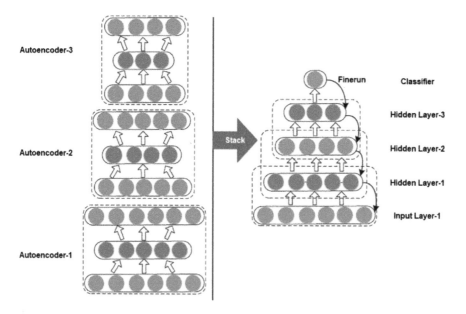

FIGURE 15.23 Structure of stacked autoencoders.

15.5.7 Extreme Learning Machine (ELM)

Extreme learning machine (ELMs) are a single hidden layer feedforward network. It randomly chooses the weights of the hidden nodes and analytically computes the weights of the output nodes. ELMs provide good performance and learn quickly.

An example code can be applied to ELM structure as shown in Figure 15.24 . The basic learning rules of ELM are presented in these codes.

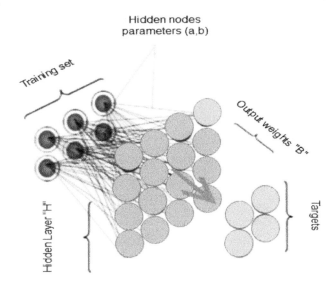

FIGURE 15.24 Structure of ELM.

```
clear all;clc
addpath('codes','dataset');
```

Load data
```
D=load('spambase.data');

A=D(:,1:57);              % Inputs

B=D(:,58);               % Targets
```

define Options
```
Opts.ELM_Type='Class';    % 'Class'  for  classification  and
'Regrs' for regression

Opts.number_neurons=200;  % Maximam number of neurons

Opts.Tr_ratio=0.70;       % training ratio

Opts.Bn=1;                % 1 to encode  lables into binary
representations

                          % if it is necessary
```

Training

```
[net]= elm_LB(A,B,Opts);
net
net =

            bn: 'binary Targets'
           app: 'Classification'
             X: [3220x57 double]
             Y: [3220x1 double]
           Xts: [1381x57 double]
           Yts: [1381x1 double]
            IW: [200x57 double]
            OW: [200x2 double]
         Y_hat: [3220x1 double]
       Yts_hat: [1381x1 double]
        BnY_hat: [3220x2 double]
      BnYts_hat: [1381x2 double]
           min: 0
           max: 1
          Opts: [1x1 struct]
        tr_acc: 0.8814
        ts_acc: 0.8689
```

prediction

```
[output]=elmPredict(net,A);
```

Important characteristics of this code:

A. It extended for usage for both classification and regression.

B. It contains functions that normalize the input samples between any desired values. For classification:

A. It allows encoding of the labels of classes into binary codes to satisfy the constraints of Activation functions boundaries.

-B. After training and in case of prediction the algorithm has the capability to decode again those codes into original labels.

For regression:

A. The algorithm also can renormalize the output values after training into original interval.

15.6 AI FOR INTRUSION DETECTION SYSTEM

Intrusion detection system (IDS) is used to save guard and secured an information system against the notorious activities of hackers and cyber attacker, the task of keeping information system secured and sustained in a secured state during the period of their usage. Therefore, Naive Bayes, KNN, and decision tree intrusion detection models can be built with a consistency features selection reduced training dataset.

The performance of intrusion detection models can be carried out by evaluating the measures from the values in the coincidence matrix also known as the confusion matrix. The confusion matrix shows the distribution of instances that are either correctly classified or wrongly classified by the models, Confusion Matrix is an N X N matrix, where N is any integer greater than 1. The diagonal elements represent the number of points for which the predicted label is equal to the true label, while off-diagonal elements are those that are mislabeled by the classifier. The higher the diagonal values of the confusion matrix the better, indicating many correct predictions. It produced four outcomes as follows:

a. TP_{class} : No of class categories classified as actual class.

b. TN_{class}: Value of Overall TP less value of class.

c. FN_{class}: Sum of incorrectly classified horizontal entries.

d. FP_{class}: Sum of incorrectly classified vertical entries

Evaluation or performance metrics are used to evaluate the performance of IDS by using ML classification algorithms. The predicted outcomes are between the range 0 and 1. The confusion matrix shows the statistical results on the basis of actual or predicted records in a dataset. The most commonly used evaluation metrics are as follows:

Accuracy:

Accuracy (ACC) is the ratio of all correct classification to the total number of instances in the test dataset. It is the estimated ratio of correctly recognized data records to the total number of data records in a given data set. The higher rate of accuracy shows that the ML model is performed better. (Accuracy [0,1]) is defined as follows:

$$ACC = \frac{TP + TN}{FN + FP + TN + TP} \qquad (15.20)$$

True Positive Rate (Sensitivity/Recall):

True Positive Rate (TPR) is the ratio of correctly predicted positive observations to the all observations in actual class. It is the proportion of the actual positives that are classified as positive by the model, it is also called sensitivity or recall. It is the estimated ratio of correctly classified attack data records to the total number of attack data records in a given dataset. The higher rate of recall shows that the ML model is performed better (Recall [0,1]) is defined as follows:

$$Sensitivity\ (or\ Recall) = \frac{TP}{TP + FN} \qquad (15.21)$$

True Negative Rate (Specificity):

True Negative Rate (TNR) is the proportion of the actual negatives that are detected as negative by the model, it is also called specificity.

$$Specificity = \frac{TN}{TN + FP} \qquad (15.22)$$

False-Positive Rate (FPR) or False Alarm Rate (FAR):

False-Positive Rate (FPR) or False Alarm Rate (FAR) is the proportion of the wrongly model negative as positive, FPR should be as low as possible to avoid unwanted false alarms.

$$FPR = FAR = \frac{FP}{TN + FP} \qquad (15.23)$$

Precision:

Precision is the ratio of correctly predicted positive observations to the total predicted positive observations. It is the estimated ratio of correctly identified attack data records to the total number of all identified data records in a given dataset. The higher rate of precision shows that the ML model is performed better. (Precision [0,1]) is defined as follows:

$$Precision = \frac{TP}{TP + FP} \qquad (15.24)$$

F1-ScoreF1-Measure:

It is the harmonic mean of Precision and Recall. The higher rate of F1-Score shows that the ML model is performed better. (F1-Score [0,1]) is defined as follows:

$$F1\text{-}Score = 2 \times \left[\frac{Precision \times Recall}{Precision + Recall} \right] \qquad (15.25)$$

The terms TP, TN, FP, and FN are used for describing the classification of Normal and Attack records in a dataset. TP (True-Positive) defines that the number of connection records correctly classified or identified into normal class of dataset similarly TN (True-Negative) defines that the number of connection records correctly classified or identified into an attack class of dataset. FP (False-Positive) defines that the number of normal class connection records are wrongly classified or identified into attack class similarly FN (False-Negative) defines that the number of attack class connection records are wrongly classified or identified into normal class connection records.

Trusted Systems

In social networks, the attacks are complex with statistical regularities, interactions, and characteristics between them. The complexity reflects into an intricate mesh of relationships between the neural network nodes. RNN is used to train the sequence data. Most attack behaviors are recorded in the form of network flow and logs in social networks. There will be trouble when the conventional RNN is used to train with a long step size, so we choose LSTM to address this problem. The training and detection algorithms are presented as follows:

Algorithm for training neural network

1. Input: features X extracted from the training dataset with labeled information

2. Initialization:

3. for channel = $1 \rightarrow N$ do

4. Training LSTM-RNN model

5. Save the LSTM-RNN model as a classifier c

6. end for

7. return: c

Algorithm for attack detection

1. Input: feature X extracted from test dataset with labeled information
2. Initialization:
3. for channel = 1 → N do
4. Load LSTM-RNN model as a classifier
5. get the result vector R of the classifier
6. end for
7. for r in R do
8. vote to get the majority element v
9. end for
10. return v

15.7   EXERCISES

1. Define AI, ML, and DL.
2. What are the common difference between the AI, ML, and DL.
3. What are the four different types of ML?
4. To what type of ML the following belong to:

   A. Optimized marketing
   B. Market basket analysis
   C. Housing pricing prediction
   D. Lane finding on GPS data
   E. Driverless car
   F. Text classification
   G. Medical imaging
   H. Customer segmentation
   I. Weather prediction

5. The classification algorithms predict the categories present in the dataset. (True or False)

6. Regression algorithms are used to solve regression problems in which there is a linear relationship between input and output variables. (True or False)

7. List the five most popular classification algorithms.

8. List the four most popular regression algorithms.

9. Supervised learning develops predictive model based on both input and output data. (True or False)

10. Unsupervised learning discovers an internal representation from input data only. (True or False)

11. For semi-supervised learning, some data is labeled but most of it is unlabeled and a mixture of supervised and unsupervised techniques can be used. (True or False)

12. The reinforcement learning algorithm uses trial and error to determine which actions yield the greatest rewards. (True or False)

13. For the three layers AI network below, the activation (transfer or Squashing) function is sigmoid (nonlinear) for the hidden and output nodes.

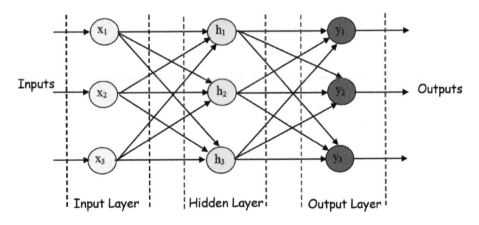

FIGURE 15.25 Exercise 13.

$$\text{Given: } \vec{I} = \begin{bmatrix} 0.6 \\ 0.2 \\ 0.7 \end{bmatrix}, \vec{W}_{input-hidden} = \begin{bmatrix} 0.8 & 0.2 & 0.5 \\ 0.1 & 0.7 & 0.1 \\ 0.3 & 0.4 & 0.9 \end{bmatrix}, \text{ and } \vec{W}_{hidden-output} = \begin{bmatrix} 0.2 & 0.6 & 0.4 \\ 0.7 & 0.4 & 0.3 \\ 0.9 & 0.1 & 0.8 \end{bmatrix}$$

A. Find the input nets to hidden layer, $\vec{X}_{\text{hidden}}$

B. Find the outputs of the hidden layer, $\vec{O}_{\text{hidden}}$

C. Find the input nets to output layer, $\vec{X}_{\text{output}}$

D. Find the outputs of the AI network, $\vec{O}_{\text{output}}$

14. Define and write the formula of AI for the following:

A. Accuracy

B. True-Positive Rate (Sensitivity/Recall)

C. True-Negative Rate (Specificity).

D. False-Positive Rate (FPR) or False Alarm Rate (FAR).

E. Precision.

F. F1-ScoreF1-Measure:

BIBLIOGRAPHY

[1] G. R. Grimmett and D.R. Stirzaker, *Probability and Random Processes.* Oxford: Oxford University Press, pp. 26–45, 2001.

[2] X. R. Li, Probability, *Random Signals, and Statistics.* Boca Raton, FL: CRC Press, pp. 65–143, 1999.

[3] R. Jain, *The Art of Computer Systems Performance Analysis.* New York: John Wiley & Sons, pp. 483–501, 1991.

[4] R. Nelson, *Probability, Stochastic Processes, and Queueing Theory.* New York: Springer-Verlag, pp. 101–165, 1995.

[5] P. G. Harrison and N. M. Patel, *Performance Modelling of Communication Networks and Computer Architecture.* Wokingham, UK: Addison-Wesley, pp. 19–48, 1992.

[6] R. Goodman, *Introduction to Stochastic Models.* Mineola, NY: Dover Publications, 2nd ed., 2006.

[7] O. C. Ibe, *Markov Processes for Stochastic Modeling.* Burlington, MA: Elsevier Academic Press, 2009.

[8] X. R. Li, *Probability, Random Signals, and Statistics.* Boca Raton, FL: CRC Press, pp. 259–313, 1999.

[9] G. R. Grimmett and D. R. Stirzaker, *Probability and Random Processes.* New York: Oxford University Press, 3rd ed., pp. 360–374, 2001.

[10] R. Nelson, *Probability, Stochastic Processes, and Queueing Theory.* New York: Springer-Verlag, pp. 235–282, 1995.

[11] D. Claiborne, *Mathematical Preliminaries for Computer Networking.* New York: John Wiley & Sons, pp. 35–42, 1990.

[12] S. M. Ross, *Stochastic Processes.* New York: John Wiley & Sons, 1983.

[13]   R. Jain, *The Art of Computer Systems Performance Analysis.* New York: John Wiley, pp. 516–517, 1991.

[14]   J. Medhi, *Stochastic Models in Queueing Theory.* Boston, MA: Academic Press, p. 31, 1991.

[15]   R. Goodman, *Introduction to Stochastic Models.* Mineola, NY: Dover Publications, 2nd ed., 2006.

[16]   O. C. Ibe, *Fundamentals of Applied Probability and Random Processes.* Burlington, MA: Elsevier Academic Press, 2005.

[17]   J. C. Falmagne, *Lectures in Elementary Probability Theory and Stochastic Processes.* New York: McGraw-Hill, 2003.

[18]   D. G. Kendall, "Some problems in the theory of queues," *J. Roy. Statis. Soc.* Series B, vol. 13, pp. 151–185, 1951.

[19]   T. G. Robertazzi, *Computer Networks and Systems: Queueing Theory and Performance Evaluation.* New York: Springer-Verlag, pp. 43–47, 1990.

[20]   S. Eilon, "A Simpler Proof of L = λ W," *Operation Research*, vol. 17, pp. 915–916, 1969.

[21]   R. Jain, *The Art of Computer Systems Performance Analysis.* New York: John Wiley, pp. 513–514, 1991.

[22]   J. Medhi, *Stochastic Models in Queueing Theory.* San Diego, CA: Academic Press, 1991, pp. 71–75.

[23]   G. C. Cassandras, *Discrete Event Systems.* Boston, MA: Irwin, pp. 349–354, 404–413, 1993.

[24]   M. Schartz, *Telecommunication Networks.* Reading, MA: Addison-Wesley, pp. 21–69, 1987.

[25]   D. Gross and C. M. Harris, *Fundamentals of Queueing Theory.* New York: John Wiley, 3rd ed., pp. 116–164, 1998.

[26]   E. Gelenbe and G. Pujolle, *Introduction to Queueing Networks.* Chichester, UK: John Wiley & Sons, pp. 94–95, 1987.

[27]   R. Nelson, *Probability, Stochastic Processes, and Queueing Theory.* New York: Springer-Verlag, pp. 295–309, 1995.

[28]   R. B. Cooper, *Introduction to Queueing Theory.* New York: North-Holland, 2nd ed., pp. 208–222, 1981.

[29]   R. B. Cooper, "Queueing Theory," in D. P. Heyman (ed.), *Handbooks in Operations Research and Management Science.* New York: North-Holland, chap. 10, pp. 469–518, 1990.

[30] P. J. B. King, *Computer and Communication System Performancd Modelling*. New York: Prentice Hall, pp. 124–130, 1989.

[31] P. G. Harrison and N. M. Patel, *Performance Modelling of Communication Networks and Computer Architecture*. Wokingham, UK: Addison-Wesley, pp. 258–297, 1993.

[32] M. K. Molloy, *Fundamentals of Performance Modeling*. New York: MacMillan, pp. 193–248, 1989.

[33] L. Kleinrock, *Queueing Systems*. New York: John Wiley, vol. I., 1975.

[34] J. D. Claiborne, *Mathematical Preliminaries for Computer Networking*. New York: John Wiley, 1990.

[35] O. C. Ibe, *Markov Processes for Stochastic Modeling*. Burlington, MA: Elsevier Academic Press, pp. 105–152, 2009.

[36] J. F. Hayes and T. V. J. G. Babu, *Modeling and Analysis of Telecommunications Networks*. New York: Wiley-Interscience, pp. 67–112, 2004.

[37] A. M. Haghighi and D. P. Mishev, *Queueing Models in Industry and Business*. New York: Nova Science Publishers, 2008.

[38] G. R. Dattatreya, *Performance Analysis of Queueing and Computer Networks*. Boca Raton, FL: CRC Press, 2008.

[39] Michael E. Woodward, Communication and Computer Networks: Modeling with Discrete time Queues, Wiley-IEEE Computer Society Press, 1993.

[40] B. A. Forouzan, Cryptography and network security, McGraw-hill, 2008.

[41] W. Stallings, Cryptography and network security: principles and practice, 3rd edition, Prentice Hall, 2003.

[42] C. Kaufman, R. Perlman, and M. Speciner, Network Security, Prentice hall, 2001.

[43] W. Mao, Modern Cryptography, Prentice hall, 2004.

[44] A. Mosenia and N. K. Jha, "A Comprehensive Study of Security of Internet-of-Things", IEEE Transactions on Emerging topics in Computing, Vol. 5, No. 4, pp. 586–602, Oct.-Dec. 2017.

[45] S. K. Lee, M. Bae, and H. Kim, "Future of IoT Networks: A Survey", applied Sciences, MDPI, Vol. 7, pp. 1–25, 2017

[46] P. Xu, M. Li, Y.-J. He, "A hybrid encryption algorithm in the application of equipment information management based on Internet of things", 3rd International Conference on Multimedia Technology (ICMT 2013), pp. 1123–1129, Atlantis Press.

[47] C. Prabhu, O. Neogi, K. Shrivastava, and N. Katre, "Review paper on security intelligence with big data analytics", International journal of Advanced Research in computer and communication engineering, Vol. 4, No. 11, pp. 453–458, Nov. 2015.

[48] Top Ten Big Data Security and Privacy Challenges: Cloud Security Alliance 2012.

[49] J. Singh, "Real Time Big Data Analytic: Security Concern and Challenges with Machine Learning Algorithm" IEEE 2014.

[50] V. N.a Inukollu, S. Arsi and S. R. Ravuri, "Security issues associated with big data in cloud computing", International Journal of Network Security and Its Applications (IJNSA), Vol. 6, No. 3, pp. 45–56, May 2014.

[51] X. Han and Y. Chen, "Research for the arithmetic of cloud computing intrusion detection", International Conference on Cyberspace technology (CCT 2015), Beijing, China, 17–18 Oct. 2015.

[52] "International electro technical commission (IEC), Internet of Things: Wireless sensor networks," White Paper, 2014.

[53] Y. Wang, G. Attebury, and B. Ramamurthy, "A Survey of Security Issues In Wireless Sensor Networks," IEEE Communications Surveys and Tutorials, Vol. 8, No. 2, pp. 2–23, 2006.

[54] I. F. Akyildiz, et al., "A Survey on Sensor Setworks," IEEE Commun. Mag., vol. 40, no. 8, pp. 102–114, Aug. 2002.

[55] A. Nelli and S. Mangasuli, "Wireless Sensor Networks: An Overview on Security Issues and Challenges", International Journal of Advanced Engineering, Management and Science (IJAEMS), Vol. 3, No. 3, pp. 209–214, Mar. 2017.

[56] K. M. Pattani and P. J. Chauhan, "SPIN Protocol for wireless sensor network", International Journal of Advance Research in Engineering, Science and Technology, vol .2, no. 5, pp. 2394–2444, May 2015.

[57] P. Pillai, et al., "Wireless sensor networks: A survey on the state of the art and the 802.15.4 and ZigBee standards", Computer Communications, vol. 30, pp. 1655–1695, 2007.

[58] I. Foster, C. Kesselman, G. Tsudik, and S. Tuecke, "A security architecture for computational grids," in Proceedings of the Fifth ACM Conference on Computer and Communications Security, San Francisco, 1998.

[59] V. C. Gungor, et al., "Opportunities and Challenges of Wireless Sensor Networks in Smart Grid–A Case Study of Link Quality Assessments in

Power Distribution Systems," Industrial Electronics, IEEE Transactions on, vol. PP, pp. 1–1, 2010.

[60] W. YuFei, et al., "Smart Grid Information Security–A Research on Standards," 2011The International Conference on Advanced Power System Automation and Protection, pp. 1188–1194, April 20111

[61] CISCO, "The Internet of Things reference model," 2014. [Online]. Available: http://cdn.iotwf.com/resources/71/IoT_Reference_Model _White_Paper_ June_4_2014.pdf

[62] H. Farhangi, "The path of the smart grid," Power and Energy Magazine, IEEE, vol. 8, pp. 18–28, 2010.

[63] The Smart Grid Interoperability Panel–Cyber Security Working Group, Guidelines for smart grid cyber security, NISTIR 7628, pp. 1–597, 2010.

[64] A. Nicholson, S. Webber, S. Dyer, T. Patel, and H. Janicke, "SCADA security in the light of cyber-warfare," Computers & Security, vol. 31, no. 4, pp. 418–436, 2012.

[65] X. Fang, S. Misra, G. Xue, and D. Yang, "Smart grid–The new and improved power grid: A survey," Communications Surveys Tutorials, IEEE, Vol. 14, No. 4, pp. 944–980, Fourth 2012.

[66] N. Komninos, E. Philippou, and A. Pitsillides, "Survey in Smart Grid and Smart Home security: Issues, challenges and countermeasures," Communications Surveys Tutorials, IEEE, vol. 16, no. 4, pp. 1933–1954, Fourthquarter 2014.

[67] M. Hentea, "Improving Security for SCADA Control Systems," Interdisciplinary Journal of Information, Knowledge, and Management, vol. 3, pp. 7386, 2008.

[68] R. Krutz, Securing SCADA Systems. Wiley, 2006.

[69] V. L. Do, et al., "Security of SCADA Systems Against Cyber–Physical Attacks," IEEE A&E Systems Magazine, pp. 28–45, May 2017.

[70] B. alloway, and G. P. Hancke, "Introduction to industrial control networks," IEEE Communications Surveys & Tutorials, vol. 15, no. 2, pp. 860–880, 2013.

[71] K. Stouffer, J. Falco, and K. Scarfone, "Guide to industrial control systems (ICS) security," NIST Special Publication, pp. 800–882, 2011.

[72] B. Lampson, et al. "Authentication in Distributed Systems: Theory and Practice." ACM Transactions on Computer Systems, vol. 10, no. 4, pp. 265–310, November 1992.

[73] M. Satyanarayanan, "Integrating Security in a Large Distributed System." ACM Transactions on Computer Systems, vol. 7, no. 3, pp. 247–280, August 1989.

[74] S. Kent, and K. Seo. "Security Architecture for the Internet Protocol." Request for Comments (RFC) 4301, December 2005.

[75] G. Audin, "Next-Gen Firewalls: What to Expect." Business Communications Review, June 2004.

[76] S. Bellovin, and W. Cheswick, "Network Firewalls." IEEE Communications Magazine, September 1994.

[77] D. Chapman, and E. Zwicky, Building Internet Firewalls. Sebastopol, CA: O'Reilly, 2000.

[78] W. Cheswick, and S. Bellovin, Firewalls and Internet Security: Repelling the Wily Hacker. Reading, MA: Addison-Wesley, 2003.

[79] S. Lodin, and C. Schuba, "Firewalls Fend Off Invasions from the Net." IEEE Spectrum, February 1998.

[80] R. Oppliger, "Internet Security: Firewalls and Beyond." Communications of the ACM, May 1997.

[81] T. Hassan, J. Joshi, and G. Ahn, "Security and Privacy Challenges in Cloud Computing Environments." IEEE Security & Privacy, November/December 2010.

[82] D. Stinson, Cryptography: Theory and Practice. Boca Raton, FL: CRC Press, 2006.

[83] R. Summers, "An Overview of Computer Security." IBM Systems Journal, vol. 23, no. 4, 1984.

[84] G. Simmons, ed. Contemporary Cryptology: The Science of Information Integrity. Piscataway, NJ: IEEE Press, 1992.

[85] A. Sinkov, and T. Feil, Elementary Cryptanalysis: A Mathematical Approach. Washington, DC: The Mathematical Association of America, 2009.

[86] V. Albino, U. Berardi, and R. M. Dangelico, "Smart cities: definitions, performance, and initiatives," Journal of Urban Technology, vol. 22, no. 1, 2015.

[87] R. Khatoun and S. Zeadally, "Smart cities: concepts, architectures, research opportunites," Communications of the ACM, vol. 59, no. 8, Aug. 2016.

[88] S. P. Mohanty, U. Choppali, and E. Kougianos, "Everything you wanted to know about smart cities," IEEE Consumer Electronics Magazine, July 2016.

[89] T. Yigitcanlar, "Smart cities: an effective urban development and management model?" Australian Planner, vol. 52, no. 1, 2015.

[90] B. Bowerman, J. Braverman, J. Taylor, H. Todosow, and U. Von Wimmersperg, "The vision of a smart city," in 2nd International Life Extension Technology Workshop, Paris, 2000.

[91] K. R. Kunzmann, "Smart cities: A new paradigm of urban development," Crios, vol. 4, no. 1, pp. 9–20, 2014.

[92] S. Dirks, C. Gurdgiev, and M. Keeling, "Smarter cities for smarter growth: How cities can optimize their systems for the talent-based economy," IBM Institute for Business Value, 2010.

[93] M. Naphade, G. Banavar, C. Harrison, J. Paraszczak, and R. Morris, "Smarter cities and their innovation challenges," Computer, vol. 44, no. 6, pp. 32–39, 2011.

[94] A. Bartoli, J. Hern´andez-Serrano, M. Soriano, M. Dohler, A. Kountouris, and D. Barthel, "Security and privacy in your smart city," in Proceedings of the Barcelona Smart Cities Congress, 2011.

[95] S. Ijaz, M. A. Shah, A. Khan and M. Ahmed, "Smart Cities: A Survey on Security Concerns", International Journal of Advanced Computer Science and Applications (IJACSA), vol. 7, no. 2, pp. 612–625, 2016.

[96] A. Guadamuz and C. Marsden, "Blockchains and Bitcoin: Regulatory responses to cryptocurrencies," Peer-reviewed Journal on the Internet, vol. 20, no. 12, Dec. 2015.

[97] W. T. Tsai et al., "A system view of financial blockchains," Proceedings of IEEE Symposium on Service-Oriented System Engineering, pp. 450–457, 2016.

[98] V. Shermin, "Disrupting governance with blockchains and smart contracts," Strategic Change, vol. 26, no. 5, pp. 511–522, 2017.

[99] M. Gupta, Blockchain for Dummies. Hoboken, NJ: John wiley & Sons, 2017.

[100] S. Manski, "Building the blockchain world: technological commonwealth or just more of the same?" Strategic Change, vol. 26, no. 5, pp. 511–522, 2017.

[101] M. Banerjee, J. Lee, and K. K. R. Choo, "A blockchain future to Internet of things security: a position paper," to appear in Digital Communication and Networks, 2017.

[102] F. Dai, Y. Shi, N. Meng, L. Wei, Z. Ye, "From Bitcoin to Cybersecurity: a Comparative Study of Blockchain Application and Security Issues", The 2017 4th International Conference on Systems and Informatics (ICSAI 2017), pp. 975–979, 2017.

[103] M. Crosby et al., "BlockChain Technology", Sutardja Center for Entrepreneurship & Technology Technical Report, UC Berkeley, Oct. 2015.

[104] P. Boucher, "How blockchain technology could change our lives," European Parliamentary Research Service, Feb. 2017.

[105] K. Christidis and M. Devetsikiotis, "Blockchains and smart contracts for the Internet of things," IEEE Access, vol. 4, pp. 2292–2303, 2016.

[106] M. Swan, Blockchain: Blueprint for a New Economy. Sebastopol, CA: O'Reilly Media, 2015.

[107] H. Chen and C.C. Yang, Intelligence and Security Informatics: Techniques and Applications, Springer Verlag, 2008.

[108] P. Samarati, "Protecting Respondents' Identities in Microdata Release," IEEE Trans. Knowledge and Data Eng., vol. 13, pp. 1010–1027, 2001.

[109] K. Liu and E. Terzi, "Towards Identity Anonymization on Graphs," Proc. ACM SIGMOD, ACM Press, 2008.

[110] X. Tang and C.C. Yang, "Generalizing Terrorist Social Networks with K-Nearest Neighbor and Edge Between-ness for Social Network Integration and Privacy Preservation," Proc. IEEE Int'l Conf. Intelligence and Security Informatics, 2010.

[111] C.C. Yang, X. Tang, and B.M. Thuraisingham, "Social Networks Integration and Privacy Preservation using Subgraph Generalization," Proc. AMC SIGKDD Workshop Cybersecurity and Intelligence Informatics, 2009.

[112] IPSwitch, "How AI Is Helping: The Finance Industry Prevent Fraud," July 2017.

[113] M. Shankarapani, et al, Kernel Machines for Malware Classification and Similarity.

[114] Analysis, WCCI 2010 IEEE World Congress on Computational Intelligence. Barcelona, Spain, pp. 2504–2509, 2010.

[115] Abu-Nimeh, S., Nappa, D., Wang, X., & Nair, S., A comparison of machine learning techniques for phishing detection, APWG eCrime Researchers Summit, 2007.

[116] Andrea, I., Chrysostomou, C., & Hadjichristofi, G., Internet of Things: Security vulnerabilities and challenges, In Proc. IEEE Symposium on Computers and Communications, pp. 180–187). Larnaca, Cyprus, February 2015.

[117] Hwang, K., and M. Chen. Big Data Analytics for Cloud, IoT and Cognitive Computing. Wiley, 2017.

[118] T.M. Mitchell, Machine Learning, McGraw–Hill, New York, 1997.

[119] R.M. Neal, Bayesian Learning for Neural Networks, Springer-Verlag, Berlin, 1996.

[120] David Foster. Generative Deep Learning. O'Reilly Media, Inc., June 2019.

[121] K. Patan and J. Korbicz, Artificial Neural Networks in Fault Diagnosis, pp. 333–379, Springer, Berlin, Germany, 2004.

[122] Ovidiu Calin, Deep Learning Architectures: A mathematical Approach, Springer, Switzerland, 2020.

[123] Apruzzese, G., & Colajanni, M., On the Effectiveness of Machine and Deep Learning for Cyber Security, 2018 10th International Conference on Cyber Conflict, 371–390, 2018.

[124] Benaicha, S. E., Saoudi, L., Bouhouita Guermeche, S. E., & Lounis, O. (2014). Intrusion detection system using genetic algorithm. Science and Information Conference (SAI), 564–568.

[125] Buczak, A., & Guven, E, A survey of data mining and machine learning methods for cyber security intrusion detection, IEEE Communications Surveys and Tutorials, 2015.

[126] Ferreira, E. W. T., Carrijo, G. A., de Oliveira, R., & de Souza Araujo, N. V., Intrusion Detection System with Wavelet and Neural Artificial Network Approach for Networks Computers, IEEE Latin America Transactions, 9(5), 832–837, 2011.

[127] Mukkamala, S. & Sung, A. H., Feature Selection for Intrusion Detection Using Neural Networks and Support Vector Machines, Journal of the Transportation Research Board of the National Academics, Transportation Research Record, No 1822, pp. 33–39, 2003.

[128] Jiang, F., Y. Fu, B. B. Gupta, F. Lou, S. Rho, F. Meng, and Z. Tian, Deep learning based multi-channel intelligent attack detection for data security, *IEEE Transactions on Sustainable Computing*, pp. 1–11, 2018.

INDEX

A

Accuracy (ACC), 557
active hub, 13
Add Round-Key Transformations, 276
AES (Advanced Encryption Standard),
    508–9
    vs. DES, 276, 277
    parameters, 270
    plaintext, processing of, 271–6
AH (Authentication Header), 436–8
ANSI X9.17 Pseudo-Random Number
    Generator, 284–6
APs (access points), 15–16
Arbitrated Digital Signature, 350–2
ARP (Address Resolution Protocol), 7
Artificial Intelligence (AI) security
    deep learning
        advantages, 536–7
        applications, 537–8
        backward propagation, 540–2
        convolutional neural network (CNN),
            544–50
        extreme learning machine (ELMs),
            554–6
        forward propagation, 539–40
        long short-term memory networks
            (LSTMs), 551
        model architecture, 539
        multilayer neural networks, 543–4
        network layers, 538–9

recurrent neural networks
    (RNNs), 550–1
recursive neural networks
    (RvNNs), 552
stacked autoencoder, 553–4
intrusion detection system (IDS)
    accuracy (ACC), 557
    FPR or FAR, 558
    F1-Score, 558–9
    precision, 558
    true negative rate (TNR), 558
    true positive rate (TPR), 558
    trusted systems, 559
machine learning
    vs. AI and DL, 527
    purpose of, 526
    reinforcement learning, 535–6
    semi-supervised learning, 534–5
    vs. statistical model, 527
    supervised learning, 528–32
    unsupervised learning, 532–4
AS (Authentication Server), 355, 397, 405
AS (Autonomous System), 8, 9
authentication schemes
    Birthday Attack, 360–1
    Birthday Paradox, 357–9
    Denning Protocol, 353–4
    digital signatures, 349–52, 376–88
    hash function, 346–9
    MD5 algorithm, 364–7, 370–1

Message Authentication, 337–46
message words in various rounds, 368
mutual authentication, 352
Needham Schroeder Protocol, 353
NEUM Protocol, 354–5
one-way authentication, 355–6
primitive logical functions, 368–70
Public-Key encryption approaches,
   355, 356
Secure Hash Algorithm, 371–5
symmetric encryption approaches,
   353, 356
two sets overlapping, probability of, 359
weak collision resistance, 363
autocovariance, 65–7
avalanche effect, 239–45

B

balance equations, 82, 89, 90, 96
BBS (Blum Blum Shub) Pseudo-Random
   Bit Generator, 286–7
BC (Blockchain) technology
   advantages of, 533–5
   benefits and challenges, 532–3
   concept, 531
   definition, 530
   features of, 531–2
   security issues of, 535–6
Bernoulli distribution, 47–8
big data analysis, 489–93
   characteristics, 490
   flow, 491
   security issues and privacy challenges,
      492–3
Binary Cross Entropy (BCE), 541
binomial distribution, 48–9, 61
birth-and-death processes, 73, 93, 96
Birthday Attack, 360–1
Birthday Paradox, 357–9
Blockchain technology *see* BC
block cipher process, 128
   CBC, 254–6

Cipher Feedback Mode, 256–9
Counter Mode, 262–5
ECB, 252–4
Output Feedback Mode, 259–62
Bridge Table, 13
brute force attack, 130, 201, 203, 247, 270
bus topology, 22–3

C

Caesar Cipher, 112, 200–2
CAs (Certification Authorities)
   hierarchical organization of, 413–14
   registration with, 410
CBC (cipher block chaining) mode
   advantages of, 256
   decryption of, 255–6
   encryption of, 254–5
   limitations, 256
CDF (cumulative distribution function),
   42–3, 63–5
central limit theorem, 56, 60–1
centralized authentication service, 391, 392
   Kerberos V.4, 397–404, 406–7
   Kerberos V.5, 405–7
   motivation for, 392
   simple authentication exchange in open
      environment, 393–7
Certification Authorities *see* CAs
Certificate Revocation List *see* CRL
CFB (Cipher Feedback) Mode, 256–7
   advantages, 259
   decryption of, 258
   encryption of, 257–8
   limitations, 259
Chinese Remainder Theorem, 189–94
cipher block chaining mode *see* CBC
cipher-text, 111–13, 116, 118, 126, 128–31,
   202, 204, 207, 221–4, 239, 240, 249, 251,
   254, 259, 262, 274, 338, 339
classical cipher schemes
   classical substitution Ciphers, 199–213
   Transposition Ciphers, 213–15

classical substitution ciphers, 199–213
    Hill Cipher, 204–7
    mono-alphabetic cipher, 202–4
    One-Time Pad, 212–13
    Play-Fair Cipher, 207–9
    Vigenere Cipher/Poly-Alphabetic
        Cipher, 209–12
Claude Shannon's theory, 223–4
cloud computing technology, 493–4
    back end, 494
    cloud deployment models, 495
    consumer service, 498
    front end, 494
    IaaS, 496–7
    PaaS, 496
    security concerns and challenges, 497–8
Common Modulus Attack, 290–2
computer networks, definition, 1
conditional probability, 39–40, 46
continuous probability models
    Erlang distribution, 54–5
    exponential distribution, 53–4
    Gaussian distribution, 55–7
    hyperexponential distribution, 55
    properties of, 57
    uniform distribution, 52–3
continuous-time random process, 62
Convolutional neural network (CNN),
    544–50
co-prime, 154
correlation coefficient, 66
Counter Mode *see* CTR
CRC (Cyclic Redundancy Check) value, 122
CRL (Certificate Revocation List), 410,
    414, 415
CSMA/CD (Carrier Sense Multiple Access
    with Collision Detection), 16–17
CTR (Counter) Mode
    advantages of, 264
    decryption of, 263
    encryption of, 262–3
    limitations of, 264–5

cryptanalysis, 112, 115, 130
cryptographic primitives, 117
cryptographic protocol, 117
cryptology, 115
CSPRBG (Cryptographically Secure
    Pseudo-Random Bit Generator), 286
cumulative distribution function *see* CDF
cyclic encryption, 283–4

D

Data Encryption Algorithm *see* DEA
Data Encryption Standard *see* DES
datagrams, 7
data integrity, 122, 124, 342
data origin authentication, 121, 338
DEA (Data Encryption Algorithm), 227
decryption algorithm, 116–17, 129, 130,
    209, 225, 239, 269, 286
decryption key, 111, 116, 118, 126, 131,
    202, 426
Deep learning (DL)
    advantages, 536–7
    applications, 537–8
    backward propagation, 540–2
    convolutional neural network (CNN),
        544–50
    extreme learning machine (ELMs),
        554–6
    forward propagation, 539–40
    long short-term memory networks
        (LSTMs), 551
    model architecture, 539
    multilayer neural networks, 543–4
    network layers, 538–9
    recurrent neural networks (RNNs), 550–1
    recursive neural networks (RvNNs), 552
    stacked autoencoder, 553–4
Deep neural network (DNN), 536
Denning protocol, 353–4
DES (Data Encryption Standard), 219
    vs. Advanced Encryption Standard,
        276, 277

critical functions of, 233–5
decryption algorithm, 239
differential cryptanalysis attack, 241–5
Feistel decryption algorithm, 230–3
Feistel encryption algorithm, 229
general depiction of, 228
hybrid encryption algorithm, 507–8
linear cryptanalysis, 244–5
multiple, 245–65
S-Box transformation, 236–7
strength of, 240–1
sub-keys, generation of, 237–8
deterministic random process, 62
DHCP (Dynamic Host Configuration
   Protocol), 7
Diffie-Hellman Key Exchange Algorithm,
   292, 450
   Clogging Attack, 296
   global parameters, 293–4
   Man-in-the-Middle Attack, 296–7
   strength of, 295
digital signature, 123–4, 292, 338
   Arbitrated Digital Signature, 350–2
   Digital Signature Algorithm, 382–8
   direct digital signature, 349–50
   ElGamal's Digital Signature Scheme,
      378–82
   Public-Key Cryptography, 341–2
   RSA digital signature scheme, 376–8
   verification of, 361
Digital Signature Algorithm *see* DSA
Digital Signature Standard *see* DSS
Dijkstra algorithm, 9
direct digital signature, 349–50
discrete logarithms, 178–82
discrete probability models
   Bernoulli distribution, 47–8
   binomial distribution, 48–9
   geometric distribution, 49–50
   Poisson distribution, 50–2
discrete-time random process, 62
distributed ledger technology. *see*
   Blockchain (BC) technology
DNS (Domain Name System), 6

double Data Encryption Standard
   decryption, 246
   encryption, 245–6
   Meet-in-the-Middle Attack, 247–8
   strength of, 247
double-key scheme, 127–8
DSA (Digital Signature Algorithm), 382–8,
   507–8
DSS (Digital Signature Standard), 382, 383

E

ECB (Electronic Code Book) mode
   advantages, 253
   decryption of, 253
   encryption of, 252–3
   limitations, 253–4
ECC (Elliptic Curve Cryptography), 114,
   300–25
   Binary Curve, 301
   efficient hardware implementation, 325
   encryption/decryption scheme, 313–25
   key-exchange algorithm, 311–13
   Prime Elliptic Curve Set, 302–4
   strength of, 311
Electronic Code Book mode *see* ECB
ElGamal Encryption Scheme, 297–300
ElGamal's Digital Signature Scheme, 378–82
Elliptic Curve Cryptography *see* ECC
emerging technology security of
   BC technology, 530–6
   big data analytics, 489–93
   cloud computing, 493–8
   Internet of Things, 498–510
   SCADA systems, 515–18
   smart city, 525–9
   smart grids, 511–15
   Wireless Sensor Network, 519–25
Encapsulating Security Payload *see* ESP
encryption algorithm, 116, 129, 130, 225,
   233, 239, 285, 406
encryption key, 112, 116, 117, 202
end-to-end encryption, 133–5
Enigma Machine, 112

Enveloped Data, 432, 434
ergodic processes, 62–3, 67–9
ESP (Encapsulating Security Payload), 439–42
Ethernet, 3
ethical hacking, 112, 115
Euclid's algorithm, 155–6, 194
Euler's theorem, 170–6
Euler's Totient Function, 168–70
Expansion Permutation, 234–5
Extended Euclid's Algorithm, 156–9, 164, 165
Extreme learning machine (ELMs), 554–6

F

False-Positive Rate (FPR) / False Alarm Rate (FAR), 558
Feistel cipher, 224–7
Fermat's Little Theorem, 166–8
field, 145–6
firewall
    application-level gateway, 484
    Bastion host, 484–5
    characteristics, 483
    circuit-level gateway, 484
    configurations, 485–6
    control access, techniques to, 483
    definition, 482, 483
    packet filtering router, 484
    state-full inspection firewalls, 484
F1-Score, 558–9

G

Galois Finite Fields, 159–266
Gaussian distribution, 52, 55, 60
GCD (Greatest Common Divisor), 154–6, 176
generating functions, 58–60
geometric distribution, 49–50
Greatest Common Divisor see GCD
group
    Abelian Group, 143

cyclic group, 144
Exponentiation in Group, 143–4
Finite Group, 141–3
Infinite Group, 141

H

hash function, 340–1, 346–9
    characteristics of, 348–9
    signed message, symmetric encryption of, 347, 348
    strengths of, 363
Hierarchical model, 9–10
Hill Cipher, 204–7
Huber loss function, 541
hybrid encryption technique, 505–8
hybrid topology, 26

I

IaaS (Infrastructure as a Service), 496–7
ICV (Integrity Check Value), 437, 438–9
ICMP (Internet Control Message Protocol), 7, 8
IDEA (International Data Encryption Algorithm), 219
    description of, 266–8
    modes of operation, 270
    sub-keys, generation of, 269–70
IGMP (Internet Group Management Protocol), 7
Integrity Check Value see ICV
Intermediate System-Intermediate System see ISIS
International Data Encryption Algorithm see IDEA
Internet Control Message Protocol see ICMP
Internet of Things see IoT
Internet Protocol Security see IPSec
Internet Security Association Key Management Protocol see ISAKMP
Intrusion detection system (IDS)
    accuracy (ACC), 557
    definition, 478

False-Positive Rate (FPR) or False
   Alarm Rate (FAR), 558
F1-Score, 558–9
precision, 558
profile-based detection, 479
rule-based detection, 479
threshold detection, 478–9
true negative rate (TNR), 558
true positive rate (TPR), 558
trusted systems, 559
IoT (Internet of Things)
   Advanced Encryption Standard, 508–9
   applications of, 502–3
   building blocks of, 499–500
   challenges created by, 504
   concept topology, 498–9
   evolution of, 499
   four-layer model, 501
   hybrid encryption technique, 505–8
   lightweight cryptography, 509–10
   and Machine-to-Machine, 500
   prevention of attacks, 510
   primary targets of attack, 505
   security requirements of, 504
   seven-layer model, 501–2
   three-layer model, 500
IP (Initial Permutation), 232, 233
IP (Internet Protocol), 7, 18
   classes, 18–20
   format, 18
IPSec (Internet Protocol Security)
   anti-replay window, 449
   Authentication Header, 436–8
   ESP, 439–42
   ICV, 438–9
   ISAKMP, 452–4
   Key Management Protocol, 450
   Oakley Key-Exchange Protocol, 450–2
   SA selectors, 445
   Secure Electronic Transaction, 460–74
   Secure Socket Layer, 455–258
   Security Associations, 442–4
   Security Policy Database, 444
   Transport Layer Security, 458–9

   Transport Mode, 445–6
   Tunnel Mode, 446–8
   Wildcard Mode, 448
ISAKMP (Internet Security Association Key
   Management Protocol), 452–4
ISIS (Intermediate System-Intermediate
   System), 8–9
ISO (International Organization for
   Standardization), 2

J

Jackson network, 108–9
joint cumulative distribution function, 45
joint probability density function, 45, 46

K

KDC (Key Distribution Center),
   278–280, 353
Kendal's notation, 77–9
Kerberos, 397–407
Key distribution
   Centralized Key Distribution, 278–80
   Decentralized Key Control Scheme,
     280–1
   definition, 277
   Diffie-Hellman algorithm, 292
   key distribution schemes, 278
Key Distribution Center see KDC
Key management
   Public-Key Cryptography, 292–7
   secure distribution of keys, 277–80

L

LAN (local area network), 15, 20–1, 436,
   482, 483, 531
Laplace-Stieltjes transform, 99
Layer 2 Protocols, 7
Layer 3 Protocols, 7–8
Layer 4 Protocols, 8
LEAP (Localized Encryption and
   Authentication Protocol), 523
LLC (Logical Link Control), 3

lightweight cryptography, 509–10
linear congruential method, 282–3
link encryption
    advantages, 132
    cipher designers *vs.* cryptanalysts, 135–6
    computationally secure schemes, 135
    disadvantages, 132–3
    and end-to-end encryption, 134
    traffic-pattern confidentiality, 134–5
    unconditionally secure schemes, 135
Little's theorem, 79–80, 95, 99
local area network *see* LAN
Logical address, 18
Long short-term memory networks (LSTMs), 551

M

MAC (Media Access Control), 3, 11, 16
MAC (Message Authentication Code), 342–3
    chosen plaintext attack, 345–6
    definition, 340
    use of, 343–5
Machine learning (ML)
    vs. AI and DL, 527
    purpose of, 526
    reinforcement learning, 535–6
    semi-supervised learning, 534–5
    vs. statistical model, 527
    supervised learning, 528–32
    unsupervised learning, 532–4
MAN (metropolitan area network), 21
marginal cumulative distribution functions, 46
marginal probability density functions, 46, 47
Markov chain, 72
Markovian random walk, 71–2
Markov process, 72–3
Master Key, 278, 279
MD5 Message Digest algorithms, 364–71, 375
Mean Squared Error (MSE), 541

M/Ek/1 queueing system, 103
mesh topology, 24–5
Message Authentication, 337
    entire message, encryption of, 338–9
    Message Authentication Code, 342–6
Message Authentication Code *see* MAC
metropolitan area network *see* MAN
M/G/1 queueing system, 97–103
Miller-Rabin Method, 182–8
mix columns transformations, 276
M2M (Machine-to-Machine), 500
M/M/1 queue, 81–7
    bulk arrivals system, 88–9
    bulk service system, 89–90
    M/M/k queueing system, 92–6
    M/M/1/k queueing system, 90–2
    M/M/∞ queueing system, 96–7
modern symmetric ciphers
    avalanche effect, 239–45
    Binary Block substitution, 220–2
    confusion, 224
    Data Encryption Standard, 227–39
    diffusion, 223–4
    Feistel cipher, 224–7
    simple substitution cipher, key size for, 223
    substitution cipher, strength of, 222–3
modular arithmetic, 151–4
    congruent modulo, 146–8
    properties of Zn, 149–51
    residue, 146
    Residue Classes, 148–9
mono-alphabetic cipher, 202–4
Multilayer neural networks, 543–4

N

Needham Schroeder Protocol, 353
negative exponential distribution *see* exponential distribution
Network Bridging, 13
network equipment
    access points, 15–16
    Bridge, 13
    end/user devices, 10

firewalls, 15
gateways, 15
hubs, 12–13, 17
network devices, 10
NIC, 10–11
repeaters, 11–12
router, 14–15
server, 16
switch, 13–14, 17
network interface cards *see* NICs
networks of queues
feedback, queueing systems with, 107–8
splitting, queueing system with, 106–7
tandem queues, 104–6
NEUM Protocol, 354–5
NICs (network interface cards), 10–11
nondeterministic random process, 62
nonergodic process, 63
nonstationary random process, 62
normal distribution *see* Gaussian
distribution
notarization, 125

O

Oakley Key-Exchange Protocol, 450–2
OFB (Output Feedback) Mode
advantages of, 261–2
encryption/decryption, 259–61
limitations, 262
One-Time Pad Scheme, 212–13
Output Feedback Mode *see* OFB
OSI (Open Systems Interconnection), 2–4
OSI (Open Systems Interconnection)
Architecture X.800, 119–26
pervasive security mechanisms, 125–7
security attacks, 120–1, 125–6
security services, 121–3
specific security mechanisms, 123–5
OSPF (Open Shortest Path First), 8

P

PaaS (Platform as a Service), 496
PAN (personal area network), 20

passive hub, 13
PDF (probability density function), 43–4,
46, 63, 65
peer-to-peer authentication, 121, 338
personal area network *see* PAN
PGP (Pretty Good Privacy)
authentication service, 420, 423, 424
compression/decompression functions, 424
Confidentiality Only service, 422, 423
confidentiality function, 423, 424
data compression, 420
data confidentiality, 419
key rings in authentications, 427
key rings in data confidentiality, 428
private key ring, fields of, 426
public keys, trust model for, 429–31
Radix-64 Transformation, 420, 424–5
receiving end, functions at, 423
security services, implementation of,
420–1
segmentation and reassembly, 420
sender end, functions at, 422
session keys, 426
S/MIME, 431–4
PKI (Public Key Infrastructure)
Certificate Revocation List, 410
certificates' chain creation, 414
hierarchical organization of CA, 413–14
public key certificate, issues of, 410
registration with CA, 410
RFC 2822, 409
X.509 Certificate, 409–17
Platform as a Service *see* PaaS
Play-Fair Cipher, 207–9
point-to-point topology, 22
Poisson distribution, 50–2
Poisson process, 74–6
Pollaczek-Khintchine formula, 100, 101
Pretty Good Privacy *see* PGP
primality testing, 182–8
prime numbers, 154, 175–8, 187, 188
private key, 113, 118, 127, 128, 284, 289,
298–300, 341, 350, 379, 410, 413,
425–31, 536

PRNG (Pseudo-Random Number Generator)
    characteristics, 282
    cryptographically generated random numbers, 283–7
    Lehmer's algorithm, 282–3
probability density function *see* PDF
probability fundamentals
    conditional probability, 39–40
    joint probability, 38
    simple probability, 35–7
    statistically independent, 40
    Venn diagram, 34
Pseudo-Random Number Generator *see* PRNG
public key, 298–300, 352, 463, 506, 535
    ring, 425–31
    trust model for, 429–31
Public Key Cryptography, 113, 118, 127
    data confidentiality, 284
    digital signatures, 341–2
    ElGamal Encryption Scheme, 297–300
    Elliptic Curve Cryptography, 300–25
    hash function, 340–1, 346–9
    key management, 292–7
    requirements of, 283–4
    RSA, 284–92
Public-Key encryption approaches, 127, 128, 339, 340, 352, 355, 356
Public Key Infrastructure *see* PKI

Q

queueing theory, 33–4, 53, 54, 77, 79

R

Rail-Fence cipher, 213–14
random processes
    birth-and-death processes, 73
    continuous *vs.* discrete random process, 62
    deterministic *vs.* non-deterministic random process, 62
    ensemble averages, 67
    ergodic *vs.* nonergodic random process, 62–3
    Markov process, 72–3
    multiple, 69–70
    Poisson process, 74–6
    random walk, 70–2
    realizations/sample functions, 32, 33
    stationarity, statistics of, 63–7
    stationary *vs.* nonstationary random process, 62
    time averages of, 67–9
random quantity, 32
random variable, 41–7, 57–8
random walk, 70–2
Recipient Non-Repudiation, 119
rectangular distribution *see* uniform distribution
Rectangular Transposition Cipher, 214–15
Recurrent neural networks (RNNs), 550–1
Recursive neural networks (RvNNs), 552
Reinforcement learning, 535–6
relative frequency, 35, 203
renewal process, 76
ring, 144–5
    public and private key, 425–31
    topology, 24
Rivest, Shamir, and Adleman *see* RSA
routing control, 124
RSA (Rivest, Shamir, and Adleman)
    decryption algorithm, 286–8
    determination of keys, 285
    ECC encryption/decryption, 325
    encryption algorithm, 285
    digital signature scheme, 376–8
    strength of, 288–92

S

SaaS (Software as a Service), 495
SA (Security Associations), 442–4

SAN (storage area network), 21
SCADA (Supervisory Control and Data
   Acquisition) system
      components of, 516
      concept topology, 515–16
      layers, 517–18
      requirements and features for, 518
      security threats, categories for, 518
secure communication, requirements of,
   117–19
Secure Electronic Transaction *see* SET
Secure Hash Algorithm *see* SHA-1
Secure Socket Layer *see* SSL
Security Associations *see* SA
Semi-supervised learning,, 534–5
Sensor Protocols for Information via
   Negotiation *see* SPINs
session keys, 278–9, 355, 426
SET (Secure Electronic Transaction)
      business requirements of, 462
      cardholder account authentication, 464
      confidentiality of information, 463
      data integrity, 463–4
      merchant authentication, 464
      participants in, 460–2
      payment capture, 473–4
      Public Key Certificates, 464
      sequence of events, 464–73
SHA-1 (Secure Hash Algorithm)
      append message length, 371
      append padding bits, 371
      MD Buffer, initialize, 371–2
      vs. MD5, 375
      output, 374
      process message, 372–4
      upgrades of, 375
shift rows transformation, 275
single-key scheme, 127
Signed Data, 432–4
simple probability, 35–7
smart city, security of, 525–9
smart grids
      active attacks, 514
      challenges, 511–12

classifications, 513–14
concept topology, 511
cybersecurity attacks, 514–15
information security risks and demands,
   512–13
layer, 512
passive attacks, 514
security objectives, 513
S/MIME (Secure/multipurpose Internet
   Mail Extension), 431–4
Software as a Service *see* SaaS
Source Non-Repudiation, 119, 342
SPB (Shortest Path Bridging), 9
SPD (Security Policy Database), 444
SPINs (Sensor Protocols for Information via
   Negotiation), 522–3
SPN (Substitution-Permutation
   Network), 224
SPX (Sequenced Package Exchange), 8
SSL (Secure Socket Layer)
      alerts protocol, 456
      change specs protocol, 455
      connection, 457
      Handshake Protocol, 455
      Record Protocol, 456–7
      session state, 457–8
SSS (strict-sense stationary), 67
Stacked autoencoders, 553–4
star topology, 23
stationary random process, 62
Steganography, 215–16
STP (Spanning Tree Protocol), 9
stream cipher processes, 128
      CBC, 254–6
      Cipher Feedback Mode, 256–9
      Counter Mode, 262–5
      ECB, 252–4
      Output Feedback Mode, 259–62
substitute bytes, 274–6
substitution ciphers, 112, 127, 204, 209,
   221, 222, 223
Supervised learning
      classification algorithms, 530–1
      data point, 529

definition, 528
regression algorithms, 531–2
Supervisory Control and Data Acquisition system *see* SCADA
Symmetric Cryptography, 114, 116, 118
symmetric encryption approach, 128–36, 356
for confidentiality, 131
link encryption, 132–6
types of attacks, 130
system security
anti-virus scanners, 481
firewall, 482–6
intruder, 477–8
intrusion detection, 478–9
malicious programs, 479–81
password management, 479
trusted system, 486–7
worms, 481–2

T

TCB (Trusted Computing Base), 486
TCP (Transport Control Protocol), 8
TCP/IP (Transmission Control Protocol/ Internetworking Protocol), 4–9
TGS (Ticket Granting Server), 397–404
theory of probability, 32
Ticket Granting Server *see* TGS
TINYSEC, 523–4
TLS (Transport Layer Security), 455, 458–9
topology
bus, 22–3
full-duplex communications, 26
half-duplex communications, 26
hybrid, 26
logical, 22
mesh, 24–5
physical, 22
point-to-point, 22
ring, 24
simplex communications, 26
star, 23
tree, 25
traffic padding, 124, 135
transition matrix, 73

transition probability, 73
Transmission Control Protocol/ Internetworking Protocol *see* TCP/IP
Transport Layer Security *see* TLS
transposition ciphers, 127
Rail-Fence Cipher, 213–14
Rectangular Transposition Cipher, 214–15
triple Data Encryption Standard
Block/Stream Cipher modes of operation, 252–65
decryption, 249–50
encryption, 248–9
Meet-in-the-Middle Attack, 251
tree topology, 25
True negative rate (TNR), 558
True positive rate (TPR), 558
two-stage hyperexponential distribution, 55

U

UDP (Unified Datagram Protocol), 8
unethical hacking, 114, 115
Unsupervised learning
association algorithm, 533–4
clustering algorithm, 533
definition, 532
goal, 533
UTP (Unshielded Twisted Pair) Ethernet, 23

V

Venn diagram, 34
Vigenere Cipher/Poly-Alphabetic Cipher, 209–12
VLAN (virtual local area network), 21

W

WAN (wide area network), 21
WSNs (Wireless Sensor Networks)
attack categories, 521, 522
concept topology, 519
defense in, 522
definition, 519
layers, 520

security protocols, 522–4
security requirements in, 520–1
WSS (wide-sense stationary), 66, 67

X

X.509 Certificate
    format of, 410–13
    one-way authentication procedure, 416

revocation of, 414–15
three-way authentication
    procedure, 417
two-way authentication procedure,
    416–17

Z

ZIGBEE, 524